"And The

James Kelman was born in Glasgow in 1946. *A Disaffection* won the James Tait Black Memorial Prize and was short-listed for the Booker Prize, which he won in 1994 for *How late it was, how late*. His most recent novel is *Translated Accounts*.

ALSO BY JAMES KELMAN

James Kelman

"AND THE JUDGES SAID..."

ESSAYS

V

VINTAGE

Published by Vintage 2003

2 4 6 8 10 9 7 5 3 1

First published in Great Britain in 2002 by
Secker & Warburg

Vintage
Random House, 20 Vauxhall Bridge Road,
London SW1V 2SA

Random House Australia (Pty) Limited
20 Alfred Street, Milsons Point, Sydney
New South Wales 2061, Australia

Random House New Zealand Limited
18 Poland Road, Glenfield,
Auckland 10, New Zealand

Random House (Pty) Limited
Endulini, 5A Jubilee Road, Parktown 2193,
South Africa

The Random House Group Limited Reg. No. 954009
www.randomhouse.co.uk

A CIP catalogue record for this book
is available from the British Library

ISBN 0 099 42184 4

Papers used by Random House are natural, recyclable
products made from wood grown in sustainable forests.
The manufacturing processes conform to the environmental regulations of the country of origin

Printed and bound in Denmark by
Nørhaven Paperback A/S, Viborg

There are too many great friends and comrades to name individually, so this is for all the team, including the ones who are no longer around.

Unity chops elephants.
old African proverb

Contents

Introduction

THIS COLLECTION IS only roughly chronological and the essay on
the novels of Franz Kafka is the earliest, dating from 1983. ' "And
the judges said . . ." ' was written much later, here revised from the
transcript of a talk I gave for students at the Glasgow School of Art
in November 1996.[1] The title is the first line of a poem by Tom
Leonard.[2] Some of the opening to the essay derives from an
attempt I made to write an autobiographical introduction to a
selection of my short stories.[3]

I devised 'Elitism and English Literature, Speaking as a Writer'
for a lecture I gave at Goldsmiths' College, London. My association
with Goldsmiths' began in September 2000 at the recommendation
of the writer Angela McRobbie who teaches there. When asked to
give a lecture I thought something entitled 'Elitism and English
Literature, Speaking as a Writer' would appeal to the students. I
wrote about four pages in preparation, then realised much of what
I was beginning to say I had said elsewhere. I did give the lecture
and borrowed little bits from two earlier essays,[4] but I used as its
foundation my introduction to a collection of writings I edited a
few years ago. This was *An East End Anthology*.[5] I was working as
tutor to a writers' group in Glasgow that met for two-hourly
sessions weekly at St Mungo's Highschool as part of an adult
education programme. The book was a selection of the group's

stories and poetry; all the artwork – the cartoons, photography and cover designs – was done by two members.[6] The individual with responsibility for this part of the education programme was a friend by the name of Cathie Thomson; she had persuaded me to take on the class in the first place. I began as tutor in 1985–86 and lasted until 1988.

Cathie formerly was married to the playwright Eddie Boyd, a major figure in Scottish radio, television and film although rarely acknowledged as such. Eddie was then into his seventies and as politically committed as ever. He was one of the many Scottish writers and musicians who took part in the Writers for Miners events organised in solidarity with the miners during their epic 1984–5 struggle to survive with honesty and with dignity in spite of the authoritarian brutality of the British State. There were four such events, in Glasgow and in Edinburgh.[7]

'Shouting at the Edinburgh Fringe Forum' is the fuller version of an address I intended to read when an invited panel-member at the 1987 Edinburgh Fringe Forum. These fora are an annual event during the Edinburgh Festival and held in the morning. On the day I was half an hour late. It was due to the most typical, practical and unavoidable of reasons for any so-called 'profit-share' touring production: the entire company was registering unemployed; if not their social security benefits would have been withdrawn. Attending to such business detail is crucial, it is the only way 'loss-share' productions survive at all. No actor ever gets paid a wage. Neither does anyone else. We all pay for the privilege of working; a typical manoeuvre in Scottish theatre.

Ironically, trying to engage at the Edinburgh Fringe Festival as a working adult artist, in spite of the economic reality, was the basis of my intended address at the Fringe Forum. I was chauffeur as well as writer, director, ticket-collector and doorman of the company and by the time I had collected everybody and driven to Edinburgh from Glasgow district the proceedings at the Fringe Forum were underway. This forum is always popular and when we arrived the place was mobbed. Somebody had been co-opted on to the panel in my absence but towards the end of the discussion I jumped up and managed to read an extract of my prepared address from the floor. It caused a slight outburst from the audience which I assumed was favourable.

The Chair called me up to the platform to finish what I was saying from behind a microphone. Technically this was better but it turned out my assumption about the audience was wrong, they did not view my contribution favourably at all. In fact many of them, and also some platform-participants, were quite annoyed by that which had become audible to their lugs. However, I finished the damn thing. The event was being televised by BBC2 and after delivery of the extract I was returning to my chair at the back of the hall when the broadcaster Joan Bakewell appeared, and whispered, in passing, that she agreed with many of my points. But none of my contribution was ever screened as far as I am aware.

I had never been clear as to why the organisers had invited me in the first place. Then a few days later I discovered a 'full-scale' controversy concerning the Fringe itself had been raging for days. It just had escaped the notice of myself and the company, we were too busy taking care of the hundred and one administrative details needing attention when one is trying to put on a play at the Edinburgh Fringe Festival with the usual no fucking dough and no fucking material resources, props or otherwise. However, there was this new formation had come into existence known as the Fringe Fringe. Apparently all sorts of people were wanting to know if this Fringe Fringe called into question the subversive nature of the original Fringe and if so whether or not such questioning was justified, i.e. had the 'real' Fringe become just another load of main-stream fucking shite. Yes cried some while others muttered No.

At last it dawned on myself and the other members of our company that yes, we did have a connection with the controversy after all. Was this actual play of mine, *In the Night*, not having its Scottish premiere here at this very Fringe Fringe venue! Aye! Fuck! So no wonder I had been invited, it was assumed I would have something relevant to say!

Obviously some of the old Fringe people suspected that this new lot, the Fringe Fringe people, which they assumed included folk like myself, were only there in an attempt to scupper the long-standing originals, i.e. themselves, the traditional rebels of the Edinburgh Arts scene. But it had fuck-all to with me, your honour. I knew nothing about any such controversy, and neither did anyone else from our Glasgow-based, so-called 'profit-share' touring-production company. Our heads were full of the same old Edinburgh Festival shite *re* our exploitation as working adult artists, and the talk I had prepared was based on that so when the day arrived I just went off on a rant, accompanied by a couple of irate actors. During the rant I further declared how interesting it was that ordinary Scottish accents were apparent only by their absence at this so-called open forum in this so-called Scottish capital city. I intended it as a comment on class and colonialism, and in opposition to the 'Received Pronunciation' (RP) voice of ruling authority but the context was gone and I was misunderstood, the comments taken as anti-English; and cries of Boo and Shame were rife.

Most of these traditional and long-standing old rebels are still subverting the Edinburgh Festival to this very day, you can identify them by their garters. (You catch a glimpse of said garments when the guys climb to their feet for another round of God Save the British Monarchy.)

One of Scotland's two 'quality' daily newspapers, the *Glasgow Herald*, noted the furore at that Fringe Forum and asked to publish a transcript of the offending address. I was persuaded there would be no tampering with the text cross my heart and right hand up to god. The journalist who made the request was an established feature writer, an older guy, and he gave me his word. But the usual shit man he was fucking telling lies. They did tamper with the text, censored the thing. The journalist made no attempt to excuse or explain what had happened, never mind apologise, but why did I fall for it in the first place?

Not long afterwards in Edinburgh the Labour-controlled Lothian Regional Council was attempting to close down the Citizens' Rights Office (CRO). A month before the closure was due I had been asked to give a talk at the Unemployed Workers' Centre. This was also being shut down by the council. There was little to choose between Labour Party policy at local Government level with the Tory Government at national level: when in doubt attack the poor.

A campaign had been formed and representatives from the Unemployed Workers' Centre were to go in front of a council committee to explain why the centre should continue to receive council funding. Attacks were taking place on a variety of community projects throughout the region at that time and people from throughout Edinburgh were involved and in attendance at the council buildings for the same council meeting. They were not there to justify a salary – most of them were voluntary workers – but the continuance of their particular community project. Each group had to stand up in front of the Councillors and deliver the same type of explanation-cum-justification and, therefore, were in a form of competition with each other. As a spectator I found it shameful; another instance of the public being treated with contempt, that singular brand professional politicians reserve for any citizen they suspect of integrity.

It was predictable funding would be withdrawn. Governments

rarely approve of places where unemployed people meet and discuss life in general. When it happened the stalwarts from the Unemployed Workers' Centre continued the campaign. Things became difficult. There was a fight to stop the eviction and shows of solidarity were called for; these included a number of writers and musicians performing a benefit night under the Artists in Solidarity banner.[8] Finally the police battered their way in to enforce the eviction order on behalf of the Labour-controlled council. The centre was shut down and the voluntary workers evicted. But the unemployed volunteers opened another centre elsewhere. It is known as The Autonomous Centre of Edinburgh (ACE) and continues in existence. All power to them. I discuss some of the proceedings in the talk I gave, included here as 'Opening the Edinburgh Unemployed Workers' Centre'.

The South African writer Alex La Guma died of cancer in 1985. Peter Kravitz knew that I liked and respected his work and asked if I would contribute an obituary for the *Edinburgh Review*. It was later amended and reprinted for *The End of a Regime? An Anthology of Scottish–South African Writing Aganist Apartheid*.[9] But the white racist regime did not end for a further three years.

Following its unbanning in 1990, the African National Congress (ANC) hosted a large conference on arts and culture in Johannesburg early in 1993. That took nerve. But there was support from abroad. Delegates and representatives of different organisations and groups arrived from different parts of the world, including a large representation from the United Kingdom. My presence at the Johannesburg conference came about via the poet and novelist Mandla Langa who then worked at the ANC office in London. He had visited Glasgow in 1990 to take part in the Self-Determination and Power Event, and we became friends. I was at the conference on a personal basis, as an observer, just as one individual writer. Having no official involvement and no defined role I was free to roam, against the advice of our hosts; at the 'safe' hotel location in Johannesburg where we met on the first day of our arrival a bomb had exploded only a day or so earlier, killing four people as I recall. Security was tight. In the reception area Margaret Busby[10] and myself were hungry and made to step outside to find a delicatessen or sandwich bar, anything. The ANC people were on to us immediately, moving swiftly from across the floor, unable to guarantee our safety if we so much as stepped outside on to the pavement.

The white racists were still in power of course and there was tremendous hostility towards what was happening. Two weeks before our arrival Chris Hani had been murdered by somebody linked to the regime. Then on the morning of our arrival Oliver Tambo died. Comrade O. T. was the only name I heard used in reference to him, always with affection. Altogether it was an emotional time and guests at the conference were aware of its historical significance. The film biography of Malcolm X had just been released and its premiere for the entire African continent was a special showing in Johannesburg for the ANC during the early part of the conference. There was a conflict that evening between a big literary event and the screening but I was glad I chose a night at the pictures.

Many of the foreign delegates and representatives were lodged at the central Carlton Hotel and it was a strange experience being in that place: bow-ties and tuxedos, and a male version of Blossom Dearie tinkling the keys of a grand piano. It was like being an extra in a Noël Coward or Humphrey Bogart movie, or a cross between the two. Other hotel residents and staff attempted not to show interest in us while a few foreign residents just seemed embarrassed. They all knew the identity of our hosts and the purpose of our visit. In the mornings taxis would ferry conference participants to the event, located right in the political heart of the city. All the taxi drivers from this hotel were white and I well remember the atmosphere inside their fucking vehicles: extreme hatred. One old guy could hardly stop himself spitting at me, his hands shaking when I gave him the money, plus a wee tip and as much of a smile as I could muster, fuck you ya bastard.

Fortunately the hotel was costing our hosts a fortune and we had to shift out after only two nights. So we wound up at a hotel in Hillbrow district for the remainder of the ten days; a tricky area to be in, an interesting area to go for a walk, but much less burdensome than the Carlton. I was attracted into one local bar, it was packed, a game of football was on television; an international match between South Africa and Zimbabwe. It was lively, putting it mildly. And I realised everybody was shouting on the opposition, who eventually scored to much cheering.

I spent some of the time away from the conference. It reminded me of the TUC annual get-together, power-broking and infighting and having to shake hands with people you hate, or vice versa. And as far as I could ascertain the ANC people taking to do with arts and culture regarded the Arts Council of Great Britain as *the* model – and not of what to avoid at all costs. It was disappointing. Among the people I met there was a sense of foreboding about the bureaucratic structures in preparation. The wheeling and dealing were evident and some of the younger township delegates were not invited into certain meetings. And there were far too many people in suits, shirts and ties.

One place I ended up was for the launch of an anthology of poetry by 'street-children'. Some of these 'street-children' had been brought in to perform extracts from the book. It was extraordinary. But nobody burst out laughing. The people I was along with took the proceedings with equanimity, more than I can say for myself, smoke coming out the ears, etc. But they were only there to fill the pockets with as much booty as possible. It reminded me of my days

8

as a young writer at Arts Council receptions in Scotland, trying to walk out with full half-pint tumblers of whisky concealed about your person; napkin-covered chicken legs stuffed into the good flannels; handfuls of fucking sherry trifle fucking dumpling and ice cream. That Johannesburg launch was full of representatives from one of the biggest banks in Africa, sponsors of this anthology of 'street-children's' poetry; all these seven-foot tall white men and women, in the name of god, one had to get to fuck, shouting about how I might be white but for fuck sake I wasnay seven foot, no even in high fucking heels. I did meet another person from Glasgow at the conference, a young woman representing her branch of the Anti-Apartheid movement; she had the good sense to spend most of her time with the younger township delegates.[11]

Until the Sharpeville massacre in 1960 the focus of the liberation struggle in South Africa had been on campaigns of non-violent resistance. At Sharpeville 'seventy five members of the South African police force fired about 700 shots into the ['perfectly amiable'[12]] crowd, killing sixty-nine Africans and wounding 180. Most of them were shot in the back.' The Pan-Africanist Congress of Azania as well as the ANC became outlawed thereafter, and 'new strategic perspectives were imperative'.[13] Comrade O.T. put it another way: 'There can be no compromise with fascists.'[14]

The South African Communist Party had been banned since 1950 and it and the ANC now strengthened links. A year later its 'leaders . . . formed a military organisation known as Umkhonto we Sizwe [MK] "to carry on the struggle for freedom and democracy by new methods"'.[15]

There are many people who feel it is useless and futile for us to continue talking peace and non violence against a government whose reply is only savage attacks against an unarmed and defenceless people.[16]

In response to this development of the liberation struggle the white racist regime stepped up its campaign of terror and oppression and 'its utilisation of emergency military and police powers . . . marked the beginning of a new phase in South African politics.'[17] Within three years security forces had captured and jailed seven leading figures. This took place at a farm in the suburb of Rivonia, not far from Johannesburg; the captured figures included Govan Mbeki, Nelson Mandela and Walter Sisulu.[18]

It was a massive blow to the liberation movement, one from which it did not recover for many years. Thousands of people were forced into exile, among them Alex La Guma. He had engaged actively in politics since the 1950s and, following five years' house arrest and bouts of imprisonment without trial, he left the country. From that period and until his death in Cuba in 1985, he worked on behalf of the ANC; in between times, where and when possible, he engaged as a writer of fiction.

The old myth that 'there is no racism in Scotland' has been revealed as a lie on so many occasions that not even politicians use it any longer. That was not the case a dozen or so years ago when occurred the horrible and cowardly murder of a young black man. This was in Edinburgh near to where the great socialist James Connolly had been born. The man's name was Ahmed Shekh, a 21-year-old Somalian student who had managed to escape from the horrors happening in his own country. Instead of finding sanctuary in Scotland he was killed by racists. He and a Somalian friend were attacked and stabbed by a group of about ten white men, only two of whom were later arrested, later acquitted.

A march and demonstration took place in his memory and to protest racist violence. What was becoming clear was the extent of the racism not only in Edinburgh and Lothian Region but throughout Scotland.

This all took place before the closure of the Citizens' Rights

Introduction

Office but it now seems clear that the few paid and unpaid workers, giving strong support to asylum seekers and other victims of racist violence, were doing their work rather too diligently for the local politicians. A few 'elected members' within the Labour-controlled Lothian Regional Council became uneasy, not with the reality of racist violence in Edinburgh, just the fact that the public were being made aware of it. They 'instructed the Social Work Department . . . to undertake a review of [the] work' done by the CRO.

Now followed widespread news of another racist assault, this one on three Asian men in the neighbouring town of Livingston. CRO workers gave support to the family and with other supporters tried to organise a public meeting around the issue. The police and local politicians were opposed and tried to talk the family out of it. A Labour Councillor made a formal complaint to the Director of the Social Work Department, that involvement of CRO workers in such a matter 'might . . . prejudice the improvement of race relations in Lothian'. What happened afterwards, to the shame of the Labour group, not only did they get rid of the 'overly diligent' workers, they closed down the entire Citizens' Rights Office. Of course this practice is consistent. Historically the victimisation of those who go to the aid of racist victims has been the second move adopted by authorities in the so-called bid to stamp out racist violence. Move number one: Appease the Racists.

Most campaigns fail. But what does it mean to win? All campaigns concern miscarriages of justice in one sense or another. They can involve the worst sorts of brutality. In many instances 'to win' a campaign is simply to have acknowledged by those in authority that a miscarriage of justice has occurred.

In Scotland, amid the civic celebrations surrounding Glasgow's winning purchase of the 1990 European City of Culture award, a number of people had shown solidarity to a campaign located in

West London. This was the Sekhon Family Support Group that formed on 11 November 1989, the day after the murder of Kuldip Singh Sekhon. Sekhon was a young father of seven children; one of the legions of low-paid workers who keep London's Heathrow Airport in business. In what spare time he had he drove a mini-cab in the West London area. It was while driving his cab that he was murdered. This case forms the basis of 'ATTACK NOT RACIST, say police', elements of which I used for various talks and discussions in the early 1990s, one I remember was a fringe meeting of NALGO trade-unionists.[19]

It was the *Scotland on Sunday* newspaper that commisioned the article by me on the closure of the factories at Ravenscraig, finishing off the steel industry in Scotland for ever. What happened is that I disapproved of the 'edited' version printed in the newspaper and, in order to counter it, I published *Fighting for Survival: the Steel Industry in Scotland* privately, in pamphlet form.[20] I wrote a Foreword and also a sort of endpiece. It should be self-explanatory.

'Philosophy and a European City of Culture' was written in 1989 and published in the *Glasgow Herald* as part of a campaign to stop the closure of the Philosophy Department, a sub-section of the Department of English at the University of Strathclyde. It can be asked why I would consider publishing something in a newspaper that I knew to operate in the typical shoddy manner outlined earlier. But when involved in a campaign I regard myself as part of a team whose object is to achieve justice on the particular issue and any individual contribution I make should be to that end, and that sort of personal compromise can be necessary. The campaign to stop the dismissal of the philosophy section was organised by a group of students and a senior lecturer, the late Hywell Thomas. I had attended Hywell's classes a few years earlier. He was a good fellow, and not scared of commitment. The outcome to the campaign was not successful and the students at Strathclyde University no longer have the option of studying philosophy to the degree level.

In 1988 I was asked to review *The Chomsky Reader*,[21] a selection of the writings of the most famous western philosopher of the present era. Back in the mid-1970s I had read some of Professor Chomsky's work in linguistics and philosophy of language as part of a degree course. If I had any criticism of *The Chomsky Reader* as an introduction to his writings it was the absence of that 'technical' side of it. As well as referring to the 'absence', my intention was to indicate some of what the 'technical' side of it might amount to, given that I was reviewing the book for a general readership. But in the early stages I was diverted by articles being published by the *Edinburgh Review*[22] on 'the distinctive Scottish tradition in philosophy'. I explored more on this, especially the work of George E. Davie. Elsewhere Davie tells of his

> Indian colleague at Edinburgh University who was very amused to find that the students in Indian Universities would all know, at least, the names of the famous Indian philosophers, if nothing else, but he had tested his students in Edinburgh and the names of the local philosophers, David Hume etc., meant nothing to them – Adam Smith they had vaguely heard of. But still, traditions can be a dead weight and it's maybe an advantage in Scotland that they hadn't bothered about traditions, that they had to start afresh, although this often meant they did the same thing again and again.[23]

Here in Glasgow during my three-year period at the University of Strathclyde the Scottish philosopher I recall being asked to examine was David Hume. The 'distinctive Scottish tradition' is said to have arisen in opposition to Hume's scepticism but the only side of the argument to be studied seriously is that of Hume. It is the only side of the argument to be studied at all, never mind seriously; there is no context as such, we must read Hume in reference to Descartes, Hobbes and Locke, etc.[24]

Hume's main rival of the day was Thomas Reid, Professor of Moral Philosophy at Glasgow University, whose advocacy of natural judgment seemed exciting to me, offering a philosophy of Common Sense without having to rely on innate ideas. It was also interesting that the focus on such matters 'coincided' with a spread of learning; an exchange and dissemination of knowledge, and a general rise in creativity, particularly among working-class people with a bit of time to spare, e.g. weavers. Inevitably, it was a time of social unrest, something with which I had been familiar, having researched the period for a play based on the lives of two weavers murdered by due process of the British State.

It took me about six months to finish writing the 'review' which I published as 'A Reading from Noam Chomsky and the Scottish Tradition in the Philosophy of Common Sense'.[25] In the meantime I sent copies of George E. Davie's work to Noam Chomsky; he seemed unfamiliar with it and I thought it would interest him. When he came to London to give a public lecture at Battersea Town Hall I wrote on behalf of the Free University Network to ask if he might travel north to give another in Glasgow. If it was possible we could work out the finer details later. His diary was full (he operates two years in advance) but he kept the request on file. A couple of months later he made contact; due to a cancellation he would be able to make the trip in a year's time.

Among other invitations to Scotland, Professor Chomsky had received one from Derek Rodger, editor of the now defunct *Scottish Child* magazine. Chomsky suggested we combine our efforts and we did. The *Scottish Child* initiative countered that of the Free University Network,[26] being rather less oriented toward anarchist politics and the philosophical context; and between the two groups we organised a two-day event in February 1990 entitled the Self-Determination and Power Event.[27] Noam Chomsky was the main speaker but George E. Davie also featured. It sold out all 300 places four weeks in advance. We received enquiries from all over the place and people travelled to Glasgow not only from different parts of the UK but from as far afield as Leningrad (three writers from the 1981 Group), Lithuania and Estonia.

There was criticism over the staging of the event, criticism too of the programme, and of participants, and so on. Hostility came from the political left and political right. Within the orthodox left the tendency is to attack any philosophy that hints of 'human nature' on the grounds that it leads to hierarchy and inequality. The Scottish Common Sense tradition certainly pushes towards a view of 'human nature'; it was always based on the notion that people think for themselves. It is not only the 'right wing' who regard the latter 'notion' as subversive.

One of the undercurrents of the hostile reaction from critics who did not attend the two days was its unofficial, non-academic structure. No doubt a few university people would have considered themselves 'Chomsky experts'. And now, right under their noses, not only had a motley crew of non-academic political misfits the temerity to invite Professor Chomsky, he had accepted the invitation. (Perhaps the nature of the 'motley crew' was a primary factor in why he had accepted the invitation in the first place.)[28]

The obvious problem for readers approaching 'There Is a First-Order Radical Thinker of European Standing Such That He Exists' is that few will have read the critique that provided the impetus. It appeared in a Scottish literary magazine a couple of years after the Self-Determination and Power Event took place. It was written by Kenneth White, a Scottish poet and academic who has lived and taught in France for more than thirty years. Not only did he not attend the conference, he admitted in the essay that he had not known of its existence until months later. It was a surprise that he attacked the event and its organisers at all, let alone so publicly.[29]

I tried to respond to the attack in a straightforward sort of point-by-point manner but I found it difficult. Here he was condemning an event without knowing properly what it was about. Maybe he thought that the organisers should have consulted him before staging the thing, or else he was just huffy – which was the case with other academics – and believed that such an event could not exist validly in the absence not so much of his physical presence but of his intellectual and spiritual aura. Or maybe if he truly believes that a worthwhile Scottish event is possible, that its only authentic location is someplace else in the world, anyplace else, preferably attended by people who are not Scottish, or who are but nowadays live abroad. No matter, his prejudice was revealed in his contemptuous attack on the work of Thomas Reid and his apparent ignorance of the outstanding contribution by James Ferrier in the context of the work of Edmund Husserl, the very man selected by White as the rod with which to beat the Scottish tradition.[30]

I was involved with the campaigning group Clydeside Action on Asbestos for a couple of years and of that I worked on a full-time basis for more than a year. I wrote much in a variety of areas during the period. The two pieces collected here were written in the space of a few weeks in the late summer of 1992. The main section of the first essay, 'Scottish Law and a Victim of Asbestos' was written for publication in September 1992 by the *Glasgow Herald* and concerns the fight for justice by Pat McCrystal, a fine man who had been poisoned by his employers and was dying of mesothelioma.

The essay opens with a Foreword which is based on the press

release put out prior to the day his case was due to be heard at the High Court in Edinburgh. The Postscript is based on the press release furnished at the time of his death. From diagnosis of his condition in February 1992 he undertook a cancer diet quite strictly and survived until a year later, which is longer than normal for a male, by some 80 per cent. The life expectancy of a male is less than six months from diagnosis, nine months for females.

When the article appeared in the *Glasgow Herald* describing his fight to get his case heard in court his union, the GMB, attacked me in the letters page as did the firm of lawyers who had acted on behalf of Pat McCrystal. He had been a GMB member for about fifty years. Apart from one solitary letter from an ex-shipyard worker from Clydebank who was also dying of mesothelioma, the *Glasgow Herald* did not publish any of the letters in support of the fight. The lawyers also attacked me personally in particular for the use of the phrase 'gun held to my head'. But it was to myself Pat made the statement and I stand by it now, as I did then.

Next follows 'Justice Is Not Money', a piece I prepared for an Emergency General Meeting of Clydeside Action on Asbestos.[31] Soon after the EGM began, one of our members collapsed and died. Some of the circumstances surrounding the tragedy I hope will become clear in the essay's Postscript which I wrote originally for publication in *Blow Out,* the journal of OILC, then outlawed trade union of offshore oilworkers. *Blow Out* was the only media organ – apart from *The Keelie* [32] – that took regular reports from Clydeside Action on Asbestos. As with some other pieces I wrote at the period, I published pseudonymously, in *Blow Out* under the name of 'Alex Smith'.[33]

In 1990 I produced 'Say Hello to John La Rose' for a collection of writings being gathered in tribute to the Trinidadian poet, publisher and activist. In it I try to indicate the importance of his contribution to British society for more than forty years. The anthology was edited and produced without his knowledge by Roxy Harris and Gus John.[34] These two, with John La Rose and Ian Macdonald QC,[35] travelled north and played a crucial part at the Self-Determination and Power Event.

It was at the invitation of John La Rose I had given a reading of my work at the 1989 Radical Black and Third World Bookfair down at Camden Town Hall.[36] Members of the Free University Network organised a bookfair in Glasgow in 1992. In 1993 and 1995, in association with the London original, a few organised the Scottish Radical Black and Third World Bookfairs.

My review of Anne Walmsley's seminal work, *The Caribbean Artists Movement 1966–1972*[37] was written for *Variant* magazine. I found the book an exciting read and wished I had known of the existence of such a tremendous alternative to the mainstream arts and literary scene back when I was living in London. The three founders of the Caribbean Artists Movement were E. K. Brathwaite, Andrew Salkey and John La Rose. I was asked to interview the latter for a future edition of *Variant*. Malcolm Dickson was editor at that time and we travelled down to London together. The interview took place in John's house in Finsbury Park. Malcolm organised the recording apparatus and he also jumped about taking photographs. Having been in the company of John La Rose quite often by this time, the only plan I had was to start him talking. Once begun he would go where he wanted and return near enough to the starting point, as long as I did not interefere too much. A reduced version of 'An Interview with John La Rose' was published in issue 16 of *Variant*, in the spring of 1994. It was our intention to publish the whole as a pamphlet but it never happened. John has agreed to it appearing in its entirety now and I thank him and Malcolm.[38] So many people are unaware of the historical depth of the struggle of black people in this country, and reading this transcription of a talk by John La Rose allows an insight into the richness of the Caribbean side of its social and intellectual tradition, a further insight into the inseparable nature of the cultural and the political.

I was in my late teens when I began reading Kafka and twenty-one when I made my first attempt at *The Castle*. I remember how it came about. The book was the Secker & Warburg 'definitive edition' published in 1953. I borrowed it from the library of the old Regent Street Polytechnic in London. It was the very first day I ever got the membership or whatever, and from the same place on the same day I borrowed Part One of *Swann's Way*; Volume One of Marcel Proust's *Remembrance of Things Past*. I was unemployed, signing on at the labour exchange office on Penton Street, and living just off Gray's Inn Road. In those days I walked everywhere. On my way home from the polytechnic the route brought me right along Oxford Street and on to Theobalds Road where there was a library of which I was also a member. I entered and borrowed *The Myth of Sisyphus* by Albert Camus. I had been reading Camus since my late teens, which was not the case with Proust. Part One of *Swann's Way* was my first and only attempt to read his work; perhaps that particular translation is not so good, so far it has put me off completely.

'A Look at Franz Kafka's Three Novels' began as a dissertation towards a degree at the University of Strathclyde. I had returned after a gap of five years to complete the course. My true objective was not so much to achieve a higher degree but to bring my novel *A Chancer* to completion with less economic hardship than otherwise. This year as a full-time student would allow me the necessary time and the Government grant towards study the necessary financial assistance to that end. Returning to university also meant I no longer had to register unemployed and that in itself was a relief. The Government students' grant was minimal but paid more money than unemployment benefit, augmenting the earnings of my wife, Marie, the major bread-winner in our partnership for almost all of our working lives.

Without doubt doing this year as a student made the difference to finishing the novel. It had been driving me nuts for ages. I began work on it around the age of twenty-four. It underwent various drafts, versions and rewritings until finally it was fit for publication in 1985. That was one year after my second novel, *The Busconductor Hines*, had beaten it into print. 'A Look at Franz Kafka's Three Novels' was never finished as far as I was concerned but throughout the years I could not summon the strength to get to work on it properly. I also was aware that to become involved in something more than a revision could lead to a reworking of the whole thing and that was to be avoided at all costs. I would have failed, I would never have finished the damn thing at all.

In recent years have come attacks on particular areas of contemporary Scottish literature by a few Scottish academics, Scottish Arts and cultural officers, Scottish media, Scottish politicians and on occasion formations like the Scottish Saltire Society. Unfortunately other writers and artists occasionally join in on the offensive. They adhere to the concept 'patriotic front'. In common they double up as voluntary workers on behalf of the Scottish Tourist Industry and attack people for letting the side down. Like many another artist one just gets fucking sick of it. Out of one bout of irritated frustration in the mid-1990s I wrote 'Social Diversity and the New Literary Order'. I intended publishing it under a pseudonym, using some upstanding Scottish protestant 'Brit' appellation:

Fergus Strachan, critic and poet; pen-name of Dr Patrick Noonan, specialist in contemporary English language literatures; educated at Glasgow's Strathclyde University, St Andrew's University, University of Ulster and Christ Church, Oxford; joint Shell–BP and British Council-funded professor at the Mosul-based British Institute for the Implementation of Linguistic and Cultural Policy.

Once I finished the piece I could not think of any place to send it, and so filed it away. When a new literary–political journal in Scotland was starting up the editors requested a contribution so I opened the file and sent it to them. Back it came. They said they were seeking something more political. Fair enough.

'Militarism and the City' was written for a talk delivered at a forum held at the University of Strathclyde in 1994, organised by students and members of the Revolutionary Communist Party (RCP). Many people on the left were wary of this group and thought they were just too well-funded. Similar comments have been made about the SWP and the WRP (and CPGB) at one time or another (which, in itself, does not mean suspicion is unwarranted). My own position is that if you are an invited speaker and have a proper platform for your own contribution then go ahead and make it.[39] In the process you can direct some of your contribution to the party members themselves. Similarly, if involved in a campaign and party members offer you support then take it, just ensure the people at the centre of the campaign retain control. Any party will try to hijack a campaign.

'Racism and the Maastricht Treaty' and 'Literary Freedom and Human Rights' were also written as talks, the former for a public meeting held in Edinburgh in 1992 to discuss some possible implications of the 'treaty'. It was organised by the Scottish Campaign Against Racism and Facism. The questions appended at the end were designed to be put to the audience once the discussion began, but I cannot remember ever putting them. The essay is here amended slightly, as is the other, and 'Literary Freedom and Human Rights', which I prepared as my contribution to a public debate organised by Amnesty International in Edinburgh, April

1995. It was in support of the Bangladeshi writer Taslima Nasrin, 'notorious' advocate of women's rights. A *fatwa* had been declared upon her in 1994 by religious leaders in her own country. *Time* magazine had quoted her comment that 'Koranic teaching still insists that the sun moves around the earth. How can we advance when they teach things like that?' In the same year she was accused of 'saying the Islamic holy book, the Koran, should be revised to give women more rights' but Ms Nasrin denied she had said any such thing.

Taslima Nasrin had travelled to Scotland to take part in the 1995 meeting. Also on the platform was Vincent Magombe, representing the PEN International Writers in Prison Committee. I have misgivings about some of these public meetings; often the reality of life in the United Kingdom is ignored, with no reference to the racism faced by thousands of people on a daily basis, nor to the outrageous and shameful treatment of asylum-seekers and refugees once they reach 'safe havens' such as Wales, Scotland and England. (Does the British State argue that 'safe havens' exist in Northern Ireland?) Shortly before that meeting I had taken part in another one in Edinburgh, also organised by Amnesty International but in support of Ken Saro-Wiwa, then held in detention by the Nigerian authorities. Seven months later the Nigerian authorities murdered him and seven other activists. Could the United Kingdom and the United States of America have exercised sufficient leverage to prevent it happening? It would be surprising if the answer to that was 'no' and by their ommission to act appropriately, both countries surely colluded in Ken Saro-Wiwa's murder.

The Nigerian writer was alive when the meeting took place on behalf of Taslima Nasrin. While she was in exile in Sweden she continued to speak out and in one lecture delivered in Ireland she discussed the role of the State in relation to the violence perpetrated against women. Later she was able to return to

Bangladesh but then in 1999 she 'fled the country for the second time'. It had been made public that $5,000 would be paid 'to anyone who killed her'. Around the same period her friend Shamim Sikdar, a sculptor and teacher at Dhaka University, had to seek 'police protection after *Islamic extremists* denounced her work and threatened to torture her to death.' The italics are my own, to emphasise the phrase 'Islamic extremists'. When the *fatwa* was declared originally on Taslima Nasrin, those responsible were not being described as 'Islamic extremists', instead they were said to be 'religious leaders'. Phrases like that can be useful cover. But no doubt Shamin Sikdar is another 'notorious' advocate of women's rights. The murder threats against her followed an exhibition of her sculpture which 'featured Bangladeshi women who fought for the country's independence against Pakistan in 1971.' The point has been made in the past, that no matter the religion, the first attack by any fundamentalist is on women.

In Scotland support for the Stephen Lawrence Family Campaign for justice started from October 1993 when the Artists in Solidarity (AIS) network organised an anti-racist benefit night in a Glasgow lounge bar. Musicians and writers performed that evening. It was a joint benefit, designed to bring publicity in Scotland not only to the Stephen Lawrence Family Campaign but to the Monitoring Group based in Southall, Middlesex in acknowledgment of their outstanding work on behalf of the hundreds of people they have supported over a long period of years.

AIS was a non-aligned body of artists and activists that came together in support of a number of campaigns over the years, e.g. against asbestos-abuse, in support of the Timex workers in Dundee; the Leland Daf workers in Glasgow, the unemployed workers based at the Autonomous Centre in Edinburgh. Such benefit nights were important for different reasons, not least to give the folk involved in the campaign a night out. AIS was anti-racist and non-sectarian not 'broadly' but as a premise of its existence. When in March 1994 my novel *How late it was, how late* was published we held the launch at the Dominion Centre in Southall. It was organised by local people as a benefit night for the Stephen Lawrence Family Campaign and the Monitoring Group. At the same venue four years earlier there had been a memorable occasion in support of the Kuldip Singh Sekhon campaign and to mark the eleventh anniversary of the murder of Blair Peach.[40]

For the March 1994 event many writers and musicians took part. A bus was hired to bring people from Glasgow; around forty travelled south. The media took no notice at all although full press releases had been dispatched. We expected some reporter or other to have made a story out of why a full coachload of Glaswegians was journeying to Southall for the launch of a novel; that coupled with the line-up of performers – surely something! Not a peep.

Among those listed to perform that evening were the South African writer Mandla Langa, the Lebanese poet Kamal Kaddourah; Trinidadian John La Rose, Jamaica-born Linton Kwesi Johnson, the Indian poet Randhir Sandhu; and from Scotland James Ferguson, Karen Thomson, Margaret Cook and the Gaelic poet aonghas macneacail, with music by the Blues Poets, one of the best blues bands in Scotland. Doreen and Neville Lawrence were also present and Doreen spoke in the most power-ful and moving terms; at that time the murder of their son had received very little media attention.[41]

In July 1995 the *Guardian* published an early version of 'Into Barbarism'. Modified versions later appeared in the *Scottish Socialist Voice* and in the journals *Militant* and *Liberation*. This was a crucial period in the family campaign. The Committal Proceedings were about to begin at Belmarsh Prison in London and if the outcome was successful then at long last the men suspected of Stephen's killing would face trial. However, if that did happen there was a strong likliehood that HM Crown Prosecution Services would move in to prosecute the case. The Lawrence Family Campaign was opposed to that and 'Into Barbarism' was an attempt to back that position.

The fact that the Committal Proceedings were happening at all was a positive step. As a member of the Scottish support group I travelled down from Glasgow to be there at 9 a.m. on Wednesday 23 August, the opening day. I was supposed to speak at the campaign meeting organised within the grounds of Belmarsh Prison where the proceedings took place. No one could predict just what would transpire on the day itself, not even the intermittent heavy rain, and the meeting took place under canvas. I had prepared a talk for roughly fifteen minutes but on the day, during a downpour, confined my contribution to less than five minutes.

Belmarsh is the top-level security prison in London and a trial of so-called IRA 'terrorists' was in progress. Different courts are housed inside the complex and 'high-risk' prisoners can be escorted on foot from their cells to the dock. There is no public transport to the prison which is located out in the wilds, beyond Woolwich and right the way across London in the diagonally opposite direction from the Southall office where the Lawrence Family Campaign then had its little office space. Obviously the location of the prison makes things extremely awkward for relations and friends. I suppose all the awkwardness is intentional. It is virtually impossible to get there other than by taxi if you do not have your own transport. I travelled with friends from Southall on the first day and on the trip home, driving west through Earl's Court I noticed it had taken us an hour and a half, and from there it would be a further forty minutes or so, thus the return trip amounted to more than four hours.

The Lawrence Family Campaign's legal team was not used to the role of prosecution; on the other hand it meant they were well aware tactically of how to play the defence counsel. In solidarity with the family, members of other campaigns attended the opening day at Belmarsh Prison, including the family of Joy Gardner. The revised version of 'Into Barbarism' also focuses on this case. People in the United Kingdom had been sickened by its horror. The brutality used on this woman, the inhuman treatment; it was shocking, people found it hard to cope. These individuals who were employed to so act on behalf of the British State had no regard for her humanity whatsoever, trussing her like an animal, 'while her five year old son Graeme looked on. She collapsed and . . . died four days later as a result of brain damage.'[42]

There is an extensive roll-call of black people killed at the hands of white employees of the British State.[43] Not long before had been the 'unlawful killing' of Shiji Lapite inside the notorious Stoke Newington police station, strangled or asphyxiated, following 'his arrest by two plain-clothes policemen'.[44] Stoke Newington police station has an appalling record of racist violation and the catalogue of shame goes back more than thirty years.[45] The 'long history of corruption, racism and brutality . . . has seen officers jailed for involvement in drug dealing and even stealing property from corpses.' A picket of the police station was organised by Shiji Lapite's family and friends. It so happens that members of the Hackney Community Defence Campaign were going to attend the picket. Prior to this they had 'carried out extensive investigations into corruption at Stoke Newington police station.' But now, the very night before the picket, their premises were broken into and 'burgled . . . The Hackney Community Defence Campaign members suspect that the Special Branch (or MI5) was responsible . . . '[46]

On the day the Committal Proceedings began my other intention was simply to pay heed and try to record what went on around. It would be of value for people just to know more of what it is like to be present at certain events, demonstrations, marches, picket-lines, protest meetings, etc. Obviously the police and other State agencies do record such stuff. Whether or not this is with a view to furthering the cause of justice and truth I cannot say, maybe somebody should ask.

One example of the police in recording mode occurred in relation to 'the first person to die [from] the . . . new US-style long-handled batons.' He was Brian Douglas, a young black man. The Metropolitan Police gave him a beating with 'the . . . new US-style long-handled batons' then left him in a cell 'for fifteen hours. He was taken to hospital, slipped into a coma and (despite being visited by four doctors while in his cell at the police station) died five days later.' There followed an inquest. A 'police consultative meeting' was arranged in Brixton so that matters could be discussed with the dead man's family.[47] But after their 'consultative meeting', members of the Metropolitan Police were caught making 'a clumsy attempt to covertly film' the family as they left the building.

Another young man, Wayne Douglas, no relation to Brian, died quite soon after in December 1995. This followed what appears to have been a savage beating by officers wielding 'the . . . new US-style long-handled batons'. In this particular case eyewitness reports indicate that Douglas, who was armed with a knife, was surrounded by fifteen policemen who were screaming at him to 'put it down, put it down'. Douglas threw the knife to the ground and was then allegedly attacked by a number of officers. The police treatment of Douglas was described as 'beyond belief' by one of several people who witnessed the incident. According to a PCA press release (5.12.95) 'he was found not breathing' in his cell an hour later.[48] None was ever prosecuted for these killings.

The security staff inside Belmarsh Prison did not allow anybody from the campaign meeting to enter the refectory to buy a cup of tea or whatever although supposedly it is 'open to the public'. I was there when they were asked why, but they would not explain why.

It seemed they had 'their orders'. They were fairly typical, as far as I could see, giving little nods to each other occasionally, designed that we might notice. I thought they were braced for confrontation. Someone commented that security at the entrance to the court was as efficient as an airport. If so, the airport would have been more akin to Belfast International than Stansted.

We can distinguish here between the police and the Belmarsh security staff. Outside the prison buildings it was the police who were on duty at the entrance and the area around the carpark. This was where the Lawrence Family Campaign had set up a marquee tent. The police did not show hostility that I saw, it seemed a different type of thing for them. If they saw the matter of the Committal and the presence of the campaign and support group as a problem then maybe it was a problem for the Crown Prosecution Service (CPS) rather than themselves. It was like they wanted us to know, or believe, that they had every sympathy with the campaign.

The public gallery is a wee room inside the court. It really is tiny, screened off by a form of reinforced or armoured glass and set high above the court itself. Numbers are controlled strictly. Security people and members not just of Stephen Lawerence's family but the families of the suspected killers were all crammed into that same wee room. The view is restricted badly and because of the reinforced glass sound is distorted. The stenographer's clack-clacking only adds to the difficulties. All that can be witnessed is the front third of the court, and we see the magistrate, the stenographer and a number of clerks. We also see the top of the barrister's head, whatever one is out giving the spiel. None of the suspected killers was visible, nor were any of the police.

If racial harassment was monitored properly by the relevant authorities, justice would be served more often. The 'People's Tribunal on Racial Violence and Harassment' took place in Hounslow, February 1996. I was invited to take part and finally undertook the role of Chairperson.[49] The Tribunal was organised to highlight the racial harassment endured by people in that and surrounding areas. There were submissions from families who had been subject to the worst racist abuses. Submissions also had been prepared by voluntary workers from the Monitoring Group in Southall, organisers of the Tribunal. Other submissions came from senior executives employed by the London boroughs of Hounslow, Ealing and Hillingdon, as well as from senior officers attached to the Metropolitan Police and the West London Office of the CPS.

But the experiences of the families giving evidence to the Tribunal made difficult listening. It was frustrating and hard not to get angry. People are living lives of unadulterated misery, their families are being attacked, they are threatened with being killed. They are being killed. What the hell is happening? Why is no one in authority doing anything apart from excusing their own laziness or inefficiency, defending their own acts or omissions? What are the police and the CPS and the politicians up to? Why are they pretending that it is not happening or, if it is, that the occurrences are extremely rare, and certainly never as bad as all the 'trouble-making politically motivated, politically correct do-gooders' like to make out.

During a coffee-break in the proceedings I was in conversation with a woman who voiced misgivings about the Tribunal and wondered if I thought the day's proceedings would prove other than meaningless. Even with the wisdom of hindsight, could I have given a satisfactory answer? Was the question itself unfair, misguided? If the Tribunal was to have any value it would be a while before that would be verified, probably a long while. Some of that value would lie in the work undertaken and accomplished by the individual panel members, how the 'findings' of the Tribunal were put to use, and so on. Whether or not the Tribunal would have any effect on the individual authorities taking part, e.g. housing, law, education, or if things might change in some other way, who knows. Like the police and the CPS, these authorities only do what they are forced to do. This does not mean they cannot be called upon to act. Of course they can. Mainstream channels have to be persevered with by somebody. And strategies such as lobbying your local Councillor, MP, or MEP; having petitions drawn up and signed by thousands of names, tens of thousands of names . . . Somebody has to get involved in that stuff. And some individuals do have the energy. But they are basic manoeuvres and take up much time and energy, far too much some would say, including the woman who voiced the misgivings. I would agree with her; there are more solid strategies. Surely nobody has faith in the political process any longer, no one involved in campaigning anyway. Sooner or later people in the black communities of this country, and most sections of the working-class, get that sort of naïvety knocked out them.

Bodies like the Southall- or Newham-based Monitoring Groups comprise a few individuals doing regular work, and most of them are volunteers. It is only through the personal will and commitment of individuals that something like the People's Tribunal on Racial Violence and Harassment in Hounslow happens at all. There was a great deal of work undertaken in preparation for the day's event and so much more work in the follow-up. In the struggle for justice people try all sorts of things. My essay 'Racial Harassment in the Community' is just part of that. There is no one way. It is by a range of actions that change can occur, through the common sense and energy of the individuals involved, based on past experience, direct and indirect; the knowledge gained via the trials and tribulations of other campaigning groups. The Lawrence Family Campaign had an extraordinary impact on this society for various reasons but it should not be forgotten that the strength of the campaign was also an expression of the political experience of the black and Asian communities, gained through struggle over a long number of years.

It matters not what powers are invested in the authorities if there is no will to change on their part; and commitment to change comes later. At the present time even statutory duties are evaded and no one has much power to do anything about that, even if they wanted to. There is little the public can do about any of it, except complain – officially that is: once you think of other methods you are on the road to reality, your own politicisation. It is better to act in the knowledge that change occurs as an effect of what happens at the bottom, from the bottom up. Those at the top only change when they are forced into it.

And this stuff about 'statutory duties being evaded' does not apply to the police. The police have no statutory duties. No doubt this applies in spades to the military forces, plus all the undercover security and policing agencies.

The next two essays relate to the plight of the Kurdish people, in particular their situation in Turkey. During the writing of this introduction some 2,000 Kurdish prisoners had embarked upon a hunger strike inside Turkish prisons and 54 had died (June 2001). It was a horrendous situation but news of it was curtailed by our mainstream media on behalf of their masters.

In 1997 Amnesty International invited me to attend the 'Freedom for Freedom of Expression Rally' in Istanbul, and report on it for them. Also present from the United Kingdom was the novelist Moris Farhi, a member of the PEN International Writers in Prison Committee, working on behalf of imprisoned writers throughout the world. Moris was born in Turkey and it must have been particularly difficult for him in the circumstances. We were among the twenty foreign writers making the trip to Istanbul; six were from Israel.

Turkey is run by the military and one surely is entitled to describe the country as fascist although the majority of the population in the UK seem in ignorance of the reality; a similar level of ignorance will apply in USA, given that

The vast majority of U.S. arms transfers to Turkey have been subsidized by U.S. taxpayers. In many cases, these taxpayer funds are supporting military production and employment in Turkey, not in the United States. Of the $10.5 billion in U.S. weaponry delivered to Turkey since the outbreak of the war with the PKK in 1984, 77% of the value of those shipments – $8 billion in all – has been directly or indirectly financed by grants and subsidized loans provided by the U.S. government. Many of the largest deals – such as Lockheed Martin's sale of 240 F-16s to the Turkish air force and the FMC Corporation's provision of 1,698 armored vehicles to the Turkish army – involve coproduction and offset provisions which steer investments, jobs, and production to Turkey as a condition of the sale. For example, Turkey's F-16 assembly plant in Ankara – a joint venture of Lockheed Martin and Turkish Aerospace Industries (TAI) – employs 2,000 production workers, almost entirely paid for with U.S. tax dollars.[50]

The Turkish State is backed not only by USA and its lackeys (e.g. the United Kingdom and Israel), collusion with the National Security Council – the military regime in control of Turkey – is rife throughout Europe, one effect of which is the difficulty in obtaining information. The south-east of Turkey is the north-west of Kurdistan but word from the interior is suppressed inside the country. In the United Kingdom it is impossible to obtain adequate news if you rely only on the mainstream media. Thus the level of ignorance among the population, although staggering, is unsurprising.

Introduction

The day after a young Turkish Kurd was murdered in a racist attack on the streets of Glasgow, the Turkish football team Fenerbahçe arrived at Glasgow Airport to play their UEFA Cup match at Ibrox Park. The television cameras reported the arrival on the BBC local news bulletin, and headed the programme with the demonstration by more than a thousand predominantly Kurdish refugees in the centre of Glasgow. Then cut to the Turkish football team and the Turkish travelling support at Glasgow airport, two separate pieces of news, and the impression given that Turkey is just an ordinary European country, that there is no possible link between it and the hundreds of thousands of Kurdish refugees across the world, not to mention the dead youth, murdered only three weeks after arriving in the country. And thousands of British football supporters travel to Turkish cities and tens of thousands of British families continue their sunshine package-holidays to safe resorts on the Turkish coast. And the curtain is draped solidly across the south-east of that same country to suppress all news of the horrors being perpetrated upon women, children and men, where

neither the right of law, human rights, nor democracy is adhered to. All that you see around you is fear and poverty. Every mountain every stone, swarms with armoured cars, tanks, those with rank and without rank, uniformed and plainclothed, thousands of security personnel bearing heavy weapons. It is nothing short of a complete war-zone.[51]

The primary purpose of the twenty foreign writers' visit to Istanbul was that we might present ourselves to the State Prosecutor with a 'Declaration of Crime!' in solidarity with the 184 people then being prosecuted by the State Security Court of Istanbul for doing precisely the same thing several months earlier, to highlight the case of the world famous Kurdish writer Yasar

33

Kemal who 'in January 1995 was tried in Istanbul's No. 5 State Security Court regarding one of his articles which was published in *Der Spiegel* magazine.'[52] Eventually Kemal was convicted of 'inciting hatred' and received a twenty-month suspended sentence. The UK media showed no interest whatsoever in this unique show of solidarity but inside Turkey itself the presence of the foreign writers at the Freedom for Freedom of Expression Rally was a major media happening. Not all twenty writers presented themselves to the State Prosecutor but the majority did so.[53]

Demonstrations and protests in Turkey are banned by the National Security Council (the military). The way folk get round it is to call a press conference and then throw it open to all; and everybody attends, including the security forces in full battle gear. At one such 'press conference' three to four thousand people were in attendance, including approximately two thousand heavily armed troops. 'The "Freedom for Freedom of Expression" Rally, Istanbul 1997' is a much-extended version of the report I wrote in the first instance for *Amnesty*.[54] The fuller version was published in *Variant* magazine; abbreviated versions of it and the following essay, '*Em Hene!*' appeared in *Kurdistan Report*, *Scottish Socialist Voice*, *Scottish Trade Union Review* and *Scottish PEN Newsletter*.

I prepared '*Em Hene!*' for a 1998 conference held in Germany, in Hamburg; organised by the Freedom for Ismail Beşikçi campaign on behalf of the writer and sociologist who has spent about fifteen years of his life in Turkish prisons for exercising 'the freedom to think'. The Turkish National Security Council does not concede such 'freedoms' to its general population and has regarded Beşikçi as its second most dangerous man. The one occupying prime position is Abdullah Ocalan, President of the Kurdish Workers' Party (PKK). Ocalan is held in Imrali Island prison off the Turkish mainland under sentence of death. How he landed there is a complicated story.[55] But according to an 'unnamed' representative of Turkey's most powerful supporter, the USA, 'We spent a good deal of time working with Italy and Germany and Turkey to find a creative way to bring him to justice.'[56]

Abdullah Ocalan offered his own account of his capture: 'that the NATO central headquarters had played the essential role in the conspiracy against him' and that 'Turkey did not have an important role'. When he landed in Kenya from where he was taken back to Turkey it was through the machinations of the Greek Government. The Greek Ambassador met Ocalan in Nairobi and told him, 'I was leading the NATO unit which had been after you for twenty years; while searching for you in the sky I found you in my hands.'[57]

At a more recent press conference, relayed by his lawyers to a press conference on Imrali Island prison, Ocalan spoke of

> the need to form 'democratic alliances' between political parties in Turkey not simply [towards] an election [but as] developed between various parties while Europe was in transition to democracy . . . [e.g.] England and Spain. A lesson must be learned from the solution of Scotland, Ireland, and Wales . . .[58]

In Turkey, for the advocacy of something as mild as that a person is little short of a rabid terrorist. Even to conduct a dialogue towards such a thing as the creation of a devolved parliament, the law would need to be changed, and even to refer to the situation of Scotland or Wales in relation to the plight of Kurdistan is a crime. 'Not one sentence can be uttered in defence of the Kurds, or of the Kurdish leader, without the charge of "separatism" or "terrorism" being levelled.'[59] That should indicate the farcical nature of the so-called trial at which Abdullah Ocalan, honorary chairman of the Kurdish National Congress, was tried as a criminal, found guilty and sentenced to death.

The exploration of the identity of the Kurdish people has been the lifetime work of Dr Ismail Beşikçi and for thirty years he has advocated their right to self-determination. In return he has received sentences of between 70 and 200 years' imprisonment by the Turkish military authorities. Another couple of years seems to get tacked on every week. His thirty-three publications are banned as 'thought crimes'. Beşikçi is one sort of academic. This essay features another sort. The 1999 launch of my collection of stories *The Good Times* was held as a benefit night for the campaign – in Glasgow and Edinburgh – to raise awareness not only of Beşikçi plight but of the factors governing his imprisonment. His publisher, Ünsal Öztürk, had just been released from prison and managed to come from Turkey for these events. He spoke at the Glasgow and Edinburgh events.[60] Events relating to the Freedom for Ismail Beşikçi campaign also took place in London and Wales.[61]

In 1998–99 I spent the academic year at the University of Texas @ Austin, and again during the spring semester of 2001. It came about through my acquaintance with Professor Mia Carter who was teaching my work on one course. I enjoyed Texas and in April 1999 travelled north to give a couple of readings in Dallas at the invitation of the poet and literary activist Robert Trammell.[62] I also agreed to give lectures on consecutive days to the students at Highland Park Highschool. 'When I Was That Age Did Art Exist?' is here revised from the original. The first part was written for an audience of 600–700 fourteen-, fifteen- and sixteen-year-olds; the second part was written for an audience of 500 sixteen-, seventeen- and eighteen-year-olds. A few parents and teachers were present on both days. Some of the first part I made use of with the older students and for the second part I borrowed from my essay ' "And the judges said . . ." '

I hope to have provided here an accurate background to the essays and talks; if there are mistakes I apologise.

"And the judges said . . ."

AT THE AGE of fifteen I had vague notions about art but it was music that excited me. We were listening to people like Buddy Holly, Fats Domino, Del Shannon, Chuck Berry, the Everley Brothers, and into my sixteenth year The Beatles exploded on to the scene, then bands like The Animals, Them, The Stones, and local bands doing similar stuff here in Glasgow, the Poets, the Blues Council, the Pathfinders and others. The major influence was blues but allied to this was country and western music. These musicians had a massive impact on Great Britain and Ireland during the late 1950s, early 1960s. They sang of their own existence, in their own voice, from their own emotion, whether rage, hatred or love. At the root of what they were about was self-respect, especially these great blues musicians, and they had assumed the right to create art. This I see as the essential thing the young working-class musicians in this country were learning. In literature if anything similar was taking place I knew nothing about it. I continued reading; aside from the lives of the Impressionists which I'll refer to later, it was mainly American literature. Stories about pioneering communities, gamblers and rounders; boys who liked horses and wanted to be jockeys or newspapermen; tramps, cowboys, gangsters; small towns and big cities. All were rooted in a life that was recognisable, more or less, the lived-in, the everyday.

One thing these fictional characters held in common was that they were not having the life snuffed out of them by an imposed hierarchy. It was a breath of fresh air. The English literature I had access to through the normal channels is what you might call state-education-system-influenced reading material. People from communities like mine were rarely to be found on these pages. When they were they were usually categorised as servants, peasants, criminal elements, semi-literate drunken louts, and so on; shadowy presences left unspecified, often grouped under terms like 'uncouth rabble', 'vulgar mob', 'the great unwashed'; 'lumpen proletariat', even 'riotous assembly' (an obscure hint that political activism by these lower-order beings was not unheard of).

Equally significant for myself was a strain in European literature that asserted the primacy of the world as perceived and experienced by individual human beings. These individual human beings were mainly government clerks or mixed-up members of some kind of minor land-owning class. It was a society far removed from my own, both in place and time. But for some reason, I could read the work of these nineteenth-century writers, mainly Russian, with a definite empathy. Gogol and Dostoevski made me chuckle in ways that seem a contradiction in respect of mainstream English literature. Irony requires some sort of a mutual recognition of selfhood, and I was not excluded from it. English literature did not allow this, people like myself were a sub-species and generally excluded by definition.

So it was from an admixture of these two literary traditions, the European Existential and the American Realist, allied to British rock music, that I reached the age of twenty-two in the knowledge that certain rights were mine. It was up to me what I did. I had the right to create art. Not that I thought in these terms, I just wanted to write stories. But I didn't have to write as if I was somebody not myself (e.g. an imagined member of the British upper-middle-

classes). Nor did I have to write about characters striving to become
other persons (e.g. imagined members of the British upper-middle
classes). I could sit down with my pen and paper and start doing
stories of my own, from myself, the everyday trials and tribulations;
my family, my boss, the boy and girl next door; the old guy telling
yarns at the factory; whatever. It was all there. I was privy to the
lot. There was no obligation to describe, explain or define myself
in terms of class, race or community. I didn't have to prove
anything. And nor did I have to prove anything about the people
roundabout me, my own culture and community. In spite of
dehumanising authority they existed as entire human beings; they
carried on with their lives as though 'the forces of evil' did not
exist. My family and culture were valid in their own right; this was
an intrinsic thing, they were not up for evaluation. And neither was
my work, not unless I so chose. Self respect and the determination
of self, for better or for worse. Most of this was intuitive, but not
all.

   It was the same existential tradition in literature that is also a point
of departure for some materialist strains of left-wing thought which,
ultimately, are as authoritarian as the right-wing. These ideologies
also debase and dehumanise individual existence, forcing people
into 'the scheme of things', not allowing them the freedom to live
as whole beings. Unlike fantasy and romance 'committed' artists
here reveal their commitment in their work – their particular form
of socialism or whatever – as a function of its representation or
approximation to 'the real world', i.e. naturalism, or 'social realism'
so-called. Stories, paintings, music, drama and so on are duty-bound
to concern 'the harsh reality', i.e. the effects of, and the struggle
against, the capitalist system. The central characters rarely have time
to tell a joke, fall in love, get drunk or visit the lavatory, although
sometimes they are allowed to visit museums, libraries and art
galleries, or do evening classes with a view to 'bettering' themselves.

The establishment demands art from its own perspective but these forms of committed art have always been as suffocating to me as the impositions laid down by the British State, although I should point out of course that I am a socialist myself. I wanted none of any of it. In prose fiction I saw the distinction between dialogue and narrative as a summation of the political system; it was simply another method of exclusion, of marginalising and disenfranchising different peoples, cultures and communities. I was uncomfortable with 'working-class' authors who allowed 'the voice' of higher authority to control narrative, the place where the psychological drama occurred. How could I write from within my own place and time if I was forced to adopt the 'received' language of the ruling class? Not to challenge the rules of narrative was to be coerced into assimilation, I would be forced to write in the voice of an imagined member of the ruling class. I saw the struggle as towards a self-contained world. This meant I had to work my way through language, find a way of making it my own.

When I was making my first stories it didn't occur to me that I was breaching linguistic and social taboos. My only concern was how to enter into my own world, how to make use of myself, my own experience, my own culture and community, and so on. Time was short and energy limited. I was having to earn a living; myself and my wife were bringing up two kids. So necessity informed my working practices, my creative methods. The problem of 'the blank page' or 'writer's block' only really arises when you have certain freedoms, perhaps essentially economic. Eventually I had as a project to write a group of stories set wholly in Glasgow, that self-contained Glasgow, not subject to the yays or nays of authority. I got into the habit of evaluating my own work, training myself to recognise when a story was finished as well as it could be finished, when it was working and when it was not working. I didn't need outside opinion, although when it came it was always welcome, even the first criticism of my work when I was about twenty-five, that I used 'the language of the gutter' and whereas I was free to do whatever I wanted I was certainly not free to thrust this language in the face of other people.

> And their judges spoke with one dialect,
> but the condemned spoke with many voices.

> And the prisons were full of many voices,
> but never the dialect of the judges.

> And the judges said:
> 'No one is above the Law.'[1]

There is a notion that art is sacrosanct and it is a dubious notion; there is also the notion that the practice of art is sacrosanct which is just nonsense. The only context in which it has meaning is political, it implies hierarchy, it assumes freedom for some and economic slavery for others; for some there is the luxury of time, not having to worry about how to get by in the world, you can be a free spirit, it is your right as an artist, you are set loose from the everyday trials and tribulations of an ordinary person because first and foremost you are not an ordinary person, with all the diverse responsibilities which that might entail, you are an Artist. It is part of the same myth, or disinformation, that as a young artist you should take it for granted that by working hard and by doing things properly economic necessity will be borne away, as if by magic on a high breeze – or perhaps on a mighty zephyr, us artists talk a different language from other people.

Maybe the only artists who ever talk about the sanctity of art and its practice in that manner either have a form of private income or are earning good money, perhaps by teaching art, or maybe they have managed to cut adrift of their adult obligations, perhaps by choosing to remain adolescents, perhaps by moving into voluntary exile, which is something most artists dream about at some point or another. It's better not to discuss artists who are forced into exile. In fact it wouldn't surprise me if the study of such artists is being withdrawn quietly from the national curriculum, if it was ever on it, since it might tempt students into pondering over the British State and its relation to people who try to seek safety in exile, asylum-seekers is what they are called.

A recent example might be Ken Saro-Wiwa, the Nigerian writer who was murdered by the Nigerian State authorities. I strongly recommend his work; read his novel *Soza Boy*, also what he says about his use of English in the author's note. Part of what the authorities found so objectionable was his commitment to his own culture, that of the Ogoni people. What would have happened if this artist had arrived incognito and unannounced in Britain seeking sanctuary to continue practising his art? Would he have escaped being sent back to the torturers and murderers, and been kept here pending a decision? Would he have survived the prison chosen for him by our Heathrow immigration authorities pending that decision? Or would he have been found dead in a British cell, suffocated in mysterious circumstances, cause unknown? Or would the Home Secretary and the British Government have made a special case for him because he was not only a well-known writer but supported by Amnesty International?

Imagine the education authorities did allow a proper study of the work of contemporary artists-in-exile, all those exiled in London at this very moment. Or better still, imagine the art establishment held a genuine Best of British art exhibition, open to any artist domiciled in Britain. Artists from the Middle East, Africa, the Sub-Continent, Turkey, Kurdistan, South-East Asia would all be eligible. I'm sure the specialist-art-authorities would have no hesitation in selecting the work on its merits. Would they have to conceal the difficult bits, the political bits? And the political bits can be the biographical bits, for the lives of these artists are themselves a political issue.

Of course us artists are not supposed to talk about political issues, we are too idealistic, we don't have a firm enough grasp on reality. We are supposed to leave that to the responsible adults, those who aren't artists. Obviously it's not only artists who are required by the State to be children, it applies across the board: as a working rule the only folk capable of making proper judgments are Cabinet Ministers, certain Members of Parliament and the House of Lords, certain members of the State and certain media-commentators. The rest of us allow our judgment to be impaired, clouded by sentiment, etc.

But being an artist is not a licence to remain an adolescent for the rest of your life. Some of the mythology surrounding art gives us to understand that a special case is made for those who create poetry, music, paintings, stories, drama, etc. – whatever the media – that artists are allowed to remain children. Either that or we are forced to remain children; it occasionally seems like this is what society requires of its artists, in one way or another, that we remain children. But I'm an adult human being and if I want to express an opinion then I'll express it. I'm not going to enjoy it if my opinion is downgraded simply because I'm a story-teller or artist. It's quite remarkable the different ways whereby the State requires its artists to suck dummytits, even when we're walking with the aid of zimmers; like kids we are to be seen and not heard.

Some of the points I'm raising here were never clearer than during the turmoil surrounding the European City of Culture carry-on here in Glasgow in 1990. This was a classic example of the exploitation of art and artists. The City of Culture Year remains a taboo subject if for serious study. One is not supposed to mention it seriously at all, just recall it hazily but with affection, as that strange time our ayn wee city of Glasgow made it on to the international map. Anything is justified because of that. Look at the publicity the city got. It was only a few years ago yet already it's a legend, a mythical kind of thing, mythical in the sense that it is not open to analysis, not available for critical examination, not then and not now. If you attempt such a thing you get called a boring spoilsport.

But it was definitely a classic exercise in respect of how art and artists are regarded by the authorities, with a mixture of contempt, distrust and fear. Once again we were children, usually spoiled brats. Those of us who refused to stand up and sing our party-piece for the visiting businessmen and other adults were sent to bed without a chocolate biscuit. The authorities were unsure how the visitors treated their own naughty children. However, some of them lost their temper and gave us a smack in public. The city's PR team, including most media commentators, responded in miti-gation, and with one or two exceptions they took great pains in pointing to how naughty we were, how sorely we had tried the patience of the adult authorities, didn't we appreciate the embarass-ment we spoilsports were causing? Surely we knew it was all for our own good, we didn't even have the wit to see this, not knowing which side our bread was buttered, how could we be so disloyal, but that's to be expected of artists, their selfishness is a byword, they luxuriate in their perpetual infancy, their rosy-hued idealism, meanwhile us adults must enter bravely into the real world, the world of the everyday, the world of compromise and necessity, if the good old adult authorities didn't get their hands dirtied why then all us artist-children would be in a right pickle and the amazing thing is we wouldn't even know it, because the world of adult authority is mysterious and secretive and beyond the ken of infants.

"And the judges said . . ."

There was another aproach to us artists, this one was utilitarian; it appealed both to our sensibilities and to our reasonableness. Okay the politicians and paid arts administration, the so-called cultural workforce, might make mistakes but it's always well-intentioned and in the interests of everybody, and come on for christ sake nobody's perfect. We all know how crass it all is but play along, don't rock the boat, you might get something out of it, some kind of commission maybe, a chocolate biscuit, a year's supply even, who knows, if not now in the long run, and if you don't maybe some other artists will, you might even know some of them.

In this scenario the then leader of the district council was portrayed as mister happy-go-lucky, a well-meaning kind of simpleton, but one who not only had a heart of gold, he was a patriot, he loved his Glasgow, he might make a wrong move now and again but it's all for the good of the cause, above all he loves his ayn wee city. And, okay, what if he is a philistine, at least he is of the unashamed card-carrying variety. And anyway, while we're on the subject, surely the preciousness and pomposity of artists need a good smack in the face now and again and this is what the leader of the district council is doing, he is showing all you artists up for the bunch of arty wankers you really are.

Yeah, that too was in there. We were being asked to show solidarity with the politicians and arts administration either because it was in our own best personal interest, the best interests of artists in general, or the best interests of the city itself. In this utilitarian argument art had nothing to do with it, art was kept out of it. And in a sense this was a paradigm of the City of Culture Year, art had nothing whatsoever to do with it. Never mind that it was precisely art as the product of individual people that was being highjacked and ripped off so mightily. The artists were being asked to conceal or disown their existence, all for the good of the cause. Part of the underlying thinking behind the authorities' strategy was that if such

45

a thing as art does exist then it certainly isn't being created in Glasgow although for some peculiar reason foreigners see things differently. I can't resist that classic line from the former leader of the Council, later recipient of Glasgow's highest office: I might not know what art is but I'll milk it for all it's worth.

It's always interesting to see how the various State authorities try to separate not only living artists from society but art itself. The educational system is one such authority, a crucial instrument of the State. Think of the resources, economic and intellectual, all that time and energy, being spent or wasted in spurious discourse, spurious activity. Areas of academic endeavour are actually devoted to theories of art where we learn that the text or artwork is all that matters, forget the artists who created the thing, their lives are unimportant, forget too the social conditions in which they worked, such things are irrelevant. When it comes to art with a capital A it makes no difference whether an artist is a multi-billionaire landowner or some poor bastard dying of malnutrition, let's examine the work. As responsible art critics we learn to establish proper criteria, criteria that are truly objective. (Note that art critics are typically responsible by definition.) As responsible and mature art critics we can award the artwork marks out of ten as a function of our unbiased and objective evaluative criteria; once we have done this we may wonder, if we are so inclined, whether or not the artist led an easy life, or if the soicety in which he moved was difficult or not, but it is unimportant, for we can both recognise and evaluate beauty wherever we find it, in a sewer or a gilded palace. All that kind of shit.

The fundamental issue concerns their own criteria. Never mind what they are, where do these 'truly objective' criteria come from. The thing is there are no ultimate evaluative criteria. It just seems that way, that there are criteria within society that somehow exist *a priori*, like god; unchanging, immutable, eternally fixed. And just like that whole set of priests, rabbis, mullahs and ministers these specialist critics and expert judges – those who bestow the final verdict – do so from a position of absolute authority. We have to take their judgment on trust, the validity of the criteria is not up for discussion. We are to have faith in the specialist art critics because their integrity is vouchsafed by an Unimpeachable Source.

But what is the source? Well, that should go without saying. If you persist in such questioning you show a marked breach of faith. There is a stage where even the most sceptical among us are obliged to bow the head not in sullen silence but in silent reverence.

The people who come armed with these special criteria always have the final word, because authority is invested in them. Aye but who invested authority in them? The wisest authorities in the land, a tiny but dedicated circle of men and women who are expert in every field imaginable, not only that but they have the qualifications to prove it. Aye but what qualifications? Many qualifications, a veritable plethora of qualifications. Who says so? And what kind of qualifications are they? Who do they 'show' them to? Where do they get them?

There was a minor furore in a West Highland town a few years back when they held a festival of The Best of British Music. The organisers were good at publicity and managed to get press releases carried in most of the national media. When the programme for the festival was released people up and down the country were amazed to find that only music composed by local musicians had been selected. That's right, with the freedom to choose from anywhere in the land the Best of British festival was entirely composed of musicians based in the town itself. This caused a real stramash. The national media arrived in force. They discovered the selection panel consisted of only one man, some local guy.

The pressure mounted till eventually it couldn't be ignored by the authorities; an enquiry was set up, headed by a committee of three 'specialist judges' from the art establishment department of music. What they wanted to know was firstly where the funding for this so-called national festival came: was it just local private money or did the cash come from the public purse, from the Scottish Arts Council or even god help us from the Arts Council of Great Britain? The next thing they did was find out about the local guy, the so-called judge. What were his qualifications and where exactly did he get them? Was it just some kind of music diploma from his local secondary school or what? They discovered he hadn't gone to the Royal College of Music in Scotland, never mind the one down in London, and when they went to examine his credentials they couldn't find any. Next they tried to examine the criteria by which the guy had arrived at his final selection but that proved impossible and what little they did pick up they just couldn't make head nor tail of them, the criteria the guy used. After that they had a quick listen to the selected compositions but that didn't help matters at all, most of it seemed to be 'West-Highland-town-type music', in the words of one of the specialist art judges. (He later apologised for his lack of clarity on that one but said he didn't know how else to describe it.)

Finally the specialist art judges approached the organisers and told them their man had no qualifications at all, they had checked his credentials, all of that, he just wasn't qualified, not only that but the guy had never been further south than Dalmally in his life, never more north than the Kyle of Lochalsh.

But the organisers defended their judge and insisted on the validity of the guy's selection, that it was both unbiased and objective. They backed him all the way. According to them he had a great ear and was scrupulously fair, it was traditional too, it ran in his family, his father and his father before him, they had been unbiased judges as well. And their township needs this kind of honest, unbiased criticism because it's also a port and ferries arrive daily, it's a cosmopolitan place. And then they flummoxed the specialist art judges; never mind his qualifications, they said, what about yours? I bet yous've never even been to the town. And they were right. None of the three 'specialist art judges' had ever set foot in the place although occasionally they flew over it on their way to art conferences in Canada or Iceland.

There was a similar sort of rumpus happened over an exhibition of Contemporary European Art which took place in France. This time there was a panel of genuine attested art critics making the selection. But the explosion here was that not one solitary piece of work by any living French artist was chosen. Imagine that, none of the art being created by the French community was judged good enough for the exhibition. It was extraordinary. It was said at the time by many French people that their country's art might not be good enough for Europe but it was certainly good enough for them. Never mind the European community they said, French art is good enough for the French community. But not everybody agreed, a few French art experts went along with the panel of judges and issued a statement to the effect that French artists should work harder in future so that they might bring their art up to scratch, scratch being the European standard, whatever that happened to be at the time.

I am a writer of fiction, of course, but here is another example that isn't fiction:

During the European City of Culture Year in 1990 there was an exhibition of British Art held in Glasgow. The director of museums and art galleries was responsible and he caused much controversy when he excluded the work of certain local artists. He is reported to have done so on the grounds that their work was not good enough.

A very interesting comment from someone holding such an office. Let's assume that his motives were unimpeachable and that he approached the task of selection in a scrupulously fair manner. Let's also assume there was no political pressure coming from the team at George Square, home of Glasgow City Council. Nor were there any sort of 'quota issues' involved, and I mean by this that if in the director's own considered opinion there had been no home-based artwork 'good enough' then nothing by the city's artists would have been chosen at all, as in the French example. As far as I know the possibility that he might choose nothing at all by local artists was not referred to by the director but in the context of this argument it is surely implicit, if not the argument is spurious. And we would just have to lump it. Top officials are often forced to make painful decisions which we might not like but which are always for our own good in the long run. It's no good us hiding our heads in the sand, if our art isn't good enough then why not admit reality and just try and improve it so that one day we can be acceptable at a national level. I mean I can imagine an exhibition of The Best of Contemporary World Art being held in Fort Worth, Texas where we find empty galleries, the judges having decided that none of the art submitted was of a high enough standard. Fortunately for the administrators of the European City of Culture, embarrassment was avoided: artwork by a couple of Glasgow-based artists was considered 'good enough' by the director.

Amid all the nonsense, I'm trying to draw attention to a couple of problems with these 'not good-enough' and 'best-of' arguments, that distinctions have to be drawn between the art of a community and the art of a community-at-large. I'm saying that the value of the art of a community seems to be a function of an extended community. We are forced to have our art evaluated relative to what takes place in this wider community. Our art is not judged on its own merits. Yet once we actually look at this wider community we find it isn't really very wide at all; in fact it's toty,

it's toty and it's exclusive, it's restricted to the values of the elite
group of people who form the controlling interest of this country.
What you find is that our society is premised on the assumption
that the criteria by which art is evaluated within this elite group are
the only criteria which truly matter. These criteria are the same
criteria by which all art thought worthy of the name is evaluated
throughout the entire country. Artwork from different cultures and
communities cannot have intrinsic aesthetic value. It may have
merit on a relative scale (which is minor by definition) but it has no
aesthetic value in its own right. Only when measured by the
standards of the elite culture, judged by its criteria alone, can the
artwork of particular cultures be awarded authentic value. Every
culture in the land is subject to it, subordinate to its standards,
controlled by those who are trained to affirm it, whether by birth,
adoption or assimilation.

But since this elite group controls most everything else anyway
it should go without saying. So much so that it's seldom said at all.
And only then by those outwith the controlling group; fringe
people, social misfits, failures, folk with chips on their shoulders;
conspiracy-theorists, provincials, racists, fundamentalists, nation-
alists, radicals, subversives, extremists, etc.

Obviously I'm not arguing that somebody who takes control of
a community's museums and art galleries must be born and bred
within the community itself. Nor am I even suggesting that s/he
has to have an intimate knowledge and understanding of a community's particular cultural traditions. The crucial point for
Glaswegians about the 'not good-enough' controversy was that
here we have somebody in charge of a community's museums and
art galleries, number one authority in control of the history,
traditions and cultural inheritance of the city, and he seems not to
understand, even intuitively, that aesthetic value is intrinsic to the
art of any community, any community at all. Enter another

hierarchy-based fallacy, that the artwork produced within one culture is superior to that of another. Now it might well be possible that the artwork produced by one culture is 'better' than that of another. That's fine by me. I'm wary of folk who adopt relativist positions; it usually means they won't take criticism. But what I do want to know is the criteria used to establish value. Surely it's not too much to ask of our finely matured art authorities.

Maybe people with an interest in other areas of Scottish life will see parallels. Why, for instance, is there no national theatre in this country? Is Scottish theatre not good enough to warrant such a thing? What do we mean when we say of a country that its theatre isn't 'good enough'? Is it possible for somebody brought up in Scotland to make such a statement? Maybe. I'm not saying it isn't, not necessarily, I just want to know about the criteria, what criteria are being applied, how is the evaluation being made, who the hell is making that judgment?

It became clear to me early on that writing stories did not offer a living, and no matter how much I resented this it was stupid to blame it on my partner. It wasn't her fault that the thing I gave most of my time and sweat to had no economic value. If I felt like changing the world then at the same time I would have to work it so that the burden of looking after the children didn't fall solely on my partner's shoulders. I didn't expect her to have three economic burdens, the two children and myself. And I remember discussing this many years ago with Tom Leonard and with Alasdair Gray, that if you couldn't be both a parent and a writer then maybe there was something wrong with being a writer. It's a perennial discussion for most artists.

The way I'm talking might sound like a denigration of art, it isn't. But we have to be able to see art in the context of society as it exists, that it cannot be separated from society. Art is not an eternal verity. Let us take it as given that life without art is so unthinkable that it may as well be a contradiction in terms of what it is to be a human being. But when all is said and done, art is created by human beings, by people; and people live in societies of people. I'm not speaking as an art historian but as a practising artist, a writer of stories.

I used to read the biographies of artists in my mid-teens, mainly the Impressionists. But it was the lives of these artists that eventually drew me to art as a maturing teenager, not the art itself. I thought Modigliani was great, he was a kind of hero. After that came his art, I looked at his art. I also thought Camille Pissarro was great, and this had nothing really to do with his painting, I didn't know it that well, it was because his home was a welcoming place. He was a generous man. Although older than the others he had no problem giving them support and a helping hand where possible. He and his wife had a pot of soup at the ready for the skint and hungry young artists of the community, including Cézanne, Van Gogh and Gauguin, and I think Utrillo when he was about sixteen or seventeen years old. As I have said elsewhere, I liked both Cézanne and Émile Zola and thought the discussions on art they had together must have been great. I was sorry about the violent quarrel they had and even though my sympathy went to Cézanne, I wanted to speak to him on behalf of Zola: 'If Émile is willing to forget all about it why can't you for christ sake Paul come on, shake hands, life is difficult enough.'

Obviously there is a romantic and I suppose sentimental side to it, but that's allowable, especially in adolescence. For several years I thought Turgenev was a stuck-up aristocratic mean-minded shit, and I didn't read him. Then at last I did read him, and found his work was great, why the hell was I so prejudiced! Dostoevski was to blame. I was so stuck on Dostoevski I had followed him blindly, even when he attacked Turgenev without telling me about his own gambling problems and how poor old Turgenev had loaned him dough till finally he couldn't any longer, and Dostoevski damned him for it. So I had graduated to a more mature understanding of the reality of that personal situation

I can't imagine somebody studying the life and work of Vincent Van Gogh and not being moved by it, not being outraged by the conventional view that suggests he was a kind of naïve idealistic madman. In spite of all that we know of the man's life the conventional view continues to be the premise, so that if we want to argue the point the burden of proof is on us. Why, why should that be? And we have a writer like Franz Kafka, we are to ignore the life of the man, we are to search his texts for its hidden mysteries, symbols and other coda about nightmare bureaucracies and despotic tyrannies as metaphors for this that and the next thing, including the immutability of a Christian god, given that Kafka was Jewish. We can involve ourselves however we like but rarely how it was to exist in Prague at the turn of the twentieth century, or the fact that the artist himself spent so much of his working time and energy trying to assist working-class people get their insurance claims settled through the various levels and rung upon grinding rung of State bureaucracy. How convenient for state authorities everywhere, that somehow or other whatever discourse there is via the normal media channels always seem to stop short of looking at the nature of society as lived in by the creators of art.

More recently, within the past fifteen years, I've come to see as exemplars artists such as the great Somhairle Mac Gill-eain (Sorley Maclean) who could not and would not be divorced from his culture, nor from his community. Throughout his life he fought all such nonsense, all such propaganda. Apart from his poetry he produced a classic work of criticism which is now out of print, a sad commentary on the current priorities of the arts establishment in Scotland. In one of his essays, entitled 'Is There a Hope for Gaelic?' he writes:

It is natural for a poet to love his own language if it is the language of his ancestors and dying, even if it were a poor defective thing. Gaelic is not a poor language, in art at any rate. Though it had only its ineffable songs, which cannot be put in other words, it would still be a priceless medium of expression. Therefore the Gaelic writer must be 'political', and in our day the teaching of the language is the prime business of its 'politics'.[2]

At the Booker Prize ceremony a few years ago I upset some people by what I was arguing, which was not a plea for separatism, nor for nationalism, nor for the world to recognise the supremacy of Scottish culture – all of which was reported by various media. Nor was it an argument in favour of the local at all costs, an acceptance of the mediocre just because it happens to be a home-grown product. I wanted simply to say that the existence of my culture is a fact and why should that be denied? It's an argument not for the supremacy of my culture, just for its validity and, by extension, the validity of any culture. There is no such thing as an 'invalid' culture, just as there is no such thing as an 'inferior' or 'superior' culture. What else is a culture but a set of ideas, beliefs and traditions held by any given community of people: a set of infinite extension, shifting and changing? Cultures will function in the same way as languages, not to mention the people who use them: unless dead they live. I'll end with a beautiful poem by Tom Leonard. It was my original intention to read this at the end of the Booker ceremony. Eventually I didn't. But I'll finish with it now:

Fathers and Sons

I remember being ashamed of my father
when he whispered the words out loud
reading the newspaper.

'Don't you find
the use of phonetic urban dialect
rather constrictive?'
asks a member of the audience.

The poetry reading is over.
I will go home to my children.

Elitism and English Literature, Speaking as a Writer

As a boy I was a great reader. I was lucky, there was a library at the bottom of my street in Govan, Glasgow, right in Elder Park. I started going along from the age of four with my big brother. There was no writer I enjoyed more than Enid Blyton and that lasted a couple of years. Then later there was no genre I enjoyed more than school stories and that went on until probably I was about eleven or twelve years old; the books featured different schools and different pupils but they all seemed related, and most seemed to be written by one author, Frank Richards. Those schools were upper-class sort of establishments.

It is a peculiar thing that children like myself could identify with the pupils in those schools. I mean it was inconceivable that I would ever in my life meet up with boys from my own background, my culture and life experience, between these pages. I'm not talking about Scottish kids in general I'm talking about Scottish working-class kids in general because it was possible to meet a scholarship boy or a boy from a colonial background, whether from Scotland or India or someplace. I cannot remember any African or Chinese boys making an entrance but perhaps it was possible, perhaps it did happen. These colonial boys would all be youthful aristocrats anyhow, back in their own country, even if they wore kilts, loin cloths or turbans, or whatever, they would be accepted as lower-rung aristocracy, and kids like Billy Bunter would give them the benefit of the doubt.

The English language as spoken by these young colonials always exhibited idiosyncratic mannerisms that were quite funny. They were exotic creatures and never made it as heroes in their own right. At the same time they were always supportive and loyal to boys such as Harry Wharton and Tom Merry. Kids like myself would identify with the last pair and other members of that regular cast of young English heroes, white Christians to the core. There was no chance of me ever making a hero out of the exotic young colonials, even if one did happen to be Scottish. At eleven or twelve years of age who wants to be an oddball outsider with no sense of style and a funny way of talking.

I had no real contact with literature while I was at school but outside of school hours I was reading various things, including adventure stories by R. M. Ballantyne. Then a major court case happened. It was a full-blown scandal to do with a novel, all because of language and sex, it was *Lady Chatterley's Lover* by D. H. Lawrence. I was fourteen. I went out and bought the paperback. My mother discovered it and burned it, but not before I browsed through some of it. Apart from a few wee juicy things I remember I was struck by the extraordinary use of language by the central male character, a salt-of-the-earth working-class country-yokel sort of guy; he used to go about saying salt-of-the-earth things like 'If thar shits and thar pisses'. I had never heard anything like that in my life, it was amazing; so that was how these salt-of-the-earth English working-class country yokels spoke! well well well. Yet, oddly, the language reminded me of the earlier school stories.

I carried on with my own reading, cowboy and private-eye novels by American writers, then branching out and from when I left school at fifteen, through the next four years, I must have devoured a great deal. One English writer I read was John Buchan.

He was actually Scottish, what you might call an assimilated member of British society. Probably that is what you would call him, British, an assimilated Scotsman. One shorthand definition of assimiliation is somebody who denies their culture. And a shorthand definition of Britain is Greater England; somebody who is content to be labelled a 'Brit' is a Greater Englander.

But perhaps it is unfair to say that someone like John Buchan denied his culture. He was an upper-middle-class guy who worked on behalf of the British Empire, and that was what he was paid for by the British State. He was very high up in Government and wrote novels in his spare time; *The Thirty-nine Steps* is one many of you will know, at least as a movie. His books are good adventure yarns, especially for the politically naïve and readers of a reactionary bent; anyone at all with a soft spot for imperial splendour. There's an entire genre of that kind of stuff. Perhaps the creator of Sherlock Holmes is part of it. Many academics and other literary critics argue that writers like Conan Doyle and Buchan should be treated with more respect. Writers of more recent generations, working in related genres and value systems, might include Ian Fleming, Frederick Forsyth and John Le Carré; others like John Grisham and Tom Clancy. I would not be bothered denying any of them was a good writer, at least not a bad writer, not unless I was pushed, but who cares. Nowadays there's a crowd of writers into that sort of right-wing secret agent stuff, CIA and MI5 heroes, high-flying financier heroes, quirky politician heroes, stalwart soldier heroes, blah blah blah.

In these genres 'white' and 'Christian' can be voiced utterances of approbation, e.g. 'His behaviour was exemplary, he was an absolute white man' or 'My horse has a wonderful temperament, he is a proper Christian.' Eventually the whole thing just done my nut. The heroes belonged to these incredible clubs that were extensions of boarding school, situated in secluded lanes around

London's West End, all with log fires and great wee libraries, and these plush, leather-bound armchairs in which crotchety old bods with handlebar moustaches would nod off in a corner over the *Telegraph* obituary columns. Certain villains might also be attached to such clubs, maybe by fraudulent means or through an administrative mess; these characters are always the 'masterminds' or 'evil brains' behind the villainy.

In such clubs there was always 'a man' to bring you a cigar and a large port or claret. It was always 'a man', never a servant. Not only did the 'man' call you 'sir' or 'lord', if not 'your Majesty', but he tucked you up in bed at night and then he came first thing in the morning and dressed you in appropriate clothes. As far as I know the monarchy still get that done for them, and not just the monarchy.

All the English heroes in that genre seem to have these 'men' in one guise or another throughout their lives, they get called various names, 'batman' for example. Maybe the young master has been a commanding officer in the armed forces and the guy now employed as his personal servant was formerly his 'batman' out in the Sudan or the Raj or the west coast of Ireland or islands of Scotland or someplace. Occasionally when a 'batman' exhibits obedience or devotion beyond the call of duty the young master will bring him home after the war to continue his personal 'batman' services. These 'servants', although they seldom get called that, can be from Africa or the Middle East, or the Near East or the Far East, they can even be indigenous Australasians. Any old outpost of Empire will do. Usually they exhibit quirky physical characteristics, or quirky behavioural patterns; these are both endearing and irritating. No matter where they come from the servants always exhibit peculiar speech mannerisms or patterns. If Scottish the 'man' will speak with what is called a 'heavy burr'. This is what the general run of lower-order Scottish people have in

English literature, 'heavy burrs'. The writers may highlight this within the text. Colonial servants and underlings are integral to English literature and different literary conventions exist to deal with them. One such convention is the apparent attempt at phonetic transcription; I mean by that the spelling of words to give an impression of sound. I say 'apparent' because there is no authentic attempt going on.

These servants and underlings do not have to be from so-called countries either, many of these so-called 'people' can be from provinicial locations much closer to Westminster and Buckingham Palace, they can be Cumbrians, Lancastrians or Yorkshiremen; they even can be born within hearing distance of Bow Bells; yes, a 'batman' can be Cockney, whatever, just as long as he is working-class, speaks funny and assimilates to the values of the ruling class, at the same time offering an unquestioning obedience to its individual representatives.

Although I still had not finished with its fictionalisation, by the time I turned nineteen I no longer identified with youthful members of the English aristocracy and upper-middle classes. This is not because I was growing up. Very many adults continue identifying with the English upper classes and the values of that culture right throughout their life. British society has been premised on that. I don't think that it is any longer, at least not to anything like the same extent, there have been a few changes in the last hundred years. There is no one reason why I gave up reading that fictionalised stuff, but I do remember one time in Manchester I was involved in some yarn with the usual upper-crust white Christian heroes. I was living in a lodging house and either I was unemployed or else working as a labourer in a Salford copper mill. It was a novel by John Buchan I was reading, one of an 'omnibus' collection. I just gave up halfway through, and that was that.

When I went to university I was twenty-nine years old and had published my first collection of stories nearly three years previously; and my second collection was due to appear in a few months' time. I had strong ideas about art: honesty, truth, integrity, justice, humanity; these were the marks of the artist. I use the term 'artist' here in its general sense; an artist can be a poet, a novelist, a sculptor, a dancer, a song-writer, a painter and so on. I felt uneasy when a writer I didn't think deserved to be called an artist was being described as 'good', and often 'major', by the academics. Even the fact that you were given such writers at university meant they were *assumed* to be 'good'. The lecturers and university authorities hold the power: they can say something is good without having to prove it. If you, as a student, want to deny that something is good then *you* are forced to prove 'it'. And proving anything is never easy. Atheists in the company will know what I'm talking about: it is never the person who actually believes in 'god' who has to find the proof, only those who don't. Proving something doesn't exist is harder than proving something does exist. Some of the greatest philosophers of the past three thousand years have been defeated by that. Anyway, at university I felt that if certain writers were going to be described as artists then something smelled about the very concept itself: art was just not as great as it is cracked up to be. So I wanted to distinguish between writers who were artists and writers who weren't artists; take for example the poet T. S. Eliot or the novelist Evelyn Waugh, both of whose elitism I rejected. Evelyn Waugh seemed to be so right-wing you'd be forgiven for calling him a Fascist. And how could you call a Fascist an artist? That struck me as by way of a contradiction in terms. Eventually I found it possible to say: here is a writer who okay might be 'good' but either s/he is a bad artist or s/he is not an artist at all, because surely someone who is a good artist cannot be someone who hates people of a different coloured skin, who hates people that speak a different language or whose racial origin differs from her/his own; surely a good artist will not be somebody who hates people of a different religion, people who come from a different cultural or economic background, who are not heterosexual, not homosexual, whatever.

But at that time I was not aware that so much of this business of the 'good' in literature, at least as it applies in education establishments, starts and ends with things like grammar and punctuation; if a schoolteacher or university lecturer calls a writer 'good' it might just mean the writer in question knows how to use colons, semicolons and paragraphs in a certain manner, or has a very large vocabulary, or uses a great variety of rhetorical devices, or exhibits a certain educational or cultural background, or shows a wide knowledge of foreign words and phrases. And all of that sort of stuff was not what good writing should have been about, as far as I could see, and certainly not what good art was about.

When I started to write stories I was twenty-two and naturally enough I thought to use my own background and experience. I wanted to write as one of my own people, I wanted to write and remain a member of my own community. That advice you get in the early days of writing, at any writers' workshop or writers' group, 'Write from your own experience!' Yes, that was what I set out to do, taking it for granted that was how writers began. I soon discovered that this was easier said than done. In fact, as far as I could see, looking around me, it never had been done. If it had, I could never find it. There was nothing I saw anywhere. Whenever I did find somebody from my own sort of background in English literature, there they were confined to the margins, kept in their place, stuck in the dialogue. You only ever saw them or heard them. You never got into their mind. You did find them in the narrative but from the outside, never from the inside, always they were 'the other'. They never rang true, they were never like anybody you ever met in real life.

There were no literary models I could look to from my own culture. There was nothing whatsoever. I am not saying these models did not exist. But if they did then I could not find them; because of this dearth of home-grown literary models I had to look elsewhere. As I say, there was nothing at all in English Literature, but in English language literature – well, I came upon a few American writers. I found folk whom I regarded as ordinary; here they were existing in stories, not as clichés, not as stereotypes. I was also discovering foreign language literature through translation; the Russians and others. I found literary models. I found ways into writing stories that I wanted to write; I could realise the freedom I had. I mean just the freedom other writers seemed to take for granted, the freedom to write from their own experience. Now I could create stories based on things I knew about; snooker halls and betting shops and pubs and DSS offices; the dole, waiting in the queue at the Council Housing office; I could write stories about my friends and relations and neighbours and family and whatever I wanted. The whole world became available. Quite a heady experience.

It was after that came the other problems. Things were not as straightforward as I thought. It had not dawned on me that there might be very good reasons why these literary models did not exist in my own backyard; yes, censorship and suppression. I quickly bumped against it through the elementary matter of my chosen artform, language.

You cannot write a short story without language. That seems an odd statement. Yet received wisdom in this society has demanded it. Yes, they say, go and write a story, whatever story you want, but do not use whatever language is necessary. Go and write any story at all, providing of course you stay within the bounds, not the bounds of decency or propriety or anything tangible; because that is not the way it works. Nobody issues such instructions. It is all carried out by a series of nudges and winks and tacit agreements. What it amounts to is: go and write a story about a bunch of guys who stand talking in a pub all day but if you have them talking then do not have them talking the language they talk.

Pardon?

Write a story wherein people are talking, but not talking the language they talk.

Oh.

By implication those in authority ask the writer to censor and suppress her or his own work. They demand it. If you do not comply then your work is not produced. That is the way it is. That is the way it always has been. You land on the assembly line of compromise, the end result of which is dishonesty, deceit, falsity. Or else silence. Our mainstream media are full of silences. Why is it the better writers never work for the newspapers, for television, radio or the movies? Do you think it is because they prefer artforms like prose and poetry? Well sometimes that is true, but often it is just because every other medium is out of bounds given their first demands of a writer are compromise and dishonesty.

Back in 1987 I edited an anthology of poetry and prose by people attending a writers' group in the east end of Glasgow. Some of the work is of a kind not readily available on the shelves of libraries and bookshops. This is because it is attempting a realistic portrayal of the lives of ordinary people. Many folk are startled to discover such a thing can be classified as 'literature'. In our society we are not used to thinking of literature as a form of art that might concern the day-to-day existence of ordinary women and men, whether these ordinary women and men are the subjects of the poetry and stories, or the actual writers themselves. It is something we do not expect. And why should we? There is such a barrage of elitist nonsense spoken and written about literature that anything else would be surprising.

The propaganda of elitism operates in different ways but those are the ways of all forms of prejudice: it makes a wide range of statements and will not allow a challenge unless it be done on its own terms, and it continues to make such statements until eventually part of the foundation of the dogma comes to be accepted as a kind of 'truth': fat women have got hearts of gold, men with red hair lose their temper, Catholics are inferior to Protestants; people from Aberdeen are greedy, Jews are greedy, Pakistanis are greedy; people on the dole are lazy; whites are superior to blacks; folk who go to university are born clever; foreigners are evil; strangers are dangerous; asylum seekers are lazy, greedy, inferior, evil, dangerous liars, and anybody who lives in a council housing estate cannot possibly be interested in reading or writing poetry or prose.

A typical misconception when beginning as a writer, when you start creating literature, is that before you get down to the writing itself you have to rush away and do a course in English. You study for your 'O' grade and then you study for your 'H' grade and then the 'A' grade and then you start thinking maybe you should go to college or university and study for your 'Degree in English Literature' – because it seems somehow obvious that the more progress you make in the study of the subject the bigger the chance you'll have of becoming an actual writer, a creator of stories or poems. Absolute rubbish. This lies at the heart of the fallacy that when you are studying English literature within the higher education system you are at the same time studying the ways in which literature is created. Some people even believe that a person who qualifies to teach English is therefore qualified to teach 'creative writing'. They would be as well to believe the person was qualified to teach 'creative sculpting', 'creative musical composition', 'creative movie-making'.

Maybe it is time to stop using the phrase 'creative writing'.

Maybe we should talk about 'literary art' or 'literature', about people creating literary art or people creating literature, instead of people 'doing creative writing'. Everybody uses language creatively, even teachers of English. If we are forced to use the phrase 'creative writing' let us insist on adopting a fuller phrase, let us call it 'creating creative writing'. But even that does not work properly, so just to avoid confusion we should stick with 'literary art' or 'literature'; literary artists create literature. Generally speaking academics will prefer the phrase 'creative writing' in its current application because it allows literature to remain their property.

When a person writes a poem, play, short story or novel the person has become involved in the creation of literary art, the person is creating literature. The one way to write a poem, play, short story or novel is to sit down at the desk with your computer or your typewriter or with your pen and paper, and start writing. Literature is no different from other forms of art: when you want to create it and you have the tools and the materials then you just get to work, you begin. The writing comes first, not the theory. When people are involved in creating literature they are involved in a practice, they are engaged in an activity; in other words they have to be doing something as opposed to talking about doing something, or listening, reading, thinking about doing something. The vast majority of those who have studied literature at an advanced level, including English teachers, university lecturers and professors, have never created one piece of literary art in their entire lives. Of course a few have. But there again, so have a few doctors and lorry drivers; painters and construction workers; shop assistants and builders' labourers; people who are on the broo, people forced to be housebound while having to raise their families. Anyone who is able to read and write has the capacity to create a poem or story. And by practising and paying attention to the work they are doing it cannot help but improve. Everything else is secondary.

Of course it is difficult to make the start and it is difficult to continue having faith in what you do, in the face of what often seems to be straightforward hostility. Writers have to develop the habit of relying on themselves. It is as if there is a massive KEEP OUT sign hoisted above every area of literature. This is an effect of the hopeless elitism referred to earlier. But there are other reasons. The very idea of literary art as something alive and lurking within reach of ordinary women and men is not necessarily the sort of idea those who control the power in society will welcome with open arms. Maybe it is naïve to expect otherwise. Good literature is nothing when it is not being dangerous in some way or another and those in positions of power will always be suspicious of anything that might affect their security.

True literary art makes some folk uncomfortable. It can scare them. One method to cope with being scared is not to look, to turn away and then kid on whatever it is does not exist. Another method of coping is to get your tormentors to stop what it is they are doing. In some countries writers find their work is no longer being published or produced. Writers in other countries can get dumped into prison or banished into exile. Occasionally writers disappear suddenly and are never heard of again. In this country writers are suppressed and censored. It takes different forms. Censors can cut out words and lines from poems, stories, plays or films. They often ask the writers concerned to substitute other words and lines. Sometimes they just substitute words and lines they have invented by themselves. The censors may search through a writer's collection of stories and poems and take out ones that offend them; the censors will emphasise the ones that do not offend them. This is a method of silencing criticism because it makes it seem as if they are dealing fairly with the writers they have just finished censoring.

The folk in control of the power in society feel safest and most prefer it when writers agree to suppress and censor themselves. This happens throughout the media. The BBC is a fine example of it. So too are all other television companies and radio stations, plus almost the entire magazine and newspaper industry. Almost every writer working for the media, and wanting to continue working for the media, accepts that there are 'dangerous' things that are not to be written about and 'dangerous' language that is not to be used. Those who break these taboos and refuse to take the censoring will very soon discover that their work is no longer being used. Writers who persist in being 'dangerous' (i.e. honest to their art) will become notorious; they will be regarded as perverse, selfish, egocentric. They will be regarded as psychologically suspect, as though they are involved in some masochistic pursuit of failure. The logic is precise. If writers were truly interested not just in 'success' but in 'getting their message across' then they would jolly well stop being so bloody difficult and start suppressing and censoring themselves immediately, just like the rest of their third-rate colleagues.

While this is going on in the media at large, preparations for it are seen in the classroom. This is where folk are first made aware of what society expects in literary art. It is here they first discover how NOT to appreciate the potential of literature as a living artform, as a dynamic activity that might involve their friends, family and neighbours. The classroom is where we discover what is 'good' literature. Very soon 'good' literature and 'literature' become one and the same thing. Literature becomes the thing we are allowed to see in the classroom. The other stuff is the stuff we are not allowed to see.

I saw a letter to the *Independent* or *Guardian* recently in which someone wrote about the film *Billy Elliot* and said how it could be used as a text by schoolteachers if only the language was not so 'bad'. Why had those responsible not thought about such a thing in the first place. Did they not realise that by cleaning up their language their work would be of use to the classroom!

It is pointless being angry at the retired teacher who wrote the letter, if it was a retired teacher. The attitudes on display are simply those of the people in control of the education system, the media and society as a whole. If a writer wants to see his or her work made available in schools then it is high time repression and self-censorship began. When work is created by those who remain honest to their art then they are going to be proscribed, their stories, poetry and whatever will be banned from the classroom and the shelves of the school libraries.

If writers cannot sell their work to the media and cannot have their work sold across bookshop counters then sooner or later they must find other occupations. There is a collection of short stories entitled *Lean Tales* which has work by Agnes Owens, Alasdair Gray and myself. Agnes is also a novelist, published by Bloomsbury, the same as J. K. Rowling. But for most of her life she has never been able to give her best time to her literary work. Instead she has had to find paying work in whatever way she could, and for long periods the only job she could get was as a servant, as a cleaner of the homes of middle-class people. In our society being a servant pays a wage whereas creating a literary art which attempts honesty in its portrayal of ordinary men and women pays almost nothing at all. Our schools and other institutions, including the media, encourage this actively.

Ninety-nine per cent of traditional English literature concerns people who never have to worry about money at all. We always seem to be watching or reading about emotional crises among folk who live in a world of great fortune both in matters of luck and money; stories and fantasies about rockstars and filmstars, sporting millionaires and models; jet-setting members of the aristocracy and international financiers. Or else we are given straight genre fiction: detectives and murderers and cops and robbers; cowboys and indians and doctors and nurses; heroic spies and nasty Communists; science fiction, historical romance, diverse pornography; ghost stories, faery stories, vampire stories, horror tales of the supernatural, and so on.

The unifying feature of genre fiction is the way it denies reality. This is structural. In other words if reality had a part to play in genre fiction then it would stop being genre fiction. This is what distinguishes it from other forms of literature. But even in the romantic fantasies mentioned above we can catch a glimpse of something approaching reality, as when a dashing financier white Christian hero is about to rush off to catch a friend's private jet to Rio de Janeiro for lunch with a beautiful albeit 'dusky' South American princess, and he just remembers in the nick of time to give last-minute orders to his 'man' to phone the restaurant, not to reserve a table, just to check out the chef is the same as last time. But that kind of detail is rare. Usually the dashing young heroes do not even have to bother with things like visas and passports, the sort of petty details that trouble other travellers, let alone the kind of basic day-to-day worries that encroach on the lives of the rest of the population.

But should we expect anything else? Should we expect those in control of power in society to promote and encourage a literature that is explicitly concerned with the day-to-day existence of ordinary women and men? and by 'ordinary' here the context is run-of-the mill day-to-day experience, as experienced by the overwhelming majority of the population. It would be quite pleasant to think this is the way things are. It would be nice to believe that ordinary women and men were being given every available opportunity to create a literature of poetry, prose, drama and song about homeless folk having to survive out in the streets or living off the edges of rubbish dumps; a literary art being created out of life on supplementary benefit, concerning itself with drug addiction, child prostitution, glue-sniffing, alcoholism, kids of sixteen being forced on to the streets; stories, poetry and song about old people surviving the outrageous costs of medicine, heating and public transport; the latest round of humiliations being endured in the offices of the DSS or the Gas Board or the Housing Department or wherever the daily humiliation happens to be occurring this morning; police brutality, racial abuses, sectarian abuses, trade-union corruption, political corruption, and everything else that comprises the reality of this country. Are we really surprised that these things dealt with properly, i.e. honestly and with artistic integrity, cannot be found in the literature promoted in schools and in the media generally? The fact is that we are consistently encouraged to accept that they have no place in English literature.

As I have mentioned before, I left school at the earliest opportunity, which in my day was fifteen years of age. I was an ordinary working-class boy making a dash for freedom at the very first opportunity the schools would allow. Like most working-class kids I was aware not only of the stigma of inferiority on my own forehead but also the one on the foreheads of my parents and neighbours. It is one of the more sophisticated features of the elitism in this country that prior to leaving school the majority of kids know not only what society thinks of them but what it thinks of their parents.

There was in Scotland a journal for English teachers entitled *Teaching English* and I remember there a review of a novel just then published. The teacher responsible for the review seemed to like the novel yet he concluded the review by saying that:

Its usefulness as a school text is unfortunately limited by the realistic inclusion in the dialogue of that element which [other writers have felt] necessary to suppress and, by references to frequent and prolonged bouts of drinking and occasional houghmagandie, the parents of your average 'S' grade candidate would certainly be moved to protest. But do read it for yourselves.

Let me tell you that 'houghmagandie' is a Scottish word for sex, not used very often, you will be amazed to hear, but it can still be heard, generally for purposes of irony. In that context it is not difficult to imagine a priest, church minister, Cabinet Minister, or even a Scottish Prime Minister using the same term. One thing it indicates is that the user of the term is at home in his culture; he is very comfortable in regard to booze, sex, drugs and rock and roll. Although he never gets too involved himself he certainly is not impressed by those who do, especially so-called writers who may want to create so-called literature around those areas for 'realistic' purposes. In his personal opinion writers who do create such work only do so for effect: such so-called 'realism' is a kind of adolescent exhibitionism.

It didn't occur to me for about five or six years after leaving school that literature was something I could be involved in. Then I discovered it was possible to write stories myself, I just had to go out and buy a couple of reliable ball-point pens and a good-sized notebook. I could even write stories about ordinary people if I wanted to. There wasn't anybody going to stop me by using physical force. After that I found out there were other people in this country also doing such things, and there were other people who had been doing such things for a couple of hundred years. It was just that nobody in any of the positions of power in society had got round to telling me.

Some of you may have noticed in the above extract from *Teaching English* how it is not just the kids being assessed, the actual parents have become S grade; only S grade parents have S grade children. Here is the relevant part of the quote:

> by references to frequent and prolonged bouts of drinking and occasional houghmagandie, the parents of your average S grade candidate would certainly be moved to protest. But do read it for yourselves.

Yes, it is presupposed that 'the parents of your average S grade candidate' will be less likely to recognise a work of 'realistic' literature than will the parents of your average O grade candidate who in turn will be less likely than the parents of your average H grade candidate who in turn will be less likely than the parents of your average A grade candidate who will, of course, be much less likely than the parents of your average 'English-Degree-at-University' candidate. This kind of shameful nonsense is horrendous when laid out in cold print; it is how matters exist in our society. At best you end up with the patronising tones of the teacher–officer of English giving us to understand that it is fine for 'realistic' novels to be read by those who are properly qualified to do so, certainly not by S grade adults. Of course there are those of us dumplings who do not even have an 'S' grade. Some of us dumplings do not even know what the hell an S grade is, including myself and perhaps Agnes Owens, the woman who wrote the novel under review in *Teaching English*. It is one of the absurdities of this type of elitism that prior to when I went to university I was not qualified to read properly my own short stories and much of my first two novels.

Aye, on ye go.

Shouting at the Edinburgh Fringe Forum

for Allan Tall

I WAS LOOKING for an excuse not to turn up this morning. I would prefer to feel that I am not really a part of Edinburgh's Fringe Festival. I don't especially like it. Yet during the past few years I have been involved on six or seven occasions. The first time was back in 1978 or 79 when I was among a group of writers doing a reading at an art gallery run by a member of this panel.[1] As I recall the event began about half past midnight and somebody's auntie turned up to double the audience figures. But the point is that whether I like the Fringe or not is irrelevant, it does concern me. And what about its future? Can it all be solved by money?

All what solved by money?

The only excuse for not turning up that I could think of was to do with economics. But eventually I decided it was better to come here and discuss these same economics. It's an opportunity not to miss, it isn't often I get the chance.

Of course being here at 11 o'clock in the morning is not only inconvenient it is costing me money. There is no fee being paid, nor expenses. But okay, I shall put up with being exploited, I am a working artist – a full-time writer – so the two things I am well used to are not being paid a fee and not being offered expenses.

There don't seem to be any other writers on the panel.

I referred to the incovenience of turning up at 11 o'clock in the morning, it concerns the little theatre company of which I am a part. In order to be here I am having to exploit five professional actors, plus stage manager, who are performing my play *In the Night*. But they are used to being exploited. This production is what is known in the theatrical trade as 'profit-share'. In practice what is shared is a variety of forms of deprivation, all of which stem from a dire lack of money, and material resources. Material resources are extremely important. Not as important as money but extremely important all the same. Artists who are 'minimalists' are not necessarily so by choice. When money and material resources are non-existent a greater imagination is required. You have to imagine your fucking sets and you have to imagine your fucking props.

This year our slot is 2.15 to 4.15 at a venue called the Fringe Fringe and it is costing us £400. Four hunner poun! For one week! So, needless to say, one week it is. To break even we needed forty paying people each of the six days, no mean figure as knowledge-able folk here will be aware, so we'll take a loss of some sort. As well as having written the play, I directed it. I am also driver of the van, for which I thank the Post Office who loaned it to us (though we had to pay the £90 insurance ourselves). Also I am doorperson, interval tea-maker, stage manager's assistant and so on. But things are running smoothly. We are not being bothered by audiences. On Monday three folk came to look. On Tuesday nobody at all.

Nobody at all!

Use your imagination on that yin. Nobody at all. This play I've slogged over, that the five actors, stage manager, musical director and administrator have slogged over . . . Nobody at all. Dear oh dear. One of the actors thought the show must go on! What a fucking stalwart. Myself and others felt differently and since there wasn't enough dough to get drunk, and it wasnay a bad day for

Edinburgh, we just went aff for a Stoical stroll on mighty Arthur's Seat, thinking wur ayn wee thoughts in wur ayn individual wee worlds.

But being the Fringe such happenings are far from uncommon. The average audience is seven apparently, a figure that includes people who get paid to attend, e.g. art-administrators, representatives of the media. Every theatre company knows the horrors of fighting for publicity, and the depressing fact that the only people guaranteed 'to win' mainstream media coverage are those performers who work in the mainstream media for the other forty-eight or fifty weeks of the fucking year. Dario Fo and people from foreign countries are always exceptions, especially if they do the English classics, productions of Alan Ayckbourn, student productions of Noël Coward, Gilbert and Sullivan, East European interpretations of Shakespeare.

We all hoped for much from the organisers of this here Fringe Forum, I speak of the *Festival Times*, newspaper to the Fringe. Last week they published a full-page interview with me which succeeded in leaving out entirely such total fucking inessentials as where and when the play was taking place. That was how we entered our first and only week. My goodness! Midway through, on Sunday last, we decided on a full-scale run-through of the play which we held up for half an hour till the *Festival Times* reviewer arrived. We thought it worthwhile because we heard from a secret source that the reviewer had enjoyed it. We still had about four days left to play, to try to recoup something of the outlay, I think our box office receipts were then amounting to £15, three oranges and a packet of Polo mints. Coincidentally the latest *Festival Times* where this review was to appear came out at 5 p.m. that same Tuesday me and the rest of the company came down from Arthur's Seat, still in wur ayn wee individual worlds. We got a hold of a copy at once. Unfortunately there was no room for the review of our play. What was that? Unfortunately there was no room for the review of our play.

Each of the company took a turn of searching every nook and cranny of that fucking organ of fucking critical fucking

sigh

We phoned the office and they advised us an editorial decision had been taken, and we were just on the wrong end of that. But they were a bit shamefaced, and of course when it comes to exploitation, they all work for nothing anyway. The reviewers of the *Festival Times* are students, it's a learning experience during their summer break from uni. Yeah, the usual.

But once one read the damn thing! Needless to say much of the space on that edition of the *Festival Times* was given over, as per bastarn usual, to all these Wonderful and Exciting TV Personalities, particularly all these millions of so-called Radical Comedians who earn their living from the BBC, ITV and other mainstream media organs man they are so fucking radical! Christ! Also there was Mr Edinburgh Fringe Festival himself, John Godber, god love him, three of whose plays were reviewed in this here edition of the then current *Festival Times*.

Turning up for eleven o'clock this morning meant assembling the company in Glasgow and Paisley three hours earlier than usual. Those who preferred not to arrive at such an unearthly hour had the freedom of choice to pay their own way by bus, taxi, rail or fucking aeroplane. Of course they were all hard done by, having already chipped in dough to pay for the fuel and van-insurance, so here they were with the choice of finding other transport and having to pay travel costs twice. (A peculiar question: how many artists do you know who can drive?) Like the other 90 per cent of the acting profession these five actors are registered unemployed and in receipt of DSS supplementary benefit. People in receipt of DSS supplementary benefit are already well below the official poverty level of this country, as members of the panel and audience will be only too aware.

I must say here and now that I am not making any complaints about the side-jobs involved with being part of professional theatre here in Greater England – sorry I mean Great Britain – as a whole. I regard it as an essential aspect of being a Great British author and playright. It connects with what the Great British Government calls the World of Art Standing on Its Own Two Feet.

And note, of course, that when I speak of the present Government I speak of the present Government, not just its Tory Administration, I include Her Majesty's Most Loyal and Trusted Opposition: the Great British Labour Party, the Liberal/SDP Alliance, Plaid Cymru, the Scottish National Party, and so on, they're all fucking in it together.

An aside: there don't seem to be any musicians on this panel.

Peculiar comments, peculiar views of the world, artists often ask peculiar questions. Here's another, it's directed towards certain members of the audience and panel here this morning: given that you are not yourself an artist, how much do you earn a year from art?

The company producing my play is Roughcast Music Theatre and it receives no funding of any sort, nor material resources. For your information I received a fee of £500 for my translation of Enzo Cormann's *The Prowler,* commissioned by The Traverse (Arts Council-supported) and playing there just now. Roughcast is a company of people whose desire is to create theatre. The musical director is Allan Tall whose involvment on the Fringe reaches back to 1969. He has composed, arranged, played and recorded the soundtrack to *In the Night.* At present, even as we speak, he is negotiating the sale of his PA system, plus one of his better musical instruments, in order to ward off a Warrant Sale of the entire contents of his household – not only his household but that of his partner, Lillian Cattigan. She is one of the five actors. But like myself they are not complaining, glad to do their bit for Great British art, making themselves pay for it in the marketplace. Very soon Allan Tall will be 'imagining' the music he could create.

He is also an actor though not in this production. Elsewhere on the Fringe he is acting, or should I say performing, or is it – well, I'm not quite sure how to describe it – reading aloud perhaps. Like many another actor on this year's Fringe he is involved in a Play-Reading.

Play-Readings are on the increase. Have you noticed? It is a brilliant idea. What is a Play-Reading? It is a thing that is not a play but you are to imagine that it is. When you go to one you are to imagine that a play is being performed. It has the great advantage of costing very little to produce. Theatre managements love the concept. The actors can be paid almost nothing, never mind the Equity minimum which is around £200 a week. Allan Tall and his actor-colleagues will be working for £50 expenses. And this is happening at one of Edinburgh's major theatres, yes, go along to the Lyceum Studio, you'll pay to see actors who are not being paid a wage. Good business though, nice to see those in authority within Scottish Theatre conforming so readily to the wishes of the Great British Government. No worries about wage-bills, proper rehearsals, sets, design, and so on and so forth, you can see the advantages. Not only is the Arts Council not condemning these Play-Readings, they are supportive, and actually helping to subsidise such ventures.

It is interesting how the Arts Council have managed to shift away from the old bottom line of a fair wage for artists. Younger folk in the audience I address you! I can remember when an Arts Council-supported event meant you could rely on being paid a fee or minimum wage. This was the primary factor about the Arts Council, it existed to support the creators of art. What a strange idea, eh!

At this year's Fringe I am involved on three fronts: 1) my own play *In the Night*; 2) my translation of Enzo Cormann's play; and 3) giving a reading of my own work at the Arts Council-supported Book Fair in Charlotte Square. The organisers initially offered me a fee of £30 for said reading. I pointed out this must be a misprint since the Arts Council's own minimum fee was £50 and they surely couldn't be offering only slightly more than half the stipulated minimum. I was not the only Scottish writer who pointed this out to the organisers and eventually they agreed to correct the misprint or oversight which everybody agrees it must have been. But me with the fish and chips on my shoulder, the sour grapes on my breath, I'm still wondering if the international giants of literature, Keith Waterhouse, Melvyn Bragg, P. D. James, David Steel, Shirley Goode and so on were being offered that same thirty quid. Probably they were working for nothing, new books on release, etc.

Questions relating to artistic merit, aesthetic value, economic value and so on hardly bear scrutiny at the Fringe. As some of you will know, one of the truly great writers of the century, Somhairle Mac Gill-eain (Sorley Maclean), appeared at Scotland's foremost Book Fair the other night, squeezed into a programme that included five other Scottish writers and 'an embellishment of saxophone music', all to take place within seventy-five minutes. In the name of fuck! I'm not sure what each of the six Scottish writers got that evening; maybe they got the same offer of thirty quid as I did, maybe they received nothing at all. Aye, and their reading event, plus the 'embellishment of saxophone music', scheduled for an entire fucking one and a quarter hours was precisely the same time the organisers allotted to actor and television personality John Cairney who was treading the boards impersonating Robert Burns.

The sad truth is that it is better not to examine the Book Fair magazine of events too closely from the standpoint of literary merit. But cash, it is good to discuss cash, good for my soul to discuss cash. Last year I earned £3,335. Under normal circumstances I don't do any readings or engagements for no fee and no expenses, not unless it's for a worthwhile cause, a political cause. People who don't have to worry about money regard my decision not to work for nothing as perverse. Some sensitive creatures actually get hurt when I say no to their invitation to come and read for no fee and no expenses. Others get annoyed and wonder who the fuck I think I am, refusing their kind offer, little shits like me should feel privileged to have been asked.

Yet others think that because my name is known to them as an author I must somehow be in receipt of a salary. Believe it or not that is a fucking common attitude man and most professional people (including arts administrators) seem to believe that being an author puts me on a par with them and usually anyone on a par with them is at the very least on a regular income, because that's what they all have, regular incomes. I don't know many artists on regular incomes. Maybe none at all. Maybe artists-in-residence who receive salaries for stipulated periods will be described as artists who get salaries but I'm not convinced this description is valid, having been an artist-in-residence myself for a couple of years and what I remember clearly is the difficulty in finding time for my own art, so that for whatever reason I was getting paid a salary it was certainly not to work on my own writing but on other projects. That is the more common experience for artists. It is a rule that people who create art don't get paid a salary. The people who get paid salaries in connection with art are those involved in administration and also art criticism, among whom are included media reviewers, people employed in radio, television, museums, art galleries, schools, colleges, universities, publishing houses, bookshops, and so on.

I wonder even about the people in this room alone, who gets

paid and who doesnay get paid, who's an artist and who isnay. Aye, here we are at the annual forum of Edinburgh's Fringe Festival, it would be interesting to list members of the panel and audience, the BBC film crew and so on. And of those directly engaged in the World of Art how many people who are artists and how many who urnay artists but administrators of art and critics of art, how many get paid and blah blah blah etcetera don't get paid. And when it comes to material resources – and forget salaries here (just for a minute), only material resources – how many of those administrators and critics have to pay for material, paper and pencils, oils and A4 paper, photocopying, and so on? Eh, how many? Fucking not many, that's for sure.

It is a weird thing to me that there are folk committed to the Fringe who maintain that the creation of art has nothing to do with cash and basic economics. It is hard to imagine an artist saying such a thing.

I wonder how many working artists are here this year, I mean overall, and how many of those are being paid to attend.

I think the ideal artist for the Fringe is somebody under the age of twenty-five years. It doesn't matter their race, creed or colour or if they are seven foot or three foot tall, the only thing that matters is that they are somebody who still believes that working for nothing is a way to secure the future. A small proportion of the students appearing this year will move into paid employment as administrators or critics once they leave university, including a few of those working for the *Festival Times*. Being an actor or otherwise engaged in the practice of art is something one does in one's youth, one grows out of it. Perhaps a couple will return as working adult artists and good luck to them. But it won't matter how hard they work at their art for events like this where luck and compromise are integral, the one thing we can guarantee is exploitation.

Nobody exploits artists so greatly as those who earn their living from art but not its creation. Ironically it is the arts administrator who could alter things in a quite substantial manner, in a quite direct way. The phrase 'a good festival' occurs to me just now. This is a phrase I've heard a bit over the past few days by people mainly engaged in administration or criticism. It is said in a sense similar to how an officer core old boy uses the phrase 'I had a good war'. Two high-ranking officials meet together and one believes it good, the other believes it bad, the one thing they take for granted is that it has no real impact on themselves; the officer core old boys who discuss good wars as opposed to bad wars have in common that certain fundamental factors remain constant either way. Similarly, for the high-up organisers who discuss good and bad festivals in this manner, a fundamental factor likewise exists whether festivals are good, bad or indifferent: one still receives one's salary.

Everybody tries to get in on the racket. Here recording what they will is the BBC, taking notes about everything so it can be brought out and used in evidence at some later date. I didn't know in advance they would be here. My only editorial control stems from my use of the words, fuck, cunt, shite, prick, bastard and so on. If I keep using them in an arbitrary fashion little of what I say will be fucking recorded for the fucking polis or whoever get their hands on the videos eventually. These fucking bastards on the fucking BBC hate paying any cunt, especially these stupid fucking pricks we call artists. A couple of weeks back the cunts asked me to appear on a fucking programme along with some fucking other writer bastards. The time and date were fucking not inconvenient so I asked the cunts about the proposed fee. No fucking fee, fuck all was being proposed at all. These bastards had the fucking downright fucking cheek to tell me I should be proud to get fucking invited because I was the fucking one and only Scottish writer they were fucking asking. All the other shites were *international* authors and none of them was asking for a fucking fee.

Imagine that, not a solitary fucking international fucking megastar writer bastard was asking for a fee. The stupid pricks were doing it for fuck all bar the glory. So that was me, good old bonny Scotland. Where was I. Sour grapes, yes.

Two years ago this company I'm involved with here, Roughcast Music Theatre, produced my play *The Busker*. We were as unsubsidised then as we are now but we aimed high and went to the Assembly Rooms. For the 2 p.m. to 4 p.m. slot they asked us for £650 for the week. Eventually they knocked it down to £450 and I'm sure it helped that the play could come under the heading of New Scottish Writing. As I recall the one and only other Scottish item on the entire programme that year was a children's puppet show. But once we saw the advertising we got for our show in relation to such mighty aesthetic larks as the Naked Radio Video Team! Fuck sake, I thought, here we go, television rules.

And it has to be said that one of the more depressing aspects of the Fringe is the arse-licking that goes on to the television companies. It is downright disgusting. As a working artist it concerns me what happens to other working artists, those who don't work for television at all or those who do the barest minimum to ward off the Sheriff Officers. All these Wonderful Television Personalities don't need any more free exposure here, they give plenty of it to each other in mainstream media outlets. Obviously those who should be supported are the artists, those engaged in the creation of art, those whose work is marginalised or exploited by television. Of course all the Wonderful Television Personalities are quite happy to come to bonny Scotland for a week or so and rough it in pursuit of art.

We know that serious dramatic art no longer exists within that medium, if it ever did, though some fantasise of a 'golden age' back in the 1960s. The medium was always corrupt. The first compromise demanded of the writer for television is self-regulation, i.e.

self-censorship; dishonesty, *a priori*. There were places, situations, people and relationships that could not be written about. Don't even consider it as a writer, not unless you accept that one demand, that there can be no linguistic freedom. Let television continue to be at the behest of those in political control, courtesy of its compromised artists. In fact to use the term 'artist' for those who earn their living from the medium is a debasement. But beyond that, why must people connected with festivals like this Edinburgh Fringe effort continue to act as though the pinnacle of achievement is to be involved with television, or invited to appear on it, or to be commissioned by it.

And see how it affects actors, musicians, dancers and people associated with the performing arts in general. I find it shameful to see some artists we know to be great agreeing to appear on television in watered-down versions of themselves. And they fail, of course, sometimes even allowing themselves to be ridiculed by their television hosts for that very aspect of their art that has led to their greatness (and to their exclusion from television). And incredible also to see these amazing young stand-up comedians all jumping about there with their radical trousers and political pullovers, you can tell how committed they are to revolutionary change, how truly extremist they are, by the fact they wear sandshoes (plimsoles) and jeans and buy their T-shirts from Asda. Do they ever wonder why they get invited on to television?

Just to finish up: my abiding impression of the Fringe is a host of very cheery and very confident young folk who in the main must be students, plus of course the usual vast majority of people who speak with the accent of the cultural élite of this country, the middle- to upper-middle-class RP voice, the voice of authority, the voice of power. As I'm from Glasgow, this festival isn't my festival, although some folk argue that it belongs to the whole of the Scottish people. What a joke. It doesn't even belong to the people here in Edinburgh. It isn't a nationalist point I'm making, I'm a socialist, and I'm talking about class.

The Fringe Festival is bound to continue to exist as it does just as long as society exists as it does. It is a sham though, a humbug, a force for hypocritical cant, and it reflects the state of art in this country, itself a paradigm of the wider society, where the vast majority of the population are plundered in one way or another by those who administer state institutions on behalf of the financiers, getting their back slapped and picking up what crumbs they may for themselves and each other.

Anyway, just to wind up, mature artists and professional companies of actors are an embarrassment here. No one really wants serious art. They want revue and comedy and reworkings of classics done in idiosyncratic ways by energetic amateurs, preferably students or state-subsidised companies from overseas, preferably from non-English language-based – preferably non-European – cultures. University students are the pinnacle of the Fringe experience. It is from such quarters that the future holders of Fringe office will emerge.

Forward pensioners!

Opening the Edinburgh Unemployed Workers' Centre

I HAVE TO confess immediately that I have been feeling a bit of a fool coming here in this capacity, i.e. a 'public figure' doing an 'official opening'. Maybe it is symbolic of something. I do not know and cannot be bothered working it out. But my decision to come and take part was based on trust. I was asked and I trust the folk who gave me the invitation, I decided to say yes. Everybody makes decisions, for better or worse. Even if you sit back hoping for the best, that is a decision.

One thing is certain, with or without me this Unemployed Workers' Centre IS opening, that is the reality. It is opening because a number of people have committed themselves to it. The people involved took their decision, they decided to fight the cuts and closure being forced on them. Maybe there is something symbolic about that. Whatever, the opening of this centre is going to cheer a lot of people up; it might give a few others the impetus to make their own decision.

It is only a couple of months ago that I first made contact with the folk involved here, and it is worth recalling. I came through to Edinburgh for the demonstration organised back in February or March by some of the workers at the Citizens' Rights Office (CRO)[1] to protest the cuts and funding withdrawals being made by Lothian Region, cuts and funding withdrawals that are going to directly affect the lives of ordinary people in what amounts to an assault on basic human rights. What makes it the more obscene, in this bicentenary year of the publication of Thomas Paine's *Rights of Man*, is that these attacks are being carried out not by the Tory Party but by so-called socialists, the Labour Party, with all their self-righteous claims about safeguarding the interests of working-class people.

After the demonstration I am referring to a friend from the CRO took me up the stairs and into the council chambers to hear some of the representation being made to the committee of political authorities led by Labour Councillor Paul Nolan. These political authorities were supposedly 'listening' to speakers from the various community advice-centres under threat who were giving reasons as to why their particular projects should not have their funding withdrawn. It is ironic that the speakers were appealing to the selfsame crew who had made the decision to do them in in the first place. So whereas getting the sympathy of these political authorities seemed unlikely, getting them to reverse their decision seemed wishful thinking in the extreme.

But there was a bad smell about the whole affair. The Labour politicians in control know fine well how important and how valuable these different projects are to the people of Edinburgh. They knew it when they made their decision to withdraw funding in the first place. Because of that there was something embarrassing, something shameful, about what was happening. Some might have called it a joke, one in bad taste, whatever, it was not funny. Maybe because I was here in Edinburgh and not at home in Glasgow I was able to distance myself from it. But I still have this image of Paul Nolan and the others sitting there trying to look interested, like 'caring officials' or 'champions of the Labour Movement' or something, sitting there being appealed to by the representatives from these different community groups, almost all of whom work as unpaid volunteers. I tried to imagine them working as unpaid volunteers on behalf of their own communities – maybe a couple of them did at some early stage in their career.

Anyway, a lot of the local representation was good; the comments made by the various groups were well thought out and so on, they stated their case well, as far as I could gather. I have to confess I was more interested in watching the politicians operate, comparing them with their counterparts back in Glasgow, all these other Labour politicians, renowned for their integrity, their honesty, their commitment to truth and justice, Pat Lally and the squad.

Is there anybody here who does not get this image of Lee J. Cobb trying to hold himself back when confronted by Marlon Brando in *On the Waterfront*!

And that reminds me of when Glasgow's Labour Party Socialists were trying to sell off a third of Glasgow Green to certain 'leisure' developers in the early 1990s. You may have heard that a demonstration and protest at that time led to the occupation of the main council chambers right in the heart of the city, in George Square. That was when the city's political authorities, the councillors, were forced to be *in the presence of* the actual public . . .

Amazing! I recommend the experience to anybody who has never seen their elected representatives in action. It is very very different from watching the House of Commons on television. Whereas when you listen to Her Majesty's Most Loyal Opposition putting in their penny's worth to their Respected Colleagues on the Tory benches, you quickly realise the one basic fact, that they have given away whatever modicum of control they had, they have got no power whatsoever – I am talking about the MPs here. Maybe they prefer it that way. Sit back and hope for the best. Put it down to luck. It makes it easier to jog along in life when you act like you have no control. And if you are a Labour politician it makes it easier to implement right-wing strategy as well, you can aye blame the Tories at national level for what you and your party decide to do at local government level. It is very likely in fact that these Guardians of the Labour Movement prefer being impotent.

Here at local government level it is a different story, you are meeting a different breed of politician. That was the thing about seeing Paul Nolan in action, just like Pat Lally in Glasgow, these Labour Party politicians in local government have got real Tammany Hall-style power, and they are well aware of the fact. They understand British democracy fully, they have it grasped right to the hilt. They know it is a total con. This is why they treat our political system with such contempt, it is what the system deserves and they understand that fully also. The only political process they have any time for is the machinery of their own party, how to seize control, how to oil your own wee set of wheels, how to build an empire. Those are the kinds of things they are are good at.

They are manipulators and nothing more, the further up the ladder they go just shows how adept at it they are. How anybody would want to put a moral case to men and women like that is beyond me. Unfortunately these unpaid volunteers were doing precisely this at Parliament Square, Edinburgh, they were putting a moral case to a bunch of Johnny Friendlys. Johnny Friendly was the gangster-heavy in *On the Waterfront*.

For these Labour Party politicians, politics is just a business. Morality, integrity, basic human rights – none of that sort of stuff has any place in their business. Power is from the bottom line. And power belongs to them. That is from where their contempt for democracy springs. As far as they are concerned, people who do not have power are little more than a joke, an occasional irritant but nothing more than that – which reminds me of the comment made by the leadership of the Labour group here in Lothian, when one of them was being interviewed in the council chambers on the day of the demonstration – somebody or other, the head of the finance department, I think, interviewed by a local journalist – he told the guy that the real enemy was not the councillors on the opposition benches, meaning the Tories, not at all, the real enemy was 'them out there'. This was his actual comment which he made to a member of the media. Extraordinary. He was talking about the folk on the street below, the men, women and kids who were out protesting the cuts and threatened closure of the CRO, the Unemployed Workers' Centre and the other community-based advice-centres. As far as this branch of the Labour leadership is concerned the people are the enemy; he has such little regard for 'them out there' he shares his view with the media.

Anyway, back to the meeting at Parliament Square, Edinburgh, watching the charade. Next up in front of the beaks were representatives from the Unemployed Workers' Centre. It took me a few minutes to realise that what they were doing was a bit different from the others. In fact I began to feel, Oh fuck, they have got no chance of getting anybody's sympathy, apart from the folk on the public benches. Then it dawned on me the man and woman from the Unemployed Centre were not appealing to anybody's finer instincts at all, they were being ironic, sometimes even sarcastic. What they were doing, they were treating the process with the contempt it deserved.

The representatives from the Unemployed Centre had no illusions, they knew the fight and they were not wasting time. It was not a case of going with the diplomatic cap on, being grateful for small mercies. They had taken control of the situation to the extent they could. There was no reason whatsoever to think you could get charity from the Parliament Square crew at all. The best you could do was show them that you knew the score, that like Nolan, Geddes and the cronies you had only contempt for the process you were expected to take part in, it was a hoax, a charade.

And maybe the first thing in any fight is to recognise the reality. If you are involved in a charade you have to recognise that that is what it is. You have to fight from that basis, because that is your starting point. And you have to do it soon because time is always of the essence. If you forget the reality and play some sort of quietist game, hoping for the best, hoping for a crisis of conscience from the political authorities, hoping for a change of heart from those in power – if that is the way you decide to conduct the struggle then you are bound to lose, and the first factor in your defeat is time, time will catch you out. Because it has to be stressed that time is always crucial. By the time you get the true picture the rug is being grabbed from under your feet. You have to fight when the going is good. Choose your time; but once you make the decision you have to admit reality. You have got to start exercising control. If you do not then at best your fight becomes symbolic. Symbolic fights are all very well but the trouble is that symbols aren't real. Symbolic victories are only won by people who lose, reality is always somewhere else.

How the Unemployed Workers' Centre will develop remains to be seen. Nobody knows.[2] But at least it begins on a proper footing, the folk there are not under any illusions. We are all entitled to dream. But dreams and illusions are not the same. You can fight to transform a dream into reality, you cannot do that with an illusion, an illusion can never exist.

The most important subgroup or subcommittee in the Unemployed Workers' Centre will probably be the fund-raisers. There is going to be a lot of work but christ almighty it is exciting. What happens here in Broughton Street will be watched carefully by many many people. Not all of them will be friends. A lot of folk will want to see that it does not succeed. They will put obstacles in the way. This is because it is out of their control and they do not like that. Many politicians will see it as a threat. I am talking about the ones that call themselves 'socialists'. As far as this issue goes the right wing are irrelevant. But definitely the Labour politicians will see the opening of this place for unemployed people as a threat. On one level it throws up their own ineffectuality, that is if they have any integrity, it is unusual to find politicians with real integrity, I mean within the power base; the structure of the party machinery exists to weed them out at an early stage.

The ones who do have power – the leadership and those around it, the cowards, toadies and bullies – unfortunately they'll have to be taken very seriously indeed. The continued existence of this centre will be a real irritant to them, the danger of a good example and all that. If it succeeds it will show them up for what they are.

There's no point hoping for small mercies and crises of conscience, not from them. You have to begin from taking control of your own struggle.

But there are going to be a great many people wishing this place well. So it'll be good if links are created and consolidated, if a network is established, communication with other groups and so on, letting other people help if they want. There's that old African proverb, in English it translates as 'Unity Chops Elephants'. Unity Chops Elephants, I have always liked that one.

Thanks for inviting me. It is an honour.

Alex La Guma (1925–1985)

'I'd like to sit down in a smart caffy one day and eat my way right out of a load of turkey, roast potatoes, beet-salad and angel's food trifle. With port and cigars at the end.'

'Hell,' said Whitey, 'it's all a matter of taste. Some people like chicken and others eat sheep's head and beans.'

'A matter of taste,' Chinaboy scowled. 'Bull, it's a matter of money, pal. I worked six months in that caffy and I never heard nobody order sheep's head and beans!'

'You heard of the fellow who went into one of these big caffies?' Whitey asked, whirling the last of his coffee around in the tin cup. 'He sits down at a table and takes out a packet of sandwiches and puts it down. Then he calls the waiter and orders a glass of water. When the waiter brings the water, this fellow says: "Why ain't the band playing?"'

We chuckled over that and Chinaboy almost choked. He coughed and spluttered a little and then said, 'Another John goes into a caffy and orders sausage and mash. When the waiter brings him the stuff he take a look and say: "My dear man, you've brought me a cracked plate." "Hell," says the waiter. "That's no crack. That's the sausage."'

– an extract from a short story by Alex La Guma, a South African

95

writer who died of a heart attack in October 1985; he was sixty years of age and living in Havana, the ANC's representative in Cuba.

I first came upon his work a few years before his death, the early collection entitled *A Walk in the Night*. One story in particular really stuck with me, 'A Matter of Taste', from which the above is taken. It is a marvellous bit of writing, telling of three men who meet over a pot of coffee in the middle of nowhere. They have a meandering conversation centred on food, then the two help the third hop a freight train heading for Cape Town wherein lies the possibility of working a passage to the USA. In the racial parlance of white South African authority the two are coloured and the third is white. La Guma himself was coloured. If the reader forgets such distinctions it won't be for long for it is always there, the backdrop to his work, inextricably bound in with the culture he worked from within. Even in that brief extract above the divisions are evident, where Whitey sees choice and Chinaboy knows differently.

The title story of the collection is the short novel, 'A Walk in the Night', a very fine piece of writing which I did not appreciate at the first time of reading. There was something missing for me which I see now as structural. In a 'A Matter of Taste' that element existed and in consequence my appreciation of the story was much more immediate. 'A Walk in the Night' is a bleak tale, set in the coloured District 6 which used to be one of the worst slums in Cape Town until it was done away with altogether, to create space for white building development. A young man by the name of Michael Adonis gets the sack after a verbal disagreement with a white man. For the rest of the evening he wanders about in a semi-daze, going for a meal, periodically meeting with acquaintances, would-be gangsters. Eventually, in a moment of stupidity he vents his anger on an elderly, white Irish alcoholic who lives in the same rooming house. The old man dies. Then the white policemen arrive and one of Michael's acquaintances winds up being mistaken for him, i.e. the killer. It is a memorable story, like most of the others in the collection. The structural element I spoke of as missing for me in my initial reading is to do with empathy; I found it very difficult to *be* with Michael Adonis, the world he moved in, it was alien to me. It was less alien on the second reading. The last time I read the story I knew the world he moved in even better.

Speaking purely as a writer it is good to feel anything and everything is possible in experiential terms. The existence of apartheid makes such a thing less easy to assume. In a good interview by Ian Fullerton and Glen Murray,[1] the South African writer Nadine Gordimer, who regards La Guma as 'the most talented black novelist since Peter Abrahams',[2] believes it is not possible for a white writer, like herself, in South Africa to write from within 'particular areas of black experience' and because of this

> cannot create black characters. The same thing applies the other way about. But there is that vast area of our lives where we have so many areas of life where we know each other only too well, and there I see no reason why a black writer can't create a white character or a white a black.[3]

There is a fine point being attempted here although at first sight it might appear contradictory. In fact she doesn't quite bring it off, to my mind, and a question later seems to back off, saying there 'is something beyond the imaginative leap'. It has to be remembered that Gordimer was replying in an interview and to the best of my knowledge did not have the benefit of being able to work out her comments on the page. I think that if she had, to risk being pre-sumptuous, she may have brought in the use of basic structural techniques like the first- and third-party narratives, and developed her argument from there. In a straightforward manner, third-party narrative allows the writer to create characters from the outside, where 'skins rub against each other', but allows the writer to draw back from certain areas of experience, the sort which are to the fore psychologically and seem to demand the creation of character from the inside, more commonly wrought by the writer through first-party narrative, although other methods are always possible.

Alex La Guma has written at least four novels; they are available in Heinemann's African Writers series, just about the most exciting list of English-language writing available anywhere, but difficult to get a hold of and at the time of his death not a solitary work by him was available in Europe's largest reference library, Glasgow's Mitchell Library. I managed to read two of the novels, on which basis I take Lewis Nkosi's point, that La Guma is only 'a competent novelist who after the flashing promise of that first collection of stories seems to have settled for nothing more than honourable, if dull, proficiency'.[4]

The Stone Country is an extended version of the short story 'Tattoo Marks and Nails'; it is written in the third party and is based on the writer's personal experience of prison. There are many good things about the novel and too there are its defects, including a bit of a rushed, fairly predictable ending. But Yusef the Turk is a fine character and the Casbah Kid also, though occasionally La Guma glamorises a little too much. And the converse of that is the deadened Butcherboy, a creation that only manages to get beyond the stereotype of 'hulking bully'. The central character is George Adams, in prison for belonging to an illegal organisation which in the case of La Guma could simply have been the Communist Party since it has been banned for some forty years in that country. The novel is certainly 'competent' and La Guma's dialogue and working of the relationships betwen the prisoners often rises to the standard of the early stories. He uses the third-party narrative in a restricted fashion, only rarely attempting to get within characters other than George Adams; thus we are seeing how folk act rather than how they think – which lies at the root of Gordimer's point as far as I understand it. This also provides a structural base for the reader unfamiliar with prison life in South Africa. I mean that to some extent we can *be* with George Adams in his dealings with an environment *alien to him*.

La Guma's last published novel seems to have been *Time of the Butcherbird* which appeared in 1979; this ended a silent period of seven years. His other two novels are *And a Threefold Cord* and *In the Fog of the Season's End*. An anthology *Apartheid*, and an account of his travels in the USSR, *A Soviet Journey*, do not seem to be available, though both are mentioned by his publisher. According to the publisher's blurb for *Time of the Butcherbird*, the author gives 'a rounded picture of all the people in a small community inexorably moving towards tragedy'. I think this is what La Guma intended but I also think he fails and that he fails in a predictable way. He uses the third-party narrative voice but does not restrict it. Instead he sets out to give the psychological workings of assorted individuals, blacks, whites and coloureds, but falls into the trap of stereotyping: the poor white woman, Maisie Stopes, and the militant black woman, Mma-Tau, are both obvious examples of this, the former being a sleazy semi-slut while Mma-Tau is a vast 'Mother Earth'. It has to be said that the writing is hurried, often clumsy, and requires a straight-forward editing. The person for this would have been La Guma himself. Failing that maybe someone at the publisher's office should have performed the job properly. And did the writer censor himself in *The Stone Country*, or was it done by another hand?

La Guma's very fine skill lay in his dealings with day-to-day existence, his precise and 'concrete observation which is the correct starting point for all materialists'.[5] The high point in *Time of the Butcherbird* is the introduction of Shilling Murile from the time that he is 'sitting in the ditch' straight through until the end of the period he spends with the shepherd Madonele, some 4,000 words later, as they move off together 'through the crumbling dunes, smelling the smoke'. This long section is beautiful, a brilliant piece of writing. It shows the true mark of the artist. Perhaps this indicates why La Guma could have felt capable of trying a novel as ambitious as this. It was a risk and he failed. In that short story 'A Matter of Taste' the risk was an easy sentimentality but he succeeded. The best artists always take risks.

Realism is the term used to describe the 'detailing of day-to-day existence' and most writers who advocate social change are realists. Incidentally, one of the areas of exclusion under the South African censorship Act is the 'advocation of social change';[6] and, of course, the writings of La Guma have always been banned there. Nothing is more crucial nor as potentially subversive as a genuine appreciation of how the lives of ordinary people are lived from moment to moment.

Ordinary people. In the African Horn the children of ordinary people are eating insects to stay alive. It is a fact of existence so alien to other ordinary people that it cannot be admitted; there is an element lacking, a sort of structural base that does not allow us *to be* with folk for whom starvation is death and not simply a concept. To face such a fact in literary terms seems to be possible only in the work of a writer prepared to encounter the minutiae of day-to-day existence. And as far as I can see any formal advances in prose have occurred directly because of that struggle; formal advances and 'imaginative leaps' may not be the same thing but they cannot easily be prised apart.

As long as art exists there are no areas of experience that have to remain inaccessible. In my own opinion those who think otherwise are labouring under a misapprehension which will lead to a belief that it is not possible to comprehend someone else's suffering, that we cannot know when someone else is in pain, that whenever I close my eyes the world disappears. It is an old problem. It has been kicking about in philosophy for several centuries. Just when it seems to have gone it reappears under a different guise and leads to the sorts of confusion we get in discussions to do with art and realism – naturalism – relativism – modernism – existentialism – and so on. One good example of this concerns the work of Franz Kafka.[7] He is probably the greatest realist in literary art of the twentieth century. His work is a continual stuggle with the daily facts of existence for ordinary people. Kafka's stories concern the deprivation suffered by ordinary people, ordinary people whose daily existence is so horrific other ordinary people simply will not admit it as fact, as something real, as something verifiable if they want to go and look. He seems to bend our line of vision so that we see round corners and perceive different realities. A few other artists also do this or attempt to; they work in the minutiae of existence, trying to gain access to, and make manifest, the dark areas of human experience, and suffering.

Most artists from oppressed or suppressed groups are under pressure of one kind or another. Time becomes the greatest luxury. Without time the work just cannot be done properly. To read *Time of the Butcherbird* is to see a writer of enormous potential labouring to perform a workaday chore. But to criticise the lack of development in La Guma's prose[8] is to assume certain general points concerning the role of the artist in society. La Guma would not be divorced from his society, no matter how hard the white South African racist authority tried to achieve it. His whole background was one of radical commitment. His father was James La Guma, a former president of the Coloured People's Congress. Both he and Alex were members of the Communist Party throughout their lives and in 1955 they were involved in the formation of the Congress

Alliance. This comprised the Indian Congress, the African National Congress, the Coloured People's Congress and the white Congress of Democrats. When the treason trials took place in 1955–61 Alex was one of the 156 leaders of the Alliance to be charged by the State. Then began the series of imprisonments and house-arrests which only ended with his departure from South Africa in 1966. He lived in London from then until 1979, although the literary people in control down there seem never to have noticed. For several years he was secretary of the Afro-Asian Writers Organisation (in 1969 he had won their Lotus Prize for literature).

Exactly one week after La Guma's death the poet Benjamin Moloise was murdered on the gallows by South Africa's white racist authority. Only a few years before that another good young poet, Arthur Nortje,[9] committed suicide in Oxford while awaiting deportation 'home'.

In Roque Dalton's *Declaration of Principles*[10] the poet can only be – as far as the bourgeoisie is concerned – a clown, a servant or an enemy. In South African society at present there is no alternative role available, whether for ordinary people or ordinary poets.

As a personal footnote; one of my treasures is a telegram I received from the man in early 1983. When I was writer-in-residence to Renfrew District Libraries and organising the Paisley Writers' Weekend I sent him an invitation to come and give a reading of his work. Unaware of his whereabouts I sent it c/o the ANC office in London; eventually, much later, came a reply from Havana:

```
THANK YOU FOR INVITATION FORWARDED ME
FROM LONDON STOP REGRET THAT AS AM
RESIDENT IN CUBA WILL FIND IT DIFFICULT
TO JOIN YOU STOP
  HAVE A GOOD WEEKEND STOP
  ALEX LA GUMA
```

ATTACK NOT RACIST, say police

RACIAL HARASSMENT, FROM various abuses through violent assault to murder, is part of the British way of life. We can deny, ignore or accept that this is reality, but if things are to change for the better then we have to acknowledge that it is the case. According to those who monitor such things it is on the increase. I suspect many people from the black and Asian communities go through different ways of coping with what is happening to them, perhaps beginning with denial, not listening to their children, seeking other explanations, in the hope of better things to come, perhaps the problem will somehow disappear or at least visit itself on somebody else.

Not long ago in a public park one evening in Glasgow two middle-aged men were attacked and viciously assaulted by a group of young white people. This was during mid-1990, at the height of the city's year-long reign as European Capital of Culture. It was a shocking attack. Twelve months later one of the victims still lay in a hospital bed, his skull crushed on one side. The man was paralysed and not able to recognise his wife and family. It was the day news came of the sentencing of the only one of the young people to be convicted.

People find it difficult to cope when they hear about these crimes. Perhaps it is not unnatural that a first response is to turn

103

your mind from the news. Yet none should be too surprised; we all know that racist abuse and violation, including murder, are the experience of the various non-European communities from John o'Groats to Land's End. This sort of incident is not untypical, it could be lifted from the catalogue of abuse and brutality that go to make up the set of horrors found under the label 'Racial Harassment', scarcely worth a second glance to those experienced in the horrors of racial violence.

It is consistent that such violation takes place on the street and, given that the British State is itself racist, people should not act as though it is some sort of social phenomenon, an aberration. But most people do not act after that fashion.

The general public rarely gets to know about everyday racism except where it occurs in front of their nose. In Glasgow an estimated 80 per cent of the victims of racist abuse do not even report the incidents nor register complaints with the police. On the day following this attack in a park in Glasgow's southside the newspaper carried a report under a headline which read 'ATTACK NOT RACIST, say police'.[1] Unless misreported, the police here were issuing a statement in which they 'rule out a racial link'. Only a few hours after the crime, without having spoken to one solitary witness never mind having caught the actual criminals; how was it possible? Apparently one of the victims had a wallet missing. I have no direct experience in police procedure, only what I pick up from reading or watching television. But surely that one finding could not make robbery the sole motive, ruling out all other motivational factors that might govern such an assault? There has to be some form of reasoning or other investigatory flaw at play, either on my part or on theirs. If we do not allow the police the benefit of the doubt on that one then there has to be some intentional act underlying their statement, it must be governed by reason of some description.

As far Glasgow's *Evening Times* newspaper was concerned the *possibility* of a racial motive was clearly established. This particular case was in conflict with everyday common sense according to which, when somebody of Asian origin is attacked by a group of white youths, *on a balance of probability*, the crime will be motivated by race hatred. In other words it is the rule. The *Evening Times* newspaper and the general public take it for granted that racist attacks occur and are not extraordinary phenomena. The term 'racism' seems more precise than 'racial hatred'. The headline, 'ATTACK NOT RACIST', states a counterpoint to the obvious, an exception to that rule. That is why it was selected. Of course it may not have been selected by an *Evening Times* sub-editor, it could have been the headline on the information piece sent to the newspaper by the PR department of the Strathclyde Police Force, but if so the argument on 'exceptions' still applies.

In the case where 'a racial link was ruled out' the day after the attack I am not arguing that robbery would play no part in it. But at that point in the procedure racist motivation was *the only factor* that could not be excluded, not until thorough investigations got underway. Surely to establish *motivation* these investigations must also concern the background of the suspect and not settle only on information such as one of the victims had a wallet missing? Does such a finding stop the investigation?

Why was racism ruled out of the frame immediately? Why is there *a need* to rule it out immediately?

In the same area of Glasgow and not long afterwards a white man was attacked and killed. On this occasion the *Evening Times* newspaper ran a headline of appalling prejudice: 'NATIONWIDE HUNT FOR KILLER ASIANS'. The widow of the dead man was 'Asian'. Presumably she was one 'Asian' in the whole of Britain who was not being hunted down. This headline may have come from Strathclyde Police or have been the work of a sub-editor.

When these brutal assaults occurred I was following the progress of a campaign for justice on behalf of the family of a man murdered in West London. It was in November 1989 Kuldip Singh Sekhon, a part-time mini-cab driver, part-time worker at Heathrow Airport, was stabbed to his death fifty-eight times. The police caught the culprit quite quickly and declared that the attack was not racist. His name was Steven Coker. An action committee was formed to support the family of the dead man the day after the murder. They conducted their own investigation of the suspect's past. Soon they discovered he had 'a history of perpetrating racial attacks on black families' and that he had already received a custodial sentence for assaulting an Asian man. Before Steven Coker came to trial the Sekhon Family Support Group stated publicly that the killing would be 'shorn of any racial motivation'. They were castigated for this by the police. Yet the evidence of motivation they had gathered and forced to the attention of the authorities was rejected. In his final summing up the judge declared: 'I would say that there is no evidence that this was a racist attack.' The detective superintendent who led the investigation had been convinced from the outset:

> Racial motivation was never a factor, right from the start. If I had found one piece of evidence, I would have investigated it to the hilt . . . Let's be honest, ninety per cent of kids like him in that sort of area are going to be racist. They're not of high intelligence, they're poorly educated, ignorant of the history of ethnic minorities in this country and the emergence of a multiracial community. It wouldn't surprise me if he was a racist . . .[2]

Apparently a man can be a known racist, convicted previously of the criminal assault of a member of the race he is known to hate;

he can be involved in diverse abuses of the race he is known to hate; and now, finally, this person comes to murder a member of the race he is known to hate: yet none of that history has a bearing on the crime. It is extraordinary. Neither the police nor the judge and judiciary see this history as having any undue significance in respect of the murder. None of it was considered sufficient to provide evidence that the perpetrator might have been motivated by his attested hatred of black people. So it seems what is happening is that in order to investigate motivation the police will examine the scene of the crime; they have no interest in the actual suspect whose previous criminal record and known criminal behaviour to date has no bearing. What it amounts to, leaving aside the ignorance and elitist prejudice, the mythical equation of education and intelligence, education and non-racism of the detective superintendent in charge, is an *a priori* denial of motivation as a material factor at all.

And where the investigating police is concerned we're talking only of the *possibility*, for surely this is precisely what the police investigation team said they had 'ruled out right from the start'. Recall the words of the Detective Superintendent: 'If I had found one piece of evidence' to suggest the possibility of 'racial motivation . . .' This upon the discovery of an Asian man murdered by a white man already known as a racist who either forgot or did not have time to rob the victim he managed to stab approximately fifty-eight times.

If we give the authorities the benefit of the doubt, and do not question their own motives in disregarding the blatantly obvious, we might understand that the difficulty they had was not so much to prove that the killer was a racist (they accepted he was a racist) but rather to prove that the attack carried out by the racist in this specific instance was motivated by racism (or that the fact of his racism was *material*). If we do award the police such benefit of the doubt then it appears to suggest that motivation somehow needs to be established 100 per cent. I thought motivation was by definition 'circumstantial', therefore grounded in probability.

As John La Rose reminds us, 'The struggle to get such attacks accepted as racial only succeeded after 1981.'[3] That was in the wake of the New Cross Massacre in London, when 'the lives of 13 black youths, all between the ages of 15 and 20 years old, were snuffed out on Sunday 18th January 1981 by a racist firebomb'. An action committee was formed and immediately organised a 'protest against the racial massacre, the indifference of the government and the media, and the inadequacy and bias of the police investigation'. The families of the dead and their friends and supporters sought to stop the 'police and coroner [proving] that the massacre had *not* been the result of a racist attack'. The action committee succeeded to the extent that the coroner was obliged to return an 'open' verdict. It surely is an indictment of the police and Crown Prosecution Service (CPS) that 'not a single person has been charged and brought to account'.

In crimes of racial violence, whether in Scotland or in Britain as a whole, it can seem as though there is an obligation on the police and judiciary to prove that the crime did not take place, that it was another crime altogether. In case after case, in crimes of racial violence, whether in Scotland or the United Kingdom as a whole, the first requirement of the State is to prove the crime did not take place; that it was another crime altogether, a crime which may well have been violent, a murder even, but not a crime that was racially motivated. Why is there such a requirement? This appalling break-down of justice has forced members of the black communities to act on their own behalf. Yet when they do they are castigated and victimised, to the extent that they themselves are criminalised. Witness the hostility directed against those who dare offer support to the victims. The reaction of the police to the Monitoring Group based in Southall, Middlesex is a prime example of that.

In this as on other occasions the family and support group were forced to risk breaking the *sub judice* law to highlight the real issues. The way the legal system operates, in order to bring these real issues to the attention of the public, people are forced to breach the *sub judice* law. There is no other way. If you don't do that then you leave social justice at the mercy of the police and the legal system, at the mercy of the institutions of the British State which as we know are themselves racist. It was Franz Fanon who made the point that racism is not some sort of phenomenon, it is a logical and consistent aspect of this society which is colonialist.

As has been pointed out often in the past, including one editorial I remember of the Campaign Against Racism and Fascism (CARF), the first priority of these campaigns is to publicise the racist motivation in such horrific and brutal violations. Time after time after time after time racist abuse, assault, physical violation and actual murder are being 'shorn of motivation'. The police appear to seek evidence of motivation only from the scene of the crime, never from the actual suspect. Amid the confusion is another murky area, the line between 'motivation' and 'causation'. The same detective superintendent who led the team investigating the murder of Kuldip Singh Sekhon said of the killer: 'None of us, not even the four psychiatrists who examined him, was able to get inside his mind.' But what could any of them have found if they had got 'inside his mind'? A fibre of 'racist cancer', a molecule of 'causal energy' buried beneath an ear-lobe? This detective superintendent seems to have thought so.

But why were 'the four psychiatrists' hired by the authorities in the first place? And who were the authorities, the CPS and the police? What evidence had the investigating team discovered 'right from the start' (or even later on) to warrant the possibility of mental or psychological disorder? Surely the perpetrator's known history of racial harassment had to have been an essential part of any such evidence. Perhaps it was not motivation they were seeking at this stage but a form of 'physical impulse', a causal factor. That might connect with the emphasis laid on the 'three pints of lager' the murderer had swallowed prior to the crime, in conjunction with evidence they had gathered of occasional 'drug abuse'. So why did the authorities not hire four publicans or four drug dealers along with the 'four psychiatrists' to give their verdict? Why not four full-time administrators of community art to give their opinion? Or four sociologists who could discuss the infinite potential of this, that and the next thing, in possible situations involving possible crimes engendered by particular cultural environments where 'ninety per cent of kids like him in that sort of area are going to be racist . . . are not of high intelligence . . . poorly educated, ignorant of the history of ethnic minorities in this country and the emergence of a multiracial community.' Maybe they could hire four experts in racist violence. Who decides? What are the criteria?

Variations on such 'reasoning flaws' have a habit of cropping up, e.g. where victims are thoroughly examined by the police or other authorities, not to discover the extent of the violation they've suffered, but to find the 'cause' of the assault on them. And what is happening here is an old story; they have turned the situation back to front, they want to know *why the victim* effected *his or her own violation*, paralleled in cases of rape where we ask of the victim: did she dress provocatively? Was she 'no better than she should have been?' Was she a woman who 'liked' men? And in cases of racist violence where a black man has been killed by white racists, why is it the police want to tell us of their own 'findings' about the murdered man, e.g. that 'he had an attitude problem'. So now the victim of the violation is transformed into its cause.

Racism is described commonly as a 'cancer' but the use of the term leads to confusion. You can't perform surgery on a person suspected of murder in order to find the motivating factor. No physical specimen lurks in the suspect's body. No matter how many biopsies are performed on the suspect there is no trace of 'racist fibre' to show the court. Evidence of motivation will be gained from an examination of the facts surrounding the crime and by an investigation of the killer's or killers' personal background and circumstances. Where racist murder is concerned the killer perpetrates the violation; why is it that the authorities feel obliged to consider the victim as the 'cause'?

Often it is the friends, families and supporters of the victims of these horrific assaults who start trying to piece it all together. Problems then arise with the police who are doing their utmost to 'rule out' the possibility of racial motivation by their cloistered examination of the immediate evidence. It becomes tricky for the friends and supporters of the murdered victims of racial violence to report their findings. It is not sufficient 'proof' to gather evidence of racial motivation. It is not enough to prove beyond all reasonable doubt that the killer is avowedly racist. None of that proves the actual crime itself was motivated by racism. The family, friends and supporters try influencing the police and the courts to accept the evidence. They find ways to help the police and judiciary to see why it is that they should accept the evidence. But nobody likes being told how to do their job, by implication meaning they aren't doing it already. And you can't force people to accept what they have the authority to reject. Eventually the police direct the prosecution as they see fit; and the prosecution will direct the judge who directs the jury. ATTACK NOT RACIST, says jury, READ ALL ABOUT IT.

And perhaps even before that another crime will have been committed, this time by the friends and supporters of the murdered victim who will be threatened and possibly charged with a breach of the *sub judice* ruling. One method of influencing the authorities lies in presenting the public with the evidence directly. But by doing this the friends and supporters of the victim are 'prejudicing' the outcome of the trial. The state condemns them for 'flouting the law', i.e. 'destroying the case for the prosecution'. This is what they are accused of when they present evidence of motivation. The police inform the victim's family that if they persist in 'claiming' racial motivation — i.e. showing evidence of the killer's attested history of hatred for the race of which his victim was a member — then the likelihood is the killer will walk free because his trial has been 'prejudiced'.

And the media will have resorted to its own devices for transferring guilt from the murderers and criminals both to the family and to supporters of the campaign. In the town of Livingston last year a friend of mine was involved in a similar situation when acting in support of two men who were attacked in a particularly savage manner. By producing a leaflet to advertise a public meeting to try and highlight the crime he brought down the wrath not only of the police, of course, but of the town councillors, all of whom were at great pains to point out that racism was 'not a problem' in Livingston. The media also attacked him and the Edinburgh *Evening News* published a silhouette profile of him on its front page just so racists on the east coast of Scotland would get more of an idea of his identity.

Thus the choice: break the law or sit by and watch the state prove, *a priori*, the non-existence of racial violation, including murder. A straightforward choice: either reject the law and settle for justice, or accept the law and leave justice in the hands of the police and the legal system. Of course it is ludicrous. It is not so much that the police and the legal system 'fail' in their job — in crimes where race is at issue it is difficult to grasp what their job actually is — but, by their reluctance to allow a racial motivation to these acts of criminal violence, justice is consistently obstructed, in fact justice becomes impossible because of the inherent prejudice on behalf of individual officers and their rejection of racial motivation in the first instance, a refusal to act upon common sense, to listen to reason.

Why does it happen? Why do so many state agencies consistently reject the obvious? Why do they turn every exception into the rule? What sort of spurious theory do they hope to fulfil by it? What are their obligations? To whom or to what do they owe them? It is never enough to charge individual members of the police, or of any other state agency with racism. This is what the State does, when backed into a corner. We are presented with 'the problem' as though it was a series of aberrations in an otherwise ordered whole. Once we examine the evidence we see the opposite. And perhaps when we do we are forced to admit that we always knew the reality anyway, that racism is endemic to this society and the state cannot be divorced from that.

One of the features of the campaign for justice on behalf of the family of Kuldip Singh Sekhon has been the extraordinary attacks directed by the police against the Monitoring Group in Southall (SMG), mainly a voluntary organisation. There have been the usual inane stupidities, e.g. that this campaign is 'politically motivated'. But there came more than that from Chief Superintendent McLean whose remarks were published by different media organs; one local newspaper carried the banner headline: RACE GROUP TOLD: YOU ARE A CANCER.[4]

A year before, this Chief Superintendent also was involved in hostilities with SMG. It followed the racist attacks on 'Ramesh K' and his family which led to them being 'hounded out of their Feltham off-licence'. The SMG had been supporting the family, having been asked to do so by 'Ramesh K':

We . . . used to ring them up in the middle of the night. We used them. We were always looking for someone who could give us help. Because they are Asian they give extra help. Being the same colour, you feel more at home. They put in a bit of extra effort.[5]

But the Metropolitan Police and Chief Superintendent McLean viewed matters differently. McLean described the Monitoring Group as a 'pernicious organisation spewing out lies and propaganda in pursuance of their own ideological aims.'[6] He also attacked Ealing and Hounslow boroughs; 'the sad fact is that the SMG are financed by [these] two boroughs, members of which are sympathetic to their aims.'[7] In view of the attacks on the Monitoring Group I looked at some of the background to its formation:

In Southall, in the late 1960s and early 1970s, the black residents were quickly shown police indifference to racist attacks when police did nothing to apprehend those who attacked shops and premises and did nothing when, in 1970, a gang of skinheads rampaged through the town. By 1973 allegations of police misconduct were so numerous that the Indian Workers' Association, the Pakistani Action Committee and Afro-Caribbean Association asked the Home Secretary to set up an independent enquiry into police brutality.[8]

There was no 'such enquiry' but an independent report was commissioned, the Pullé Report, which in 1973 'concluded that there was a *"prima facie* case against the police on charges of brutality and partial conduct against the immigrant community in Ealing" [which] report aroused a storm of protest from the Metropolitan Police.'[9] Not the police brutality itself, just the fact it was reported, verified and made public. Three years later 'a Sikh schoolboy called Gurdip Chaggar was murdered. Seen symbolically as the first racial killing; it led to the foundation of the Southall Youth Movement.'[10] John Kingsley Read was then chairman of the British National Party (BNP) and at one meeting he declared:

> 'Fellow racialists, fellow Britons, and fellow Whites, I have been told I cannot refer to coloured immigrants. So you can forgive me if I refer to niggers, wogs and coons.' Then, referring to the murder of Gurdip Singh Chaggar . . . Read said, 'Last week in Southall, one nigger stabbed another nigger. Very unfortunate. One down, a million to go.'

For this he was charged with incitement to racial hatred. At the trial in 1977 Judge Neil McKinnon 'directed the jury that the law against incitement to racial hatred did not cover "reasoned argument in favour of immigration control or even repatriation."' The learned fellow concluded that 'it was difficult to say what it is that this defendant is alleged to have done that amounts to a criminal offence.' Accordingly the jury found John Kingsley Read not guilty and Her Majesty's judicial representative gave him some cordial advice for the future: 'By all means propagate the views you may have but try to avoid involving the sort of action which has been taken against you. I wish you well.'[11]

A little more than a year later came the run-up to the general election that brought Margaret Thatcher's Tory Party into power. Prior to this the Tories were promising 'a new nationality law . . . along with new restrictions on the entry of dependants, husbands and fiancés.' Enoch Powell had 'returned to the subject of race after a relative silence of some years [and] racial violence reached a new height in 1976.'[12] Amid acts of horrific brutality enacted against black people in general, including murder, sickening attacks on immigrants came not only from street thugs acting unlawfully on the street, but from thugs working lawfully and unlawfully in police and prison uniforms, and thousands of other thugs working in civilian clothes on behalf of Her Majesty's Department of Immigration. Include in this sorry catalogue not only paid employees of the department itself but all the thousands of others who perform occasional dirty work on its behalf; this list is inexhaustive and includes people who work in airports, hospitals, the DSS, the education system and so on. Further attacks on the diverse black communities came from local, regional and national politicians, and of course the media. During this period and in the run-up to the 1979 general election the behaviour of many media organs was particularly loathsome:[13]

> the incidence of racist attacks has been closely related to the level of government and media-inspired mass resentment against immigration. Of the sixty-four racist murders that took place between 1970 and 1986, no fewer than fifty occurred in the five years – 1976, 1978, 1979, 1980, 1981 – when immigration scares reached fever pitch.[14]

On 17 April 1979, Margaret Thatcher 'stood by her statement . . . of the legitimacy of "British people's fears" about "being swamped".' In a few weeks' time 'the National Front vote collapsed'[15] and so began eighteen years of Tory Government. But before then the National Front (NF) was stepping up its own 'reasoned argument [against] niggers, wogs and coons'.

Among other things they 'organised a public meeting in Southall on St. George's Day',[16] the very place where the fourteen-year-old schoolboy Gurdip Chaggar had been murdered. The meeting held by the NF on 23 April was countered by an 'historic community mobilisation' from Southall itself.[17] However, Her Majesty's forces of law and order had also assembled to protect the freedom of ordinary racists, including those going about their legal entitlement of 'propagating views' that might end in the slaughter of 'a million niggers':

> the police cordoned off Southall . . . thus creating what they revealingly called 'a sterile zone' in the town centre, they did so in order 'to teach Southall a lesson' for the past. In a police action without precedent in Britain, 2,756 police officers, including units of the Special Patrol Group, occupied the areas. In the ensuing confrontation, the police killed one man – Blair Peach – fractured the skull of another, caused innumerable injuries to hundreds, arrested 700 people and charged 342 . . . No police officer was ever prosecuted for Blair Peach's death even though the inquest jury, in returning a verdict of 'death by misadventure', accepted that he had been killed by the police. Eleven eye-witnesses told the inquest under oath that Peach had been hit by a police officer; there was no evidence that he had resisted arrest, assaulted police, or even tried to flee.[18]

A report on the day's events concluded that police behaviour had 'left a scar on the people of Southall that will take years to heal. The racial abuse that accompanied the violence, the wanton destruction of property . . . and the pursuit of persons running away and/or trying to seek shelter, all give the lie to any suggestion that the police were merely defending themselves, and are consistent with Superintendent Hurd's comments early in the afternoon that Southall needed to be "taught some discipline".'[19]

The funeral of Kuldip Sekhon was an historic occasion in Southall. A march and day of mourning took place to com-

memorate his life and it brought more than 3,000 people together.
Local shopkeepers all closed their doors in solidarity, even the
betting shops.

There was a bus hired to journey south from Scotland in support
and a crowd of Edinburgh folk travelled. Many images are
imprinted in my own memory. One when a contingent of young
punks and mohicans, having been invited into a temple by locals,
were taking off their shoes, then being dished out dal and pastries
by two or three elderly Sikhs. Another image I have is of the dead
man's ex-workmates, mainly white taxi drivers, forming a guard of
honour. A third clear memory I hold is from an Evening of Culture
and Resistance held in April, organised jointly by the Blair Peach
Anniversary Committee and the Sekhon Family Support Group.
Tom Leonard and myself were among the writers and musicians
performing that evening and I remember being sold raffle tickets by
two wee girls with big grins, obviously sisters; I realised later that
their father was Kuldip Singh Sekhon.

In the interval between his murder and the funeral an eleven-
year-old girl, Tasleem Akhtar, was raped and murdered not far
from her home in Birmingham. A sixteen-year-old white youth
was eventually convicted for the crime. 'Crowds of demonstrators
and protestors gathered outside the court during the trial.' The
judge said that it was 'quite plain from everything I have read and
heard that the sole motive for this terrible crime was sexual and had
no racial association in any way.' The Akhtar family thought
otherwise and the girl's uncle spoke of the 'tension [and] racial
hatred [within] the community . . . [and that we] will carry on
demonstrating until such murders and killings stop.'[20]

In spite of the wishes of the family, Kuldip Sekhon's body had
been retained by the authorities for a very long period, from the
murder on 10 November 1989 right the way through to 31 January
1990 when at last the funeral was allowed to take place. The body

was in a badly decomposed condition. It seemed another needless hardship to be endured by the family. In keeping with religious practice the coffin would remain open during the funeral. Many people thought that the reason for such a scandalous delay could only be political, having more to do with dampening the emotional temperature in Southall. Either way there was very little regard, if any at all, for the sensibility of the murdered man's family, and that lack of regard by the State authorities for the families of the victims of racist violence is a common thread.

Finally, just to rub in the salt in the wound 'two Punjabi teenagers . . . the niece and nephew of Mr Kuldip Singh Sekhon [were] banned by the Foreign Office from entering Britain to attend their murdered uncle's funeral because they failed a test on how many water buffalo their father owned.'[21]

Fighting for Survival: the Steel Industry in Scotland

For the steel workers and their families,
and the struggle to come

Foreword

A VERSION OF this appeared in the *Scotland on Sunday* newspaper,
20 May 1990. It was 'edited'. The reason given was 'lack of space'
which I find not only hard to believe but close to impossible. I
think it has more to do with distortion and is in keeping with
recent developments within the *Scotsman* group as a whole, perhaps
in particular the censorship and suppression scandal connected with
the *Scotsman* Letters Page last year. The purpose of publishing it in
pamphlet form is simply to produce it in its entirety; by displaying
the 'edited' bits in **bold type**, emphasis will be given them:
attention will thus be drawn to certain aspects of the overall
argument, like the way in which the *Scotsman* group, by the act of
deletion, obscured it.

The Arts Page, like any other newspaper page, has been
involved in censorship battles for decades. Myself and other writers
have been experiencing this for most of our working lives. There
is nothing new about it. But it is important people understand the
levels on which it continues to operate. And further, that as a direct
consequence of suppression within the media, many important
factors never gain entry into the arena of public debate, e.g. the
collusive role of the TUC in the right wing's progressive war on

the Labour Movement and the left in general.

In the past it has affected myself and other writers of fiction and poetry in different ways. If you write a story or poem through the eyes of a man or woman whose daily use of language includes certain words which are conventionally regarded as 'taboo' then there is never any likelihood of your story or poem being used by the media – not only the *Scotsman* group but every other group, including the BBC and IBA. As recently as last year, when my novel *A Disaffection* was published, an Arts Page member of the editorial team at the *Scotsman* was not allowed to publish extracts from it. Eventually extracts from a novel by P. G. Wodehouse were used instead.

Yet somehow the general public has come to regard this form of suppression as fair enough, to the extent that most people – including most political activists I meet – don't regard it as 'real' censorship at all. But there is only censorship. Freedom of expression either exists or it doesn't. In this country it never has. When a voice is being suppressed it is being suppressed. These things have to be hammered home. It so happens that the voices being suppressed with the utmost consistency are those from that group of people herded under the somewhat anachronistic label of 'the working-class'. But it also includes people from so-called 'different' groups and communities, including those on the front line of the battle against racist violence by which I mean the black community. How many members of the TGWU, let alone the Labour Movement in general, will be aware that the worker who was stabbed to death some fifty-eight times in the head last year,[1] apart from being 'black' was also an *active* TGWU member, one who did the weary legwork with a collection-tin on behalf of the miners' struggle? How many TGWU members are now involved in the campaign on behalf of his widow and five daughters? Ironically, true solidarity is almost always obscured, or repressed, by the existence of 'bipartisan fronts'.

One aspect of my argument is the need to examine 'Thatcherism'. The term is misleading, it distorts the issue and the left should scrap its use immediately. The Prime Minister is simply a cog in a much larger machine. The world of capital is more sophisticated than the use of the term implies. Those within the higher reaches of power in this country weren't sitting about waiting for a leader to be born. She was selected. When a person is selected people are responsible for that selection. If she hadn't been around somebody else would have been chosen. The very notion of 'Thatcherism' suggests what is now happening in this country began with her: and will therefore end with her.

The history of high politics in the 1950s, 60s and 70s is one of collusion, of covert operations and not only in Ulster. One of the more interesting features in UK politics is not the part played by folk on the right, but those on the so-called left, especially those linked to 'the core organisation in these anti-communist (anti-socialist) manoeuvres in the British labour movement – the Trades Union Congress.'[2]

It is very easy to be dismissed as a 'conspiracy theorist' but great caution must be exercised whenever people within established authority circles start clamouring on behalf of 'united fronts' and 'bipartisan campaigns'. We don't have to hypothesise too much. There are precedents. We can look at earlier groups from 'right', 'left' and 'centre' who campaigned on 'united fronts'. It is always instrumental to see just who is uniting with whom, and what possible interests they could conceivably share; in the face of what possible 'common enemy'.

This takes us beyond the scope of a 'foreword'. Yet, in passing, it is worth mentioning some of the pressure groups who have pushed for 'united fronts' in the past – organisations like Common Cause and Industrial Research and Information Services to name but two in which folk from the 'left', 'right' and 'centre' marched shoulder-to-shoulder: Labour MPs and TUC full-time officials; Liberal MPs and Tory MPs, and certain other individuals either directly or indirectly connected to such 'bipartisan' organisations as Moral Re-Armament, the Economic League, MI5 and MI6, various CIA-funded European 'united fronts', e.g. the Information and Documentation Centre, Anti-Bolshevik Bloc of Nations etc., etc.[3]

I am not suggesting for one moment that any of the above-mentioned sinister outfits can be linked to the campaign to save 'Scottish' steel. However, it is difficult to be anything but cynical when you see Thomas Brennan[4] and Malcolm Rifkind,[5] plus diverse other MPs, party politicans, full-time union officials and members of the church all shaking hands and praising each other profusely for the great campaign they are now leading. There are simply no grounds on which this sort of posturing can be trusted. Only the opposite. If people do pin their hopes on such a right/left/centre deal then they'll be living in a form of fantasy world, similar to folk who buy Murdoch or Maxwell newspapers in the off chance they'll win a million pounds in a beauty contest. And as far as obtaining the support of 'Labour-controlled' Strathclyde Regional Council is concerned: this organisation is the largest employer of low-paid workers in Scotland.

The miners' struggle continues to set the precedent for the men and women engaged in the steel industry. Things like productivity are little short of joke issues in the contemporary world. It doesn't matter how many 'man-hours' are required to produce a ton of coal if a company has unlimited men to draw upon and the 'price' and working conditions of the men is on an unlimited downward spiral, thanks to 'sensible' settlements by 'realistic' trade union officials in 'negotiation' with 'determined' management, backed up by 'strong' Government 'forces', i.e. the police and the army.

It is a big world of private enterprise out there; one in which freedom to choose and freedom to exploit amount to the same thing, freedom for them and bondage for us.

In the act of denationalisation – of having what belongs to us sold on behalf of us to us – we lose the right to have any meaningful debate in decisions that affect not only ourselves as individuals, but the future of our families, communities and countries. We become 'interferers' in things that don't concern us. Matters of economic strategy are purely 'commercial' and are the property of big business corporations. They must be entrusted to those whose 'job' it is, the so-called experts, men like Sir Robert Scholey and Sir Ian MacGregor. The folk who control the national and multinational corporations of the world also control the communities of the world. It is old news everywhere; except, apparently, as a point of order in the continuing struggle between organised labour and capital. But any so-called agenda which isn't premised on 'the news' is a fraud.

The article was commissioned by *Scotland on Sunday* on the Wednesday the closure was announced, and is the first and only piece I ever wrote for them. I was given a personal guarantee: no political interference; they knew my work and knew what to expect. The first version I gave was thought to need more personal reflections at the outset, an editorial point which I accepted and still regard as sound editorial judgment. I got the finished version to them on Saturday at around 9.30 a.m. and I believe they went to press an hour later. I don't know who was responsible for the final 'editing'. Perhaps a couple of bits were 'unintentional'. Who knows. Many acts of suppression are. People working within the mainstream media often presume the validity of an existing, political reference point and by tacit agreement never challenge it. By presenting the full version here readers will be able to judge the 'intentionality' or otherwise for themselves.

Fighting for Survival

While in the Ravenscraig area the day after the announcement of
the strip-mill closure, a steel worker in a pub told me that this was
a time for bipartisan action, that the Scottish people must adopt a
united front in an all-out effort to save the steel industry. His was
roughly the same line as that being offered by a large majority of
folk, including most of the media and most of our parliamentary
politicians, with opinions perhaps diverging only on the extent to
which investment should be private or public. Even Michael
Forsyth and other Scottish advocates of **what is now known as**
Thatcherism seem to be 'pledging the Tory party to campaign to
save the mill'. In the words of the current STUC general secretary,
'All of Scotland must unite behind the campaign and set aside the
sniping and points scoring we have seen in recent times.'

The last time in this area I confess I was going to Wishaw
dogtrack with two friends so my mind was elsewhere, I didn't
notice the 'Craig skyline. I was reminded of this a couple of days
ago when a television programme led off the topical interest side of
its report by showing a steel worker whose job is under threat,
coming home from walking his greyhound – a practice that's
always appealed to me, living in Glasgow, for the way it forces you
to breathe fresh air. There was a nice open field across the road
from this particular dog owner's house so he wouldn't have had to
walk too far to find space, although I'm not sure how fresh the air
is. I used to work in a copper mill which is different from a hot steel
strip-mill; that was twenty-five years ago, the factory was down in
Salford. I was nineteen years old and I used the experience for the
background to one section in my novel *A Chancer* where the young
central character touches a white-hot copper bar with the toe of his
shoe, it bursts into flames instantaneously. I remember going back
up to Glasgow and my mother at some point washed my

workclothes. She was surprised by how green the water kept turning. I also remember the taste of sweetness every time I smoked a cigarette.

The best time for an outsider to see the Ravenscraig skyline may well be at night although I confess a bias; it can't be as bad as Port Talbot, but only because of the concentrated nature of the South Wales operation. Everything is so hemmed in and stifling down there. It's only the proximity of the sea makes it bearable. Years ago I used to drive quite frequently between Swansea and Cardiff and once you hit the Jersey Marine road the skyline resembled a form of hell, the flames erupting from enormous chimneys, the smoke dense and in assorted colours. During the day you still see the fire and smoke, but the image is more down to earth: you become immediately aware of the rows and rows of housing where the steel workers and their families live, tucked right beneath the enormous chimneys. You also see washing hanging out to dry and are maybe struck by the thought the clothes will come in more dirty than they went out. In the Ravenscraig area the families are luckier, if only because of the space, although it now seems this is about all they'll be left with.

My sympathies are with the steel workers; like the miners, many of them may still be engaged in the type of work where avoiding death or serious injury is a technique to be applied three or four times per hour. Working conditions such as these can provide an easy sentimentality for outsiders, they are also easy to mythologise. I don't want to get into that. But there is no question that the men who do such work have every reason to take pride in what they do. And a certain bonding always exists between those involved in dangerous jobs. It involves a quite particular irony, which can make an outsider feel slightly insecure in their presence. The men I spoke to are angry, they are absolutely angry. It is very predictable. But there is also a sense of hopelessness, and if as an outsider I can never reach the depth of the steel workers' anger, it is this sense of hopelessness which induces the anger in myself.

How do the men and women directly concerned in this latest disaster fight what is happening to them? And among all those shouting so loudly over the past few days who is going to offer genuine support? Or even genuine hope? Are there any solid grounds for hope? What sort of precedents have those with any political clout set such that the steel workers in Scotland – or any workers in Scotland – should be feeling cheered by the prospect of 'united fronts' and 'bipartisan campaigns'?

The man I spoke to was not alone in thinking the fight for survival needed more than the Ravenscraig workforce to achieve success. **To engage in a struggle with the present face of British capital that has to be true.** But is bipartisan action of the kind being suggested an authentic possibility? Can folk from right, left and centre of the political spectrum call a truce in order to address a 'truly serious' matter, i.e. one that somehow **isn't 'merely' political but** concerns the nation as a whole **(given that we can refer to Scotland as a nation)**. This idea that the interests of the country at large can be expressed irregardless of political and economic differences is very suspect indeed, **which is one reason why myself and many other folk continue to avoid the SNP, not to mention the rest of the parliamentary parties**.

What do we actually mean when we talk about the 'interests of the country as a whole'? At what point do the interests of the individual citizens who actually live there enter the argument?

Even in the event of the steel industry being saved, whether by private or public investment, or a mixture of both, what then? Here **we are** in the middle of 1990: in what sense can a country such as Scotland 'have' a steel industry? As things stand I no longer know what this entails, although as far as Sir Robert Scholey **and other corporate managers are concerned,** it is certainly a time for caution at the upfront end of the market, by which I mean primary production.

In the ever-expanding market economy now being 'made available' to private capital both in Europe and elsewhere at least one thing is clear: a country can compete or not. But if it does compete then the 'fair price' of its product may well be reckoned alongside the same product from a country where labour relations are a function of the War Department. Who could compete in a 'free world' coal market, for example, where the price is set somewhere around that obtaining in South Africa under the present white racist regime? The outraged voices of Scottish steel workers, politicians and others, arguing over the tremendous productivity at the 'Craig is understandable, but in such a context is irrelevant and something of an anachronism.

There is no room for sentimentality in business. Nor is there room for 'politics'. There is no room for any sort of outside interference at all. People are to stick to their own backyard and not meddle in what doesn't concern them. Somewhere **along the line** we seem to have lost not only the 'right' to work but the right to even discuss the matter. Upper management must be empowered to perform its job as it **alone** sees fit, for it alone has the expertise to judge on matters of commercial enterprise. And if the production of steel does not 'pay' in this country then it may well pay in another — **perhaps Poland or Hungary or East Timor** — but if not then it will be time to move out of steel altogether, perhaps into another industry, culture for example, or waste disposal. **The fact that steel production or coal production or ship production has traditionally been at the heart of a country's economy cannot be allowed to stand in the way. As Sir John Harvey-Jones reminded sentimental corporate managers recently, in reference to the 'biggest mistake' he ever made while engaged in the oil business,**

'beware of the allure and attraction of your own creation'.
In the same column Sir John gives an interesting insight
into the expertise of corporate management when he tells
us that prior to the last few years

> **business theory was in favour of vertical integration.**
> **That was largely because companies were able to**
> **measure the benefits, but they couldn't measure the**
> **risks. It was only from the early eighties that everyone**
> **[sic] realised that vertical integration means putting**
> **most of the capital behind the front end of the**
> **business, which has the highest risk (***Independent on***
> ***Sunday***, 13 May 1990).**

If there is to be an attempt at a bipartisan campaign to save
Ravenscraig let it begin with an appraisal of the situation now
facing the workers and their families, and all those others whose
livelihood depends on the steel industry, directly or indirectly. I
mean a genuine appraisal.

For hundreds of thousands of people throughout Great Britain
the last decade or more has been a form of nightmare. The plight
of the steel workers and others in the Ravenscraig economic belt is
a direct effect of the past twenty or so years' strategy of those who
make decisions on behalf of Government and big business.
Elsewhere throughout the land other groups and communities
have been assaulted and battered. This is why folk don't need to
visit the area to appreciate or sympathise with the steel workers'
plight. Unfortunately we are inured to bad news.

The steel workers themselves have been coming to terms with
the inevitability of Sir Robert's decision to terminate their working
lives for some years. They've also had to cope with the knowledge
that there is next to nothing they can do to save the industry, not

on their own. Given the present circumstances the harsh truth is that it isn't their industry at all, it is part of the property of British Steel. And if by any chance there is a takeover at the Scottish end it still won't be their industry, it will belong to the shareholders, Scottish or otherwise.

Sir Robert Scholey will have made his decision to close some long while back; only the timing has mattered. **He is the head expert.** It is his job to make such decisions, as Conservatives **Ian Gow, Nicholas Ridley and now the Prime Minister herself** have all reminded Malcolm Rifkind.

Margaret Thatcher had prepared the way in her recent televised declaration of how utterly – **and no doubt morally** – wrong it would be for the state to interfere in the internal affairs of a private enterprise. **As far as those who control the Tory Party are concerned the ultimate closure of the steel industry in Scotland has nothing to do with the people who live there, it's strictly business, a question of management;** the argument should therefore be conducted by the appropriate managerial team. In this respect Sir Robert Scholey has a good and true track record, his expertise has been instrumental in transforming the industry during the past few years into a 'hugely profitable concern', at the slight cost to date of some 90,000 job losses.

If there can be such a thing as a national campaign then it must also be a time to stop talking about 'redundancies'. The 800 jobs lost with immediate effect at Ravenscraig plus the estimated 15 to 20,000 that may eventually follow are not the personal property of individual people. If jobs can be said to belong anywhere it is to the community at large. Like the 529 tobacco workers in Glasgow who were given their closure announcement last week, the steel workers are all too aware that a job is something other folk can have as well as yourself. When somebody leaves or retires somebody else takes over. A job isn't a 'thing' to be bought and sold. In accepting the concept of redundancy payments the Labour Movement accepted a quite straightforward Tory principle. But at root the concept is fraudulent.

The main spectre haunting the steel workers is not so much the closure of Gartcosh rolling mill: it is the 1984–85 miners' strike. It is no coincidence that Sir Robert Scholey and Sir Ian MacGregor used to 'hit it off well' together, **to quote from last week's *Scotsman*, with both 'their Thatcherite faith and Sir Robert's belief in the need for great secrecy about corporate operations' helping them to get along.**

Almost every worker in the country has 'learned his or her lesson' from the assault on the miners, but those involved in the steel industry have particular cause. Like the rest of us they were forced to watch the horrific treatment meted out to ordinary men and women whose one crime was to fight for the economic survival of their communities. Ironically, however, as John McCormack (one of the victimised miners) pointed out in his fine book *Polmaise: the Fight for a Pit*, 'The biggest battles with the police in Scotland came at the pickets of the Ravenscraig steelworks and the Hunterston terminal in Ayrshire where foreign coal stocks for Ravenscraig were landed.'

For the steel workers the miners' lesson is especially bitter. In the pubs and clubs and other places people meet in dialogue, images of the miners' strike will not be erased easily and must colour all talk of 'united fronts'. The events of the 1984–85 struggle are more than a memory, just ask some of the sacked miners who are still being victimised, or the widows and families of the men who died. **Those within the inner circles of Government power executed that particular battle quite ruthlessly. And though a good deal less shady in their own dealings over the affair the STUC, as well as the TUC, as a collective body, did**

little more than allow the isolation of the NUM leadership.

The steel workers are also having to cope with the stark fact that so many of them declined to 'hang themselves on somebody else's cross' six years ago, their support of the miners left something to be desired. It was members of the Iron and Steel Trades Confederation who unloaded the 'foreign' coal down at Hunterston. These things have to come out into the open. If the spectre of the miners cannot be erased then any campaign on a united front is scarcely more than a joke in very bad taste. The miners, ex-miners and their families know better than anybody the sorts of pressure the Ravenscraig men were under; it isn't a time to bear grudges, the steel workers were fighting for survival even then, and that was before Gartcosh.

Nowadays it is common knowledge that the strategy of confrontation was planned by those central to Tory power as far back as the early to mid-1970s, funnily enough, around the same time those at the helm of big business had become 'very disillusioned'. This strategy seems also to have included the adoption of a strong right-wing figurehead − a role the current Prime Minister, Margaret Thatcher, fulfils very adequately − which makes it the more crucial that those in opposition to the 'apolitical' business directives of the present Government give up acting as though the toppling of Margaret Thatcher is the end of the road. At best such a position is simply naïve. At worst it is more than a farce, it is straightforward collusion. But unfortunately 'collusion' is one of the frequent outcomes of the bipartisan united front approach. The first meeting to discuss the campaign was held yesterday morning, it included members of the STUC and Strathclyde Regional Council. It will be interesting to see how matters develop.

And what will happen if the steel workers' struggle for survival fails and this last bastion of industrial Scotland collapses? Perhaps it is simply time to move into another industry, culture for example, or waste disposal. This is 1990 and it is difficult to avoid cynicism if you live in Glasgow which might be described as cultural capital of Strathclyde Regional Council as well as European City of Culture. Last Wednesday, in common with many thousands of other people involved in the campaign against the Poll Tax, I received my warrant notice at last: fortunately for myself, being a writer, the sheriff officers acting on behalf of Strathclyde Regional Council won't poind the word-processor on which this is being composed, it is a tool of my trade.

Wednesday was also the day that the announcement of Sir Robert Scholey's decision was made. That same evening Glasgow's cultural vanguard attended Luciano Pavarotti's concert, for which the singer received a 'six-figure sum' and the orchestra nothing at all, apparently. Perhaps Sir Robert Scholey attended, he too is a man of culture, in fact he is an opera buff. There is nothing wrong with opera. I happen to like it myself. In cultural competition with Pavarotti's concert was the international football match at Pittodrie Park, Aberdeen; the night it became very difficult – even for wee boys – to dream of a successful conclusion to the campaign for Scottish World Cup glory. This same day a portrait of Van Gogh's doctor, painted several days before the artist's suicide, was sold in New York for £49m.

It is hard to make any unifying sense of these distinctly different events. Perhaps there is no 'unifying' factor at all, it just seems as though there should be.

Further elements can be introduced, depending on your political persuasion, the fact that the announcement took place precisely one week after the Scottish Tory Party Conference, precisely two weeks after the country's local Government elections. Some people also argue that all the significant announcements only come when the public's attention is otherwise engaged. How long the argument holds I don't know. If I had not read through a couple of old newspapers to catch up on last week's events I would have missed the news about the closure of the tobacco plant down at Alexandra Parade (the removal of the operation to Bristol in preparation for the assault on the coming European Market in 1992). For the five or so hundred women and men of the tobacco plant, and their families, nothing will be more important at all at this moment and perhaps they'll even feel slightly aggrieved that their own news is now largely a forgotten item, like the shocking betrayal of the distillery workers at Stepps. How many bipartisan ex-campaign members of that united front are still resolved not to drink Guinness?

The closure of the strip mill at Ravenscraig suggests the final moment of Scottish heavy industry approaches rapidly. There seems no workable pretence available to 'our' politicians any longer.

Folk are in a state of shock generally. So many attacks are being launched on people that anyone not engaged in this struggle directly will have to work at it to discover why it is any more important than another. These things seem to me *always* relative. During the miners' struggle some years back the controversy over the importation of foreign coal to Ravenscraig was occurring somewhere around this very week, at one point 1,500 pickets were confronting more than 1,000 police down at Hunterston. What was being forced on the miners is now being forced on the steel workers. Not that ex-miners will want to gloat, not even those who were sacked and are even now, five years later, still being victimised for the part they played in trying to safeguard the future of their own industry. It was then that our Prime Minister spoke of those on strike as 'the enemy within', and further 'compared the miners to the Argentinians'. How the steel workers' struggle will develop and how the Whitehall Government responds is a question of time.

But certain things can be predicted. Some of us can remember when there was a car plant at Linwood, not to mention actual ships (as opposed, for example, to oil platforms) being built on the Clyde. There is no point in relying on 'our' Government to resolve matters favourably. And judging from the track record of the major parties of Her Majesty's Loyal Opposition, there is next to nothing to be gained by pinning any hopes there either.

One other item of news this past week concerned the shooting of a Major International Motion Picture in what used to be a large fishing port before becoming what used to be a booming wee oil town – Stonehaven; according to latest reports the citizens here are now envisaging a future working life as film-extras. Perhaps the people of Motherwell can be put to similar use. Other types of employment may be forthcoming during the periods when the Major International Motion Picture Industry is elsewhere engaged. In some of the wealthier sections of the USA the stylish party host and hostess employ members of the unemployed to stand in their gardens and houses as living statues. But the last thing required by the steel workers and their families is another dose of humbug.

Philosophy and a European City of Culture

for Mags Thomas

GIVEN THE STATE of intellectual life in this country, the latest academic news seems depressingly predictable: the philosophy section at the University of Strathclyde is to be closed down by the academic authorities. As far as the prevailing self-congratulatory climate in Glasgow is concerned the news is of a kind more normally associated with satirical revue. Philosophy is to have no future at the heart of the 1990 European City of Culture. The very premises of existence can now be taken as read, first principles are no longer at issue. Henceforth not one single student within hailing distance of the city chambers will be encouraged to challenge the foundations of truth, of belief, of faith. All that sort of critical nonsense can be dumped for what it is, a peculiar anachronism, a left-over from a time when folk had the leisure to sit about discussing the meaning of life and related questions, e.g., the right of one group of people to hold total power over another. From now on we can get down to tackling the real work, we can confront the major issues, *viz*. the diverse strategies for the diverse interests of big business. And while we are at it we shall devise methods for acquiring funding for our own department at the expense of someone else, we shall work out ways of safeguarding our own security of tenure at the expense of a colleague, of advancing the interests of our own kids at the expense of a neighbour, my health at the expense of yours, get rid of your job to keep my own, and so on and so forth.

In present parlance such forms of thinking or rationalisation come under the heading 'new realism': how best to safeguard what we have right now, at this present moment, given the reality of right now, this present moment: for the one thing beyond discussion, right now, at this present moment, is the reality of the existence of the present Government.

These days there seems to be an unhealthy and overriding desire among political parties of all persuasions to testify to that reality. It is as if there is a badge of honour (or chain of office) awaiting those who 'face' up to the 'truth' – never mind that somewhere along the line in the admission of that 'truth', ultimate authority and the right to that ultimate authority have been conceded. It is a malaise which seems to have become the basis of contemporary thought – not only in our seats of Government but across the spectrum of society as it spirals downwards through the politics of local Government, the politics of health and welfare, the politics of education etc. It is what gives rise to the peremptory closure of schools and other community resources, that new way those at the top now refer to students or even hospital patients as customers, not to mention the selling-off of books by our libraries – which last point is perhaps not too surprising when we note that what used to be known as Librarianship at this selfsame Merchant City University now lurches around beneath the title Information Science, that what used to be known as the Department of Politics is now entitled the Department of Government.

I went to this university at the age of twenty-eight, a good age for attending such an institution. Although a published author and the father of two children I was still naïve enough to believe that the department which 'taught' English Literature was a good place for a writer to enrol. Fortunately, there was a semi-independent section within the department; this was the philosophy section and it had a staff of three lecturers. It quickly proved to be the only section that really mattered for many students. The lectures in philosophy had to be attended at all costs – even when it was your round in the Press Bar or The Dunrobin, you had to ignore the cries and rush back up the hill, for here was where you learned to question at the level most likely to irritate authority. This was the place that equipped you to ask a different type of question: e.g. can poetry be taught? what does 'teach' mean? what is art? what do we really mean when we say this story is good literature and this other one is not? by what authority does this department have the right to say Philip Larkin is a poet to be studied while Karen Eliot is not? what criteria are being used and are they valid? and so on.

If the study of philosophy leads to anything it is to philosophising itself, raising the fundamental question, of challenging a 'truth' being taken for granted, some basic premise which we sense intuitively to be wrong (what does 'The European City of Culture' actually mean?). What can a university possibly amount to if the techniques of general appraisal/criticism are no longer to be acquired by its students? It is a singular coincidence, in view of the infrastructural upheavals in contemporary Britain, that the ever-dwindling numbers of young people allowed to enter higher education are slowly but surely being starved of these very techniques. How long before the right of criticism itself is 'conceded'? What will the consequence be when the foundations of truth are not available for discussion? Unfortunately this is all too predictable – in fact it is already happening in most parts of the planet, including this one; writers, artists, philosophers, scientists and thinkers in general will be forced to account for themselves, before the self-appointed guardians of ultimate truth. Some will be censored, some suppressed, some will be gaoled, sent into exile, some will be tortured, some threatened with execution while others again, like the young Scottish student of philosophy back in 1697, will be put to death. This is the general outcome when the servants of the State put an end to criticism. It is a time when the citizens are called upon to Rejoice for what they have, and to be thankful that those in power are being 'realistic' enough to make such nasty decisions as might be necessary in order to keep it. And you voices of possible dissent from within be warned, this is a time when the nation must pull together and be as one, just so we can remain secure from 'the enemy without'; self-criticism is certainly not on. It strikes me that a university which does not have a philosophy section has lost the right to be known as a university.

A Reading from the Work of Noam Chomsky and the Scottish Tradition in the Philosophy of Common Sense[1]

IN 1982 POLLS indicated that 70 per cent of the US population believed the Vietnam War to have been 'fundamentally wrong and immoral'[2] whereas 'virtually none of the really educated class or articulate intelligentsia ever took that position.'[3] Thus in the face of more than two decades of relentless media propaganda on behalf of the ruling group the great majority of ordinary people had the wit and the will to judge it for themselves. It is absolutely central to Chomsky's thesis that 'there is no body of theory or significant body of relevant information, beyond the comprehension of the layman, which makes policy immune from criticism.'[4] Everybody can know and everybody can judge. Unless we are mentally ill or in some other way disadvantaged all of us have the analytic skills and intelligence to attempt an understanding of the world. It just is not good enough 'to be bad at mathematics'.

The skills demanded of an elderly person for playing several cards of bingo simultaneously or for studying thoroughly the form for a big sprint handicap in the 'heavy going' at Ayr Racetrack in an effort to pick the winner; the skills demanded of parents on welfare trying to cope with a family of young children, just seeing they stay healthy from one week to the next: all such skills are there to be developed and could be applied to any subject whatsoever, including subjects like a country's foreign policy or, nearer home, the correlation between cuts in welfare and infant mortality; between cuts in welfare and suicide; cuts in welfare and death from hypothermia; cuts in welfare and local crime and violence; cuts in welfare and drug abuse, alcohol abuse, gambling abuse, prostitution, madness.

No matter the subject under scrutiny, certain factors remain the same, we apply our reasoning devices and these devices are inter-disciplinary. We apply them in physics, in astronomy, in domestic economy, in horse-race betting, in joinery, in the creation of art. Logic is a reasoning device; so too is mathematics. They are also activities. We engage in them to find solutions to problems all the time. They are also skills, they can be refined and improved.

By approaching different kinds of problems we apply our reasoning skills in different kinds of ways. We start reflecting on how we use them and see how other folk are faring; we make comparisons and connections, construct theories. This is why poets can discuss methodology with people involved in sculpting marble or rigging up electrical circuits. If we are restricted to one subject only then our ability to reason may stagnate; it will become difficult to reflect on what other folk are doing when they are engaged in subjects not directly related to our own; we will forego the opportunity of keeping an eye on 'the experts'.

Although his name had been known to me, I first became aware of Chomsky's work while at university as a mature student, but my reading was confined to what he was doing in linguistics and I did not persist; the technicalities of the subject did not interest me especially. One of his earliest works was published in Holland when he was twenty-nine years of age; this was entitled *Syntactic Structures* and it

revolutionised the scientific study of language . . . the revolutionary step that [he] took . . . was to draw upon [finite

automata theory and recursive function theory] and to apply
it to natural languages, like English, rather than to the artificial
languages constructed by logicians and computer scientists . . .
He [further] made an independent and original contribution
to the study of formal systems from a purely mathematical
point of view.[5]

Both finite automata theory and recursive function theory are
crucial not only in abstract disciplines like mathematics and logic
but in disciplines such as physics, economics, botany, art theory,
anthropology; they are also central to the analytic method known
as 'structuralism'.

But an understanding of these theories is not at all necessary to
appreciate Chomsky's demonstration that an argument used by the
US Congress in 1984 with regard to 'the right to bomb Nicaragua'
could be adopted by the USSR with regard to 'the right to bomb
Denmark'.

There again but it is good to know things, not to let ourselves
be put off by technical phrases like 'finite automata theory'. We
don't have to go away and look up a specialised dictionary, we just
keep such stuff in quotation marks.

I want to know about physics. By knowing about physics people
have split 'the atom'. Most people do not know what an 'atom'
actually is yet by splitting 'it' the world can be destroyed. The
worlds of Nagasaki and Hiroshima have already been destroyed, an
event described by the thirty-third President of the United States
of America[6] as the 'greatest thing in history'. I want to know why
the most powerful figure on Earth can say that, and if there is any
connection between it and the fact that by the end of World War
Two the nation of which he is supposedly the boss owned 50 per
cent of the planet's wealth. Yet this same nation had only 6 per cent
of the planet's population.

And of that 6 per cent (some 220 million folk) about 90 per cent would have owned next to nothing at all. So, in other words, if we take the 6 per cent and divide it by 100 and multiply that by 90, and so on, we see that less than 0.6 per cent of the world's population owned half of the world's entire wealth and material resources. This was back in 1945. I wonder what the figures are now. Maybe also, if I had been given examples like that in primary school, instead of things like apples in baskets and quantities of water in leaky tubs, I might have become 'good at mathematics'. Who knows.

Chomsky's boyhood in New York had been spent hanging around his uncle's news-stand at 72nd Street and Broadway

which was sort of a radical centre . . . in part Jewish working-class . . . Communists . . . very much involved in the politics of the Depression . . . all night discussions and arguments . . . Freud, Marx, the Budapest String Quartet, literature . . . [From adolescence he was] deeply interested . . . in radical politics with an anarchist or left-wing [anti-Leninist] Marxist flavor, and even more deeply interested in Zionist affairs and activities – or what was then called 'Zionist', though the same ideas and concerns are now called 'anti-Zionist'. [He] was interested in socialist binationalist options for Palestine, and in the kibbutzim and the whole cooperative labor system that had been developed in the Jewish settlement there . . . but had never been able to come close to the Zionist youth groups that shared these interests because they were either Stalinist or Trotskyite and [he] had always been strongly anti-Bolshevik.

His father had been a linguist and from the age of twelve he was put to an experimental, progressive school. His years at college and university were also noncomformist. He came under the influence of the philosopher and mathematician Nelson Goodman. And also Zelig Harris, one of the foremost names in linguistics, although Chomsky has said that 'it was really his sympathy with Harris's political views that led him to work as an undergraduate' in the subject. Apparently Harris used to conduct his lectures in a café and continue them during the evening back in his flat.

These details can be decisive; so-called background or personal information is often the difference between taking us into the work of somebody or not. Just knowing that Zelig Harris had 'political views', that his lectures and personality could keep students stimulated for hours, it's interesting stuff. What kind of a man was he? What was it about linguistics that drew him to the field? The way most present-day educational systems operate we are to study the work and leave the somebody out of it. Never you mind if that literary critic does happen to be a Fascist. You are hereby sentenced to spend the following year studying his theoretical work on the art of poetry. And for the rest of your life you are duty-bound to take it into account whenever the topic of literature arises.

During a recent series of lectures[7] Chomsky was asked about his method of investigation, given that he appears 'to reject Marxism and materialism [and] investigation involves' both. While denying that he does reject them Chomsky demonstrates the often irrelevant and stultifying effect of fixing labels to ideas. Ideas are not static; they do not belong to anybody, they are simply the outcome of the 'common intellectual background of reasonable people trying to understand the world.' 'Marxism' consists of an indefinite number of ideas and in terms of the history of ideas 'it' has already been incorporated. And as for 'dialectical materialism', he 'personally, has never understood it [but] if other people find it useful then fine, use it.'

Chomsky went on to say, during the same lecture series, that he has no particular method of investigation at all, what he does is 'look hard at a serious problem and try to get some ideas as to what might be the explanation for it, meanwhile keeping an open mind about all sorts of other possibilities.'

Such a statement might sound surprising, almost like an exercise in mystification, as though he is trying to make what he has achieved accessible but the route by which he travelled inaccessible. This is common among professionals and 'experts' generally, including many so-called teachers. We try to follow the process by which they arrived at a solution, then discover the destination becomes as mysterious as the route.

It is a serious problem. Whole areas of experience and knowledge are hived off from ordinary men and women and children. Society is controlled by those who are 'paid to know', the specialists. In recent years the most famous international expert on global affairs has probably been Henry Kissinger, someone whose downright 'ignorance and foolishness' Chomsky describes as a 'phenomenon'. Nevertheless, when sponsored by the might of the US military, the power exercised by such a person is life or death – as in Angola for example, where the same man 'tried to foment and sustain a civil war simply to convince the Russians that the American tiger could still bite.'

Human suffering is of no account and the economic cost is next to irrelevant since in political affairs of state such costs 'are always public' anyway; only the 'profits are private'. All talk of morality as a value is naïve. If morality does exist it is to be regarded as a separate field of endeavour, like experimental physics or mechanical engineering or opera. Even genocide is consigned to the realm of tactics and becomes 'wrong' only when its 'effects are debatable and are likely to provoke hostile reactions in world capitals.'

But at its official level international reaction is fairly predictable. It depends on who is doing what and to whom, and the profit involved. In 1974 the country of East Timor, with a population less than that of Glasgow, was attempting to determine its own existence; like Angola this was after the horrors of Portuguese Fascist colonisation. Four years later a quarter of its people had been massacred after an invasion by Indonesia, 90 per cent of whose military supplies came directly from the USA:

> but while [they were] the major foreign participant in the slaughter, the others tried to profit as they could and kept their silence. In Canada, the major Western investor in Indonesia, the government and the press were silent [while in France] *Le Monde* reported in 1978 that the French government would sell arms to Indonesia while abstaining from any U.N. discussion of the invasion and in general doing nothing to place 'Indonesia in an embarassing position.'

This is only one instance from an enormous number cited by Chomsky. But after a time statistics dull the senses, including those concerned with wholesale slaughter, as he reminds us:

> You see what they mean when you look more closely at the refugees' reports: for example, a report by a few people who succeeded in escaping from a village in Quiche province [Guatemala] where the government troops came in, rounded up the population and put them in the town building. They took all the men out and decapitated them. Then they raped and killed the women. Then they took the children and killed them by bashing their heads with rocks.

Reports by refugees of atrocities are difficult to cope with. We are not used to such testimony, not unless, perhaps, the refugees are in flight from the same ideological enemy as ourselves.

A Reading from the Work of Noam Chomsky

If Chomsky has a specialist subject then some would argue it is not linguistics, nor the philosophy of language, rather it is US global policy, with particular reference to the dissemination of all related knowledge. When he says he has no 'method of investigation' we would be as well asking to what the phrase could refer. Is having a 'method of investigation' the same thing as having a system of rules and procedures worked out in advance so that we know how to proceed in problem-solving? Should we be thinking of 'induction' or 'deduction', or 'dialectics' or 'structuralism'? What do these things mean? Before going off to investigate something are we supposed to go away and learn a method of investigation?

Maybe by 'method' some people just mean they prefer working with a fresh pot of tea at the ready, a packet of cigarettes within reach and soft music in the background. They might even be referring to a preference for observation and experimentation as opposed to sitting about chatting and thinking aloud, in the style of some old Greek philosophers (and some contemporary ones as well, not just from Greece). What seems clear is that restricting yourself to one particular method will just make life more difficult. Everything and anything should be available, including intuition. Einstein was a staunch believer in intuition. Without such a reasoning device a great many scientific advances would not occur. It is the ability people have to soar above the boundaries of one field and land not in another field but in a street.

In his introduction to Chomsky's work in linguistics, John Lyons suggests that it is necessary to meet him 'on his own ground'. This can imply the need to embark on a concentrated study of linguistics or the philosophy of language. But an insight into the technical, the formal problems confronted by Chomsky may be possible without that. It also may be possible to see where these formal problems impinge on matters of more general, political concern.

Rousseau is an important thinker for Chomsky. It was what Rousseau perceived as the strength of the will to self-determination that led him to propose 'the struggle for freedom [as] an essential human attribute'. Rousseau also concluded that

> the uprising that ends by strangling a sultan is as lawful an act as those by which he disposed, the day before, of the lives and goods of his subjects.

The sultan has no inherent rights. Beyond civil society there is an authority to which he is as subject as the retinue of men who helped him dress for breakfast that morning. This authority does not derive from outwith the realms of humankind. It is not God. It is not superhuman in any form. This is the authority of natural law which inheres in every woman and child and man.

Rousseau sent the essay in which that appeared to Voltaire whom he much admired, aside from his atheism which he detested. But Voltaire did not appreciate the argument at all; he said it made him feel like 'walking on all fours'.[8] He thought the essay was affirming some sort of 'golden age' where primitive folk would be free to be primitive once the shackles of civilisation were burst asunder.

But Rousseau's argument is more powerful than that. When he saw 'multitudes of entirely naked savages scorn European voluptuousness and endure hunger, fire, the sword, and death to preserve only their independence' he was seeing a basic premise that had to be true beyond any shadow of doubt: it is

> from human nature that the principles of natural right and the foundations of social existence must be deduced . . . the essence of human nature is human freedom and the consciousness of this freedom.

Human freedom is so inalienable a right that it can scarcely be described as a 'right' at all, it is the very essence of what it is to be a person.

When Chomsky started in linguistics he accepted the orthodox view which was that semantics had nothing to do with the subject. Semantics involves 'meanings', the way that people actually *use* language, whereas linguistics was to concern language as *it already exists*. In other words, the subject was restricted to the study of syntax and phonology. To start bringing in 'meaning' was very risky since it implied 'mentalism', having to get involved with events and activities that take place in the mind; and this was awkward, things that happen in the mind are not readily available to observation – we cannot see into minds.

Earlier linguists like Zelig Harris and Leonard Bloomfield had sought to provide a collection of procedures which would 'yield the correct grammatical analysis of [any] language'[9] once applied to the raw data. But a formal difficulty in this presents itself over the idea of 'the correct analysis': how can we ever know for certain that the analysis we have is *the* correct one? Maybe it will just turn out to be one of many.

There is a proposition by Ludwig Wittgenstein, that 'when all possible scientific questions have been answered the problems of life remain completely untouched.'[10] At a glance this could suggest a separation between science and life of a kind that will lead to mysticism; but at the core of the proposition and of Wittgenstein's 'picture-theory' in general lies the theory of structure. Two central features of any 'structure' are (1) that they are not theoretical constructs (they are not 'man-made' but 'natural'); and (2) that they are sealed off from description.

In this sense no science can ever hope to describe life; it is not possible. 'Man is uniquely beyond the bounds of physical explanation'[11] and will aye remain so. There is even a mathematical proof we can offer as a demonstration of this courtesy of a theorem formulated by an Austrian mathematician, Kurt Gödel. His theorem makes use of both finite automata theory and recursive function theory.

Chomsky was well aware of Gödel's Theorem. Even back when he accepted the orthodox view of linguistics – that semantics should be excluded from the study – he had his own distinctive approach:

> a linguistic theory should not be identified with a manual of useful procedures, nor should it be expected to provide mechanical procedures for the discovery of grammars . . . We cannot hope to say whether a particular description of the data is correct, in any absolute sense, but only that it is more correct than some alternative description of the same data . . . The most that can be expected is that linguistic theory should provide criteria (an *evaluative* procedure) for choosing between alternative grammars.

In comparison to the Bloomfield/Harris objective, as John Lyons points out, Chomsky's objective here seems quite unassuming, but ultimately it is more ambitious. Einstein's physical system is greater than Newton's because it is more powerful, it copes more adequately with the raw data of the universe. His system can do what Newton's can do, but it can do a great deal more. Yet nowadays we know enough about systems in general to appreciate also that the Einstein version is not the last word, not in any absolute sense. Eventually another system will come to supersede it. Once this point is realised, Chomsky's ambitions become clearer, he is seeking a form of ultimate criteria, *universal* principles by which different grammars may be evaluated.

At least one trap was lying in wait for those social scientists who saw nothing peculiar in isolating language from people; it becomes exposed through the following statement by Bloomfield:

> although we could, in principle, foretell whether a certain stimulus would cause someone to speak and, if so, exactly what he would say, in practice we could make the prediction 'only if we knew the exact structure of his body at the moment'.[12]

Those who assume freedom as the natural right of all people should reject the statement *intuitively*. The extended line of thought is instanced again and again by Chomsky, straight from the annals of imperialism, where as late as the mid-1960s a 'think-tank' of eminent, mainstream intellectuals – US scientists – had to go to their work in order to arrive at the startling conclusion that 'you cannot isolate [counterinsurgency] problems from people'.

Bloomfield's position does recognise that every human being is unique; he knows that no one can ever hope to fully comprehend anyone else. But his particular brand of behaviourism can make no allowance for any genuine freedom in the way a person handles language; there is no room for linguistic creativity. What remains is a kind of pathology, where syntactical components and phonemes are assembled so that eventually a body of language gets constructed, but any resemblance between it and a living force is very slight indeed; the introduction of semantics is akin to the breath of life.

In one of his more illustrious book reviews, Chomsky attacked the extreme branch of behaviourism as it appears in the shape of B. F. Skinner and that approach to psychology which seeks to affirm that 'what a person does is fully determined by his genetic endowment and history of reinforcement'. Chomsky can barely conceal his contempt: 'It would be hard to conceive of a more striking failure to comprehend even the rudiments of scientific thinking.'

But it is integral to his approach that you should not halt at the point where something is revealed as false: from there you will make further discoveries by asking 'what social or ideological needs' are being served by such a theory. In the case of Skinner-style behaviourism this is quite straightforward; in fact Skinner himself has suggested that 'the control of the population as a whole must be delegated to specialists – to police, priests, owners, teachers, therapists and so on, with their specialized reinforcers and their codified contingencies.'

Yet a tacit acceptance of this sort of behavioural approach is a feature of those who exercise the controlling interest in western society. It lies at the core of the dogma of imperialism and the unswerving belief that a colonised people has neither the wit nor the will to determine its own existence. Every insurrection becomes the effect of foreign infiltration. There is no such thing as a self-motivating populist movement. Ordinary working people never go on strike except when hypnotised into it by crazed external agitators who have penetrated the shopfloor. Within the terms of this argument folk like Arthur Scargill,[13] like Castro, Allende, Mandela, are always puppets of a foreign regime. It is inconceivable to such authority structures that individual persons may create strategies of their own, close to a logical contradiction.

Chomsky offers a great example of this in the person of Ho Chi Minh. For years a variety of western intelligence agencies tried to establish his connection with Moscow but it could never be done. Such a connection could never be discovered: but to suggest the connection might not exist would have required a mammoth leap of the imagination. Instead came the following:

No evidence has yet turned up that Ho Chi Minh is receiving

current directives either from Moscow, China, or the Soviet legation in Bangkok . . . It may be assumed that Moscow feels that Ho and his lieutenants have had sufficient training and experience and are sufficiently loyal to be trusted to determine their day-to-day policy without supervision.

It is only by an extension of the same logic that the fortieth President of the United States – Ronald Reagan – begins wondering, apparently in all sincerity, if Auld Nick, the very Devil himself, could be responsible for the current wrongdoing in the world. It is consistent. The global policy of his Government has presupposed the existence of an international conspiracy forever engaged in novel methods of advancing its own 'Communist interests while preserving the fiction of "autonomous" national liberation movements.' Thus if the authorities are never brought any evidence of 'spying' they are entitled to suppose their intelligence agents are falling down on the job. If eventually they are forced to concede that their agents are doing their work properly, then they will have to look elsewhere for an answer. At this stage, instead of re-examining the actual premise of the argument – the existence of an international Communist conspiracy – the authorities go veering off into the outer reaches of the theory: enter the alien infiltrator, the superhuman force of evil, he of the cloven hoof. It may be the stuff of comic books but the logic is consistent.

Generally, both logic and mathematics operate as systems of deductive reasoning; they begin from assuming the truth of one fundamental premise or set of premises, and from there any number of statements or propositions can be produced. And all of these statements or propositions will be true for as long as that original premise, or set of premises, itself remains true. But once they start showing too many signs of collapse there is no point trying to shore them all up, the entire edifice probably needs to be reconstructed, and that means a new foundation, one that will hold everything together.

Philosophers have been preoccupied for centuries by the search for that one thing they could see to be true beyond any shadow of doubt. It was this search that led René Descartes to his *cogito ergo sum* (I think therefore I am), the one statement about the world he felt able to rely upon absolutely. It made no difference what he was thinking about, just that he was thinking, this was the fact. From that one foundation he went on to demonstrate the existence of God.

The years previous had been difficult in Europe; among other people Galileo, Kepler and Copernicus were discovering things about the physical world that did not seem compatible with the prevailing wisdom, especially that which held the Earth to be the centre of the universe. The implications for the Church by this modern line of reasoning were all too apparent to the ecclesiastical authorities of the day – the history of persecution is probably the history of the defence of false premises.

Just about the first move any dictatorship makes on procuring power is to have its right to that power placed beyond challenge. This is achieved by diverse methods; one such is by having the right established not simply in law or by force of arms, but as an actual 'fact of nature', i.e. a law set beyond the reach of mere mortals. Thus comes about the divine right of kings and the infallibility of religious leaders.

The less blatant method is to frame the right in a constitution and have as its first principle that all challenges to The Constitution shall be deemed 'unconstitutional'. In South Africa the African National Congress is the representative voice of the overwhelming majority of women and men who live there; but that voice is always excluded the 'right' to be heard when any 'official' talks begin. Yet if the racist group who hold power there were to include the ANC in these talks they would, in effect, be conceding their own illegitimacy: their 'right' to power is premised solely on their appropriation of the right not to recognise the overwhelming majority of people who live in the place.

And civilised western societies like Great Britain and the USA are content to concede them that right, they are quite willing to allow the argument from tyranny to reign supreme; so yet another murderous dictatorship is entitled to do whatever it likes, it can change or not change but in the last analysis it is entirely up to itself.

During his revolutionary work in *Syntactic Structures* Chomsky has abandoned a purely behaviourist approach, accepting the primacy of semantics in the study of language, and 'a large part of [it] is devoted to precisely that question, that any linguistic theory would have to be judged adequate or inadequate on the basis of its ability to account for semantic facts.'[14] Some of the universal principles he sees as part of 'human nature' are grammatical, e.g. rules of transformation, and these he had worked out before his movement away from orthodoxy. But once the way in which language is actually used by people is introduced into linguistics the full complexity of the study becomes apparent, for the matter is thrown right back to what Chomsky calls 'Plato's Problem'. This is where

> Socrates demonstrates that an untutored slave boy knows the principles of geometry by leading him, through a series of questions, to the discovery of theorems of geometry. This experiment raises a problem that is still with us: How was the slave boy able to find truths of geometry without instruction or information?

In his own attempt at solving the problem of how folk seem to know things they have never before experienced, Plato landed in other worlds and previous existences, along with other thinkers both before and since. An extension of the problem concerns creativity in language – not the creativity of people involved in literary art forms, but the daily creativity of men and women and children as they go about their daily business:

> in normal speech one does not merely repeat what one has heard but produces new linguistic forms – often new in one's experience or even in the history of the language – and there are no limits to such innovation.

The importance of this fact for any theory of knowledge is underlined by Chomsky. Language is so rich and sophisticated, capable of such infinite possibility, that no strictly empirical approach can hope to account for its existence. Once we are engaged in its study at this level we are in at the heart of the study of mind; 'linguistics, psychology and philosophy are no longer to be regarded as separate and autonomous disciplines.'

The step Chomsky takes around this point is very bold, very courageous; it leads him away from the vanguard of contemporary linguistics. In philosphical terms he becomes, like Plato himself, a 'rationalist': somebody who believes there are *a priori* forms of knowledge, i.e. forms of knowledge available to people outwith any experience they may have gained from being in the world. This allows of a solution to 'Plato's Problem' and also to the 'creativity' extension of it referred to above, which derives from another rationalist, René Descartes.

The problem is knowledge, how to give a satisfactory account for its acquisition and for the unique application each one of us makes of it. There are some things we know from our experience of being in the world but there are other things we seem to know just by the workings of our own individual minds; mathematical truths, for example, the kind of 'truths' that the 'untutored slave boy' knew.

But there are other, similar sorts of truths, such as the 'properties' of God, i.e. 'goodness', 'perfection', 'immortality'; then too there is our knowledge of the connecting links and relations between things and events, e.g. our certain knowledge that the sun will rise tomorrow morning, and so on. For Chomsky these *a priori* forms of knowledge will include certain principles of universal grammar; these principles enable human beings to use the language or languages of whatever culture they chance to be born within.

Through the Middle Ages society had been segmented. In matters of the intellect individual disciplines were inclined to keep themselves to themselves, the physical world consisting largely of a confused jumble of raw data, and it was up to each to make what sense of it they could. Alongside the breakthroughs being made in the sciences from the latter part of the fifteenth century onwards there developed a critical interest in mathematical reasoning. Also communication was becoming more public; discussions were taking place between people. Then a hundred years or so later Descartes had his tremendous insight into the possibility of *one* theoretical foundation being provided for *all* the sciences. Even bolder, a system as powerful as the one he envisaged might provide a way of working out the connecting links and relations between God and men and things.

Yet he could find no foundation of truth in the world about him, the physical world; there was nothing he could perceive there as being true absolutely. Every last thing was open to doubt. The one and only certainty he had (I think therefore I am) was true by the light of his own reason: Descartes knew that he existed *only* because he was thinking. There was no evidence for it outside of himself, beyond his own mind. It was a *natural* judgment, one arrived at purely through his own reason, his own common sense.

Nowadays much of the antagonism toward rationalism results from dogma, straight prejudice against (and confused by) the very idea of 'mind' being 'a place', where principles of reason are 'stored'. In his later writings Chomsky refers always to 'mind/ brain'; this is a way of distinguishing his own conception. It can deflect the confusion that may arise from conventional thinking, where brain is 'body' but mind is 'mental', somehow 'not body' at all. This sort of 'dualism' is associated with Descartes and others; it makes a clear separation between body and mind, where body is 'physical' and mind is 'metaphysical':

> When we speak of the mind, we are speaking at some level of abstraction of yet-unknown physical mechanisms of the brain, much as those who spoke of the valence of oxygen or the benzene ring were speaking at some level of abstraction about physical mechanisms, then unknown.[15]

Arguments against rationalism and the entire idea of innate forms of knowledge usually revolve round the existence or otherwise of metaphysical entities like 'mind' and 'soul'. But in the above Chomsky is carrying the defence a stage beyond, by suggesting that there is no longer any adequate explanation of 'body'. At the present time of inquiry what we are left with 'are a variety of forces, particles that have no mass, and other entities that would have been offensive to the "scientific common sense" of the Cartesians.' He seems to be proposing that if the most elementary 'thing' in the physical world is an infinitesimal bundle of energy – instead of an infinitesimal particle of matter – then there may well be 'places' where innate forms of knowledge can be located after all.

A Reading from the Work of Noam Chomsky

But that aspect of the problem may well turn out to have no solution at all, which last point provides another sharp distinction between Chomsky's beliefs and those of the great metaphysicians like Descartes for whom it was central that the system he hoped to construct would be powerful enough to supply the answers to *everything*. Chomsky dismisses that as an illusion; no theoretical construct can ever be capable of such a thing.

A way of avoiding the problem is thought possible by some via the work of other folk involved in theory of structure. Jean Piaget once suggested that Chomsky seemed aware of only two alternatives in the acquisition and application of knowledge: (a) innate principles of reason and (b) knowledge that we derive directly from the world about us. Piaget does refer to a third process, that of 'internal equilibration', a process 'governed by general laws of organisation' which is 'self regulating'.[16] Chomsky, however, was aware of Piaget's line of argument, he rejected it:

Piaget and I actually took part in a lengthy discussion about these topics a couple of years later [after publication of *Syntactic Structures*]. The problem is that there simply is nothing to the third process that he mentions. It's impossible to formulate, and it turns out to be nothing but metaphor and empty rhetoric. By now I think these ideas have largely been abandoned in cognitive psychology simply because they don't get anywhere.[17]

Piaget cited the findings of a group of French mathematicians ('Nicholas Bourbaki' is the group's pseudonym); in particular their 'discovery of three "parent structures", that is, three not further reducible "sources" of all other structures'. The three structures referred to are (1) Algebraic (2) Order (3) Topological. This trio encompasses the kind of activities associated with judgment and an entry into this line of thought comes through a look at the Common Sense tradition as it developed in Scotland. Chomsky sees 'libertarian conceptions [being derived] by Rousseau from Cartesian principles of body and mind', then being 'developed further in French and German Romanticism' and on through the 'libertarian social theory of Wilhelm von Humboldt'. But this view may underestimate the ramifications of the intellectual struggle going on in Britain around that time. Rousseau was influenced by Andrew Fletcher (1655–1716) who favoured the Greek ideal of the little nation whose 'seat of government [would] remain in a city small enough to contain a face-to-face community where people could be under one another's eyes most of the time.'[18] Fletcher wanted federalism and was strongly opposed to being governed by remote control, whether from London or anywhere else. George Davie points to the influence here of 'the reformation ideal of a constitution finely balanced as between church and state'.

It is too easy to disregard this from a late-twentieth-century western perspective but the 'ideal' can provide a system of checks and balances 'through the cooperation of a pair of mutually complementary assemblies, the one concerned with politics and law, the other with the sphere of ethics and faith.' If this sounds anachronistic it should be compared to the present system of western democracy where voting is usually just a method of 'ratifying decisions that have already been made' by one or two people in an office.

In Scotland during the last years of the seventeenth century between a third and a fifth of the people were reported as 'having died or fled' due to the effects of famine.[19] The Darien Scheme had just collapsed and the economy was more or less bankrupt. On a wider intellectual level this was a decade or so after the German thinker Leibniz and the English thinker Newton, unbeknown to each other, had been locked in the simultaneous creation of differential calculus. Meanwhile in Edinburgh certain premises were still not open to challenge and a nineteen-year-old student by the name of Aikenhead was executed for having dared to demand 'evidence for the dogma that the moral blindness of natural man can sometimes be overcome by a grace-inspired reading of the bible.'[20]

What developed from all of this was a fierce debate on the problem of how to reconcile economic expansion with the moral and intellectual consciousness of the population as a whole. For those unfamiliar with George Davie's work on the Scottish Enlightenment this can appear a rather surprising 'problem'. It may be thought obvious that the greater the technological and economic progress in a country the greater the benefits that must accrue to the country as a whole. But in reality such conclusions are only guaranteed in party political broadcasts.

One clearly defined route to economic expansion lies in the production of highly skilled and trained individuals who are to take on specialised employment. This can lead to the demand for an educational system geared precisely to the production of experts and specialists. Under the influence of John Locke and others this was happening in England and many folk north of the border were pushing for the same thing. Andrew Fletcher was *not* one of them.

Fletcher argued that an educational system devoted to the production of specialists would result in a situation where none of the educated community would be fit to govern the nation, given that being fit to govern the nation entails the capacity for decision-making in general contexts. This capacity involves the power of judgment and critical evaluation, which is developed more potently by the ability to see beyond the limits of your own discipline. If the educational system is to thrust groups of people into separate compartments then none will be equipped to take the wide view necessary. No longer does it become possible for the poet to discuss methodology with sculptors and electricians. Reasoning devices like mathematics, logic and intuition will stagnate, this being abetted by the decline in subjects thought to be impractical, e.g. philosophy, the classics, the study of languages and other cultures, these very subjects which encourage a general approach to the world.

In this scenario actual knowledge itself becomes at a premium, cut off from those who are not 'specialising'. And gradually the majority of men and women and children become divorced from those areas where 'experts' reign supreme. What remains is not only repugnant but disastrous:

> a society spiritually split between over-specialised boffins on the one hand and unthinking proles on the other is not merely repellent from a moral point of view, because of its tolerating or even encouraging the intellectual backwardness of the masses, but at the same time is also inherently an unstable basis for the material progress it seeks to sustain [and] the stultification of the majority [will] affect the mental balance of society as a whole . . . [21]

If there is any irony at work at all in this nightmarish world being envisaged by Davie it could lie in its resemblance to the medieval order of ignorance which Descartes had sought to eradicate by constructing his unified system of knowledge. At the root of the matter is the segmentation of knowledge, the push for individual disciplines to keep themselves to themselves; and in line with that the creation of 'experts' and 'keepers-of-the-faith' ('priests, owners, teachers, therapists and so on, with their specialized reinforcers and their codified contingencies'), whether they be monks in a monastery or members of a government planning department.

As far as Fletcher could see, once Scotland became incapable of creating its own governing élite it would cease to be free, it would become an intellectual desert, having to import an élite from the English upper-classes. He advocated a return to the 'solider sorts of learning'[22] as in Oxford and Cambridge, for it is to be noted that both these seats of higher education continued as before, prior to the new approach and altered curriculum, designed to hasten economic progress. It could be argued, perhaps, that the classical approach being so rigorously defended by the Oxbridge traditionalists was devoted to that most subtle of all specialisations, the production of a *leadership class*. This class dominated most of the English-speaking world then, and for folk who live in countries connected to the former Empire very little has changed, certainly not in Scotland.

The continued erosion of the generalist approach to education ensures that the entire system comes to exist as a straight reinforcement of the prevailing right-wing authority. Beyond Oxbridge about the best we can hope for is the paternalistic liberalism of a William Cobbett, whose

> ideas of democratic or mass education seem to have been drawn from his experiences in the army. The model of mass education is for him the N.C.O. explaining the 'naming of the parts' to the recruits.[23]

And it is within this context, no matter how well-intentioned are its orthodox left-liberal principles, that the educational system comes to be nothing more than

> a reification of the notion that culture is synomomous with property. And the essentially acquisitive attitude to culture, 'education' and 'a good accent' is simply an aspect of the

competitive, status–conscious class structure of . . . society as a whole.[24]

Thus, across the mainstream political spectrum, from 'hardline' left to 'extremist' right, different games are being played with the same set of rules. The end product is hierarchy, whether it be a form of meritocracy or a mix of that with the usual hereditary privileges for rank and/or riches.

This is a world where the scepticism of Locke, Berkeley, Hume and the rest has led to the ideological behaviourism of those responsible for the global and domestic policies of western civilisation during the past couple of hundred years. It is a world where there are no universal principles, whether of freedom or anything else. People are 'blank slates' upon which anything is to be scraped by those who have assumed the right to power. Knowledge gets doled out in the form of rewards and punishment exercises. Those who have been produced to govern on behalf of the rulers decide the curriculum: history will concern the lives and loves of famous personalities; politics is a field of endeavour best left to those who specialise in it, i.e. Members of Parliament and Members of the Media; poverty and deprivation become the concepts of social science, death and disease the experience of the medical profession.

Both the Cartesian Common Sense tradition as developed by Chomsky and the Common Sense tradition developed in Scotland are premised on forms of natural reason. In the former this becomes grounds for rationalism whereas in the Scottish philosophical tradition such a *necessity* does not arise, there is no *need* to become involved in innateness hypotheses. Each shares a belief in fundamental principles that are inherent in all people. These include the faculty of judgment which lies at the heart not only of reason, but of the will to freedom. This faculty is neither learned nor is it taught. But neither is it a 'thing', whether material or immaterial.

The skills involved in judgment are mathematical, logical, intuitive; they can be refined and improved; or else they can remain fallow. It does not follow that highly educated folk will prove more capable of good judgment than those who 'fail' within the mainstream educational system.

Chomsky destroys any presuppositions about the relationship between higher education and the ability to think clearly and critically. The educated classes have more access to information than the vast majority of ordinary men and women but it is rarely in their own economic interest to seek it out and see what it amounts to. This does not have to imply a deliberate policy, let alone the existence of a conspiracy:

> the intellectual elite is the most heavily indoctrinated sector [of society], for good reasons. It's their role as secular priesthood to really believe the nonsense they put forth. Other people can repeat it, but it's not that crucial that they believe it because, after all, they are the guardians of the faith. Except for the very rare person who's just an outright liar, it's hard to be a convincing exponent of the faith unless you've internalized it and come to believe it.

An interesting example of this is the novelist Saul Bellow, 'a propagandist's delight', according to Chomsky in his review of Bellow's *To Jerusalem and Back*,[25] which he describes as 'a catalogue of What Every Good American Should Believe, as compiled by the Israeli Information Ministry.' He concludes the review by referring to the 'critical acclaim [the book] has received [as] revealing, with regard to the state of American intellectual life.'

But that applies equally to Great Britain where Saul Bellow is always being pushed by the mainstream literary establishment, including the 'radical' younger writers; all defer to Bellow as the one infallible source of American integrity and clarity of vision. When a fine introduction to Chomsky's political writings was published recently, the *Independent* newspaper gave it for review to Auberon Waugh. At first sight it appears the kind of jolly, xenophobic prank which members of the British media like to play on major thinkers from other countries (I seem to recollect Clive James being employed by one of the 'qualities' to write the obituary of Sartre) but it is as well bearing in mind that Waugh, while content to be allied to the far right, has in the past been revealed as an 'occasional mouthpiece for some highly sensitive "gossip" or intelligence smears' which those in control of British society have wished to see public.[26]

Finding new ways of denying reality is a key function of the mainstream intelligentsia. Language provides unlimited opportunity for it. Before it is possible to enter any debate about the unspeakable atrocities being perpetrated on people every day of the week in all parts of the world a slow trudge through semantics has to begin. What do we mean by pain? What do we mean by suffering?

Around this point the terms get surrounded, captured by inverted commas – e.g. what do we mean by 'torture' – thus throwing into doubt the very existence of the experience. A distinction is created between the actual experience and the 'concept of the experience'. In creating this distinction a closed system is put into operation: only those who specialise in discussing concepts will be admitted. The actual experience of atrocity becomes redundant. It becomes the predicate instead of the subject; we no longer refer to atrocity we refer to the 'concept of atrocity' where concept is subject and atrocity predicate. Refugees' reports are excluded. So too are folk who are likely to be affected by such reports:

> The ardently opionated, the ardent in all forms, the raisers of
> voices, the thumpers on the table, the 'swearers', the
> passionate, those who burst into tears – these are all absent . . .
> For the 'professional' exists through a language that acquits
> him of personal involvement . . .[27]

Such specialists are paid for their experience of experiences they
never encounter, their experience is conceptual. They get paid for
their experience of every concept under the sun; from the concept
of happiness to the concept of torture, from the concept of
malnutrition to the concept of dampness in council housing and its
relation to the concept of death from lung disease. They exclude
the actual experience from the terms of the argument, they
'categorise in the *absence* of that which is being categorised',[28] they
get rid of the premise.

One year after the European Convention on Human Rights had
'found the British Government guilty of "torture, inhuman and
degrading treatment"', a famous judgment was delivered, it was
soon known as the 'Torturers' Charter':

> after a torture case had been brought against the Greek
> Colonels . . . the Commission defined 'inhuman treatment' as
> 'at least such treatment as deliberately causes severe suffering,
> mental or physical.' 'Torture' was 'inhuman treatment which
> has a purpose, such as the obtaining of information or con-
> fession, or the infliction of punishment, and it is generally an
> aggravated form of inhuman trearment.' 'Degrading treat-
> ment' was 'treatment or punishment of an individual which
> grossly humiliates him before others or drives him to act
> against his will . . . '[29]

which gives us a fair idea of what the Callaghan–led Labour

Government had been found guilty of in 1976.

But this judgment occurred one year *after* that, when four men and one woman found themselves in front of the Belfast City Commission. One of the four men was a boy of sixteen who complained of Assault During Interview by the RUC. The experiences he complained of included being 'struck thirty times mostly to the stomach and having his hair pulled' during the first interview; receiving 'dozens of blows' during the second interview; while in the third

> he said he had been punched in the stomach, the kidneys and the back more than fifty times and slapped around the face with an open hand. He said that his mouth had been burnt with a lighted cigarette, that he had been made to strip and was struck in the testicles and around the kidneys.

How do we describe that? A report? A report of what? Torture? Rough treatment? Hard luck? Interrogation? Being interviewed?

Defining experiences is notoriously difficult, especially those experiences endured by other people. State authority thinks it a job best left to the experts. In this particular instance above the expert was Lord Justice McGonigal, 'former Second World War commando and a founder of the S.A.S.' He was quick to indicate that 'a certain roughness of treatment' was allowed by the European Commission according to the definition outlined earlier; and this could

> take the form of slaps or blows of the hand on the head or face and also underlines the fact that the point up to which prisoners and the public may accept physical violence as being neither cruel nor excessive varies between different societies and even between different sections of them.

A Reading from the Work of Noam Chomsky

Such equivocation allowed Lord Justice McGonigal to draw that wee bit closer to the elimination of the experience altogether when he did his own exercise in semantics:

> Inhuman treatment is . . . treatment causing *severe* suffering. Torture is an *aggravated* form of inhuman treatment and degrading conduct is conduct which *grossly* humiliates.

At which point experts who specialise in encountering concepts can instigate a further debate on the meaning of grossness or severity, or the meaning of the concept 'aggravation'.

This kind of dualist thinking has a long tradition, it is reminiscent of an ancient line of thought which believed every single thing in the world had its own tiny god. It also lands us back with Descartes and the rationalists in one corner, the British empiricists in the other. While in between is the problem of knowledge and how to connect reason with experience, thought with extension (mind with body), essence with existence.

The argument given on behalf of the British Labour Government above is in sharp opposition to common sense and natural reason. It amounts to the following: people who have been tortured do not have valid grounds for knowing what torture is.

When refugees' reports are heeded it is usually as an aid to apportioning blame, to discover which *individual* is responsible. During this the position of the victims will be brought into question: are they innocent or guilty, are they innocent victims or guilty victims. It so happpens that in the case mentioned above the sixteen-year-old boy was released. It was conceded that he might have been treated roughly but if so then any statements made by him were 'not admissible in evidence', which not only refers to any so-called confession, it also refers – surprise surprise – to the complaints he made concerning the RUC and their Assault During Interview.

The relativist position of the European Commission should be kept also in mind. By extension there is one legal system for the powerful and another legal system for the powerless. But nobody expects anything else anyway, not even the powerless themselves, and that seems the only justification. 'Terror and torture' governments should just exercise caution occasionally, lest they 'provoke hostile reactions in world capitals'.

The crucial feature of scepticism is that it subjects premises and principles to scrutiny; it takes nothing for granted; 'truths' are no longer allowed to be assumed, they must be put to the test and verified empirically. This has obvious dangers for metaphysical theories to do with 'mind' as also for truths connected with religious belief and faith. But in the early eighteenth century people in Scotland wanted to fight clear of the dogmatic prejudice that resulted in the State killing of the student who dared to demand 'evidence'.

The critical method of John Locke and others seemed to offer this possibility through its rejection of innate forms of knowledge. Nothing would be admitted as true unless it was seen to be true. Unlike Descartes they did not want to construct one unifying system to yield ultimate knowledge of all the mysteries of the universe. They were content to clear away the muddle of conventional thought, thereby allowing the scientists to get on with the real work, applying the proper methods of observation and experimentation. Unfortunately formal problems over the 'two' kinds of knowledge still arose.

Empiricist approaches become bogged down in the theory of knowledge, tending as they do toward 'atomism', the belief that suggests it is possible to discover the nature of the whole by a strict examination of the parts. The ancient form of this philosophy centred on the notion that 'the whole visible universe has arisen by the cohesion of small invisible particles, the atoms.' This further applied to the mind which was composed of 'very smooth, delicate and round [atoms]; or, as Lucretius put it . . . the smallest, roundest and most mobile that there are.'[30]

But if we do come to know things only piecemeal, via our sensory experience, then 'Plato's Problem' must crop up sooner or later. How can we know the properties of a triangle if triangles do not exist in the world? How do we know of the connecting links and relations between things if none of those links or relations can be discovered as things in the world roundabout us? And if we learn of the whole by assembly of the parts how are we able to recognise the whole when it is complete? Davie points to the influence of Irish philosophy as decisive on the Scottish tradition here, in particular the work of George Berkeley (although Francis Hutcheson is also of importance).[31]

There is a vague similarity to Chomsky when instead of worrying over the existence of 'mind' George Berkeley proceeds to dispense with 'body', he rejects the existence of matter altogether. A body exists only when it is being perceived. We never know any objects in the physical world at all, only our own perceptions of them. But this does not mean that bodies come in and out of existence, or that the world disappears when we close our eyes. These were common charges against him, and still levelled against him into the twentieth century. Thus 'we have not so much reason to admire the strength of Berkeley's genius, as his boldness in publishing to the world an opinion which the unlearned would be apt to interpret as the sign of a crazy intellect.'[32]

His influence in Scotland was primary, none left a greater mark on the Scottish Enlightenment. He personally wrote to congratulate a group of youths from the Edinburgh Students' Society on their understanding of his 'system' and his

paradoxical and provocative argument that there was perhaps
less difference between Locke and his illiberal opponents
whether Scottish or otherwise, than was generally supposed,
and that, properly sifted and consistently developed, the
experimental pragmatic principle which was Locke's greatest
contribution was likely to lead men back to a God-centred
philosophy not unlike that of Halyburton.[33]

But one of the most powerful voices raised in opposition to the
Irish philosopher was not of the 'unlearned' section of society,
rather it was the 'learned' Dr Johnson. Johnson held the Gaelic
language in contempt. While visiting Scotland he scoffed at the very
idea that it might also have had a written form. Rather than telling
him to fuck off, Scots in the vicinity offered arguments, which the
'learned doctor' refused to accept. Of course it was not the
'unlearned' of whom Berkeley was so scathing but his colleagues
and peers, the 'learned', in the areas of philosophy and science; those
unable to trust 'their own senses . . . and [who] after all their
labouring . . . are forced to own that . . . self evident or demon-
strative knowledge of the existence of sensible things' is just not
possible.[34] Their work led to 'forlorn Skepticism', foundering on
the belief that we know our ideas of reality but never reality itself.
If what these 'learned' believed were true then it is impossible for us
ever to know the world at all, we are doomed to remain in a state
of ignorance for all eternity. The 'illiterate bulk of mankind . . . walk
the high-road of plain, common sense . . . governed by the dictates
of nature, for the most part easy and undisturbed.'[35] This because
their belief in God is absolute, as with Berkeley himself.

Berkeley was answering John Locke who had distinguished
between 'primary ideas' as representative of 'primary qualities'
existent in the world, e.g. size, shape, extension, and 'secondary'
ideas representative of 'secondary qualities' that cannot exist in

themselves, e.g. smells or sounds. The existence of these 'secondary qualities' is dependent upon the agency of an active being, e.g. a thing smells only if it is being smelled, the wind sounds only when it is being heard.

But Berkeley demonstrated that 'primary qualities' – qualities as they are in themselves – can never be represented truly by our ideas of them. He further argued that 'primary qualities' are every bit as dependent on the perception of an active being as are 'secondary qualities'. Nothing at all exists, said Berkeley, not unless perceived by an active being or itself a being capable of perceiving. He was a Bishop of the Anglican Church in Ireland, based firstly at Derry City then later at Cloyne, and his solution to the problem lies in the existence of God: matter is always and eternally being perceived by the Almighty.

The existence of God is the premise of his philosophy; the world is always in His presence. It is a line of thought in the tradition of the concept of Divine Illumination – there is never a time when we are not in the presence of God, through Him the world is revealed, and so on – and can be traced back to Augustine and earlier Neoplatonists, Christian and non-Christian. Berkeley argued that we experience the world 'immediately', as brute data; there is nothing between us and it. And further, that these brute data are elements of a divine language, the language of God Himself. Science may describe the world but not explain it. He formulated a theory of vision and an alternative approach to geometry, stressing 'touch' as distinct from 'sight', leading

the way in shewing how we learn to perceive the distance of an object from the eye . . . He made the distinction between that extension and figure which we perceive by sight only, and that which we perceive by touch; calling the first, visible, the last, tangible extension and figure.[36]

As far as Berkeley is concerned 'the externality we attribute to the objects of our senses consists simply in the fact that our "sensations occur in groups, held together by a permanent law." '[37] In terms of straight empiricism this offers good progress in the theory of knowledge but his position still lapses into atomism; the gap between our sensory experience of the world and our actual knowledge of the world remains as wide as ever.

An escape from the difficulty appears through the work of the Scottish philosopher Thomas Reid whose insight is of significance in the development of theory of structure:

> Every operation of the senses, in its very nature, implies judgment or belief, as well as simple apprehension . . . When I perceive a tree before me, my faculty of seeing gives me not only a notion or simple apprehension of the tree, but a belief of its existence, and of its figure, distance and magnitude; and this judgment or belief is not got by comparing ideas, it is included in the very nature of perception. [These] original and natural judgments . . . make up what is called the common sense of mankind.[38]

Our knowledge of the world does not derive from singular sensations of brute physical data. It comes about through an elementary synthesis. Knowledge *begins from judgment*. When we sense something we are perceiving it at one and the same time. There is no gap between coming into sensory contact with something and the knowledge of what contact with the something amounts to. And this 'knowledge of what contact with the something amounts to' *includes* an understanding of connecting links and relations such as must be essential for 'a belief of [something's] existence, and of its figure, distance and magnitude.'

This strand of thought distinguishes Reid not only from

Berkeley but from his great rival, David Hume. Hume was opposed to the idea that experience could ever bring knowledge of connecting links or causal relations. We cannot experience these 'necessary connections'; what happens is that we 'feel' such things to be true.

But in common to both Scottish philosophers is an acceptance of a form of natural reason. In the case of Hume this seems to end at 'instinct'; Reid goes further, common sense is a faculty of judgment held in common by all members of humankind. The Common Sense tradition, whether of Chomsky, Descartes, Reid or Rousseau, is not a question of instinct, not unless by instinct we mean something that can comprise logic, mathematics and intuition.

The key feature of Reid's position is irreducibility; it is in opposition to any form of atomism. If it is at all possible to discuss a reductive process then it can only be something along the lines of the 'Bourbaki' 'parent-structures', the algebraic, order and topological. These are the processes of understanding, of thought. And in terms of further exploratory work here, it is of interest to note that if we stick to mathematics in the slipstream of Thomas Reid then we enter the field of spherical geometry in which he was engaged some fifty years ahead of his time.[39] The concepts of time and space have loomed into view; not only in the world of science but in the world of ideas generally.

And for the politics of late eighteenth-century Scotland a philosophical context is also set for the libertarian consciousness that was developing through thinkers like John Millar and Dugald Stewart, both of whom believed in the general dissemination of knowledge.

George Davie describes this period as the 'pinnacle' of Scottish philosophy, when came the creation of its many great textbooks. There are obvious parallels here with what was happening in

France, with the rise of discussion groups among tradesmen and craftsmen, bound in with the basic notion that if people can think for themselves they can also determine their own existence. In Paris around the turn of the eighteenth century it was not uncommon for the great mathematicians of the time to lecture to as many as 1,200 folk at a sitting.

Needless to say radical lines of thought were not confined to any single field of endeavour. How could they be when the very essence of the argument concerned the universalisability of knowledge, that no boundaries were to exist. Ideas of freedom and self-determination, the attempted unshackling of bolts and chains, were being discussed in different parts of Great Britain. In Scotland the work of the poets was of significance, not only that of Robert Burns,[40] but also poets like Robert Tannahill, Sandy Rodgers and Alexander Wilson – the last two of whom were gaoled at different times for sedition. Both Tannahill and Wilson were weavers to trade; eventually the latter was under so much pressure from the authorities that he emigrated from Paisley to the USA, where he went on, in the best generalist tradition, to become the founder of American ornithology.[41]

Another weaver by the name of Wilson was in communication with Thomas Muir, the radical lawyer, and involved in organising discussion groups with other workers from an early age. Many years later, while in his mid-sixties, this man was hanged in front of 20,000 people in Glasgow. He was James 'Purly' Wilson, so-called through his invention of the purl stitch. Official history for the next 150 years described him as an illiterate half-wit, that he had been led astray by infiltrators.[42] He had been in direct contact with John Baird, the Condorrat weaver hanged at Stirling alongside Andrew Hardie. The three men were executed in 1820 for their part in the Scottish Insurrection (there were 88 counts of high treason in Scotland during that year).

A Reading from the Work of Noam Chomsky

The name of 'The Ettrick Shepherd' might sound unlikely in the above context. Yet in a sense the work of James Hogg is every bit as crucial in this generalist, Common Sense tradition as is the life of Alexander or James Wilson. As well as being a noted poet he published a great deal of prose. His novel *The Private Memoirs and Confessions of a Justified Sinner* appeared in 1824 and is his masterpiece. But within mainstream departments of English literature this novel is regarded as a fluke – that is, when it is being regarded at all. If evaluated solely within this restricted field the novel seems destined to remain a fluke for ever.[43] Nowhere else is there to be found even a suggestion of that strange and deadliest of ironies which Hogg perpetrates, bending reality, in the latter pages of the story.

This is the point where real-life members of the contemporary literati of Edinburgh are suddenly introduced into the tale thereby offering an illusion of 'natural reality' while lending their own personal weight to the 'authenticity' of the narrative. The literati being portrayed by Hogg were in the main contemptuous of his inferior social standing. As well as being a famous poet he had spent much of his life as a shepherd and he spoke in the language of his own cultural background (until his late teens he was close to illiterate). There was a tendency amongst his peers to patronise the poetry while failing to appreciate the prose. Hogg's novel is written in the ordinary standard English literary form of the period. When he brings the literati into the story he has them speak in that same standard form.

But then he introduces himself into the story and this 'self' is the man who is employed at wheeling and dealing in ewes, lambs and rams at country markets; not the 'self' as writer. He has this shepherd 'self' speak in the phoneticised language of someone who, by English literary standards, is a certain social inferior. The irony works on different levels but the most hair-raising one of the lot is that which is structured on the premise that somebody who speaks in a 'culturally debased' linguistic form could not conceivably create this prose masterpiece in the imperial language of English.

But such preposterous élitism is still rampant in contemporary literary circles where in a recent interview with the poet Craig Raine there was yet another example of 'the intellectual elite [as] the most indoctrinated sector' of society. In a discussion of the medium in which he works in relation to his 'working-class' background Raine was quite willing to concede that the actual art form itself, poetry, belonged to the upper reaches of society. But the folk from his own 'working-class' background do have their own art forms, he was at pains to point out, his father for instance had been a 'fine raconteur'.[44] Waal! Thanks Craig. But this kind of myopic nonsense is extraordinary. All it takes to disprove the point is a walk into the local library – although from there you might have a search, of course; the poetry written by people who 'fail' our educational system is more likely to be discovered in the 'local history' section.[45]

The year after the publication of Hogg's novel, the French mathematician and astronomer, Pierre Laplace, had summarised 'the development of deterministic mechanics'[46] as follows:

We must envisage the present state of the universe as the effect of its previous state, and as the cause of that which will follow. An intelligence that could know, at a given instant, all the forces governing the natural world, and the respective position of the entities which compose it, if in addition it was great enough to analyse all this information, would be able to embrace in a single formula the movements of the largest bodies in the universe and those of the lightest atoms: nothing would be uncertain for it, and the future, like the past, would be entirely present to its observation.

A Reading from the Work of Noam Chomsky

With slight adjustments here and there this could be turned into a textbook approach to semantics-free linguistics or, perhaps, for any purely behavioural approach to the study of mind. And with other slight adjustments it becomes an argument on behalf of the existence of God. But the God so conceived would stand in brooding opposition to human creativity and the principle of natural reason, utterly opposed to any puny demonstrations of self-determined activity and the will to freedom. It is a conception of God abhorrent not only to such as George Berkeley but also to William Blake and Søren Kierkegaard.

The Anglo-American tradition approves of David Hume the great empiricist and skeptic but is less certain of the Hume 'who spoke of those parts of our knowledge that are derived "from the original hand of nature" and that are "a species of instinct".'[47] Chomsky does pick up on that side of him but without being aware of him in the context of Scottish Common Sense philosophy. The thing that excited Immanuel Kant about Hume's thought concerns the theory of knowledge and the Scotsman's denial of 'the existence of necessary connections in nature' and his severing of any 'logical relations from those of the real world . . . ' And, paradoxically, this also influenced thinkers of a view diametrically opposed to his own, e.g. the Christian mystic Johan Hamann whose regard for Hume is somewhat reminiscent of Rousseau's regard for Voltaire.

But it is worth noting the influence of Hamann on Kierkegaard and existentialism, which can be readily appreciated from the following:

Nature is no ordered whole: so-called sensible men are blinkered beings who walk with a fine tread because they are blind to the true and profoundly disturbing character of reality, sheltered by it from their man-made contraptions; if

179

they glimpsed it as it is – a wild dance – they would go out their minds. How dare these pathetic pedants impose on the vast world of continuous, fertile, unpredictable, divine creation their own narrow, desiccated categories?[48]

The important factor being derived here is the ultimate unknowability of the brute physical data of reality. For thinkers like Johan Hamann, in the wake of David Hume, a return is now sanctioned to that conception of God premised on absolute, and *logical*, incomprehensibility.

In the same year Laplace died, 1827, another blow was being struck against deterministic mechanics and its 'anti-existential' implications. A Scottish botanist from Montrose by the name of Robert Brown observed

the behaviour of pollen grains – particles from various plants which . . . measured something like 1/5,000 of an inch – when immersed in water. What he discovered was that these particles perform a constant, agitated, and apparently erratic motion which has nothing to do with any currents moving in the water . . . 'These motions were such as to satisfy me, after frequently repeated observation, that they arose neither from currents in the fluid, nor from its gradual evaporation, but belonged to the particle itself.'[49]

As with Reid's elemental judgment, there is an 'irreducibility' being posited here, a structure that simply cannot be broken down into any 'constituent parts'. The particle is a network of impulses or motions of a self-determining/self-regulatory kind, i.e. it seems to be governed by itself and for itself (but a confusion here could lead to the difficulty Descartes had and the split between 'I' and 'I think').

This phenomenon has become known in the world of science generally as 'Brownian Motion' and was the subject of a decisive paper by Einstein which finally 'convinced the sceptics of the existence of atoms'. These atoms differ from those of the ancient materialists; they are *structures* as opposed to elemental, indivisible 'bits': when these atoms have been 'split' worlds have blown up.

People confined by the parameters of their own specialisation probably assume Einstein discovered his physical system by a close reading of the collected works of Isaac Newton, but ideas develop and shift in innumerable ways. The concepts of 'irreducibility' and 'elementary synthesis' are implicit in some remarks of the Spanish cubist painter Juan Gris:

> the architectural abstraction of the elements in a picture must be explored by the painter as if he were his own spectator . . . Until the work is completed he must remain ignorant of its appearance as a whole. To copy a preconceived appearance is like copying the appearance of a model . . . From this it is clear that the subject does not materialise in the appearance of the picture, but that the subject, in materialising, gives the picture its appearance.[50]

at which level the technical problems to be resolved by the artist concern space and time. These have been the preoccupations of – among other artists – Cézanne, Claude Monet, Gertrude Stein, James Joyce, Franz Kafka, Carlos Williams, and also W. S. Graham and Samuel Beckett. Tom Leonard writes of the last two named and

> that area of present-time consciousness [they] give to their personae; and their personae in turn pass it on to the reader. It's a very political thing to do, since it seems to assume that

the only – and equal – value that can be placed on any human being is in the fact that the human being actually exists.[51]

The most crucial aspect of James Hogg's achievement is linked to this 'present-time consciousness' and the way in which he succeeded in embedding himself in the text. Any attempt to isolate him from the 'reality' of his 'fiction' leaves the reader stranded in strange loops and warps; a technical term for this is 'recursiveness'.

In the summary of deterministic mechanics given by Pierre Laplace a formal problem arises. Is the 'intelligence' he refers to capable of 'embracing itself' while 'embracing the universe'? If the 'intelligence' is itself a part of the universe then that should go without saying. This means it must 'embrace itself' while 'embracing the universe', as it 'embraces itself' 'embracing the universe' 'embracing itself' 'embracing the universe . . .' and so on *ad infinitum* throughout the spiral of eternity. If the 'intelligence' is not of 'this' universe then the concept 'universe' requires redefining. Perhaps one solution will be to create a second universe, one more powerful than the first, so that the 'intelligence' can belong to it and be capable of embracing the smaller one.

When that happens a separation takes place between 'intelligence' and 'universe'. But probably the first implication concerns the power of the 'intelligence'; it simply cannot be as powerful as we thought since it is bound to run up against the 'embracing itself' problem, and can never become capable of embracing this second, more powerful universe. Maybe a third universe is the answer.

It is a problem that turns up in various disciplines and involves finite automata theory and recursive function theory. It was central to the theorem formulated by Gödel and published in 1931[52] as a response to *Principia Mathematica*, a three-volume work on mathematical logic by A. E. Whitehead and Bertrand Russell.

One thing demonstrated by Gödel is that if there is any 'system comprehensive enough to [embrace] the whole of arithmetic'[53] then there cannot be any method of proving it — not unless the proof can employ rules and procedures different from the actual system itself. But if a different set of rules and procedures is allowed then how are we to find out if the set is valid or not? This seems the gist of any approach that seeks to discover '*the* correct analysis'; and if there is no logical possibility of proving *a* correct analysis to be *the* correct analysis then we would be as well dispensing with the search for one altogether.[54]

Sir William Hamilton edited the works of Thomas Reid. In his day he was a famous and controversial Common Sense philosopher, whose 'notorious hostility to algebra'[55] was no doubt influenced by Reid's rejection of atomism and experimental work in the 'space and time' of spherical geometry. Two of Hamilton's pupils have to be mentioned here. The first is James Clerk Maxwell, one of the greatest mathematicians of all time, he has been likened to Michael Faraday as 'Newton was to Galileo and Kepler'.[56] There is an interesting personal detail on Clerk Maxwell provided by Faraday, where the old physicist compliments the young mathematician — forty years his junior — on his ability to break down even the most esoteric formulae in such a way that somebody who is not a specialist is able to comprehend the issues involved.

The second of Hamilton's pupils was James Ferrier (poet and philosopher), and it is Ferrier who

> sorts out with a sure hand, the incredible complexities of the empirically based self-knowledge which lies at the root of common sense . . . combining with this Wittgensteinian aperçu the complementary insights, due to Sartre and Merleau-Ponty . . . [on] the relation of sight and touch . . .[57]

– the aspect of David Hume's thought that is known to have influenced the phenomenology of Edmund Husserl.[58] The development of the Common Sense tradition in Scotland here allows for an escape from rationalism while managing to keep that fundamental will to freedom, the very heart of natural reason. This should be borne in mind when, in reference to his overall view of the study of mind,[59] Chomsky speaks of

> studies by British Neoplatonists of the seventeenth century that explored the categories and principles of perception and cognition along lines that were later extended by Kant and that were discovered, independently, in twentieth-century gestalt psychology.[60]

When Chomsky dispenses with the search for '*the* correct analysis' he brings in the search for an 'evaluative procedure' that will enable us to 'choose between alternative grammars'. The question may then be asked, How will we know that the 'evaluative procedure' is valid? It will be valid if it is capable of doing the job; and it will prove its power if it can achieve what the last one achieved, and then achieve a little bit more: the proof of the pie will lie in the eating.

Arguments from human nature and fixed principles are usually regarded as reactionary by the orthodox left. Their inference is that such a road must lead to hierarchy, people being born to rule or to serve; people being born lazy or talented, being born selfish, being born good at mathematics, or dancing or painting pictures, etc. Such arguments are thought to suggest that we are not born free at all but are chained to our essential selves and thus are our own lives, and the lives of our children, determined for us in ways for ever beyond our control. There may be elements of this that can be framed validly. Chomsky looks on 'human nature . . . as a system of a sort familiar in the biological world, a system of "mental organs".' Against the 'left-liberal spectrum' his defence takes the following course:

> Human talents vary considerably, within a fixed framework that is characteristic of the species and that permits ample scope for creative work, including the creative work of appreciating the achievements of others. This should be a matter for delight rather than a condition to be abhorred. Those who assume otherwise must be adopting the tacit premise that people's rights or social reward are somehow contingent on their abilities.

But for most mainstream intellectuals a true democracy *is* a form of meritocracy, a system whereby highly educated specialists will be rewarded in accordance with the quantity of knowledge they have consumed in their specialist subject. In this form of society a twenty-three-year-old university graduate will commence his or her working life at a salary some two to three times that of a woman or man who has spent the past thirty years working on a factory production line. As Chomsky has said of meritocracies, 'insofar as they exist at all, [they] are simply a social malady to be overcome much as slavery had to be eliminated at an earlier stage of human history.'

I cannot conceive of someone reading Chomsky's work honestly and failing to be moved by it. The basic principle of humankind is freedom, the right to not be tortured, the right to not be raped, the right to not be violated, the right to not be colonised in any way whatsoever. It is an inalienable right; whether it is deduced or whether it has to be discovered in any other manner is not of great significance. And such questions can only be of *ultimate* interest to those whose ideological position is served by obscuring the issue. Either we do battle on behalf of the basic principle or we do not. This seems to me to be Chomsky's position. It is not a new one but it remains as dangerous as ever. His writings are banned in some countries and are anathema to the ruling minorities of most of the rest.

There Is a First-Order Radical Thinker of European Standing Such That He Exists: or, Tantalising Twinkles

THIS FIRST-ORDER Radical Thinker of European Standing (FORTES) leads us toward the very realms of metaphysicality by a form of phenomenal falsity which in its transcendental otherness conveys itself as truth established, unapproachable even by the most wayward of disbelievers because ultimately founded on the sludge of Higher Radical Learning. He does so by brooking no distinction between his own commonsensical perception of the world and the world-in-itself (indeed The World). FORTES transforms his own judgment into an ultimate judgment (indeed The Ultimate Judgment). Armed with this formal technique he is then at liberty to be 'pretty sure' of finding a like-mind in whomsoever he pleases, including radical thinkers of World Renown.

And where have we come?

Let us resurface to a point beneath the outer crust of the earth. There we arrive at the very marrow of the Mediocratic Controversy that so bedevilled, almost two and a half centuries ago, both the Great European, David Hume, and his sonsie near-contemporary, the Minister at Newmacher, near Aberdeen (son of a Minister at Newmacher, near Aberdeen).[1] Following in the path of our Radical Thinker we are pretty damn sure that if by chance we err along the way then that selfsame error is irrelevant in the Greater Scheme.

Liberated from these and other cross-time constraints we now apply that cross-age critical method whereby we see 'from a distance without getting fankled in the details'.

These are Radical Categories, seldom found in Humdrum Philosophies. And if the remotest part of this hints remotely at ane springboard of local coloration, an axiomatic approach long interred in the prosaic soil of Ach Caledonia to wit that commonsensical reliance upon so-called First Principles, then have at thou imprisoned soul!

We go more deeply, to a train of thought derived from a far weightier structure (indeed the Deeply-most Structure because Universal) that thus we may, when the whim takes us, allow a sideways step from the common ordinariness that besets those who would plough through datum after datum in order to build towards a sound theoretical foundation. (Think here of Descartes, born 31 March 1596, at La Haye, near Tours, educated by the Jesuits, teacher of Queen Christina of Sweden, catcher of a cold that deteriorated into an inflammation of the lungs which resulted in his death in the year 1650.)

But earlier we used the term 'whim' (in Latin *libido*). Unlike the deviationist erstwhile Jesuit student (who did not know of David Hume's existence, having died prior to the latter's birth and whose assessment of the man's work is not, therefore, to be divined via dull Mediocratic Methods), the religious and moral convictions held by the minister at Newmacher, near Aberdeen, were in opposition to the implications of the work of Hume (okey-dokey colleague of Radical European Greats), and played a crucial role in his Hostile Criticism.

We would doubt the very possibility of that criticism ever being valid, either then, now, or during. If called upon further we shall seek to disqualify from all serious discourse the Reverend George Berkeley (born Kilkenny 1685, Ireland, studied Trinity College,

Ireland, later Dean of Derry, Ireland, Bishop of Cloyne, Ireland). Like the erstwhile Newmacher minister and the former Jesuit student from La Haye, the good bishop's philosophical explorations were also founded on the rock of Divinity, notwithstanding his seven-year sojourn in European Settings. We would further disqualify (it should go without saying) the sonsie Immanuel Kant (born Königsberg 1724, lived, worked and died there in 1804, having been brought up in the puritanical strictness of Pietism without having visited Paris). Let us turn aside again as further we disqualify the good saints Aquinas and Augustine, not to mention that most miserable moral prig and despiser of Kierkegaard: Schopenhauer (who shared his bachelor existence with a dog named World Soul (or *Atma*)). Seen from a distance we are pretty sure you will too.

FORTES sternly reminds us that 'Napoleon's France was looking for a humdrum philosophy [and] found exactly what it wanted in the "Scottish School".' Some will say that countless people are always finding exactly what they want to find in the work of any number of writers. Think here, say, of Mediocratic Nazi Germany's reading of Nietzsche (disciple of the afore-mentioned most miserable moral prig and pet-owner, despiser of Kierkegaard) and also of Heidegger (Husserl's successor at Freiburg; disciple of Kierkegaard; translator of sublime Hölderlin – close friend of Schopenhauer's arch-enemy number one, Hegel – the 'historical panorama of [whose] poetry consists in a chain of [god-like creatures] rising like single luminous peaks in a mountain range which stretches from prehistoric times down to the poet's own age' and for whom 'the link between past and present is genius').

Instead we pass on, our penetration ever more deeply, delagging the channels of Cross-Temporality and on toward the Remote Illumination of Outer Cosmic Schemata wherein dull particulars are not simply irrelevant but redundant. Recollect that Milton made use of 'the hypermetrical or redundant line of eleven syllables' first noted by the same Dr Johnson whose excitable young amanuensis Boswell, erstwhile Convert to Roman Catholicism, unlike fellow-countryman Hume, was not only acquainted with Rousseau but with a certain Thérèse Le Vasseur.

Yet onwards we must proceed, ever-vigilant in the face of those for whom 'the smug prison of pedantry conceals the yoke of a nationalist yawn-factor', in the words of Qing Ru Yan (our own translation of the footnote to para. xxiii of the ninth section of his seminal INTELLECTUAL RESURRECTIONISM: or, *Why We Must Pulp the Books of the Previous Generation Now That Its Last Member Has Lately Deceased*).

Yet must we journey deeper, deeper and yet deeper, not to Confucius, nor yet to his sixth-century contemporary, the mysterious Pythagoras; not as far as that, but to Plato (arch-enemy of the irreligious) and from whose mighty presence we emerge bounding cheerfully on via Ferguson, Smith, Hegel and Proudhon to the Medioterialist Marx and his Manchester-domiciled associate Engels, who narrates of the word *gens*, that it is

derived, like the equivalent Greek word genos, from the common Aryan root gan, signifying to beget. Gens, genos, Sanskrit dschanas, Gothic kuni, ancient Norse and Anglesaxon kyn, English kin, Middle High German kunne, all signify lineage, descent. Gens in Latin, genos in Greek, specially designate that sex organisation which boasted of common descent (from a common sire) and was united into a separate community by certain social and religious institutions, but the origin and nature of which nevertheless remained obscure to all our historians.

And on not to Husserl but to that sonsie contemporary of Kierkegaard, James F. Ferrier, of whose relation both to the work of the Austrian-born Husserl and the Common Sense school associated with such as Reid, Hamilton and others of the ilk we pass over in that discursive arrestment that allows of arrant relief.

The jump goes like this: earlier we used the phrase 'sonsie'. It was of course ironic. The term 'irony' comes from the Greek εγρωυεγα, especially in reference to the efficacy feigned by Socrates as a means of confuting a real or imagined enemy without retiring into outright sarcasm or fisticuffs. He too was a skeptick. Yet further he was an academic and teacher and yea though a holder to the rule of Old Gods is not to be confused with those who yea are of a somewhat more Modern Article.

Similarly when the Mendievil Metaphysics were instigated by the disinterring of the works of Aristotle some thousand years after his commitment to the prosaicness of soil a Great Irrationalism came into being. Hence Euclidean Geometry, being disinterred by mathematicians from Aberdeen, Scotland, who were not in deference to an Exciting Europe but part thereof, whose reliance on the humdrum algebraic point had resulted in a lack of a sense of 'curve' insofar as when we see a 'field' we do so in the knowledge that if we draw a line, or attempt to draw a line, from one fixed point to another, the line we see is neither straight nor bendy, it is simply an extended point, no matter what the good Zeno may have to say on the matter, let alone Albert Einstein who owed nothing to anyone but acknowledged that selfsame anyone, including Clerk Maxwell (friend of Kierkegaard's sonsie contemporary, likewise pupil of the Arch-Defender of the works *of the minister at Newmacher, near Aberdeen,* the good Lord Hamilton, and too Thomas Brown (born Montrose, educated Aberdeen, son of the manse).

Earlier we used the term 'Mendievil'. This was to doff the

bunnet to the Moorish Modern, Averroës (in Arabic Ibn Rushd) born Cordova 1126, son of the local Cadi and later a Cadi himself. He, if we remember, held Universal Reason as indivisible but shared in by all, and successfully eludes the stranglehold of that Christio-Islamic non-void. One is inevitably an integral part of one's culture and Averroës was no different (the trick is not to become enmeshed in it), but he successfully shied clear of its consequences, expounding the Qran according to Aristotle, pupil of the pupil of Socrates, teacher of Alexander the Great (who roved the lands of the ancients, at one point setting fire to Persepolis, wonder of the world, while drunk and incapable, according to legend, at the hands of a certain Athenian courtesan).

We suspect the douce Cadi had discovered a hitherto unruffled disjuncture performed *in abstinentia* by that humankind whose world's-eye view is downrooted by the unvisionariness of an opaque fixity, irrevocably glued in its atmospheric void, its accursed lack of (in)voluntary exile a sad reminder of shameful non-modernity. These are existential terms. The 'Mendi' and 'evil' we adopted as a play upon words, or pun – origin obscure – but when we search for it in our dictionary inevitably the pages fall open at 'pub'. But we are pretty sure the Cordovan Cadi would share our opinion on pubs.

Thus FORTES is correct in surmising our 'Linguistics Philosopher' would have found Common Sense ideology 'pretty thick on the ground' in Govan, Glasgow. The World-Famed Professor perhaps predicted as much prior to accepting that invitation, due partly, we conjecture, to the generative effect of a structure far deeper than dull naturalism has heretofore intuited: an Open Mind, his cross-time motivation in transversing the ocean in an ever-developing pursuit of the Abstract Actual, in stark confutation of the Power of the Precious.

Let us return down the disinterred ladder, removing all

diversionary phenomena associated with backandforthicity.

We arrive on the flat, experiencing an immense gasp of liberty, and we set to with gusto, unfankling the chains of musty breathlessness, blacking out the merest hint of all deviational futurism (mere potential reality of a socio-politico sameness). Now we kick away the chains and leave them to rust. We chop down the ladder but do not sell the sticks. We burn the wood yet do not heat our hands. Rather do we attend the cross-spiritual, communing with the quintessentialsthetics of supragenius. And in a split simultaneity we now regain that long-lost *bon vivre*, that hearty *bon vivre*, so beloved of parties the wide world over. Behold the fierce flames of a new dawn. We offer an Art for the time, a prose for the period, a living lexicon of philosophicology.

BIBLIOGRAPHY:

Chambers Biographical Dictionary
Shorter Oxford English Dictionary

Scottish Law and a Victim of Asbestos

Foreword

A MILLION OR more British television viewers became aware of Pat McCrystal's plight recently when a BBC2 *Newsnight* devoted much of its programme to his story. It highlighted the drastic financial effect that the death of a victim has on damages in Scotland. Under Scots law a major proportion of the settlement dies with the victim. At present Lord McAulay is pursuing a bill through the Lords in relation to this.

Ex-Clydeside worker Mr McCrystal is suffering the terminal illness mesothelioma which can only be caught by exposure to asbestos. No Scottish victim of mesothelioma has ever made it into court before. It appears that in this singular instance a form of 'fast-track' process took place.

The Glasgow area (including Greenock and Clydebank) is one of the 'black spots' on the world map of asbestos-related diseases. There are many myths surrounding these diseases. One is that only asbestos workers are at risk of infection. That simply is not true. People from different walks of life are contracting these incurable illnesses, many only in their thirties and early forties. Pat McCrystal, however, is one of thousands of Clydeside shipyard workers contaminated by the poison since the end of World War Two.

There are different reasons for the lengthy delays in the judicial process. Civil actions take anything from one to seven years. Some argue that delays are used to obstruct proper compensation payments to asbestos victims. The hard truth is that many of these people will be dead long before the law finally runs its course. Many will have settled for 'out-of-court' payments which groups such as the Clydeside Action on Asbestos (CAA) charity would have described as inadequate.

Pat McCrystal's case was regarded as a test-case by CAA, bringing public recognition to the campaign for justice being faced by terminal victims of asbestos-related disease. Glasgow is described as 'cancer capital' of the world but a proper context, taking into account the mammoth incidence of asbestos abuse, is rarely offered (80 per cent of asbestos-induced terminal cancers are not mesotheliomas but lung cancers). Instead the usual factors are always mentioned; tobacco, alcohol, cholesterol-saturated food, and so on.

The motto of CAA was 'justice for the living – remember the dead' and members were calling for a global ban on asbestos. Pat McCrystal stated that his only reason for pursuing his claim through the court was to highlight the plight of Scottish victims of asbestos.

Scottish Law and a Victim of Asbestos

A unique event in Scottish legal history did not take place in Edinburgh's Court of Session last Thursday. Mr Patrick McCrystal did not become the first mesothelioma victim to hear his case championed in a Scottish court. But the proceedings that did occur demonstrate the absurdity of the concept 'justice' in respect of the fight through the legal system by victims of asbestos-abuse against those reponsible for inflicting them with progressive, ultimately terminal illnesses. Mr McCrystal's life and imminent death was settled against his wishes in an out-of-court financial deal between his legal representation and that of the Defenders. In early August Mr McCrystal was given four months to live by a Glasgow-based specialist in respiratory disease. Supported by Clydeside Action on Asbestos, the charity of which he is a member, it had been his intention to take the case all the way. This proved impossible.

For the lay observer the out-of-court settlement occurred in the most shabby manner. He suffers the horrific asbestos-induced disease mesothelioma. Outside the West of Scotland and certain other parts of the world it is regarded as a rare terminal illness. In the Glasgow and surrounding area, mesothelioma can hardly be described as rare, and its incidence is nearly eight times higher than the UK average. This is the 'official' figure. The disease has the reputation of being notoriously difficult to diagnose. The actual figures could be much higher. Twenty thousand shipyard workers alone are known to have contracted asbestos-related diseases since the end of World War Two.

Mr McCrystal's case was funded by his union, the GMB, who employed their own lawyers. Yet in the opinion of Mr McCrystal he was browbeaten into the financial settlement by the legal representation, his lawyer and QC. The use of terms such as 'browbeaten' must be used warily in respect of the legal profession. It is hoped that the account which follows will justify its use, which was applied in context by Mr McCrystal in my own hearing.

He and his niece, his friends and fellow members of CAA (90 per cent of whom are also victims of asbestos-related disease) were prepared for the worst. The majority have their own cases in process – progress is not the right word; the system generally rolls on for years. They had predicted the end result. Unlike his lawyer, neither Pat McCrystal nor his friends were surprised by the 'astonishing' last-minute news that his appointed QC was set to resign from the case if the latest 'cash offer' was not accepted. Even so Mr McCrystal felt himself rendered powerless by what was described as 'legal blackmail'.

The Defenders had accepted liability. Thus there was 'no case'. The admittance of liability establishes that some of the more illustrious Clydeside names, e.g. Fairfield, Blythswood Shipbuilding, Harland and Wolff, exposed their workforce to a deadly fibre and that they did so knowingly. In consequence Mr McCrystal, like so many other exshipyard workers, will shortly be dead.

The first cash payment offered to him in lieu of compensation was £18,000. He rejected this and also rejected the second sum of £22,000. A week before his scheduled court appearance the offer was increased dramatically to £50,000. He rejected this and again stressed to the solicitor that the money was immaterial; he sought 'justice' rather than financial compensation.

Two days before the court appearance he was called through to Edinburgh for a meeting with the lawyer and the QC. The meeting lasted two hours. The offer of £50,000 was confirmed and he was advised this was the very best he could hope for. Again he stressed his position. By 'justice' he meant that the full guilt of his former employers might not only be revealed in public but become subject to a form of court ruling that might aid other asbestos victims. He explained that the fight was not simply on his own account but those thousands of workers who suffer, and will continue to suffer, a fate similar to his own.

It was evident that those professionally involved were unable to grasp the point. It was explained to him that civil actions were about money and if he wanted justice he should 'go to Westminster'. He was also advised that the court was not the place for 'feuds' (a strange legal euphemism for the submission that one party may have poisoned another to his certain death). Mr McCrystal remained adamant.

"And the judges said . . ."

During the days prior to his scheduled court appearance and on the morning itself, there was great activity on the part of his legal representation. The financial settlement had to be delineated item by item and £1 for £1 in the way that such matters occur. Mr McCrystal did mention in passing that there had been a full six months in which that business could have been conducted. In view of his fast deteriorating physical condition coupled with the current psychological stress, he was not in the best state to deal with it at this late stage in the proceedings.

The day before the hearing he was again asked what sort of settlement figure he had in mind. He suggested to the lawyer that since they had filed for a sum of £100,000 originally they should ask for that. (He told me later that he strongly regretted mentioning any figure at all but that he was tired and the pressure was getting to him.) The lawyer then advised him they always filed for this same sum, £100,000, that it was a formality, but to ask for such a sum in 'real life' was outwith the bounds of reason.

The court hearing was scheduled for 9.45 on Thursday morning. At 6.30 a.m. the lawyer phoned, requesting certain information and again asking what sort of sum of money he had in mind. He replied that he was 'going to court'. Three hours later, in company with his niece and the group of friends and fellow-asbestos victims he arrived in the hallowed halls of justice Scottish-style, Parliament Square, Edinburgh.

The negotiations moved up a gear. It was now explained to Mr McCrystal that there were two unfortunate factors in his case which might entail a reduction in the settlement. One factor had been worked out at £5,000. Mr McCrystal accepted this 'loss'.

The other factor concerned 'future loss of earnings'. When he had reached retiral age he was asked by his employer if he would consider working on until he was seventy. Mr McCrystal had agreed. It was now suggested by his legal representation that his

198

employer had only offered him an extra few months' employment. This was an important consideration and if true it meant another drop in any settlement figure. Because of these two factors he was advised that the £50,000 was an extremely good offer and if he went through with the court hearing it was likely that the 'in-court' figure would be substantially less.

As an added bonus to the 'out-of-court' settlement the Defenders would admit their liability. Mr McCrystal was further advised that 'they' were not too enamoured with the media interest in this potentially unique moment in Scottish legal history; tactically such public interest might prejudice his case. But he was unable to have it explained satisfactorily to him by his legal representation why this might be true, nor to whom the 'they' referred.

Things had become hectic at this stage, with toings and froings from both sides. It now appeared that this 'out-of-court' settlement would further be announced in court. Thus although it was 'out-of-court' it had the trappings of the 'in-court'. This was a difficult point to have clarified. But it would appear that he had achieved what he had set out to do and thus would be said by everyone to have 'won'. The legal representation were doing their best to clarify it all. Even so, neither Mr McCrystal nor his niece and friends could quite grasp the nature of the 'victory'. In their experience of the horse-dealing operation that the establishment refers to as Scottish Civil Law this seemed another stitch-up, but this time in the form of a 'ringer'; here was an 'out-of-court' settlement being sold as an 'in-the-court' something or other.

Pat McCrystal declined the offer. For six months he had prepared for court and he would go through with it come what may.

The lawyer departed for further consultation with the QC. At this point Mr McCrystal and other experienced members of

Clydeside Action on Asbestos predicted the QC would now withdraw from the case. Further, that the lawyers acting on his behalf would suggest they too might be forced to withdraw, for one reason or another.

The mean life expectancy for male mesothelioma victims is six months from diagnosis and this courageous and determined man had been diagnosed back in February, seven months ago. From the first meeting two days prior, right the way through the morning in question, the QC had refused point blank to allow any of Mr McCrystal's friends to be present during discussions. Nor at any time did the fact of his terminal condition seem to be taken into account. It was just expected that he would travel to meetings and hang about waiting, and waiting.

And now came the offer he could not refuse. Pat McCrystal's QC had released the 'astonishing news' that he was duty-bound to withdraw from the case if the current 'out-of-court' settlement was rejected. The lawyer said this had never happened before. Even so, it was explained to her, the move had been predicted by Pat McCrystal and his friends. A couple of months earlier another asbestos victim, who had expected a settlement of £70,000, was obliged to accept less than £10,000 when faced with the same ultimatum.

The question was put, in the event of the QC's withdrawal, would it be possible to hire another counsel?

Answer: No, not really.

There was an additional factor: although the lawyers were indeed acting for Pat McCrystal they were being funded by his union, the GMB (who receives 10 per cent of any settlement figure for its own costs, etc.). And the GMB could be unable to continue funding the case if the 'out-of-court' settlement was refused. They would base that decision on the worry that if the case did go to court then the settlement figure awarded by the judge might prove less than that offered 'out-of-court'. And that would present other difficulties in relation to costs and so on. After explaining the situation the lawyer left to phone the GMB and find out the situation for certain.

Mr McCrystal and friends now had to plan what to do in the event of being left stranded. They had talked around this probability for the past two days but were unable to find a satisfactory alternative. CAA is a self-supporting charity funded almost exclusively by donations from its members and sympathisers. In the event of Pat's union, the GMB, withdrawing support, was it conceivable that the money could be raised elsewhere to continue? Could any of the members don the QC mantle and fight the case in court? Or would 'they' not allow it. Who were 'they'? But if such things are possible in criminal law what about civil law? And if it was allowed, was there time to prepare an adequate submission?

One of Pat McCrystal's group spotted the Dean of Faculty in a conversational walk with a colleague. Could he be approached? But some astute, legal advice was essential. And there was no time to go to the library and read up on the subject. Imagine being in such dire need of legal advice while standing in the vast hall of Edinburgh's Court of Session, surrounded by the silks and gowns of the legal profession.

It seemed impossible. If Pat McCrystal did insist on going into court the only practical route might lie in a request for a new hearing in light of the 'unusual' circumstances. This would allow time to come up with some realistic alternative. But it was noticeable that he was now very tired indeed. Remember too about asbestos-related diseases that every breath can be a struggle. Given the inner strength that had sustained him these last months there remains the physical reality of the condition.

And there is always the 'Scottish' factor to consider, the 'effect of death on damages': under Scottish law if Mr McCrystal died before settlement then the bulk of the claim would die with him. Bearing in mind that ALL asbestos-related diseases are incurable this is the trump card that every last Scottish victim has had to confront. Pat McCrystal confessed to us that he would be dead by the time any new hearing began. It had to be today. He was obliged to concede defeat. There was no alternative.

The GMB's lawyer was instructed to inform the QC that he need not withdraw from the case after all, surprise surprise, the settlement figure had been accepted.

At 11.45 a.m. the court assembled to hear news of the settlement. Both counsels spoke for a brief period. The judge also spoke. The counsel for the Pursuer asked for it on record to the effect that Mr McCrystal was a courageous man. The counsel for the Defenders asked for it on record to the effect that his clients had shown their gracious consideration of Mr McCrystal's imminent death by allowing an early hearing. Etc. Etc. and Blah Blah Blah.

In fact the speed of this court hearing was the only thing unique about last Thursday's events in Parliament Square, Edinburgh and may have had something to do with the recent media interest in Pat McCrystal.

But what cannot be forgotten is the disclosure of liability. The hard reality is that all of those world-famous Clydeside shipbuilders were aware of the deadly effects of asbestos exposure but took no precautions to safeguard their hundreds of thousands of employees. For nearly a hundred years successive British governments have been well aware of the terrible dangers. In 1898 factory inspectors had already expressed concerns about 'the evil effects' of asbestos dust. Only ten years later 'a Parliamentary Commission confirmed the first cases of asbestos deaths in factories and recommended better ventilation and other safety measures.'

As far back as 1929 the world's largest asbestos corporation, the US-based Johns Manville, was served with writs by asbestos victims. The claims were settled 'out-of-court' with 'secrecy orders'. In Scotland nothing much has changed except the public disclosure of 'liability'. There seems no process in law by which guilty people can be brought to account for their blatant disregard of human life. No matter the opinion of the Scottish legal profession, the only victory on Thursday belonged to themselves and the Defenders. For the victims of asbestos abuse it was one more nail in the coffin.

Postscript

Pat McCrystal died from mesothelioma on 23 February 1993. He was a leading figure in the campaign to help ex-Clyde-shipyard workers suffering from the effects of working with asbestos. Pat was a dignified figure who appeared at many meetings and on television to argue that thousands of workers who had been exposed to asbestos were now being denied justice. He fought a tremendous battle for justice which was the subject of a BBC *Newsnight* special report. A member of Clydeside Action on Asbestos described him as a unique man: 'Pat would never like to be regarded as special but even in his critical condition he was still in fighting spirit.'

A mass was held for him at St Constantine's Church, Govan and he was buried at St Conval's Cemetery. In Pat McCrystal's memory, Clydeside Action on Asbestos named their office in Briggait, Glasgow after him.

Justice Is Not Money

for Peter Boyle and Janette Sawers, *in memoriam*

RECENTLY WE WON a major victory for one of our members, a woman who died of mesothelioma; she was a schoolteacher. Her husband is also a CAA member. It was an important victory because it means any worker who becomes an asbestos victim, even a white-collar worker, now has a way to beat the DSS. It will not be easy but we have shown the door is there to be chapped, or at least kicked in. All it takes is time and effort, some knowledge about the issue, and the will to fight. The will to fight is essential. We were disappointed not to receive backing from the schoolteachers' unions.

But we should not kid ourselves on, a victory like that is very unusual, but even as we speak the DSS authorities are looking for ways of appealing the decision to try and get it reversed. We are confident they will not succeed but you can never tell.

Sometimes you feel that the DSS give us occasional victories just to string us along. They have shown time after time they can put the block on any victim more or less as they like. Everybody that comes into the CAA office to fill in a form is a victim of asbestos. We know it and they know it. So too do the medical authorities, and still they deny diagnosis. The doctors will not even tell folk what diseases they have. It is no wonder so many of our members have to make a conscious effort not to hold the medical profession in contempt.

People are catching incurable diseases and not getting proper treatment and care. And when the diseases are industrial they are not getting their proper welfare benefits. They are forced to spend their time fighting to get their rights instead of being allowed to cope with the mental torture of having a disease which they know is incurable and from which it is odds-on they will die, sooner or later. Remember that these DSS benefits and allowances are *rights*, they are not favours. This Government is duty-bound to allow them to any victim of industrial disease. Yet even when a man or woman dies of mesothelioma and the doctor admits they died of mesothelioma, the DSS will still do all in its power to stop the person's widow or widower getting their posthumous entitlements. The DSS 'doctors' will argue that the victim died of something else altogether. In fact what the DSS 'doctors' do is exactly the same as what the so-called 'doctors' employed on behalf of the asbestos industry and its insurers have been doing for nearly a hundred years.

Let us be clear that in 99 cases out of a 100 the employers know about the dangers of asbestos. That is why they admit liability in those out-of-court settlements. They know they are putting men, women and children to work in conditions that not only will damage their health, but might kill them. The British Government also knows and, like the employers and the insurers, has known for nearly a hundred years.

The employers knew they could get away with it and they did get away with it. And in far too many cases they are still getting away with it. And the Government is still not doing anything about it. Worse, instead of attacking the guilty people the Government attacks the victims. Instead of making the employers pay for their crimes the Government pays lip-service to the plight of the victims and, if forced to do so, the DSS will dish out a few benefits and allowances.

The Government acts the part of an insurance company for the employers. And what a great deal it is. The employers do not even pay for it! Who does? The workers. Yes, the actual victims. The workers pay health insurance and the Government gives them their money back to compensate for the fact that their employer has poisoned them! Some deal. This is like a potential murder victim having to pay money on the off chance he gets murdered, and then when in the process of getting poisoned to death he gets it back in the form of compensation. Great stuff. And the victim is supposed to see that as justice. And then watch the murderer get off scot-free. No criminal proceedings will be taken. It is a matter for civil law. And that means also that the burden of proof moves on to the victim. Yes, okay, you think they are poisoning you to death: fine, prove it. If you succeed the Government will pay you some sort of welfare entitlement. And if you get the energy to fight on for a few years you might even get an extra few quid from your poisoner's insurers.

The DSS and their medical authorities will do all they can to deny diagnosis, and their legal practitioners will do everything they can to wrap you in red tape, anything to avoid paying benefits, entitlements and allowances, they will skin the victims out of every last penny.

That is the way the British Government operates, just like the employers and insurers, and the asbestos industry in general. The fight against the DSS is like taking on the Defenders in a civil-action claim. The DSS is in the role of the insurers. The Defenders are just the usual Defenders, the employers and the asbestos industry. As a victim you do not get justice. There is no chance of that. All you get is the promise of disability benefit, of financial compensation.

In Glasgow a few weeks ago asbestos was removed from a school in a big housing estate. Asbestos was discovered littering the playground.[1] The people we are talking about do not care if they contaminate the playground and poison our children. They do not care. How many times do we have to shout this out. They do not care. There is no punishment. The business firm responsible in this instance has already been fined but they are still doing it and still getting away with it, and *still being employed* by the council authorities.

We know about asbestos in schools and public buildings and we know that the children and ordinary public are at great risk. If any of them are unfortunate enough to contract one of the asbestos-related cancers they could die without even having a claim against the company that has killed them. It would not be classified as an industrial disease, there would be no claim.

In Australia and South Africa there are reports of children dying of mesothelioma. How soon before we hear about that in this country? Maybe it is happening already and we do not know about it. The way the system here operates the parents would have to prove what disease it is that their children are dying from.

What about justice, morality, blah blah blah? The problem is, if you are a victim, you get so caught up in the struggle to get your DSS benefits and compensation that there is no time for anything else. You are forced to run the gauntlet; the authorities line you up against a battery of medical experts who begin from denial. They put you down as having anything from bronchitis to emphysema, from tuberculosis to asthma, lung cancer caught by smoking – whatever, but always *in the absence* of asbestos-related disease. There is great physical and mental stress on victims, caused by the process of doing the doctors' job for them, of trying to establish proof of their disease. And if your disease is at a later stage there are the obvious – but rarely discussed – issues around family life; in other words, how do you prepare the people closest to you for the true nature of your condition and its probable central effect, an earlier death than expected? A high proportion of victims of asbestos-related disease die in the process of establishing their right to compensation, an outcome which does not upset the Defenders one bit, for the obvious reason, it means they have to pay out less cash.

Justice and morality, justice or money. Pat McCrystal summed it up in his fight with the legal profession. Remember how he told the lawyers and anybody else that would listen: I'm not interested in your money, I'm not interested in your financial compensation. They asked him, What is it you want? Name the price. There is no price, is what Pat told them, no price.

How can you put a figure on somebody's life? Pat McCrystal talked about justice. And what happened when he talked about justice? What did the legal profession do, the lawyers and the QC? Nothing. They just looked at him. It took a few minutes for them to work it out. They did not even know what he was talking about, not at first. Eventually they advised him that justice is not what his case was about, and anybody who thought it was was plain naïve. His case was about money, it was about financial compensation. That is what every case is about. That is what the law is about. It has nothing to do with justice, not as ordinary people understand it. What Pat's lawyers said, his legal advisors, they said if he wanted justice he should go to Westminster. Go to Westminster if you want justice: that is what they told him, which makes them very naïve indeed, that is if they were being serious, but I doubt if they were.

The law is about levels of compensation and it is about financial deals and negotiations, it is about bartering and it is about the marketplace. In Scotland the 'great hall' of the Court of Session is just another marketplace, but an especially élite marketplace. The money-dealers are members of the legal profession. Sometimes they wear their uniforms, the black growns and the white wigs, that kind of stuff. Then off they go backwards and forwards tipping each other their winks and their nods, a five grand here and a ten grand there, and twenty in the corner, any advance on twenty!

The lawyers are correct to say that it is not about justice, justice is not financial compensation. But for groups and charities like ours the fight should also be about justice. Obviously for any victim of asbestos-abuse, compensation must come into it. There is no choice about that. But it is also about justice. If it is not about justice then it is not about anything and bodies like Clydeside Action on Asbestos would be as well shutting the doors for good and just leave it to the lawyers and the welfare rights office.

This has been a major issue within the trade-union movement. All we ever talk about is cash settlements. An extra couple of quid for a shift, a hundred pound for the loss of a pinky, two hundred for a thumb; a couple of thousand to your widow if you are unlucky enough to get killed by your boss's ignorance, inefficiency, or downright greed. That is the extent of it. Nobody remembers about justice. We have to watch about falling into the same trap here at CAA. We spend most of our time, effort and energy in trying to win these individual DSS claims and civil-action claims. Much of the work we should not even be doing, not as unpaid volunteers, it is the work of welfare rights officers, it is the work a solicitor should be doing.

The Government and the asbestos industry and their insurers have always been happy to let us think the fight is about money. Name your price! Here we go again, the guy is walking up to you and saying: okay I admit it – now that I've been found out. Yes, it is true, I have been killing people for years. And now I'm forced to give you a bit of bad news: you're one of them. And by the way, did your wife wash your jeans or your dungarees? If so maybe I've killed her as well. Awful sorry. What about your weans by the way, did you wash your hands before you played with them when you came home from work? Did your wee boy try on your bunnet? Pardon me. How much dough can my insurers offer you to square the account? I do not mind if you get something, that is what I pay them for. Mind you, whatever you do ask for they'll fight you tooth and nail, every step of the way, to the last breath in your body. Aye and see once you're dead, they'll fight your widow as well.

No matter what happens, they are never going to stand trial. It is all just a bribe. That is essentially what it is, that is civil law. The guilty people are paying us off. That is what the criminals are doing; the asbestos industry, the employers, the insurers, the Government.

This is how they have destroyed the lives of hundreds of thousands of working-class people for the past hundred years and that is how they are still destroying them. And they will go on destroying them and screwing them down until we start remembering properly what the fight is about, that justice is not the same thing as bribery. Some would argue that the history of health and safety within the trade-union movement is a history of bribery, of financial settlements, out-of-court deals. And where you get these deals you find corruption to some degree, the one follows the other.

This is not an argument against trade unions. The very opposite. Almost anybody who fights in a campaign to do with health and safety is committed to the trade-union movement. Everybody here is, or has been, a trade-union member. But there are trade-union officials who cannot take criticism. They like to kid on that a criticism of them is a criticism of the movement. But the very reason these individuals get criticised is because they have failed the movement. And too many of them have shamed the movement, by their corruption, and most of all by their cowardice.

When we talk about justice we are talking about bringing killers into court, getting their names known to the public; letting the public see what has been going on and what is still going on, showing them about wrongful diagnosis and misdiagnosis and the denial of diagnosis and the shameful and inhuman way asbestos victims are getting victimised in this society.

There is a famous quotation known to anybody who ever read *Blue Murder*, that great little book on the struggle against asbestos-abuse. The quotation comes from the first lawyer in Australia who got committed to the struggle. He was an exceptional guy altogether. He made the statement when he was first taken to meet a group of ex-workers from Wittenoom in north-western Australia where they were mining blue asbestos. He listened to all that was being said, until finally it dawned on him, a revelation, that there he was sitting in the same room with a bunch of people in various stages of dying: here was somebody with mesothelioma, another with asbestosis, somebody else with lung cancer, and so on. I quote from memory here – and I've got to, because somebody stole my book, and no apologies for the language the guy used. Okay he was a lawyer, one of the few. He was upset and angry, and he said: What the fuck's going on, here's a roomful of people dying and nobody's doing anything about it! And it was just that realisation, when it hit him about the reality of the fight faced by the Wittenoom miners and their families.

It would be great to see every asbestos victim fighting to get their case into court. It is important. The legal profession and the medical profession and the politicians' profession and the trade-union officials' profession cannot grasp why we think it is important. It is not so you get the chance to tell the court about the extraordinary injustice you've suffered personally. The way we see it is to try and get the judges forced to make some sort of ruling, about the gross negligence, the reckless and irresponsible, downright wilful behaviour of the asbestos industry and all these employers who have poisoned so many human beings and who have killed so many human beings. We want judges forced to start to make rulings in court.

People act like the law was laid down by God. They forget the law was made by people and can be changed by people. What about the campaign to do with the Effect of Death on Damages, that campaign we are all involved in, that is what that's about, we're looking for a change to the law.[2]

But what we see as the one unpredictable factor in the compensation process is what in the USA they call 'punitive damages'. Here they call it 'exemplary damages'. Punitive damages are awarded where 'a company has acted in an utterly outrageous manner'. In the struggle against asbestos abuse punitive damages were first awarded in 1981 in the USA against the Johns Manville corporation. Another judgment happened in Australia in 1988. And some of you might have heard about 'the Baltimore Judgment' in the USA a couple of months ago, one of these big multiple actions they get there, about 60,000 people were all tied in together, and they won it.

Who knows what would happen. But what is the situation in criminal law if you can prove your workmate's death was a result of the acts or ommissions by the boss who possessed the knowledge or belief that death or grievous bodily harm could result? Personally I don't know what would happen. I wish I did.

How do we make use of the law to get employers tried for corporate murder or manslaughter? Can it be done? Civil law might be an early step in the process. Maybe if we can push cases into court the public will start witnessing what goes on, again and again, and maybe the judges will be forced to make rulings that allow us to start the ball rolling over criminal proceedings. And maybe support a conviction of murder? I don't know, stranger things have happened. There might be better ways of doing it. But these are issues we should be raising as well, instead of just talking about dough and benefits and entitlements all the time. Everything to their place.

Postscript

Among the 120 or so CAA members in attendance on Saturday was ex-shipwright Pat McCrystal whose out-of-court settlement of £50,000 had occurred in controversial circumstances two weeks previously. Most were victims of asbestos-abuse, also present were families and friends. During the opening minutes a 58-year-old man collapsed with a heart attack. The ambulance men arrived swiftly and fought long and hard to save his life but he died without regaining consciousness.

Some thought the meeting should be abandoned, others that it was important to continue. The Chairman of CAA, who suffers asbestosis, pointed out that the tragedy could have happened to any one of them. Asbestos victims have to live and cope with progressive lung death; this affects the bloodstream and oxygen flow, placing abnormal strain on the heart. Eventually it was agreed the meeting should continue. A proposal came from 'the floor', given that it was also a time for anger and positive action, that a deputation should meet with the Lord Provost first thing on Monday morning to protest about what had happened and to demand an official inquiry.

One of the CAA voluntary workers had phoned the City Halls on the Friday to have it confirmed that access for disabled people would be available for the EGM. It was confirmed. But when people arrived on Saturday morning the disabled-access was closed off and none of the janitorial staff was there to help. Everybody was forced to return outside and walk around the street to a side entrance; here there was no lift, they had to climb a tortuous, steep staircase to the third floor. Some of the members could not attempt it and had to return home. One guy in a wheelchair was carried up the stairs by voluntary workers. Some who made the attempt were in great physical distress by the time they got upstairs to the meeting room. A short walk can be a problem for people suffering lung disease. They have to slow down, they have to stop for intervals. Some need regular access to oxygen. It is impossible for some of them to ever attend meetings, even if they had a couple of people alongside them, one carrying an oxygen bottle and the other pushing the bed.

What angers the members of CAA is the unwillingness on the part of the authorities to acknowledge the truth about their physical condition. Is it a con or is it a genuine problem? Is it because the body's organs are 'invisible' and the effects of the contamination cannot be seen? Should asbestos victims get their lungs and heart tied round their necks with a bit of string, so the legal and medical authorities can inspect them at their pleasure. If the DSS allows somebody a claim for an asbestos-related disease then that person has to be a minimum 20 per cent disabled. And as any victim would tell you, once you have fought to get the DSS to admit you are 20 per cent disabled then the one thing you do know is that you are more than 20 per cent. Why do they persist in using the word 'breathlessness' to describe the crippling effects of lung disease? It is a shocking abuse of language.

It had turned 10 o'clock on Monday morning when about thirty asbestos victims and supporters arrived at Glasgow's City Chambers, to express their outrage to the political authorities at what had happened to their friend and fellow member of Clydeside Action on Asbestos. The media had been alerted and journalists and television cameras were waiting to record developments. In the lobby of the City Chambers the group was met by uniformed staff. They were told they could not see the Lord Provost because he had a meeting to attend. However, if two delegates from the group were appointed then somebody from the Town Clerk's Department would meet with them to discuss the matter. The proposal was rejected at once. The 'uniforms' were advised it was the Lord Provost or nothing. One of the ex-pipefitters put it differently, 'We've come to see the organ grinder, we're no dealing with any monkeys.'

But it was clear the uniformed staff had no understanding of the situation. At one point the 'head man' lost his temper completely and looked ready to call in the police or else get physical on his own. The usual was happening, they could not see any significance in the fact they were dealing with people with asbestos-related lung disease. These were not violent protestors but disabled persons, and one of their fellow disabled persons had just died because of that same lack of respect for the condition.

The 'head man' managed to calm down, and stepped aside to phone 'upstairs'. Down came a 'PR suit' to meet the deputation. He said that the Lord Provost could now agree to meet two appointed delegates. He was advised that that was not good enough, it was either the whole deputation or nothing. There were only thirty of them. What was so difficult about the Lord Provost meeting them all inside one of these huge rooms they had, the City Chambers was full of them. The 'PR suit' thought this unreasonable. He was advised that whether he thought it unreasonable or not was irrelevant, his job was to report back to the Lord Provost. Off he went upstairs.

The Lord Provost agreed to meet the full deputation. The meeting was to take place on the second floor. And the inevitable happened, the asbestos victims were shown to the great staircase to begin their way up on foot. They explained they were unable to undertake the climb. It was because they were disabled. They would require the lift. It was allowed.

The Lord Provost was in company with two of his colleagues, one of whom was the Councillor in charge of the 'Halls' department. The deputation called for an official inquiry into the events that led to the tragedy. The Lord Provost said he would look into the matter and while the television cameras rolled he signed a charter calling for a global ban on asbestos (BBC news bulletins showed this during the rest of the day).

Who knows what it will amount to. The victims of asbestos abuse have very low expectations. Some said that it took a man's death to gain the attention of the political authorities. Those who said it are naïve. In Scotland the political authorities would have to be deaf, dumb and blind not to know the reality. The situation in West Central Scotland is notorious. The only reason a couple of them listened in this particular instance is because they were embarrassed by a deputation of asbestos victims who found the energy to voice their outrage in person, in the presence of the media.

Say Hello to John La Rose

A FEW YEARS ago a friend urged me to drop in at New Beacon Books the next time I was in London, and say hello to John La Rose. There were two or three 'next times' before I got round to it. It is awkward going to meet somebody you have not met before who is not expecting you and who most likely has not been advised of your existence. Crossing certain social barriers, in this instance colour and racial, does not help matters. But the friend urging the visit is a persistent guy and I knew there would be no rest till I made the visit. On the credit side, any independent bookshop is always of interest. He had given me information on what it might stock so I was looking forward to seeing the shelves. Eventually one Saturday I had about five hours' free time before travelling back to Scotland. I arrived just after lunch-time and it was quiet; behind the counter were three women. In the shop area was one other person, a youngish man with a fair pile of books at his feet; he seemed to know his way around and I reckoned he had to be an employee of some sort. I was looking for certain things and eventually asked his help. He assisted me as comprehensively as I would have expected from an employee. He told me what was available and where to find it, then indicated some poetry he thought could be of interest.

Soon he lifted his pile of books and went to the counter. I heard him speak with one of the women there, then the till rang; he was not an employee at all, he was a customer paying for the books. I continued browsing. My own pile was steadily building; magazines, books and pamphlets. I had to call a halt. I went to sort out the cash. It came to more than expected, but included the occasional duplicate I was buying for a friend back in Glasgow. I paid by cheque then had to find the social whatever-it-is to ask if John La Rose was around. The fact that I would be asking a white English woman really did not make this easier, I'm always aware of 'voice' down south and this woman's accent is one I always have difficulty with – upper- or upper-middle-class it sounded to me, so to hell with that really, is what I thought. However, having come this far . . .

She told me John theoretically was retired from the shop nowadays and also had not been too well recently, but said I should still call on him and gave me the home address. Once out on the street I considered heading back to Finsbury Park tube station but instead I gritted the teeth and continued. I think having these treasures in the carrier-bag made a difference, things I had never expected to get, many I had not known existed, I was quite elated really.

Along and round the corner the man himself answered the door; after my introduction he paused for only a moment then brought me past the piles of books in the lobby, upstairs to the kitchen, introduced me very briefly to somebody already there – lo and behold the customer from the shop, the guy I had first taken for an employee. The conversation I had interrupted now continued. Both were polite and very occasionally glanced at me; this indicated I was not being excluded. I was given a cup of tea, and offered a sandwich which I declined. Later myself and the other chap were offered a choice of rums; I did not recognise any of the labels; we had small ones. The host did not imbibe.

I found the conversation extremely interesting, little of which I now remember except that it touched on various matters; economics, literature, politics; languages in Africa and the prominence of Hausa. I thought the content a bit explicit politically considering I was a stranger and put this down to the fact I was there at all; that in the act of bringing me upstairs John had made his decision – maybe initiated by his trust in the mutual friend back in Scotland. My contribution to the conversation was negligible. In strange company you do your best to keep your mouth shut, especially if much of what is being said is new to you. One point in passing; at that time I had given up smoking – which helps me date this to sometime in 1987 or early 1988. A year or so later, being back on the cigarettes, I do not know what the social ramifications would have been if I had asked for an ashtray, given Mr La Rose's well-known aversion to cigarette smoking.

The conversation halted after about an hour and a half; John suggested myself and the other guy share the journey back to where we were going, he to Brixton and me to Victoria. The two of us hardly had exchanged more than an occasional nod until then, with John doing most of the talking. Whether the other guy found the suggestion as novel yet as obvious as myself I do not know; but we accepted it and made the best of it (by the time we reached Victoria we were exchanging addresses). John had shown us to the door, the leave-taking was courteous but he looked tired. I think it had been a bit of a strain for him.

That was my first meeting with John. There is nothing significant about it beyond the immediately personal: it is not often I meet three people who become friends in the space of a two-hour visit to anywhere; in this instance a black man from the West Indies, a black man from East Africa, a white woman from what seemed to be somewhere in the upper social regions of England. But there are a couple of additional matters which have further significance; again these are personal. John's life has been one of full commitment to what he believes in and I am very aware that I do not know the half of it; but I now find at least two areas of his commitment have touched on matters relating to myself directly; the connections, though strictly of the personal-coincidence variety, are important to me.

In the late 1960s I was twenty-two and in London, working as a labourer for Turriff & Co., one of the building firms on the new Barbican development (just up from Smithfields meat-market, you had to walk past a pub where a pint of Guinness was available at 7 o'clock in the morning). Next door to Turriff was the firm of Laing, generally regarded by the semi- and unskilled labouring force as the top outfit on the entire site. It was about my fourth job on a building site so I did not have all that much building trade experience but the working conditions with Turriff were unexpectedly good. What the position was at Laing I do not know except that assuming it was superior to Turriff it must have been special.

Semi- and unskilled building workers belonged to the Transport and General Workers' Union (TGWU) but having been a member of this union on a couple of earlier occasions I had no respect for it at all. It was about the largest union in Britain and very weak on the ground. Back home in Scotland the general conditions of the busworkers bore witness to that. In 1965 female conductors were still being paid less than male conductors; around £9.50 for a 40-something hours six-day shift-working week. I remember starting there as a nineteen-year-old youth and making more than a woman who had worked in the job for thirty years. For all busworkers, earning a livable wage meant foregoing your one day off and trying for as much overtime as possible on the other six. As far as conditions went, it was run like the army; when you stepped out of line you were up on a charge; the role of bus inspector was equivalent to that of serjeant-at-arms. Office 'staff' did not wear uniforms and were said to wear 'civvies', and were ranked in some indefinable way; always they were treated with deference by uniformed busworkers. The head man, the Garage Superintendent, had the power of a field marshal; outside of ordering someone's execution for bad timekeeping he could do just about anything he liked.

Beyond the buses I was used to working in places where conditions illustrated the level of union organisation. Any overtime working was a secret whisper between worker and gaffer and seemed to hinge either on arse-licking or forelock-touching, or else relationships like family, lodge or religious denomination. As far as safety conditions were allowed to function in these places, you would suddenly notice the guy standing next to you in the washroom was missing several fingers. In such factories elderly men in dungarees addressed twenty-one-year-old youths who wore suits, shirts and ties, with self-effacing hesitancy, firstly having grabbed a brush to look busy. Top-brass upper management were legendary figures in pin-stripe suits and crombie coats and you had to catch your breath in awe as they strode purposefully home at half past two in the afternoon. Even elderly men in dungarees did not have to grab that brush in the presence of the legendary figures, they were beyond such earthly matters. I doubt if TGWU branch officials were even granted an interview with them. We were all invisible, the entire workforce. Well, that is not quite true, the merest hint of an infringement of company rules would have been spotted at a hundred paces. At least two factories I worked in were run by Christian fundamentalists. If you went to church they let you work overtime.

But typically the unions in these places were worse than useless. If you thought you had a grievance your hardest struggle was with the union itself, branch officials first and then the full-timers. The primary duty of most union officials lay in revealing that what you thought was a 'genuine' grievance was not really a 'grievance' at all. At the monthly branch meeting the half-dozen folk who bothered to attend would stare at any strange face – not wondering if you were an infiltrator from Special Branch and/or the Economic League: no, they would be trying to work out if you were some sort of radical left-wing Communist Trotskyist anarchist trouble-maker just arrived in from Vladivostock. These were the kind of meetings where 'politics' are kept strictly in quotation marks and where individuals yawn or else sigh very loudly whenever anything resembling that dastardly subject crops up. And if it does crop up a voice from the back of the room will shout, '*Ultra vires*, brother', probably even if you are a woman.

At twenty-one or twenty-two I knew enough to know that other forms of union activity could exist; from the age of fifteen to seventeen I had been an apprentice compositor and member of SOGAT, one of the small but powerful print workers' unions.

So taking all of that into consideration, down in London the idea of resuming membership of the TWGU in the building trade was not too appealing. But I soon discovered things were different on the Barbican site. For a start, you were not forced to work a 60- to 72-hour seven-day week for a livable wage. Nor were you forced to toe the line in order 'to win' the chance of working these long hours. At Turriff & Co. everybody worked a 46-hour five-day week; the basic 40 plus 6 hours' overtime. Those 46 hours were all that could be worked. The wage at the end of the week did not make you a millionaire but it was livable, it was the highest hourly rate I had ever earned in my life. There was no 'officer core' either. At that time I was living in a tiny room at the top of a three-storey house in Calthorpe Street, WC1. The kitchen was way down in the basement; scrub your plate, pot and table *before* cooking (most folk lived on toast and cheese, with weekend visits to Indian restaurants), so I had good cause to appreciate the on-site subsidised meals in the Turriff canteen. Huge platefuls of grub, big potatoes, meat and gravy. I cannot recollect if the grub was tasty or otherwise, but with portions of such a size that made no odds, the quality was the quantity. Also I remember hearing some good ska and rock steady music in the canteen, accompanying the grub, from the likes of Derrick Morgan, Jimmy Cliff, the Ethiopians, the Maytals.

This was the period of the long strike down at Thamesmead, and men left the Barbican to travel to there once a week to join the picket-line in solidarity with the strikers. They left from various Barbican sites. Every Friday the half-hour lunch-break was followed by the weekly, half-hour branch meeting. I found attendance compulsive if not compulsory. The 'unskilled' workforce was Irish and West Indian with a tiny sprinkling of Scots; the shop steward was a white middle-aged Londoner, a very businesslike guy. On the door going into the canteen a couple of branch officials – one of them Scottish – sold the *Morning Star*; and whether or not your politics were to the left, right or centre of the Communist Party it was good having the choice of a non-establishment line in a daily newspaper.

Eventually I left the Barbican and returned to Scotland at the tail end of 1969 with Marie; we had just got married and were expecting a baby, and with only one wage there was no chance of finding a proper place to stay in London.

So it was back to the buses once again. I had worked already on four occasions for three different bus companies. There was never any other work in Glasgow, not that I could find, where an 'unskilled worker' could earn the semblance of a livable wage, given you had to cram in the equivalent of a fortnight in hours every week to get it. This meant a return to the old TGWU, not as bad in this new garage as it had been in the others. In fact it was not bad at all, driving out of Partick Garage for Glasgow Corporation transport, the conditions were so much better than they had been for the private companies. But still nowhere close to how things were at the Barbican. I finally left the buses four years later, to start mainly nightshift work in a factory, lurching back into the TGWU dark ages, of which enough said.

I did not help change much in any of the jobs I held but if latterly I succeeded in irritating a few people then my experience at the Barbican branch of the TGWU was crucial. Through my time as an apprentice compositor I knew strong unions existed but my time with Turriff & Co. revealed a more interesting point: any union at all can be strong, even those I thought a joke, such as the TGWU. They might well be a joke in general, and at the upper reaches of full-time officialdom both morally corrupt and politically bankrupt, but on the ground, the shop-floor, their strength was a function of the branches, individually and separately (as opposed to collectively which only comes later). And each branch was as strong as the commitment of the rank and file, the ordinary members. Everything hinges on that. Relying on those at the top to further the cause is useless. Sometimes it is difficult to differentiate between full-time union officials and a team of industrial-relations experts sub-contracted from the CBI. For any group engaged in struggle, success arrives from the ground, street level: even where the leadership is strong, if commitment is lacking at the bottom then problems are unavoidable, the strength is superficial, an illusion.

Twenty years after leaving London, and perhaps a year after my first meeting with him, a chance remark from John La Rose and I discovered he had been one of the TGWU shop stewards at the Barbican. In fact he had been working on the site next door; Laings, the best operation there. He had left the job about two years before I started. Perhaps it is not a big thing that he happened to be working there, I do not know, I have yet to hear the full story from him, how things were, what sort of fights were having to be fought to reach the organisational level the unskilled workforce were then at. But I saw a consistency, that John should have been involved as a shop steward for the outfit with the best conditions on the new Barbican site during a period in the building trade when genuine grass-roots strength did exist.

Shortly before starting there I had begun writing my first short stories and early in 1973 a small press in the USA published my first collection. The morning after receiving my 'payment' by parcel post – 200 copies of the book in lieu of cash – I was driving a bus out the garage at 4 o'clock on a February morning; just the thing to destroy any romantic illusions about being a writer. Like most small presses this American one had no dough either. As far as Britain, Europe, Africa, Asia and Australasia were concerned, I was sole distributor and marketing manager for the 200 books. It took me a few years to get rid of 199 of them (I still have one left but I am keeping it).

Fortunately in Glasgow there were other folk around aware of the reality: unless you are involved in mainstream Eng Lit it is not enough just to write the stuff, you should also prepare for the rest of the business, the printing and publishing and distribution. Every writer should face up to startled, bored or hostile bookshop proprietors at some time in their life, I mean when you are trying to place copies of your own books, even giving them away on that 'sale or return' deal, the one where they get tucked out of sight on the remotest of shelves and lie dormant for years. And you are too embarrassed to return in the off chance they might have been sold. Maybe you manage to pluck up the courage. When you do nobody in the shop has ever heard of the damn thing, title and author, they assume this is some newfangled shoplifting method.

My next collection of stories, *Three Glasgow Writers*, was also small-press, myself and another two writers, Tom Leonard and Alex Hamilton. The one after that was called *Short Tales from the*

Nightshift, published by a co-operative some of us had set up at Glasgow Print Studio in 1976–77. As I recall we were aware of the need for something more than what we were doing but it was plenty at that time, and we did not take it beyond that stage. At this time of writing – 'Glasgow 1990 City of Culture' – there is no alternative bookshop worthy of the name in the entire place.[1]

Since my late teens, early twenties, along with the European writers that meant much to me, I had been reading black American writers like Wilbur, Wright, Jackson, Cleaver, Malcolm X, Baldwin and Ellison as well as white American writers like Kerouac, Algren, Hemingway, Salinger, Crane, Anderson. One of the first contemporary, non-American authors working in English who did mean something to me in terms of prose technique was a West Indian, Sam Selvon. Eventually he spent a year as writer-in-residence at Dundee University in Scotland in the mid-1970s. A story of mine was published in a magazine to which he also contributed. His was an extract from *Lonely Londoners* and I thought his approach similar to where I was myself.

It was a couple of years on from there that I discovered a wider range of writing, during my first writer-in-residence job at Renfrew District Libraries. The man responsible for my appointment was Chief Librarian Joseph D. Hendry, a true believer in the power of the word. Joe had transformed Renfrew District Libraries into the second-highest book-spending service per head in Britain (second only to the City of Westminster). Among other innovations he introduced a system of no fines on overdue books. Central to his philosophy was the belief that if somebody in an ordinary, working-class housing scheme felt obliged to hang on to a copy of Franz Kafka or James Joyce then he would gladly replace it. Like many other people Joe has had to leave Scotland to get proper work.

Here in Paisley Central Library 1979 I noticed a small shelf standing by itself. But it was a 'complete section', and had the title 'Ethnic', and was also labelled in Urdu and other languages. When I browsed there I found the majority of books were in English, and included fiction, poetry, drama, politics, economics, etc. It contained something of a marginalised English literature. In this 'Ethnic' section I found Ayi Kwei Armah, Amos Tutuola, Alex La Guma, Okot p'Bitek and others. Although using the English language, these writers were NOT working to assimilate their own cultural experience within standard prose form which is possible only through ultimate surrender. Surrender was the last thing on their mind. They were attacking and the attack was formal and methodical; like Sam Selvon they were laying claim to the language, allowing their culture to breathe in it. What they were doing was not new to me and nor did it define what I was up to myself. In Glasgow I had had the benefit of the conversation and ideas of close friends Tom Leonard and Alasdair Gray for the previous six or seven years. But coming on these other English-language writers from other marginalised cultures reinforced the position, speaking personally, and helped clarify the situation.

It was there in Central Library I also found a couple of interesting catalogues which seemed responsible for most of the books in this 'Ethnic' section. One was the Heinemann catalogue for the African Writers Series and the other belonged to an independent publisher and distributor. I kept both in the room at the library where I had my typewriter. And when I left the writer-in-residence job I took both catalogues home with me. It was only a few months ago that I discovered I still have them. The small independent one turned out to be the 1979 New Beacon catalogue, the same New Beacon enterprise run by Sarah White and John La Rose, thus many of the important writers I had come to know ten years earlier in Paisley were courtesy of their work.

Any marginalised culture is a culture under attack. Accept the marginalisation and act on it. Spread the information; share the experience; disseminate the knowledge. If the struggle succeeds it will succeed from the bottom up. Be methodical. Take what exists and lay claim to it, transcend it, get beyond it. You write, publish, co-publish or otherwise acquire the books, pamphlets, magazines, tapes or whatever; then you advertise, distribute and sell them, if possible in your own bookshop, a place where people will eventually drop in, just to say hello. No lines of demarcation, no restricted zones; outsiders may enter and are welcome but the goal is self-containment, for the operation will continue to function either way, and with maximum commitment it will flourish. It has been along these lines that New Beacon has continued, and its work has been of great importance to such a great number of people, and not only in the United Kingdom.

As a variation on something John once said himself, to make a revolution at least (and only) two people are needed. His is no one-man-band. Far from it and nowhere near it, and that too is to his credit.

An Interview with John La Rose[1]

JK: You knew Cheddi Jagan, I noticed your name in the index of a book I have by him, in fact his autobiography.

JLR: Yes, Cheddi Jagan came when I was there, in Venezuela, and I introduced him to various people, because he was trying to come to terms with the problems of the rice industry and the Federation. Leaders were trying to tell him to come and enter the Federation and he was finding it very difficult, because the Indians did not want to enter the Federation. They saw themselves being swamped by these Africans in the islands. That's the central political mistake Cheddi made. Nevertheless he came there to sell rice and I was able to help him to sell the rice to keep his Government going, because he was under pressure from the British Government, the United States and from the Caribbean Federation leaders. So with that, coming to England in 1961, it meant that I brought all that experience.

JK: Okay, so maybe now, picking up on CAM, the Caribbean Artists Movement.

JLR: CAM was very significant because of the fact that this was a movement that sought to deal with the artist as a totally vulnerable person engaged with other artists in a very vulnerable way; and that kind of engagement had been unusual in Caribbean society and that made the experience extremely valuable in elucidating our own lives as individuals and as artists, as people involved in politics and so on – because we would have these long nights of discussion. Cabral says, 'It begins with culture and it ends with culture.' With CAM we always began with culture, in the sense that it was always a cultural subject for discussion. But it took in everything, so that when we had a private discussion subsequent to the public discussion, we would need to talk about literature, politics, music, culture; everything in society. And in talking about everything we were exploring ourselves, exploring society and societies. Coming from the Caribbean you had a really great experience of societies. In Trinidad we have the Chinese, French Creoles who came with the French Revolution from within the Caribbean to Trinidad, we have the Spaniards who had been original conquerors of the Carib and Sarawak Indians in Trinidad, we have the English who took over from the Spaniards, then we have the Africans who were brought to work on the plantations. Although we're not a classic plantation society like Barbados or Jamaica. What happened was because of the need for labour after 1838 when slavery came to an end. We had the first Chinese who were brought to work on the plantations and we had the Indians. I grew up seeing Syrians selling cloth and I went to school with them. All these people, it meant you were really familiar with different societies. I am very familiar with Indian society, I have a feeling of growing up with it. That's what's so peculiar about it all. I was taught by an Irish priest. He taught me Greek at St Mary's College in Trinidad. I hadn't known white people attacking other white people but here was this man attacking the English for the Black and Tans. He was obviously an Irish Nationalist. I did not know that white people could talk about other white people like that. The idea was that it was black people who were like that, you know, 'black and chicken can't do nothing'. Those kind of self-deprecatory, self-contemptuous sayings which have been imposed on society. But the revolutionary movement and the cultural movement weaken all these things, all the time. Every time it moves forward it shows that it is not true: we can do these things, we can deal with the British. 1903 was a situation where we almost had power in our hands in Trinidad. The place where the Government had its seat of power, the Red House, it was totally burned down in the water riots. The Governor was tarred. There's a *kaiso* [calypso] about it.

JK: One of the things about the publishing side of it at New Beacon is it is like reclaiming the radical history and your own history in publishing.

JLR: That was very much part of what we were doing. We were doing it very actively as a political movement involved in popular culture. Popular culture in Trinidad, the *kaisos* in particular, do make reference to all these events in our society. For example, there was a big march to Woodford Square, Port of Spain led by Butler the radical, popular leader in the 1940s. In those days transport was not easy from one end of the island to the other, and they marched for seventy miles into Port of Spain to protest what the Government was doing in the oil industry and so on. They got into Port of Spain and invaded the Red House and after that they went round to the Governor's House. And there's a *kaiso* about it: 'The man in the garden hiding/ hiding from Butler/oh come outside Mister come outside.' That's the Governor they're talking about. 'Oh come outside Mister, come outside/Mister do not hide, oh come outside/ Butler want to bust your ah ha!' You couldn't say bust your arse in the *kaiso* so 'Butler want to bust your ah ha'. Our *kaisos* do incorporate all that experience from 1925 when we had our first elections on a limited basis. We have 'Who you voting for

Cipriani?' Captain Cipriani was the leader of the Labour Party in those days. We had had the Working Men's Association and then the Trinidad Labour Party came out of that. We were part of the International Working Men's Movement, as were all the movements in the Caribbean in the 1920s.

JK: These kind of Working Men's Associations were crucial places; you had them – or slight variations – in various cities, London and Glasgow, New York, Warsaw. Books were available, so you could go in there and just read, talk to people.

JLR: Ours had been the Trinidad WMA, which subsequently became the Trinidad Labour Party. I knew all that history extremely well, both in terms of our oral history and I also made a special study of it in our libraries. We had a Trinidad Public Library since 18-something. They had the West Indian section in the Public Library – that's where the West Indian books were kept!

JK: We have Scottish sections in our libraries right now. And in the bookshops, Scottish bookshops, they still genre-ise our own culture; you get these wee sections tucked round a corner, often in quotes – 'Scottish' – that's where you find Scottish writing, contemporary literature or recipe books for haggis, what's the difference.

JLR: I didn't realise how funny that was until much later. But in the West Indian section I was able to go and read extensively and borrow books. I did a comprehensive study of all that for quite some time as part of the political, cultural work we were doing; this included a production of a poetry reading in the library, you'd be surprised that one of the books I was looking for was by Rabindranath Tagore, he was quite famous among us. I couldn't get this particular book by Tagore, the *Gitanjali*, till a friend who was the Deputy High Commisioner for India in Trinidad got me a copy for the poetry reading. It really meant that when we came together in CAM we got a lot together.

JK: It is also the organising, you are bringing this tremendous organising experience from various outside things, which is crucial.

JLR: You see Kamau Brathwaite had been to Africa after he finished his studies at Cambridge University. He got this job in Ghana. It was that experience that made him understand the traditions of African society and the Caribbean in the way he understands it and writes about it in his books. He was also involved in the education movement there and he wrote a play for schools, very much used in Ghana. Although he had done history at Cambridge he was also very interested in literature. He is still regarded as a historian but he's really more interested in comparative literature and histories.

JK: The key term you're using, 'comparative'. With you and Andrew Salkey and E. K. Brathwaite, apart from the fact that there's all these different societies, you are from three different countries basically, so you are bringing a whole kind of range of different ways of working in comparison.

JLR: But you see there was a common experience coming from those islands, which had to do with the fact that we were colonial territories of Britain, fighting against British colonial domination, what we called battleship democracy. They were not as actively involved in that because they left the Caribbean younger than I left. I left when I was thirty-one, Kamau at eighteen and Andrew at a similar age too. I was much more formed within the Caribbean experience than they had been. Nevertheless they had been attached to that experience all along, both in terms of their study and their work.

JK: And they were anti-assimilationist as well.

JLR: That's right, they were not for that. Not only that but Andrew and Kamau came from very interesting families. In

233

Barbados there's a house called the Bay House, where Kamau grew up – it is in all of his poems – the sea's at the back of it and the Roman Catholic cathedral on the opposite side of the road. That's where he grew up as a young person. His grandfather lived inside the country. Barbados is a small place but it is the country where they're concerned, and it is in all the poems. Kamau's sister wrote a piece – there was a celebration for him recently at the Community College in New York – and his sister, called May Morgan, wrote a very brilliant piece on Kamau's work, showing all the references from the place: the *genius loci*, it is all there and she knows it. No other literary critic could pick that up, but she describes it in great intensity.

I would think that coming here to England: firstly none of us were starry-eyed about Britain. I knew a lot about British history, I was anti-colonial. I knew of Churchill and his corruption and all his family in the Cabinet; things of that sort. There's nothing here to impress me, I was not impressionable about British society. I was very detached, looking to understand more of this colonial experience out of British society. I made contacts from the top to the bottom of British society. Just like I did when I lived in Venezuela, I mean I had meetings with the President right down to the bottom of the people. I had all these connections because I genuinely wanted to understand the nature of this colonial experience and how it had affected us and colonial societies, culturally, politically. Socially in all kinds of ways, and what that interaction means. And we were doing all that here, exploring all of that all the time within CAM – exploring it in terms of the writers and their writng.

JK: We were talking earlier about the autonomy of New Beacon. There's a kind of related thing that I have found an exciting notion about what you've been involved in, the way I have interpreted what you've been doing and thinking about it.

Besides being a publisher and writer you are creating a whole autonomous community in the sense that you have the publisher, you have the writers; with luck you have a sympathetic printer, you have the shop – to sell the work you are creating, you are your own customers. So there's a complete self-sufficiency within this, it in a sense is the ideal.

JLR: It happened by chance. Firstly my going into book publishing was not by chance but the question of bookselling was by chance: partly because of the fact that here in London all the books I wanted to get and read, there was no place I could buy them. So I decided at some stage that we would really do the international book service. That was the very first book service of its kind ever done from the Caribbean. I was a Caribbean specialist so it meant that I did a booklist in French, Spanish and English. The very first catalogues we sent internationally to everywhere, so it meant that people came here all the time. This was still in the 1960s, people came to our house and worked downstairs – here in Albert Road, Finsbury Park, London. I talked to so many people writing their Ph.D.'s or post-doctorate research for hours downstairs. It was that kind of place. It was a home, you couldn't just walk in, you had to get permission to enter and once you entered you were made comfortable. These were friends really and they came from the United States, Africa, the Caribbean, Asia. But they were all Caribbeanists, some were Africanists. So it was that kind of international connection we built right here in this house. The bookselling was partly encouraged by CAM because at that stage there were new writers being published every now and then. Some of the sessions involved discussing the new work, some of the sessions might have been private but it was always a free autonomous thing. It is a question of interacting with ideas and between personalities. People should not suppress what they think for this or that reason. Encouraging free and open discussion was a very important part of what we were doing. And in a certain sense you are making yourself vulnerable by discussing all you think personally, your own feelings – which is important for the artist, to talk about your feelings and intuitions as well.

JK: That vulnerability is almost a contradiction of what society in Britain is, a real kind of anathema.

JLR: And we really made an intimate relationship among ourselves. But it was not a constraining relationship, it allowed for – the phrase I used – 'free development of free individuals', which is a famous Marxian phrase, that's what was happening within CAM.

JK: Would that be one of the reasons why it was so attractive to so many people? One of the things again that I found exciting about it was the cross-generational thing. You had the young Ngugi, Linton Kwesi Johnson and Darcus Howe, a lot of young people; and you also had C.L.R. James being excited by it, who was forty or fifty years older. Thinking about the kind of influence you can infer about what Ngugi has been doing in and out of Kenya. And also what L.K.J. was doing in his poetry, and also moving into the 70s, the different things they were involved in, having derived in a way from much of the ideas and interplay of CAM – cultural activists, but also there was the political side continuing after CAM terminated.

JLR: Linton was involved with CAM in a way that Darcus was not. A lot of people from Britain and abroad became involved with us post-CAM but they understood and valued the experience.

JK: Which also includes an organising capacity, seeing an organising potential, and strategy.

JLR: Correct, and it really makes politics, culture, social life one indivisible experience.

JK: You see, I felt in my own case, that that was missing in Scotland. It was the organisation that was missing. There was a lot of kind of tentative good things going on. You had writers' conferences in the mid-70s, various things were happening in the 60s. But these organisational and comparative things, this crucial point about how do things go on in other societies, what these people have been involved in. All these things are so necessary.

JLR: It is strange but we always thought highly of the Russian writers. We felt a distance of geography only. My personal interests were in music and literature and I came across Gorky quite young, when I was about thirteen. I had never read anything like Gorky's short stories. Later on when I was interested in music in a much more serious way I was very interested in what are called the 'Nationalist Five': the Russian composers Cui, Borodin, Mussorgsky, Rimsky-Korsakov, Balakirev;[2] I became very interested in what these composers were saying. Now it subsequently connected me up with the meaning of the Russian revolution. Later when I met Sarah [White] she was researching the reception of Darwinism in Russia in the nineteenth century for a Ph.D. at Imperial College and that told me a lot more about how to read world society. But that all began in my teens.

JK: Knowing how other people organise, though, I read a biography of Sun Yat Sen. What they did was just incredible. But again it is this organisation, looking at the way they organised.

JLR: We had a direct link with Sun Yat Sen in Trinidad through a man called Acham Chen, a Trinidadian Chinese who'd left to go to China and was part of Sun Yat Sen's movement. He became the Foreign Minister. Of course we knew a lot about what was going on in India because the Indian Congress movement sent representatives to Trinidad. Wherever there were these overseas Indian populations they sent them. So in Trinidad people knew about the Congress movement.

JK: The same in South Africa.

JLR: Like with Gandhi yes. We knew about the Congress movement and what they were fighting for, the fact that people were being banned from going to one place and another. If you read something which we published not long ago about the history of the Negro Welfare and Cultural Associations, it is about movements I connected up with after reading Maxton's *Lenin.*[3] I went looking for these organisations, looking for the study group movements and so on. Eventually we formed a connection with the remnants of the Negro Welfare Cultural Association. They had been the organisation which had been organising the workers and the unemployed in the north of Trinidad, joining up with the Southern Workers' Movement in the 1937 General Strike and Popular Insurrection. They had this connection whereby they knew what was going on in the Indian struggle for independence. One got that kind of information second-hand. I had not then read Nehru or Gandhi's books. So we were really connecting up with all that was going on in the rest of the world. For example, later on in England I was the Chairman of the Committee for the Release of Political Prisoners in Kenya. When they were struggling with the Mau Mau – the Kenyan Land Freedom Army – and we identified with the Mau Mau struggle, we were getting information on it through the Communist Party in England. We called our own colonial collaborators 'loyal Kikuyu' from listening to radio reports on the BBC. We were pretty well-informed about India too from the Indian Communist movement. There was all that behind us.

JK: It was a good influence from India, the influence of various people from there in exile in the United States, etc. I was just thinking of moving back into the post-CAM period. There was a good statement you made, I'm paraphrasing: the time is over, there was a communion, we shouldn't worry about that, that's how it goes, there's something else we can develop – the embers from the fire. And I am looking from the outside but there seems to have been more of a concentration on political activism *per se*; now I am not speaking of yourself, but the kind of CAM experience in *Race Today* or whatever, and also some of the campaigning that goes on. Did art and culture remain important in that campaigning, for example?

JLR: It was always here in London. For example, I became deputy chairman of the West Indian Student Centre, where we met mostly. Andrew [Salkey] had been there because he was still fed up over one of the parties run by the West Indian governments. During that time there was a lot of activity stimulated by the presence of CAM at the centre. When we began to talk about the Black Education Movement and so on, it stimulated the students to get involved with it. There was a dance group and you know the poem by Okot p'Bitek called 'The Song of Lawino', they produced it. I introduced the book to them, told them who Okot was, how important the book was. It is interesting how they did it, in a small room with no stage; and they followed it up with articles which we discussed, where you can make theatre, how you can make it. You can make it anywhere. Now they would have taken that out of the centre into various things that they were doing. For example, I became involved in establishing the South East London Parents' Organisation [SELPO], which became involved in this political struggle in the area. Part of what they did was to write plays about the police and the courts. So the cultural activity was always part of what they were doing. It was not something we organised, they organised. These organisations organised as part of what they had seen out of the experience of CAM, because CAM was interested in both, doing productions as well as discussing issues. It was very important to all those youngsters. They are now into all kinds of things in British society. An explosion of black creativity took place, interestingly, in the plays and the poetry.

JK: Particularly in the performance. The performance has been so important in poetry, in other contries too: Kenya, Peru, South Africa. That includes the performance of writers.

JLR: With CAM 'performance poetry' began with Kamau's performance of *Rights of Passage*. It influenced a whole lot of that generation.

JK: I am thinking of that time in Scotland, about Jim Haynes who was there then. There was a famous event at the Fringe Festival round about 1961, when Trocchi and McDiarmid met on the same platform. Burroughs was there I think, John Calder too. Who else? Mailer? But the fight was Trocchi versus McDiarmid, it still gets discussed. I think Jim Haynes was directly involved in the organisation of the event.

JLR: We knew of his paperback bookshop in Edinburgh and we knew of his work in theatre, and then he comes down here with the Traverse to the Jeanette Cochrane Theatre. We had met him through Sarah's father who almost lost his job because he gave Jim and his theatre a grant and Lord Goodman – the Chairman of the Arts Council – did not like it. We found we had a common experience, he had grown up partly in Venezuela. He was also open to what we were doing.

JK: But it is the idea that performance is so crucial. And when there is struggle, performance also becomes an exchange, that's also taking part in an experience within your own culture.

JLR: That's why the play is such an intimate connection. I

remember a friend saying, 'Why is it that you are not publishing more plays? Plays are a very significant element of the interchange within the culture, a direct form of interchange.' I said that I really hadn't thought of it in that way. We were having a big argument about it in Barbados – we were about to publish that book by Kole Omotoso on Caribbean theatre – I did not realise that we had missed out in that kind of discussion about the immediacy of theatre.

JK: I think it is important that plays are published, but you can not publish the performance of a play.

JLR: One of the things that happened in London that I recognised as an element of what had happened with us in Britain was this explosion of Black theatre. It affected British theatre in very significant ways, because there were these people meeting in small halls. That was what excited me about Jim's theatre. All the plays he put on – Sarah and I saw nearly every one of them – were by living playwrights, which made it a very contemporary theatre. Some of them became quite famous. That play *Loot* by Joe Orton, we saw it there where it was first produced. Jim told me he had made a mistake, he had not taken out all the rights; so when the play became famous and made so much money they were not making the money they ought to have made. So when I heard Kamau reading *Rights of Passage* I thought that this was the place where this ought to be produced and told Kamau right away. I did not know if I could produce a whole reading of a long poem but I knew that Kamau would be a very powerful reader, so we could do a dramatisation and stage it at the Cochrane.

JK: Part of the objective thing, getting it away from only one writer. It's a central element so lacking in mainstream literature, is this indigenous aesthetic, this validation of particular cultures, your own culture. Talking about what's happening here, there's

all these different things: here's a writer, here's a poet and here
also is a working language. All these things that say this is our
culture, this is our language. We can discuss it, here are artworks,
all of that. These things are central to a person becoming valid as
a person. You can only do that once you've seen this is your
culture, you do not have to turn away in embarrassment because
you've met someone from your own place, or someone stands
up in public and reads something from your own background,
your own culture. Whereas, part of the colonial experience – as
it is also in Scotland – is you're taught to be ashamed of your
own culture, you know, inferiorisation. If you're down here in
London and a guy starts talking in a strong Scottish accent you
wind up blushing with embarrassment. Thinking about that
effect in the 1970s where that is part and parcel of the self-
confidence of going into the street, of challenging authority and
not being put down by authority: the right to self-defence. All
these things become part of valuing yourself and your
community.

JLR: You are absolutely right. The young people who became
   involved in all those struggles; there was a girl, Althea Jones, she
   was doing chemistry, but she came out of the cultural experience
   in Trinidad, and she came to London and straight to CAM. She
   knew about me from Trinidad; she came into a cultural and
   political situation here that she had just come out of back home.
   She later went and joined the UCPA which became the Black
   Panther movement. By that time she became part of the
   Mangrove Nine case. She was finishing a Ph.D. thesis and she
   was a very powerful orator. It was to them that John Berger gave
   the money when he got the Booker Prize, which made a
   scandal. They bought a house on Tullington Park Road in our
   area, Finsbury Park, which they used as their headquarters. She
   came out of the same experience as myself where politics, art and

culture were one holistic thing. I found it very difficult to understand the nature of artists in British society who somehow kept themselves away from these things, compartmentalised and out of a constantly vibrant and changing social life.

JK: They're trained to, they're trained to separate them.

JLR: In a certain sense they become entertainers. You'd go to opera or plays and I would talk – especially the English élite – the first thing they would say is 'it was a success' or 'it was interesting'. On the whole I noticed that the language was not an effective language of communication and interchange with the artist and his work. Not that they were not critical people. But they were critical people who worked for the newspapers. They were not prepared to commit themselves to an independent original opinion which they might have, which they should have, about a work of art they'd seen on the stage. I was always freely committing myself to what I thought.

JK: That's part of the education system, that you are taught not to do that. You are taught that personal experience and responses are invalid.

JLR: I would freely make a comment about how I saw it and try to engage the others about their feelings about it. I thought those things were important, not simply the intellectual presentation of it and the intellectual understanding, also their feelings, how they intuitively responded. Intuition is so important.

JK: The intellectualisation is a rationalisation. That becomes a reflective thing anyway, you are moving right away from experiences.

JLR: I always noticed people used these bland phrases about their experiences. In my view you couldn't really move your society with bland expressions, you had to really engage in a serious interchange between both individuals and social groupings. Within CAM we'd gone to the ultimate to do that with the people who were intimately involved with the work of CAM. The private sessions we called 'Warishi' nights – from the kind of things the Amerindians in the interior and the Pork Knockers used for carrying heavy loads on their heads.

JK: I was thinking of the separate way in which art and politics are here. It is interesting the way that art is devalued because of that. The kind of disinformation that says the function of art is basically decorative or whatever. Even within the left that's the case; art generally is devalued from within the left, because it is regarded as being predicated on the fact that it is not political – unless it is a particular case, a kind of 'well here's political art' and 'here's a still life' and 'here's a portrait'. It is really weird but of course it is part of the education process anyway, a very essential part, kids being kept disinformed.

JLR: As I told you about Venezuela, they were all political people, all very artistic, cultural people, so that all these things had been interconnected all the time in their life-experience, on a daily basis. It was not something they'd separate one from another for particular occasions, because politics is so much part of the experience of life it means that with the intimate experience of politics you are also experiencing life in a particular way. My subsequent understanding of it is that people bring to politics what they are. They can not bring anything else. So if you are a highly developed person, you bring that to politics, whatever way you've developed you bring that to politics. There's nothing idealistic about politics, in that sense you know, there's nothing idealistic about politics. There's a phrase, 'come the revolution'. I say there's nothing like that. My argument is the very opposite: it is the very process by which we live and so that makes this a continuing constant process. There's no end or beginning in a revolutionary process: it is a continuing process.

JK: These kind of statements are made, people say things so they do not have to examine reality. It has always been beyond me the way people can say that art has been divorced from politics. It is as if they'd never looked at what's in front of their nose. So many writers talk about, 'Well you cannot change things, nothing gets affected by what a writer does.' It's total nonsense. If we just look at the opposite side of the coin, let's look at a negation of that. Let's take countries that are in struggle, people who are in struggle: what do the governments there do to their writers and artists? We might well say that artists and writers do not think that they affect things, okay, but State authorities and the right-wing, they don't think that. Christ, they kill them! It's too obvious to even discuss, the only question is how come we still get the propaganda. And taking something like early reggae, I mean rock steady, ska and all that, blue beat, and the subversive qualities. Gordon Weller talks about it in terms of language: the actual language that people are using is so creative.

JLR: It is all there in the language of the *kaisos* and in the language of the reggae, of all these popular arts and songs. The songs retain that tradition longer than the political experience, long after people have forgotten what Burns said and why he said it, they're still singing the songs. And it is important that we try to understand what these songs were in their context, because it gives us a reference with this changing human experience. I know that because it is so pronounced in the *kaiso*. The *kaisonians* themselves were from the working-class and their focus is from within the working-class looking at the rest of society, from within the experience, from below.

We did not begin to study what the British did in the 1930s until recently – how they were seeing us, what we were doing to counter British oppression and colonialism – and it showed what all the different groups of the working-class were doing at that period. There were three people, the Governor and a man called Nankivell. Although he was Colonial Secretary he seems to have been a radical and he met with the people. Now when the General Strike, uprising and insurrection took place in Trinidad he was looked at by the Colonial Office as the guy who was not behaving properly and eventually he was sent away after the strike. I found that interesting because another guy came over as a colonial administrator and he made a statement about oil and the fact that the oil companies had been saying the oil was *not* going to dry up. And they'd been saying that it would dry up for the last twenty years but that wasn't true and so he too was sent away. A researcher told me that Nankivell died on a train and I said, 'MI6 pushed him off.' I am almost certain that MI6 did it to him, he was part of the movement in the 30s and the Colonial Officer was very annoyed with these Trinidad administrators who couldn't handle the strike well enough for them. Susan Craig writes about this in *Smiles and Blood*. There we were looking at how they were responding to us and the movement for the transformation of Caribbean society and against colonialism and the British connection in that particular period. What in my view is significant is that it shows the creativity of ordinary people in society. People do not look at creativity as political creativity, they see it only in terms of cultural creativity, the writers, the artists. But when you look at what that creativity is, especially in the case of the Caribbean in the 30s, it is working people who learn how to understand the colonial experience, who find ways, all kinds of ingenious ways, of dealing with that situation, confronting it and winning battles against it.

But a significant section of that grouping – there's a similar kind of group which Malcolm X and people like that came out of in the United States – they are semi-unemployed or unemployed and they become highly articulate, highly creative in terms of how they organise other people. That happened here in 1981 with the Brixton riots, the Uprising. The people who took on the police were not active political people, they were ordinary people whose sense of Britain was a sense of tremendous police action in the area, plus all kinds of social oppressions, from school to unemployment and so on. They took on the police in a very military way, attack then retreat, then simply disappear. And that's how the unemployed behaved in the Caribbean in the 1930s. So I understood that creativity does not simply mean a writer or a musician, creativity means social creativity as well, which involves all these people whom other people regard as the 'ordinary zero' in society.

JK: Again it's just this disinformation that is right the way through our society. People are taught to think of themselves as being a zero, that you are part of the 'lumpen proletariat'. Even activists within the left, they have this debate about it. Again it's like what's in front of your nose; look around, the poll tax, or whatever the activities and experiences are that ordinary people are doing and having. The forces of the right always see a need for that infiltrator, they don't see self-determination. In Scotland recently with the Timex struggle, the quality Sunday papers made such a great play about that sort of stuff, 'It's Militant or the SWP responsible.' They would not allow the Timex workers the right to think for themselves: 'They're being led by the nose, all the things that occur, occur because of these infiltrators.' It's like the old US State propaganda from the 1950s about Ho Chi Minh or something, every time something happens their agents are sent out to find the proof and the proof is the arch villain Ho Chi Minh, he's got to be lurking about somewhere, doing his infiltrating, and even if they don't find him they'll say Ho Chi Minh is keeping himself out of sight, they can't imagine him not being involved.

JLR: Creativity is something that we've got to look at. I was very
familiar with it, much more than Andrew [Salkey]. It was for us
a total education. What is this creativity, and how this creativity
operates within societies. And how it changes a culture. How
does it move a culture into different kinds of areas which previously it had not attacked. For example, these black youngsters
here in London who say 'Self-defence is no offence.' It was their
slogan. And 'Come what may we're here to stay.' It was their
slogan. I did not invent it. Their parents were not saying that. I
belong to the parent generation. I always knew I could go back
to the Caribbean if I wanted. Even those who had come with
the intention of going back in five years, when Powell came
along and said, 'You'll all have to go' – talking of repatriation
and so on – they had to face up to the reality of their situation in
Britain. Some of them took the money and went back home.
The youngsters, they're the ones who faced up to the police in
Brixton and everywhere in London. The police were framing
them up all over the place. Those slogans, 'Come what may
we're here to stay', were their slogans. It also affected how
people in France thought. They began to say 'J'y suis, j'y reste.'
I am here and I remain here. This is ordinary creativity. It was
very much part of what we understood a popular movement to
be. It teaches people how to organise themselves so they become
part of their own independent autonomous organisation, taking
on these matters that affect them.

JK: That could take you into Carnival.

JLR: Carnival is that kind of activity as well. Again, you couldn't
study *kaiso* without carnival, carnival and *kaiso* went together.
What is interesting about carnival – in Trinidad it is similar to
Brazilian carnival – what is common to all of these is a certain
Catholic relationship with the Africans. Within their culture, the
place they find themselves, Brazil, Louisiana, very Catholic

countries; what they do is they creatively respond to that. Because the carnivals that these others brought were an end to the flesh. Sin and so on. It comes before Lent. Two days of total and absolute abandon. Lent comes and for forty days you are supposed to be repenting in the flesh with physical and mental flagellation. So you have two or three days of total abandon. Now that's the carnival and you are on the streets. At that stage the white people introduced some of their tradition into the Caribbean, in Trinidad, and in the other islands who had some French connection. So the Africans entered into that in the 1830s because they are now free, and they reinterpret that in terms of their own festival experience, which is drum, singing and so on. In Africa there are a lot of praise-songs but there are other songs, other traditions, where you sing songs about what you do not like and what's bothering you, the song that satirises what is in society, and that's what the Africans reinterpret.

JK: Just as an aside, I was also thinking of these Soweto singers. In all the townships there would be these variety events, where these popular events would have singers singing satirical stuff, things about local people, anecdotal even.

JLR: This appears in the carnival. Now what they call 'Jouvay' [*jour ouvert*], daybreak, it usually began on the Sunday night, the field slaves would march through and terrify the town. They would do that because they were re-enacting their loves theatrically and musically in the carnival, in the road, on the streets. Now that led to the riots in the 1880s and the British suppressed the carnival, which is very like what I see in the carnival in London. I see the connection there very easily. So they suppressed and regulated the carnival. Instead of it starting in the night and terrifying people – they also had torches, that was the danger – they were in the streets, enacting their past and as a result of that these riots happened. The authorities in the

1880s regulated the Sunday night, started the carnival at six in the morning until the night. The carnival has this revolutionary tradition. Its popular creativity has been immense, with everybody doing what they can in the situation, music, dance, song and the organisation. So the carnival is all that plus it is the greatest popular festival, which incorporates most of the society for three or four days.

Then there's the carnival that begins after Christmas, with the *kaisonians* in their tents, where the *kaisonians* are moving the population. It is preparing the people for carnival with all these songs about what's going on in society, with all these political comments, all these tribunes who are the *kaisonians*. Especially at the stage before 1925 when we had the first elections in Trinidad. Even up to the 1940s there were two main aspects of the *kaiso* which were very pronounced: first, the *kaisonian* as tribune, speaking for the people, because there were no elected representatives, not by adult suffrage, not until 1946. So from the *kaisonian* as tribune out come all the grievances and all the problems and aspirations of the working-class. Then there is the *kaisonian* as entertainer: that was becoming more pronounced after the 1940s, after the war, when we were moving towards independence; and with all the Americans who came to the country, people were entertaining them for the kind of money they never got before. These two traditions intertwine and one of them is more dominant than the other at particular phases in the life of the *kaiso*. The *kaiso* is what presents the whole situation and creates the atmosphere for the carnival. It begins right after Christmas and continues up to the carnival. In the earlier days the chantwell or *chanteur* of the *kaiso*, the singer, was in the band and the band was the chorus. So it was really a very communal experience and that's what makes carnival a very strong tradition. What makes people stronger is that the bands were completely autonomous. Each band chooses to play what it wants to play, how it wants to play, who is going to sing what song. Nothing to do with any other band or the Government or anybody else. It is totally autonomous creative expression. All the creativity in the population – in the kinds of costumes they would make, what colours they would use – is totally autonomous. It is a very democratic tradition, very anti-authoritarian.

This is another aspect of the question that makes carnival such a dangerous thing. Nobody asked the police or Home Office for permission to make carnival. When they went into a group and wanted to play carnival they simply went on the road. It was such a normal thing to do in the Caribbean. And they won that right. There's a *kaiso* about it: 'The road made to walk on Carnival Day, the road is ours.' All these governments recognise how dangerous it is. People on the streets are always dangerous to governments anyway. The time when Fidel Castro made an attack on the Moncada barracks to overthrow Batista on July 26th, it was the moment of carnival in Santiago, with all these massive amounts of people on the streets. There's always that danger with carnival for the authorities, but it's freedom of self-expression and creativity for the mass of the population.

JK: One of the legal things here is that there is no actual right to do anything else when you are on the streets other than walking, to get from A to B. You do not have the right as such to be in the street. You have the freedom to assemble but there's no right for it. I was also thinking of Breach of the Peace. If the police exercised the powers that they have – theoretically, as I understand it – then they could charge every single person at any time of the day, even being asleep, with Breach of the Peace. And if the full weight of that was ever attempted by the State, it could be revolution, it could be finished in a day. I think the example of carnival demonstrates something about it. You were talking about how people were scared of this thing. It reminded me of the time when 20,000 people marched in London, bringing the city to a halt, I always have this image of the gents in bowler hats looking out the window saying, 'What the hell's this coming over the bridge!'

JLR: The Black People's Day of Action for the New Cross Massacre was on the 2nd of March 1981. I will never forget that. It was something that had not happened since the Chartists, back in the 1830s. People had not marched across London into the City. We had to negotiate with the police, I would chair the meetings. And that decision came from within the meetings of the Black People's Assembly. People would be saying, 'Man we have got to do something about this thing. The police can not get away with this thing!' That kind of talk went on. And they said, 'Yes we'll go on a march.' 'Where are the guns?' That kind of talk: 'We want some guns!' And I said, 'Have you heard of a man called Brigadier Kitson, *Low Intensity Operations*?' If you haven't read his book then you should read it. Because if you are talking about going to Parliament with guns you have to take on Kitson.' He had been the Commander in Northern Ireland, he was GOC in Britain.[4] I said, 'Let's talk seriously, you are starting at the end, let's start at the begining.'

We had that sort of interchange all the time at the meetings, very open, free meetings. So they said, 'OK we'll go on a march.' We said, 'Well, what day are we going to march?' Because the normal marches took place on a Sunday, when nobody's working, everyone's home, the people said that they wanted it to be on a day when the British are bound to take notice. So what day? We had to disrupt British society, that was absolutely clear. That is what we were saying in that movement. We wanted to snarl up traffic all over London.

So we decided it must be a Monday, that came from within

the audience. We wanted to make this place realise that we're serious and we're going to disrupt the whole of British society. We aren't going to work that day. People had been talking about the question of a Black general strike since 1964. That was highly impractical at that time, but the idea was there.

We already had the experience of the first demonstration of about 2,000 outside the house where the massacre took place, there in New Cross Road on the Sunday after the 18th January 1981. We stopped there for hours. The police could not move us from the street. We disrupted the traffic coming from the South of England. They were trying to move us but they did not dare. They could see people were going to burn down the place or something. It ended peacefully and people went away. But on the other day, when we met with the police from the City of London as well as from the Metropolitan Police, one guy – Superintendent Paul Kinghorn I think he was – he came with a map and told us where we could go and so on. I said, 'You listen carefully, we have decided that the route we're going to take is the route. And we're going as far as Blackfriars Bridge. We have to have a further meeting of the Assembly, and when we're finished with that, we'll come back to you again and tell you where else we want to go.'

Paul Kinghorn had never met people talking to him quite like that. He was trying to intimidate us. The leading officer from the police never said a word during the negotiations that we had. Then we told Kinghorn, 'If you do not take us seriously – you are just the police, we are a political grouping – if you do not understand that then we will deal with the Home Secretary, not with you. So the next time you come to negotiate, you better bring someone with authority.'

That's what we told him. The next time they brought the Deputy Assistant Commissioner and his aide. By that time we had finished the second part of the route. But the route he wanted to take us was different. But we had the route we wanted, we had it decided. The police are very informed, and we learned a lot about negotiating with them. The police never tell you what their own plans are, they only want to know what your plans are.

What demonstrations in the past usually did was to march on Hyde Park into Whitehall. We said we were going to go where the people are going to know that this is happening, we're going to march in all those areas – like Peckham – before we come into Blackfriars Bridge. That way you are going to hit that area of London with all those people who are really concerned about what's happening in the whole New Cross area, and then march through the financial centre, the City, and shake up the place, terrify them.

JK: It is amazing how people allow demonstrations and marches to be totally controlled by the police. In Glasgow they always start them on a Saturday in a quiet part of town, office buildings, nobody's there. It is crazy, they've allowed the agenda to be set about the nature of their protest. In Britain most of the organisers of these things are all part of the official Labour movement anyway. They deal with the police all the time, they negotiate with the system. It is just a total contradiction.

JLR: We were confronting the system, quite deliberately and clearly. I had to go to the House of Commons because of what happened. They did nothing about it. We saw them the day before the demonstration and they said, 'Why do you not stop at the House of Commons sitting that day, to show how you felt about those people who were killed.' The MPs we spoke to then put on an Early Day Motion, about what had happened at New Cross.

JK: It may be quite important to say here that with the New Cross

Massacre thirteen black teenagers were murdered and no one has been charged with this thing, and it's twelve years later. People just don't know that.

JLR: We could benefit from our experience. Michael Mansfield and Ian Macdonald, other lawyers, were involved in that case and we were handling most of the major cases of that kind at that particular stage, dealing with those major cases ourselves.

What had happened was that the police were trying to pin the event on some youngsters who were at the party. Because of that we were able to prepare ourselves for the inquest. Because of our experience in fighting all those cases prior to 1981 we knew how the police handled those cases in court and at inquests. It is the police who decide what is the evidence before calling an inquest. We had to prepare ourselves and get collecting the evidence ourselves. We collected evidence from people who were themselves involved at that party. We had a lot of evidence to give to our lawyers. So they were not relying on the police, even in the evidence, and at the inquest they could question the police.

The police were rotten throughout all that business. The coroner behaved abominably. The whole press saw it. Because of the kind of influence we had we got the inquest held in the chamber of the GLC. It lasted for thirteen days.

So that evidence that they were trying to pin on those boys – this is what they had done in other cases, the Guildford Four and so on – they failed in doing that. They spent about £250,000 doing that. They had about fifty policemen doing that. Having done it, saying that 'These are the boys who did it', they couldn't come back now and say who else did it. When we went to court again about this particular matter they admitted they'd been wrong trying to pin it on the boys. But they had no further evidence to apply as to who else may have done it. They never pursued it. But what they were not able to do is what they had done in the case of the Guildford Four and others, to pin it on those boys. They failed to do that.[5]

JK: Thinking again about these fights against racist violence, the brutalities. What in effect the campaigning group was doing was of course police-work, the work of the police. And they also have to go and get the evidence because it has already been decided by the police what the crime is, and the first thing they always say is, 'It wasn't racist.' Thinking again about that way of confrontation, where it becomes a genuine protest, the other thing is you have to break the law. In the sense if it's serious, any campaign, if you are going to do it properly, because it is always in their power to do you for *sub judice*, or hold that up to you.

JLR: I had some legal training in Trinidad. I had come here to study law but I abandoned it within the first year. Nevertheless I knew a lot about law. So here I knew what you had to do to present statements about your case and not break the *sub judice* rule. Darcus knew. He'd trained in law as well. We were also dealing with most able, brilliant and sympathetic lawyers. Most lawyers whom you deal with in these matters want to control the case themselves, and we knew much more about these particular matters than they did. We also knew exactly the line of defence you've got to take in the cases, and we won most of them. So coming to that inquest in 1981, the New Cross Massacre, we were really much more prepared than any other grouping in British society would have been to handle that inquest. That is why we were able to defeat the police in their manoeuvres. Because they went all out to show politically, that what this group of people were saying from the beginning was not true, that the people who had done it were the boys themselves at the party. That's the line they were feeding the press at the very beginning. That's how the press reports these matters. The police give them the information and they report it.

But we had a strategy to deal with that. We formed our own Independent Commission to investigate this particular matter. And we also fed information to certain members of the press about what was happening. So it meant that there was a counter to the general police media strategy. We countered it ourselves in the radio, TV and so on. The police did not have as free a sheet as they would normally have had in dealing with a political matter of this kind. The other important factor was that because we understood the inquest we knew that it was there they would make their stand to publicly denigrate all that had happened: all that we had done; the Black People's Day of Action, the previous demonstration, the campaign we were organising, and so on. Therefore we knew we had to prepare for that inquest very carefully to counter their influence, and we did.

They were really encountering a different kind of political process from what they were normally accustomed to, when they walk through a thing – almost without any opposition. Everyone benefited from the experience that we introduced into this way of handling these matters. Because after that all kinds of groupings knew how to handle these matters. We made our way, our method of dealing with these matters, as widely understood as possible. People were ringing us from Bradford, Manchester, Birmingham – all over the country. And we'd go and help them to organise their cases. We got involved in teaching them how to do it. That's another aspect of creativity that people do not really take as creativity. It is creativity.

JK: Again, our system is designed to do the opposite. It is designed that you do not do that, that you give it to this guy who gets paid £50,000 a year, and he goes and whatever, talks your politics for you.

JLR: It was very much part of what we understood to be a popular movement, and what it has to do. It teaches people how to

organise themselves so they become part of their own independent, autonomous organisation, for taking on these matters.
After a time I do not have to go there at all, they know it and
see it through themselves.

JK: It is the opposite of a vanguard in that sense.

JLR: That's right. They understand what they will do themselves
and they will do it. What happens with that experience, with all
the ultra-leftist organisations like SWP, where we're making
something they're not accustomed to make . . .

JK: They cannot cope with it.

JLR: No they cannot cope with it. They couldn't cope with us
during that New Cross Massacre campaign, or any of the major
campaigns. For us the courts were also an area of political
struggle.

JK: Just finishing up, John, a word maybe on CAM again, I was
thinking about the visual arts.

JLR: We were all interested in the visual arts, some of us were
practitioners like Carl Craig. He went back and became Head of
the Jamaican School of Art. So we had all that experience, were
very vitally concerned about it and interested in it. I thought that
the articulation of ideas and theories about art was less intense
within CAM. Unlike the other arts – novels, plays, poetry, etc.
– what I discovered really was, we had not done for the visual
arts what we had done for the others, where a serious kind of
discussion went on. That was another aspect of the activity.
Trinidad was awash with art and music. Because carnival is
fashion-art, it is a day of art with all kinds of artistic creations on
display, music, song, dance. Yet we never had the same kind of
theoretical discussions. But we had brilliant artists, like the
painter Aubrey Williams, and Althea McNish, and the sculptor
Ronald Moody, and we interacted with them. And they and
their work influenced us and our experience.

JK: It raises some of these points about art and how we do it, as artists, from the indigenous culture. But some of these questions had been raised in CAM anyway, to do with 'What should I paint in the painting to show my commitment.'

JLR: It is a hangover from the question of the role of the artist in society, from art for art's sake, to the question, for example, of art in the Soviet Union, Social Realism.

JK: And there's that quote about figuration being missionary art.

JLR: That kind of discussion went on, although not to the same intensity in the public events in CAM. It took place in the private events which don't figure in the documentation. But we were in general exploring and discussing, and creatively self-expressing.

JK: That was actually the bottom line, of initiating CAM anyway, as a place where artists can talk together.

JLR: Yes but it is not on the record. When you ask what it is that we'd discuss on Warishi nights, the only answer is about everything. And it went on for hours, like we're talking now. That's what made it so important for the artists in the long run. Obviously the artists were not really creating in those nights. The artists were still taking back to themselves whatever creative ways they could view that experience, to create both in theory and in practice. I understood that in politics things go like that too, you have periods of intense creativity, so I knew it would happen in the cultural experience we were having as well. I did not expect it to last for ever. I expected it to last as intense as it was, then it would go away. It bonded us in a very important way; Andrew, myself, all the people who were part of that experience, immediately part of it. It lasts for ever really, it has bonded us in very significant ways. It doesn't impinge upon anybody's autonomy but nevertheless involves a deep interrelationship, which does not require a lot of restatement of things really.

The Caribbean Artists Movement
1966–1972

'CAM starts by saying that liberation begins in the imagination. We do not have an official membership. We do not have
officer responsibility but worker responsibility. People find
this structure hard to grasp.'

John La Rose

THE CARIBBEAN ARTISTS Movement lasted from 1966 to 1972
but its impact was far-reaching. 'The concept behind its informal
structure was that of a community.' Its founder members recognised one fundamental issue, that for the artists of a marginalised
culture there is little or no assessment of their creative output.
Genuine criticism will not exist within a context defined by the
dominant culture. Even where such creative output is noticed by
the dominant culture it remains subject to it, judged by its criteria
of what is 'good'.

Ultimately the sure basis for critical recognition by the establishment is assimilation. The greater the distance you place between
your art and your culture the more the guardians of the dominant
culture will grant you that recognition. Assimiliation does not
guarantee reward but it sets you on the trail. If you exercise your
freedom of choice to reject assimilation you will be rewarded by
critical neglect, not to mention a dire lack of dough.

During the 1950s and 60s West Indian art was not unknown in
mainstream circles, particularly its literature through the work of
writers such as V. S. Naipaul, George Lamming and Derek

Walcott; perhaps also Sam Selvon and Wilson Harris. But other artists were around and a critical context was missing. One of CAM's founder members was the poet and educator E. K. Brathwaite whose published work had received almost no attention whatsoever, neither from the dominant culture of the ruling British élite, nor from his own West Indian community: 'Our problem is that we have been trained for over 300 years to despise [our] indigenous forms.'

Brathwaite had worked in Ghana during the period of Nkrumah and independence and become 'immersed in the rural community life and traditional culture' of West Africa. At the first public meeting of CAM he argued the case for 'a jazz novel', that there was 'a correspondence between jazz and contemporary Caribbean culture . . . the basic elements of word, image and rhythm; the nature of improvisation, of repetition and refrain'; and that the 'oral tradition provided a model for West Indian literature . . . suggestive of an indigenous aesthetic for West Indian creativity and criticism.'

The influence of Caribbean music was crucial. A later public meeting was devoted to 'Sparrow and the Language of the Calypso' and another founder member, the poet and publisher John La Rose, had already written on *kaiso*, calypso music.[1] From an early age La Rose had been politically active in Trinidad. Former General Secretary of the Workers' Freedom Movement, he later held the same office for the West Indian Independence Party, at the same time 'producing *Voice of Youth*, a fortnightly radio programme'. Still in his twenties, he was forced into exile.

The third founder member was Andrew Salkey, who often met La Rose at the same protests and demonstrations in London. Salkey was a free-lance broadcaster (interviewing Martin Luther King on three occasions) and had a very wide network of contacts. As a student at London University he also 'devised an alternative learning plan' for himself: 'I damn well wanted to talk to Jamaicans about Jamaica in the long poem I was hoping to write.'

Of the broader political agenda Salkey makes a key comment in relation to the different formations that existed during the 1960s – including the Black Power groups – that 'no one group had it all, and I figured I had [to] serve nearly all and be useful to all.' CAM was always 'a movement'.

But it would be a mistake to place too great an emphasis on the founder members; they were acquainted with a circle of committed individuals, many artists among them. One of the impressive aspects of CAM is the number and multiplicity of its participants (ages ranging from C. L. R. James to the young Ngugi and even younger Linton Kwesi Johnston). It was an extremely ambitious project and, given the nature of its structure, could not have succeeded to the extent it did without such commitment.

CAM began quite simply as a means by which 'writers, artists and people interested in literature, art and culture' could come together. Literature was the predominant artform but painters, musicians, sculptors and theatre workers were also involved. From informal gatherings held in the homes of members it was broadened out to public meetings and 'included talks and symposia, readings and performances, art exhibitions and films . . . and a newsletter, bookselling and contact network.'

At its first conference the historian Elsa Goveia argued in her keynote speech that artists have a choice

> between the inferiority/superiority ranking according to race and wealth and the equality which is implied by one man one vote (and) until then we cannot be really creative as individuals because our energies are going to be absorbed by the terrible job of working from two completely different sets of premises . . .

She also established the point 'that the creative arts were at the forefront of . . . social change.' This raised all kinds of questions, e.g. the 'sort of art the committed artist should produce', 'which art forms were most effective', 'how the artist communicates and to whom', etc. The painters Aubrey Williams and Clifton Campbell who 'both worked in predominantly abstract styles were concerned to defend it as no less socially committed than figurative painting . . .' Williams 'asked for freedom for the artist to explore his own style: "If our painters must grope and search and forge ahead, we do not as yet know the language they should speak."' He spoke of his doubts on '"narrative painting" as "hand-me-down missionary art" in danger of becoming "tourist representational art".' The response from the audience to the work of the visual artists under discussion forced him to 'conclude that the level of visual art appreciation among intellectuals is very, very low . . .'

The conference was such an exciting and unique event that how to follow it was a major problem. John La Rose was moved to write to Brathwaite that

> CAM is a movement . . . not a structure. We . . . have struck a chord. With such things, in my experience, people take out of it what they are looking for and bring what they must give. Then the communion is over. And it lives; and we inherit it; and it passes on. The vital spark of life and spontaneity, as I have discovered, in my own life, is not long-lasting. Glowing embers remain and we mistake it for fire. I mention this only that we would know what to expect.

That was in 1967, some five years before CAM's eventual demise. It is impossible to do justice to the impact and legacy of the Caribbean Artists Movement, both culturally and in the broader political context, perhaps particularly to its organisational influence in the struggle against racism – certainly in the United Kingdom – throughout the past twenty years. Anne Walmsley's book is seminal, it should be required reading for any artist or activist.

The Caribbean Artists Movement 1966–1972: A Literary & Cultural History by Anne Walmsley
(New Beacon Books Ltd, London, England 1992).

A Look at Franz Kafka's Three Novels

Introduction

CRITICS HAVE ADVANCED theories that attempt to provide 'the meaning' of the work of particular literary artists. A familiar example, although a bit old-fashioned nowadays, could be one that seeks to treat the writings of Franz Kafka as Christian allegory. In *The Trial* we might find Joseph K. being pursued by Divine Justice while in and around *The Castle* the Land Surveyor is involved in a search for Divine Grace. The Supreme Source of justice or authority in such an interpretation can be benign or not but is always implacable, the authority itself God-given and the authority-figures justified. Yet in both these novels the natural goodness of the Supreme Source is at least problematic; if God does exist his workings are so remote from mankind that they are or have become incomprehensible.

In the same writer's short story 'The Great Wall of China', the narrator offers the reader a parable to elucidate the difficulties faced by those who build

> a superficial culture mounting sky high round a few precepts
> that have been drilled into people's minds for centuries,
> precepts which, though they have lost nothing of their eternal

truth, remain eternally invisible in this fog of confusion. [p. 74.]

In this country which is so vast 'its multitudes have no end', an Emperor sends a message to one solitary individual. The messenger's task is impossible. The individual is aware of this himself but will continue to remain by the 'window when evening falls and dream it' to himself. No exposition is given by the narrator who eventually suggests not only that the Emperor does not exist but that the multitudes are aware of the fact; and lest this incredible self-deception should be thought a 'weakness' the narrator quickly points out that it is one of their 'greatest unifying influences'.

For many people, among them literary critics, the implications of this are horrific, doubtless contributing to the arguments of those who condemn Kafka's work for its 'pessimism'. The idea is related to that which occurs in Dostoevski's *The Brothers Karamazov* where in Ivan's poem of 'The Grand Inquisitor' obedience to God has become a ritual devoid of anything beyond itself. Here Jesus Christ reappears on earth but in fifteenth-century Spain and the townsfolk do not recognise him. They pay their homage to the old Inquisitor who has become more than the symbol of their ritual, in fact he is the supreme authority. Yet a certain optimism remains in Dostoevski's novel: no matter how remote the people are from God, at least He still exists. In Kafka's work there is nothing to suggest any source of power beyond humankind itself, but whether or not this represents grounds for pessimism depends on the individual reader's own beliefs.

In one sense it makes no difference whether an 'ultimate source' exists or not, not if its workings are so infinitely remote that they are for ever inaccessible to mere mortals. Here on earth the authority of this 'ultimate source' will become subject to the interpretation or 'translation' of individual human beings. But what individual human beings should be empowered for such an undertaking? And how will people know that that interpretation or translation is a true account, or an authentic element of the authority, or that it derives from the 'ultimate source'?

People who do hold a religious belief which seeks to posit a 'supreme power' external to mankind occasionally propose that authority is invested in certain individuals by the authority itself, directly or indirectly. They may put forward an argument to the effect that God has representatives here on earth; priests and ministers and so on, messengers perhaps, people who pass on 'the word'.

Others in receipt of a religious belief might argue that the way to God, or any 'supreme power', cannot come via other individual members of humanity except incidentally. It is a logical absurdity to hear 'the word' from another mortal being. The only way to a true understanding is through a form of spiritual transcendence and this is to be achieved by individuals on their own: 'only one attains the goal' (according to St Paul).[1] There is no evidence to suggest that Kafka did have faith in a 'supreme being', nor in any power external to humankind. But if he had perhaps he would have placed himself in the latter grouping; above all others it was the Swedish philosopher Kierkegaard to whose work he returned, and continually, throughout the last decade of his life.

If Kafka has 'a place' in literature it is within the tradition known as 'the existential'. I shall assume this. By the time I reach a conclusion to this essay I hope to have justified the assumption, at least so far as his novels are concerned.

One unusual element to these three works that I find is the lack of irony as a structural basis. Within the existential tradition the distinguishing feature, typically, is the use of the first-party narrative. This 'I' voice is not that of the author but the central protagonist of the story. The story takes an ironic form which is based solely upon the assumption that author and prospective reader hold reality in common. We are always aware that the 'hero' of Gogol's 'The Overcoat' or Dostoevski's novel *Notes from Underground* somehow has to be kept in quotation marks; this in the knowledge that the figure being cut by the 'hero' is less than heroic, and frequently hysterical if not ridiculous. It is important to recognise that the vision of the world held by such a first-party narrator is strictly singular: the 'hero's' perception of reality and reality in itself should never be confused.

Kafka did attempt versions of his three novels in the 'I' voice but he finished them in the third. He confines his use of first party to the short story. When his precursors switched to the third-party voice it was in fairly traditional mode, the narrative retained the flavour of convention, conventional reality that is; thus reality as perceived by Ivan Karamazov may appear distorted to the majority of readers but reality itself is never to be doubted. The world inhabited by Alyosha, as well as by the narrator of the novel, is the same as that of Dostoevski and the prospective reader. This is not so much an assumption as a presupposition. Irony does not form the structural base for the third-party voice as employed by writers such as Gogol, Hamsun, Dostoevski or even Sartre. While this may hold true also of Kafka it should become clear that the function of his third party is different from the others.

The conventional perception of third-party narrative derives from a naturalistic view of the world and sees it as objective and unbiased. If somebody is giving us an opinion from within the narrative we are informed that this is what we are getting, an opinion; and by definition opinions are subjective. The traditional third-party narrative, as a general rule, takes the form of an 'unbiased', 'objective' voice that reports, depicts or describes reality in a way that allows the term 'God-voice' to appear valid. The 'voice' of the third-party narrative tells us 'what happened' and we take it for granted that this 'voice' does not tell lies. It presents us with 'reality'. Yet when we examine the 'voice' we discover these third-party narratives are saturated with the values of its contemporaneous society, the society within which the author lives and works.

Kafka's technical achievement cannot be overestimated. Far from placing the reader as 'objective' bystander within reality, he removes the reader to the level of genuine observer; one who is occupying an almost exalted position, roughly equivalent to that which a 'supreme authority' would hold in order to cast value-free judgments, on a plane outside reality. Kafka is a major artist if for no other reason than this: that he has advanced creative possibility within his medium.

The existential tradition in literature is generally associated with the work of European writers but contemporary opinion might link writers such as Sterne or Blake to its development. I must draw immediate attention to *Confessions of a Justified Sinner*. Written some twenty years before 'The Overcoat' and about twenty-five years after *The Sufferings of Young Werther*, James Hogg's masterpiece fits very snugly into the tradition. Yet there is one striking distinction between it and any other novel I have come across. It lies in the deadliest of ironies which Hogg has included in the last few pages. The story contains two voices. In common with Goethe's *Young Werther* it begins with a conventional first party and proceeds to the point where the 'Confessions' begin as 'written by himself', the actual 'Sinner' of the tale. When this 'I' voice ends his account, the 'editor' resumes to conclude the novel and during this a few real-life members of the Edinburgh literati are introduced into the tale to add weight to its authenticity. Then suddenly Hogg is himself introduced to the literati – but *not* in his role of author. The novel is written in standard English literary form and the Edinburgh literati use precisely that linguistic expression when involved in dialogue. But when Hogg gives himself a couple of lines in reply to them he speaks in the supposed culturally inferior dialect of a couthy Scotch shepherd. It is an incredible irony. It is also suggestive of a 'third' reality. There is reality as perceived by the 'Sinner' which we already know to be distorted, and conventional reality as presented by the 'editor'. But on what plane does Hogg's ironic introduction of himself fit?

One feature of the 'modernist' movement was the recognition that other cultures might not necessarily be inferior to that of highly educated Europeans. As the product of one such 'inferior culture', Hogg had already demonstrated the point by creating one of the few genuine masterpieces written in Britain during the first half of the nineteenth century. His ironic use of language was a direct challenge to the self-appointed linguistic authority of his cultural 'superiors'; but sadly, if unsurprisingly, the irony was lost on the literati of the period as also to the 'modernists' in English literature a century later who never seemed to realise that what they regarded as an 'inferior' part of their culture was, in effect, a different culture. In my discussion of Kafka's original contribution to the novel form, the name of James Hogg may be kept in brackets.

Individuals are constantly being confronted by the demands of society in Kafka's tales. In 'Metamorphosis' Gregor Samsa subsumes his own potential as an ordinary young man in order to fulfil the function of 'dutiful son'; for his pains he is transformed into an enormous beetle and dies ignominiously with an apple embedded in his back, a symbol of the life he has rejected for the sake of his family, and by extension society itself. Part of the tragic nature of the tale lies in the fact that in performing his duty Gregor only hinders his family; with his son out the way the old father shelves his advancing senility and returns to work while Gregor's sister is transformed into an attractive young woman.

Punishment also awaits the 'junior manager of a large Bank' in *The Trial*. Joseph K. is another individual content to perform the role society appears to have given him. Then he is arrested. Eventually it should become clear that it is not so much people have been 'telling lies' about him but that his perception of reality is grounded in a form of self-deception. Even allowing for this, it can still be argued that Joseph K. has been condemned for breaking a Law he never knew existed.

An individual is confronted by authority from birth. One reason why children have such a highly developed sense of injustice is because they are frequently breaking rules of whose existence they are unaware. In general they know these mysterious rules may exist, it is particular cases that present problems. This is why many children go around as though expecting a sudden retribution, a sudden strike from the hand of an adult. In a sense growing up is an exercise in hermeneutics; a child is learning the rules and thus how to survive, observing and interpreting the behaviour of various authorities within society. By the time adolescence is reached a fortunate individual will have learned to distinguish authority from authority-figures and, further, to distinguish between authority-figures. Karl Rossmann has difficulties over this in *Amerika*. He does not always recognise that adults can be obliged to punish, not for personal reasons but on behalf of society which makes its own demands on parents, teachers and other adults. And as will be seen in Kafka's first novel, the exigency of society supersedes both family bonds and those 'eternal principles' people like to assume as governing the movement of mankind. The phrase 'eternal principles' is here and elsewhere in the essay to be regarded as interchangeable with phrases such as 'universal truths', 'the moral law', 'the word of God', 'the ten commandments', etc.

Many readers will experience a sense of outrage at the fate of some of the 'heroes' in Kafka's fiction; after all, most are conforming to the expectations of society. If Joseph K. is guilty then surely everybody must be guilty? Yes, and this is the gist of Joseph K.'s 'defence'. But he still has to face execution. Perhaps the best that can be said for him is that he is not so much innocent or guilty but a mixture of both: he is ignorant. Ignorance is an essential concept within the work of Franz Kafka. By paying heed to this perspective it will allow us to see Karl Rossmann as an ordinary boy and not some sort of adolescent paragon to whom things always seem to happen.[2]

If individuals have the power to make things happen they also have the power to make things not happen. There is a short piece of prose from the *Diaries* of 1914 that I shall quote in full to illustrate the point:

> 'Don't you want to join us?' I was asked recently by an acquaintance when he ran across me alone after midnight in a coffee-house that was already almost deserted. 'No, I don't,' I said. [p. 217.]

Here the 'I' character is alone but not lonely. By accepting the invitation he would be creating the conditions for a different group of possibilities for the outcome of the evening. He does not want this. He makes things not happen by remaining at his own table. I think here also that something is being shown about the creative process, about the making of stories, artistic possibility: Kafka has created the conditions for a 'story' but taken the ultimate possibility, he negates it. Yet, paradoxically, in so doing he has still written a story: extremely brief, yes, but a story in its own right and worthy of standing as such. Should anyone bring out an additional collection of his prose fiction in the future, there are a couple of 'new' pieces that may be discovered in his *Diaries*.

Both Joseph K. and young Rossmann can be regarded as making

things happen by default. It is an accusation that cannot be levelled at the Land Surveyor. Ignorance is probably his greatest asset in his quest to enter *The Castle*; that he should have undertaken such a challenge in the first place reveals his determination to transform his life. As in the earlier two novels, questions of guilt and innocence are central but they arise in a more curious form. Any faith the reader has in 'eternal truths' proves more of a hindrance than usual in Kafka's writings. The more we dwell on typically moral issues the more it becomes clear that standard criteria are insufficient; in themselves they simply confuse the questions. Like the Land Surveyor we must make the attempt to be 'freed from prejudice' [p. 238] for only in this way can we hope to understand why Amalia should be guilty and the obvious culprit – the official, Sortini – somehow placed outside the scope of our judgment. The efforts of the Land Surveyor to penetrate beyond the Castle doors can be likened to the reader's initial attempt to enter the actual novel.

Kafka's three novels may be seen not only as separate units; there is a distinct progression thematically and in the author's formal development within the medium. Before *Amerika* he had created some very fine short stories, including the 'Two Dialogues'.[3] The episodic nature of the first novel shows the difficulty in making the transition from the shorter medium; *Amerika* is by no means a 'perfect example' of the novel. And the same can be argued of *The Trial* for reasons I shall mention later. *The Castle* is the masterwork.

Part 1 *Amerika*: Innocence and Ignorance

Kafka's prose fiction is regarded generally as difficult. A critic has put his own response to the work in the following words: 'while there is much in Kafka that I do not understand, I believe that I do

273

understand some things in Kafka by understanding my not understanding.'[1]

Of the three novels, *Amerika* is certainly the least difficult. Karl Rossmann's struggles, if never typical, will be fairly familiar to most folk who can bring to bear a basic knowledge of literature since in one way or another the problems of adolescence have been well documented. *Amerika* is as convincing a portrait of this stage in life as any I have come upon. The author said it was his 'intention . . . to write a Dickens novel, but enhanced by the sharper lights I should have taken from the times and the duller ones I should have got from myself.'[2] In the same passage he criticises the English writer for his 'rude characterizations'. Kafka's desire was to create individuals rather than 'images'.[3]

The novel begins with the boy not yet sixteen years old, having arrived in New York harbour.[4] He has been sent into exile for a sexual misdemeanour with a 'servant girl' more than twice his age. He has never questioned this decision of his parents. The nearest we come to hearing how it was reached is when his Uncle Jacob tells of the letter he has received from the girl. Apparently the Rossmanns were worried about 'scandal' and having to pay 'alimony' (p. 35). Family kinship did not weigh too greatly in at least one middle-class home in Prague.

If it had not been for the 'servant girl', the boy's uncle would never have known about the incident, nor of his nephew's arrival. Perhaps the family did not want the shame to reach across the Atlantic Ocean. The fact that Uncle Jacob regards it as his duty to meet Karl aboard the liner heralds the gulf between the values of the Old and New Worlds. It so happens that Karl's uncle is also a senator and a millionaire.

At the turn of the century hordes of the European lower orders were emigrating (fleeing might be a more appropriate term) to the USA, usually in the belief – however vague – that hard work was the only requirement to becoming rich and successful. And Uncle Jacob appears the living proof that this was possible for at least one individual. The sense of a limitless freedom is symbolic in the Statue of Liberty and young Karl Rossmann is overwhelmed on first seeing it.

So much so that he mistakes the actual torch for a 'sword' (p. 13), thereby strengthening the notion of boyish adventure. A darker aspect to the symbolism is struck by this hint of the more rapacious side of frontier capitalism. It is not immediately certain if the 'sword' was intended by the author as a true picture of the Statue, in other words it might have been a mistake. Heinz Politzer discounts the idea that it may have been a slip on Kafka's part which is fine, but I think he is mistaken in believing it to be 'pointed against Karl Rossmann's conscience'.[5] If it is so 'pointed' then it can only be done by a narrative 'voice' and in view of the way the narrative functions, that is unlikely. This point shall be developed within my discussion on Kafka's handling of 'reality'. At this stage I am content to repeat that the 'sword' is simply the boy's own perception being stated indirectly, within the narrative.

Throughout the opening chapter various ironies are in evidence. If we are considering Karl as a typical juvenile hero we do so in the knowledge that he cannot step down into the 'land of the free' without having his 'umbrella' to hand. He must go below decks to find it. After blundering into a strange cabin he becomes responsible for a situation in which the Captain of an ocean-going liner, having just arrived from halfway across the western hemisphere, is forced to listen to the pettiest of pleas from a 'notorious grumbler'.

Young Rossmann is of the opinion that an injustice must logically be rectified if once brought into the open. In the New World justice must surely apply across the face of society; even a man as low in rank as a stoker cannot be robbed of a 'recognition that should certainly be his' (p. 23). Karl's idealistic enthusiasm modifies when his uncle makes his identity known. Gradually it becomes valid to wonder why he is rushing to defend a crewman's minor grievance since he has never paused to question the ruthless action meted out to himself back in Prague.

The irony then assumes a harsher note: through Uncle Jacob the servant has assumed an identity; she is Johanna Brummer, thirty-five years of age. His uncle is the only person from the Old World to have advised him of the situation. A fuller picture of the sexual misdemeanour is given and it now seems rather pathetic. The Senator spares his nephew, he does not regale the company with all the details. He need not have bothered. Karl has 'no feelings' whatsoever for the woman and could not have cared less had the letter been read in full (p. 35). He is content to consider making her 'some return' at an unspecified date in the future for having taken the trouble to inform Uncle Jacob. How she and their baby boy are to survive in Prague does not enter the equation.

If we return to the opening page of the novel we can see how, by placing Karl as object grammatically in 'a servant girl had seduced him and got herself with child by him', the author has faded the line between seduction and rape so well that it has almost disappeared. But he was seduced, and the act requires a degree of assent, however minimal. Ultimately he acceded to her demands; he must therefore bear a slight degree of responsibility in the affair. Karl has allowed himself to be absolved of all responsibility. His readiness to defend the stoker – someone of a similar rank to Johanna – may well have owed a little to a sense of unease over it.

From disinterested upholder of moral imperatives he assumes the role of Senator's nephew, his attitude to the stoker correspondingly alters. He toys with the man's fingers as a child might play with a puppy, and continues the defence in a half-hearted fashion. Uncle Jacob quickly advises him to 'understand your position' and not 'mistake the situation' (p. 40). The Old and New

Worlds may be dissimilar in a variety of ways but the nephew of a Senator is still a different sort of individual from a stoker. In Prague Karl had gained experience of the subservient nature of family bonds when in opposition to the authority of middle-class society (presumably he did not need to be reminded of the subservient role of servants). Here in New York harbour he is being confronted by a similar form of authority and also being offered a glimpse of how authority-figures can interdepend. Aboard ship the Captain's authority is supreme, not even a Senator can gainsay him, let alone the nephew of one. The episode closes with Uncle Jacob leading him ashore. He is in tears. The umbrella is still lost and, to compound matters, he has forgotten his trunk.

At this stage it is already difficult to make out a case for young Rossmann as an 'image . . . [of] natural goodness and innocence'.[6] He seems a fairly average boy from what may have been a fairly average middle-class background of the period. His individual characteristics include an inability to see beyond immediate horizons; the umbrella incident serves as an example, as much as his implicit belief in the right of certain individuals to hold authority over others, in all matters. He is self-centred but capable of genuine warmth to other people, as his affection for the stoker revealed. He also seeks warmth in other people, indicated by his 'terrible feeling of yearning' at the end of the affair with Johanna (p. 36). Lastly, as a true adolescent, he both desires and fears freedom. Faced by freedom he rushed back for the umbrella. Then he lured the stoker into the 'trial' in the cabin, only to turn away from him, subjecting himself to the authority of his uncle.

Karl's perverse streak, to the fore throughout the next chapter, further suggests a vague awareness of freedom. Perhaps his willingness to accept his parents' decision was due to his seeing exile as an appealing prospect, an escape from the restrictions of family life. Now, on the brink of adventure, he has been led into captivity by the Senator and is being expected to conform to another set of rules and regulations.

Soon he is tempted to leave by an associate of his uncle, just for an overnight trip to a country house; as a bonus he is to meet the man's daughter. Although Uncle Jacob's reaction to the proposed trip is ambiguous, he allows Karl to make the decision. Karl is content to allow the persistence of Mr Pollunder to prevail, and is driven to the country.

Uncle Jacob's misgivings had been veiled but Karl was right to have made that inference when the mysterious Mr Green, an associate of the Senator, arrives unexpectedly. At the dinner table Mr Green brings the conversation round to the subject of 'fidelity' and at once the boy feels nauseous (p. 63). He soon desires to return home at all costs. Too late. The consequence of his latest seduction has already been decided.

At sixteen years of age Karl is not mature; it is an individual characteristic, others of the same age could have been more responsible. When his uncle spared his feelings in the Captain's cabin it was because he did not want to embarrass him in front of the other men who were obviously regarding him as 'a bit of a lad'. Neither Uncle Jacob nor anyone else perceived how truly a case of seduction it was. Perhaps Uncle Jacob had realised his error; it would be one obvious factor in why he should have been opposed to the visit. Money is another factor. Pollunder's financial affairs seem extremely dubious. It transpires that he is not after all the owner of the house, just the tenant. Mr Mack, his daughter's fiancé, is the owner. Prior to that revelation, Karl has been dismayed by Mr Green's behaviour towards the girl. Pollunder must also have noticed the behaviour but he managed to ignore it; he seems prepared to exploit his daughter in any way he can.

Karl was amazed to find that the young couple already 'shared the same bed' (p. 89) in a room next to the one the girl had brought him. Perhaps her father had intended having him caught in a compromising situation with her. But when Miss Clara gets him alone she ends up having to 'lock him in a well-applied wrestling hold' (p. 69). As usual in Kafka's work, ambiguities abound; in this case it is one drawback for the boy that not only women are physically attracted to him. Pollunder is continually touching him, at one point going so far as to draw him 'between his knees' (p. 78). The leitmotif of finger-stroking, a sign of affection from Karl to the stoker, is explicitly sexual in both the later novels.

Once the fateful letter is delivered, Karl attempts to offload responsibility on to the messenger's shoulders. He accuses Mr Green of exceeding his instructions (p. 93) by detaining him until midnight. It would have made not the slightest difference to his fate if the letter had been read earlier on, as a brief look at the contents will clearly reveal: the Senator had reached his decision almost as soon as Karl had reached his decision to be tempted away by Pollunder. His pedantic niggling with Mr Green is a straight-forward expression of his unwillingness to face up to a difficult reality, made all the more difficult by being an effect of his own decision-making (p. 94). The experience he had in Prague could have prepared him for such an eventuality. Young Rossmann might have realised that a disobedient nephew is, first and foremost, a disobedient member of society.

Society can be regarded as a labyrinth of authorities whose powers are functional. Aboard ship a Senator will 'understand his position' and not try to wield authority over a Captain. Had an equivalent 'trial' occurred within an office in the House of Congress no doubt the Captain would have allowed Uncle Jacob to take control. Lines between one authority and another are not always so clear-cut, frequently they can clash; but in normal circumstances a sort of pecking-order exists of which most adults are aware. A child is not always aware. It can be confusing when a teacher is continually contradicting what a parent has been saying in the home, and vice versa. Karl's confusion at the dinner table was caused by his increasing awareness that Pollunder's authority was subservient to that of the mysterious messenger.

His own authority has also become problematic. Perhaps Prague girls of his own status would have acted much more diffidently towards a male than Miss Clara. As a member of the European middle classes he would no doubt have been used to a certain deference from servants. Here in the New World he bumps into an idiosyncratic old man whom he reasons is logically bound to be a 'faithful servant' because they have allowed him to 'wear a beard' (p. 75). Karl acts towards him as though expecting to catch the old man having a quiet laugh behind his back. It is becoming evident that his authority is only as authentic as his place in society's hierarchy. This is about to vanish. At the end of the episode he is being ejected into freedom with a ticket for San Francisco, across the opposite side of the continent from his relative.

An amusing instance of decision-making occurs here. Instead of taking Mr Green's advice the boy *chooses* 'a chance direction' (p. 94). He seems to be already preparing his next defence; should things turn out badly he can always blame 'chance'. It transpires that he is awakened next morning 'by someone tickling him under the armpit' (p. 100). He is at the feet of two disreputable tramps. This is a good example of how the Czech writer will realize the most conventional of clichés: from the highest level of American society young Rossmann has landed right at the bottom. Later on, from the balcony of Brunelda he will witness free beer being distributed to the workers, donated by a candidate for the judiciary who is being carried aloft on the shoulders of a giant (p. 229).

Earlier I suggested that the 'sword' was not part of the narrative as such. Kafka manoeuvres narrative more subtly than that; caution is necessary to distinguish interior reflection – the thought processes of Karl – from the reality being presented. An obvious example is the way a reader could continue with the novel under the illusion that seduction is rape. A blatant instance occurred when the boy was accusing the messenger of applying delaying tactics, something we know to be utter fabrication. Even so we find that 'Karl looked at Green with shrewd eyes and clearly saw that shame over this exposure was conflicting in the man with joy at the success of his designs' (p. 93).

Most writers will feel obliged to inform the reader when the switch is being made within the narrative, thus we have something like 'He thought that Green was ashamed' or 'He thought, "Green is ashamed."' Part of the basic craft of writing is telling a story with as few extraneous words as possible. An author who inserts too many 'he thought's' into the tale is obstructing the flow of narrative. One obvious reason why Kafka is a truly great writer is that he has taken such great pains to rid his prose of superfluous words. A more crucial issue enters the affair. If a writer is continually having to intercept the narrative in order to make a concrete distinction between reality and the characters' perception of reality then it must imply the overall lack of distinction: by extension, perhaps there is no fundamental distinction between the two. If this conclusion seems harsh, the argument will become clearer in the next section. It is within *The Trial* that Kafka presents reality in his highly original manner. This would not have been possible without his continual battle to submerge interior reflection within the narrative.

In Pollunder's country home the seamier aspects of American society were in evidence. The boy had the chance of seeing for himself that an individual's right to authority does not derive from any moral propriety. He is ignorant of how society functions. It would be wrong to call him innocent, for if he was then all boys of his background, age, experience, etc. would have to be adjudged the same. Kafka's own experience was almost precisely similar to his fictional character, although he never visited America. Yet at sixteen years of age Kafka was a committed socialist, resolutely opposed to the authority exercised by his father over the people employed in the family business.[7]

In America capital is more explicitly central to how society functions than it was in Europe during the time of the Habsburg monarchy where the role of class in itself meant power. Whereas a bankrupt aristocrat would have retained some authority in Prague, he or she might simply have been a bankrupt member of society in the New World; here it was always possible for someone to achieve the 'American dream' and work his way up to becoming the foremost member of society whereas it was literally impossible, i.e. a logical contradiction, for anyone from the lower orders to become head of the Habsburg monarchy – just as it is still an absurdity that a 'commoner' can ever become 'sovereign' of a kingdom such as Saudi Arabia, or Great Britain. Mr Pollunder was a banker; his authority in society might be said to have decreased in relation to his dwindling financial assets. Karl is not yet in a position to question whence authority derives; he assumes that because society exists as it does, it must be entitled to do so.

His inherited authority is directly challenged by one of the tramps, the Frenchman Delamarche; it is he who will cast doubts on Uncle Jacob. When they come upon a cavalcade of trucks containing men it transpires that 'dock labourers' are being recruited by the 'Jacob Despatch Agency' (p. 103). Karl is surprised by the tramps' lack of interest in employment by this method. Delamarche explains that the method is 'a scandalous fraud and the firm of Jacob . . . notorious throughout the whole United States' (p. 104). Then we find that a strike is in progress within the building industry. The largest employer is Mr Mack's father. Being in the company of workmen at the time, the boy hears another side to the affair than he would have at the country house of Pollunder. Whatever the other side is, he refuses to give it credence, unable to 'believe a word of what was said by these badly informed and spiteful people' (p. 108). Again his comments are stated indirectly within the narrative and are as value-free as were the comments on Mr Green's 'shame'. In the next episode he gathers further experience of working people; he gets a job at the Hotel Occidental.

Prior to this he had always regarded lift-boys as somehow 'ornamental' (p. 125). Now at the hotel he finds they work fourteen-hour stretches at a time on night-shift and live in totally inadequate surroundings; not even a bed is given to individual boys. Unlike Karl, they do not seem to see their 'present lot [as] provisional', their outlook on life being largely grounded in a society within which they function as lift-boys. It is important to recognise why young Rossmann has an enlarged perception of the world in comparison to his colleagues. Like the Land Surveyor in *The Castle*, the boy is an outsider, not only through being a foreigner, he hails from a class whose members are authority-figures to such as lift-boys. He also had first-hand knowledge that the 'American dream' can actually come true for at least one individual, his millionaire uncle, a senator. Regarding his present circumstances as temporary, Karl makes the best of it and takes a pride in the cleanliness of his lift.

His leisure time he devotes to improving his command of the English language, assisted by Therese who works as secretary to the manageress. Her story of her mother's death is described by Edwin Muir as a 'fortuitous beauty'.[8] But it does have considerable importance in the development of the novel. Karl is an adolescent, an individual on the verge of manhood. This stage in life is one where events can have great bearing on the future. Therese's story is exactly the sort of thing to exercise influence on a young person, perhaps making the difference between a responsible adult and one who abnegates individual responsibility in favour of unquestioning obedience to the authority of society. Edwin Muir may have considered it a coincidence that the girl's mother was killed either by falling or jumping from a half-finished building, given that in the past she had to survive by working as a hod-carrier. But one of Uncle Jacob's associates is a 'captain of the building industry' and Therese recounts her story while the strike is in progress. One prime factor in the optimistic ending of the novel is the boy's rejection of a secure job within society as a clerk; just as well when we remember the fate of Gregor Samsa and Joseph K.

After Therese has told the story the boy is reduced to silence for one of the very few times in *Amerika*. Her story is presented indirectly, through the narrative, and captures a kind of objectivity. The girl was five years old when the incident occurred and this objectivity is that which we could associate with the perception of a child; to that extent it remains free of bias. Readers of Kafka will find something else unusual for one of the author's 'stories within the story'; there is no exposition offered. But nor should it be expected in light of the 'coincidences' referred to in the previous paragraph. The girl's story is never referred to again.

The relationship between Therese and Karl develops from a point where she has entered his bedroom at midnight. Under the misapprehension he is being groomed for her own job she tacitly offers herself to him through a mixture of bribery, insecurity and loneliness. Unlike Miss Clara and Johanna Brummer she does not take the initiative but allows him to assume the traditional male role. He is not yet mature enough. Their relationship will eventually become that of sister and brother. Even so, Therese still has hopes it might progress and continues to bring him presents, including sweets and a big apple which gives 'out a strong fragrance' (p. 148). The apple is a sexual symbol but in both

'Metamorphosis' and *The Trial* the apple is more associated with life itself. That Therese gives him sweets as well as the apple perhaps indicates his ambiguity for her, he is both a boy and a man.

Although Therese does not particularly value her body 'beyond all else', she is untypical of Kafka's female characters, and not in the manner of Olga, Frieda or Pepi (*The Castle*) or Leni (*The Trial*). Nor does she resemble Amalia (*The Castle*) and she carries none of the enigmatic qualities of Fräulein Bürstner (*The Trial*). Possibly if there is one figure in *Amerika* who does represent 'natural goodness' then it is this girl Therese who is prepared to offer love to Karl. He remains ignorant. Perhaps it is all too much for him. He will eventually delude himself into believing that it is she who has 'influenced [him] in coming to the conclusion that [Delamarche] was a dangerous man' (p. 147), never mind that we have witnessed the Frenchman consistently deceiving and stealing from him. Karl seems to be seeking an end to his association with the girl altogether in order to retain his freedom.

The little experience he has gained of society is forgotten when he is hauled in front of the Head Waiter for neglecting his lift. Instead of acting as lift-boy who wants the indulgence of authority, he conducts his defence on a 'man-to-man' basis. He fails to 'understand his position'. An additional charge is levelled against him by the Head Porter (another man who continually tries to touch Karl). He is accused of 'bad manners' (p. 161). Just as well the latter offence is being committed in *Amerika* and not 'In the Penal Settlement' where the lower orders face the death-apparatus for similar transgressions. Apparently the boy has failed to 'greet' the man each day. He has also been guilty of speaking to the man as a paying guest would to a member of the hotel staff, rather than in the way a lift-boy would address a Head Porter.

During the 'trial' his patron, the German Manageress, attempts to intercede on his behalf; she and the Head Waiter are engaged to be married. But, unlike Uncle Jacob, she is guilty of 'mistaking the situation', using personal bonds to exert pressure on an individual who is merely fulfilling a function. The Head Waiter is performing an obligation on behalf of society and its demands outweigh all other considerations. A lift-boy who deserts his lift is guilty of neglecting his duty and must be dismissed instantly. The Head Waiter dismisses Karl instantly. Once again he is ejected into freedom. This time it is almost total; his identification papers were in the jacket he had to leave behind in the tussle with the Head Porter.

When he is caught by Delamarche his initial reaction is to escape but gradually he becomes quite content to remain as servant to Brunelda, the ex-opera singer.[9] Earlier in the story the Frenchman had accused Karl of using him until something better turned up. Although the boy denied this, it was true; as soon as the German Manageress took him in he was happy to dump the tramps. But there again he had little option; his self-centredness is ensuring his survival; he is still only sixteen years of age. Now he will stay in their apartment until joining The Nature Theatre of Oklahoma.

Since his arrival in New York harbour he has consistently been faced with individual responsibility and freedom of action: he rarely accepted the former, managing to achieve the latter mainly by default. Signs of approaching maturity are surfacing. While in conversation with 'black coffee', the student, he seems quite prepared to recognise his academic limitations. He decides to stick it out and try for a job in an office that he hopes will contain a career-structure. In this he can be said to be accepting reality far more than the student. With very little chance of improving his lot, 'black coffee' appears set for a mental and/or physical breakdown. *Amerika* peters out after this. Kafka never completed the chapter (but it was much longer in earlier drafts) and there is a jump from there into the 'nature theatre'.

When a clerk of the 'nature theatre' asks if Karl has come to join them, he answers: 'I read the placard your company put out and I have come here as I was requested' (p. 252). He is still not accepting responsibility for his own actions. His manner of coming to the 'nature theatre' can be paralleled to the Land Surveyor's ambiguous arrival at *The Castle*, and notice too that the Land Surveyor must 'cross a bridge' to enter the actual district. When everyone else hesitates outside the 'nature theatre' it is young Rossmann who will 'cross the platform' (p. 249) to be first to sign on.

Amerika can be seen as preparing the way for the later novels. Almost as soon as he finished it, Kafka was on to 'Metamorphosis' then *The Trial*, both of whose central protagonists have accepted reality. No doubt Uncle Jacob for one would have been pleased had the boy stuck to his decision to become a clerk. Instead of that he settled for the 'celestial witchery'[10] of The Nature Theatre of Oklahoma and thus escapes turning into a beetle or being executed. Uncle Jacob would have found such retribution incomprehensible, for the boy would simply have been accepting reality and doing his duty as a citizen. But anyone who concedes his or her individual selfhood in the face of society's authority is never making a 'manly decision' (p. 91) in Kafka's prose.

In common with Joseph K. and the Land Surveyor, Karl Rossmann is an individual confronted by authority. His struggles are more accessible to the reader because they occur within a conventional framework. His innocence is that of a child and his guilt that of any individual who makes things happen by default, i.e. by not making things happen. His ignorance is that of youth and intellectual immaturity. With unquestioning obedience he assumes the right of society to function as it does; as a member of the middle classes, of course, it is usually in his best interests to do so. Yet when he transgresses its authority he will become a victim the same as anyone else. Kafka was sceptical of a straightforward socialist solution to the misery of ordinary working people. The world is composed of individuals. Ordinary working people are as guilty of accepting reality as those who profit by it. He saw capitalism as

> a system of dependencies, which run from within to without, from without to within, from above to below, from below to above. All is dependent, all stands in chains. Capitalism is a condition of the soul and of the world . . .[11]

As a preparation for the later novels, the author has provided examples of his preoccupation with messages and messengers; the first two episodes have letters central to the storyline. Eventually the significance of this question becomes crucial to the distinction between man as function and man *qua* man. The Czech was well acquainted with ancient literatures, and was no doubt intrigued by the old Greek custom of killing the messenger who brought the bad news. Karl wanted to blame Mr Green for bringing bad news from Uncle Jacob. In *The Trial* Joseph K. gets annoyed at those who act on behalf of the Law.

Kafka's *Amerika* may be his most conventional realization of the novel but it should not blind us to his technical achievement. The narrative is hardly a recognisable third-party voice at all, unless it is presenting Karl Rossmann's interior perception of how things are. The ending envisaged by the author is not relevant since he appears never to have set it down in draft form let alone included it in his final version. In *Amerika* there is really no place for 'celestial witchery' and perhaps he was wise to stop work where he did. The freedom in which we leave the boy is optimistic but it is also a reflection of the freedom implicit in the writing itself: 'The Nature Theatre of Oklahoma' is an enormous leap for Kafka himself. No longer will his creative imagination be governed by the authority of conventional reality.

Part 2   *The Trial*: Ignorance and Guilt

Like the boy exiled to the New World, Joseph K. has been liberated from the burdens of immediate family life; he was reared as ward to his Uncle Karl.[1] All the more socially praiseworthy, perhaps, that he has achieved the position of 'junior manager of a large Bank' (p. 48). The security he has is in part a realization of the fantasy had by young Rossmann when he watched 'the clerk . . . that morning' from Brunelda's balcony (*Amerika*, p. 248). It was something in the man's contented bearing that had him considering life in an office as a career. Joseph K. has his place in society and, for the boy, this place would have been enviable. Not only has K. accepted society, society has appeared to accept him — something that was always being denied young Rossmann.

Efficiency and punctiliousness are traits of Joseph K. but are also those we expect of any competent bank employee. It might be argued, therefore, that the character is more of a type than an individual, but this is not the case. Perhaps the 'public' and the 'private' Joseph K. have merged to the point where there exists only one being such that he is the 'junior manager' Joseph K. For all that, he retains certain characteristics or habits to mark him from the crowd: he carries a small mirror about with him and takes pains to dress for the occasion. At thirty years of age his only relationship with the female sex is a weekly visit to a cabaret 'skirt-dancer [who is] neither soft nor kind, nor would she be capable of sacrificing herself for him' (p. 122). It is noticeable that the idea of sacrificing himself for her never occurs to K. Within his society it is hard to imagine anyone sacrificing him or herself for anyone else.

The Trial begins in what could be described as typical Kafkaesque fashion; the more thoroughly the opening paragraph is examined the more obvious it becomes that the only thing clearly established is the need for thorough examination. From the famous opening, 'Someone must have been telling lies', it will continue on until Joseph K. is reflecting that if his arrest truly 'is a comedy he would insist on playing it to the end' (p. 11). During the intervening 1,500 words or so Kafka has drawn the reader into the complexity of the tale with none of the extraneous detail a lesser writer might have felt compelled to put forward by way of explication. While witnessing K.'s arrest we gain insight into the mysterious nature of this Law. He himself is revealed: we see how he relates to other human beings both within and without the Bank. We also observe that he lives his life on the assumption that nothing exists outside of society, either that or 'the something' which does exist is irrelevant. Yet we can further witness that such an assumption is fallacious. This Law exists. It exists outside of society as he knows it. He has been ignorant of it. He has been living under a misapprehension. For the remainder of the novel we follow the proceedings right until the final outcome, his execution, when we may reflect that the outcome has been inevitable ever since the closing line of that opening paragraph.

Kafka's opening paragraphs are always of the utmost relevance; frequently they are paradigmatic of the stories themselves.[2] But this does not mean there is no movement. The author's central characters are never quite the same individuals they were when their stories began.

On his thirtieth birthday Joseph K. seems a well-adjusted member of society insofar as he is never in danger of misunderstanding his position within it. Life has become a closed system of rules and procedures. In his town it is beyond the realm of belief that a dustman could associate with a doctor on any 'man-to-man' basis of equality. There is no room for a moral life. If universal principles were to apply it would require men and women to recognise one another, first and foremost, as men and women, unique individuals. But Joseph cannot even recognise three of his colleagues from the Bank when they step beyond that context, no longer at their place of work but standing in a room in his lodging-house. Once advised of their identity he is able to recognise 'the stiff Rabensteiner swinging his arms, the fair Kullich with the deep-set eyes, and Kaminer with his insupportable smile' (p. 22). The keenness of the description shows how observant he can be when objects and people are not out of place.

So far his attitude towards the arresting officers has been ambivalent. He has difficulty in determining their reality from their appearance. At first he could not take them seriously because their uniform resembled a 'tourist's outfit' (p. 7). On the other hand, they are acting as though in authority over him. This is very puzzling. Even if they actually are arresting officers 'they could only be warders' (p. 10) and thus should be socially inferior, giving him his 'place' as 'junior manager'. From this circumstance alone he is able to intuit that the men are somehow beyond society. And so he wonders, 'What authority could they represent?' (p. 10).

Upon 'seeing' his colleagues, he can regain some composure and act as though nothing untoward is happening. He addresses the trio as though in the security of the Bank, with the careless air of an official speaking to three minor employees. Henceforth all scenes between Joseph and his colleagues will take place amid an under-current of mutual awkwardness. If this is in any way familiar it is worth remembering the author's regard for both Gogol and Dostoevski, both of whom occupy prime positions within the existential tradition in literature. There is an affinity between Joseph K. and the 'heroes' of stories like Gogol's 'The Nose' and 'The Overcoat', and also Dostoevski's 'A Nasty Story'. In the latter, after the dreadful débâcle of the previous evening, crowned by his ridiculous behaviour at the home of an underling, Ivan Ilyitch must show his face in the office next morning in the knowledge that the entire body of underlings will know of the

incident. His horror is absolute when he sees that their embarrassment is so great that it cannot be concealed behind their 'uniforms'.
In Dostoevski's story the private and public Ivan Ilyitch have
merged into the one individual, and this individual is an utter fool.

Joseph K. is always on the brink of losing control but just
manages to conceal his shame although never quite sure how
successful he is. Why for instance does the Deputy Manager treat
him in so offhand a manner? Is it because his work is suffering as a
result of outside pressure? Or is it because the Deputy Manager
knows the truth?

K. is surprised to find his first Court appearance scheduled for a
Sunday morning which is a day of rest for bank employees. He also
assumes the Court will assemble as for office hours and turns up
shortly after 9 a.m. only to discover he has kept everyone waiting,
and waiting for ages. He then proceeds to treat them all as his social
inferiors which they are by his own criteria, his criteria being those
of society as he perceives it; but society as he perceives it and
society 'in itself' are not the same thing. Not only do the Court
officials fail to appreciate his professional status, they mistake him
for a 'house-painter'. When he corrects the error it provokes a
'hearty outburst of laughter' (p. 48). Yet Joseph is convinced the
object of derision must be the Examining Magistrate, the man
responsible for the error. The trouble is that any authority held by
him is purely a function of his job description. As far as the Court
is concerned he is not an accused 'junior manager of a large Bank':
he is an accused person. Little wonder he cannot bring himself to
take it all seriously. If he was to accept the Law as an authority
greater than society then he would seem obliged to admit that his
life to present was based on a form of deception. He continues to
maintain his innocence. By the time Uncle Karl arrives from the
country he is less sure.

Joseph had expected to be consoled by the man; he is taken

aback to find him more worried than he is himself. Uncle Karl is also worried that the scandal may touch other members of his family. He warns Joseph that his behaviour is not that of 'an innocent man'; in fact, to look at his nephew, Uncle Karl 'would almost believe the old saying: "A litigant always loses"' (p. 108). Joseph is grateful for his offer of assistance but is secretly dismayed to be 'driven to a poor man's lawyer' (p. 109).

He still hopes that his status is somehow relevant to his defence. If not, he may have grounds for feeling uneasy about this mysterious Law. Yet at this stage he has had ample evidence that its authority is not governed by the values of middle-class society, and neither can it safely be shelved to somewhere beyond society so that its power is meaningless. It has already invaded the bank. While strolling down a corridor he hears a commotion from a small 'lumber-room', inside his warders are set to strip off and be flayed by a man 'who was clearly in authority over [them] and . . . was sheathed in a dark leather garment.'

And Joseph K. is responsible. If he had not complained about their behaviour, retribution would have been unnecessary, even had they been caught stealing from him. After the initial shock he regains composure and is able to inquire: 'Can that birch-rod cause such terrible pain?' (p. 96). This disinterested curiosity in the mechanical aspects of the torture instrument is reminiscent of the Explorer's questions in Kafka's story 'In the Penal Settlement', and linked thematically to the issue of messages and messengers. At one stage in the 'lumber-room' with 'the Whipper', Joseph K.

gave Franz [a warder] a push, not a violent one but violent enough nevertheless to make the half-senseless man fall and convulsively claw at the floor with his hands; but even then Franz did not escape his punishment, the birch-rod found him where he was lying (p. 98).

Note how K.'s action is seen as physical violence but the physical violence of the Whipper seen merely as punishment. The individual has become divorced from the act; it is the 'birch-rod' which 'finds' the culprit. Man and wood are irrevocably bound together as the institutional instrument of retribution. K. can accept this without question. He is accustomed to accepting the authority of society as an inalienable right.

The beating can be likened to a message and the Whipper is performing the role of messenger. He may be bringing 'bad news' to the warders but he cannot be held responsible for it; the punishment he metes out is nothing to do with him. Whereas Amalia in *The Castle* and Karl Rossmann in *Amerika* take issue with the messenger, Joseph K. is too much a product of his society to make that mistake. A Whipper is an individual who whips. How can a man be blamed for the mere performance of his duty? It would be as foolish for Joseph to hold the Whipper responsible as for a stage-manager to blame the dummy if the audience are insulted during a ventriloquist act.

And equally absurd to hold a soldier individually responsible for killing an enemy. Thus we are on course for a logically based discussion relating to whether or not the defendants at the Nuremberg Trials were soldiers simply carrying out their duties – conveying messages of death – or individual human beings to be held accountable for their actions. The actual recipients of the 'bad news', the victims, are not always relevant. The message is very important and so too is the messenger, and so too is the authority on which such a message could be sent, but the people who 'get the message' somehow vanish from the equation.

Perhaps a different logic could put forward another question: faced with genocide, why should logical points concern the authorities to such an overwhelming degree?[3]

But by its nature that kind of question seems unreasonable, as if the person who asks it has failed to appreciate the complexity of the problem. This is exactly how a reader who believes Amalia to be innocent will feel eventually. Anyone asking such a question is made to feel extremely naïve, or ignorant of the ways of the world. Once we have sorted out the logic behind Amalia's misfortune it is a straightforward thing to find her guilty, she has insulted the messenger. If a condemned man should fight his way free of the hangman we can see how he may be found guilty of obstructing the due course of the Law and assaulting an officer of it but we would find it ludicrous if the condemned man was found guilty of evading death at all costs, which seems to derive from an entirely different logical system.

The issue of messages and messengers is a continuing pre-occupation of the author and there is a variety of examples in his work. Yet the main thing established is the need to judge each example as an isolated case, that the logic of each is internal; or perhaps that logic is less rigorous than we thought.

The violent side to Joseph's personality has been in evidence. He is a member of a violent society so it is not too surprising. The Whipper scene was no symbol of sado-masochism, it was a concrete expression of it. Joseph showed particular interest in the 'birch-rod'. Earlier, on his first visit to the Court, he interrupted a group of children and reminded himself that if ever he returns he must 'either bring sweets to cajole them with or else a stick to beat them' (p. 43). On his second trip to the Court he is given a guided tour of its offices by an attendant whose wife he has tried to procure. Some of the other accused are pointed out to him and he sees one who obviously 'belonged to the upper classes'. Instead of acting as one would have expected from a 'man of the world' towards a social inferior, the elderly gentleman acts deferentially towards the attendant. Joseph is so incensed by the elderly man's 'humility' that he grabs him and flings him 'with real force' (p. 75).

If he is continually repressing his aggression he is also having to repress his sexual needs. The women of his own status do not surface in his story. The nearest we observe are Elsa the 'skirt-dancer' and the enigmatic Fräulein Bürstner. Leni describes the former in precisely the phrase used by Robinson in *Amerika* when speaking of Brunelda prior to her liberation by Delamarche: Elsa is 'very tightly laced'. And Joseph expects nothing from her although he carries her photograph around on his person. Apparently he is only capable of directing his physical needs to women of the lower orders. In his pursuit of the attendant's wife he was willing to risk the wrath of her lover, plus that of her prospective lover who happens to be the Examining Magistrate, to say nothing of the actual attendant. Then at the height of his interview with the Advocate Huld he is quite prepared to bolt from the room to find Leni; in doing so he is risking the wrath of Huld, and his Uncle Karl, not to mention the Chief Clerk of the Court who is sitting in the shadows. And later, outside the door to Titorelli's attic, Joseph is as agitated by the sexuality of the young working-class girls as by any other aspect of their behaviour.

His most blatant loss of control occurs with Fräulein Bürstner towards whom he behaves 'like some thirsty animal' (p. 7). This girl's part in the novel is very important. She is an enigma; Joseph cannot 'place' her within society. When the old landlady hints about her being seen with different men he is furious, unwilling to believe such a thing possible. In the wake of the incident he attempts to rationalise his wild behaviour by referring to her as 'an ordinary little typist' (p. 92). If her social status truly is inferior to his own then his actions towards her are irrelevant. Yet he cannot convince himself. On the road to his execution he sees either her or some sort of image of her, and gains an insight into his predicament. Perhaps if he had been able to see the girl first and foremost as another human being, just like himself, he would not have been under arrest in the first place. At that point she still remains an enigma, and the symbolism of the 'white blouse' is rooted in an ambiguity which ultimately ends in paradox; while its colour signifies purity the fact that it hangs from her bedroom window suggests sexual availability.

Uncle Karl had described Joseph's behaviour as compromising. In fact he is approaching a level of awareness such that whether he is innocent or guilty is irrelevant, his 'trial' will continue. The Advocate Huld consolidates this line of thinking. Even the provision of proof of innocence appears of little concern to him. Joseph becomes discouraged by the way Huld is handling his case and feels he can do a much better job. But he cannot fathom what the nature or substance of his guilt might be and so cannot defend himself adequately. His only recourse is the preparation of a 'written defence' based on 'a short account of his life' (p. 126). He hopes that the Court will know his guilt and thus recognise the 'crime' in question when it appears in the 'short account'. Obviously the misdemeanour will have been an important event. By inserting as many important events as he can recall into the 'short account', he reckons he should manage to include that particular one wherein lies his guilt. His defence will be based on the brief explanation he intends to append to each event, stating 'whether he approved or condemned his way of action in retrospect' (p. 126).

Enough of the proceedings have been observed for the reader at this stage to see that Joseph is being honest as far as it goes. If he is guilty then he has no knowledge of it, although ignorance is insufficient reason to be released from the charge. If he is to prove his innocence perhaps it will require not just 'a short account of his life' but an exhaustive examination of his entire twenty-nine years.

But can he be guilty on the available evidence? And can *we* judge him guilty on what we know from our reading of *The Trial*?

This is different from arguing whether or not Joseph K. should be capable of seeing his own guilt. Some critics[4] have argued that his 'guilt may remain indecipherable as long as it is sought within the confines of the novel' but Joseph may be found guilty by the reader who pays attention only to the story itself. Kafka does not have to 'define' the young man's guilt; he has presented it. Heinz Politzer has described the author's 'failure' 'to motivate' the guilt as possibly the 'major flaw in the construction of the novel' but what he regards as a 'major flaw' is an outstanding technical achievement. We are not forced into committing 'an intentional fallacy', we do not need to 'extend the story into Kafka's biography'.[5] All we are required to do is make a judgment founded on what exists within *The Trial*.

Franz Kafka did not create art within the reality inhabited by his fictional characters. The narrative of this novel serves two primary functions; it provides reality as perceived by Joseph K. and gives us a glimpse of the reality in which he exists; we are given a glimpse of the reality of his society, unfiltered through his perception.

For an example of the world as perceived by Joseph K. we need refer only to the opening sentence of the novel. Clearly not everyone in his society would agree that 'lies' are being told about him. Neither is it an unintentional bias in his favour from the anonymous third-party narrator. It is the character's own evaluation of the situation. It is Joseph's own reflection on the situation, embedded within the narrative, of the sort I drew attention to in reference to *Amerika*. The following extract offers an example of another aspect of society, one Joseph is in contact with but does not 'see'. He has decided to dispense with the services of the Advocate Huld and, acting upon the advice of a 'manufacturer', thinks to obtain assistance from Titorelli the Court-painter. He rushes straight out from the Bank to the address where the painter lived, in a suburb which was almost at the diametrically opposite end of the town from where the Court held its meetings. This was an even poorer neighbourhood, the houses were still darker, the streets filled with sludge oozing about slowly on top of the melting snow. In the tenement where the painter lived only one wing of the great double door stood open, and beneath the other wing, in the masonry near the ground, there was a gaping hole out of which, just as K. approached, issued a disgusting yellow fluid, steaming hot, from which a rat fled into the adjoining canal. At the foot of the stairs an infant lay belly down on the ground bawling, but one could scarcely hear its shrieks because of the deafening din that came from a tinsmith's workshop at the other side of the entry. The door of the workshop was open; three apprentices were standing in a half-circle round some object on which they were beating with their hammers. A great sheet of tin hanging on the wall cast a pallid light, which fell between two of the apprentices and lit up their faces and aprons. [p. 156.]

This is the reality of K.'s society. This is the route through which he must pass to reach the Court-painter. If he were to pause a moment and use his eyes and his ears he would bear witness to elements of his world which by no stretch of the imagination can be classified as 'good news'. But Joseph is in great haste, pre-occupied by his own predicament, and he 'flung only a fleeting glance at all this, he wanted to get out of the neighbourhood as quickly as possible . . .' (p. 156). It is not surprising he would want not to be there. This is the underside of that society; its filthy and verminous living and working conditions, as experienced day in day out by people at the 'diametrically opposite end of the town from where the Court held its meetings.' K. cannot abide the place and wants away, perhaps he might be robbed; also the longer he stays amid such desolation – and this is the crux – the less likely he can remain in denial of that reality.

In the above passage the author has hoisted us into a place where we admit horror as a fact of Joseph's society rather than an opinion. Kafka achieves the effect via a correlation of quite functional language. The horror can be 'skipped' if we read too quickly, or it can be ignored. But neither action negates its existence. There are three evaluative terms in use; 'poorer', 'darker' and 'disgusting'; 'poorer' and 'darker' are concrete, relative terms, referring to that particular district in relation to one K. had visited previously. The third – 'disgusting' – refers to the 'steaming hot . . . yellow fluid'. In early readings I found this an interesting term in context, either it was extraneous or K.'s own perception of reality as opposed to reality in itself. For although the nature of 'the yellow fluid' was ambiguous the proximity of the 'tinsmith's workshop' across the way had me inclining towards metal waste, molten tin, something like that. But given the location of the 'gaping hole', and the appearance of the rat, the 'yellow fluid' is surely human waste and in this context it may be argued that 'disgusting' is a non-evaluative term if, as a general rule, any human being would regard the 'yellow fluid' as disgusting.

But it is through his avoidance of relativistic, value-laden language that Kafka creates, so to speak, a 'new reality'. Rather than say of him that he 'distorts' reality,[6] here in *The Trial* it is as though there are three 'realities' posited. James Hogg had hinted at some such possibility a century previously in his *Confessions of a Justified Sinner* and it connects to the 'distorted vision' of earlier 'anti-heroes' in the existential tradition. The first of the 'three realities' is the world as perceived by Joseph K., technically the same as that perceived by Dostoevski's 'Collegiate Assessor' in *Notes from Underground* and the rest of these 'I'-voice hero/narrators. The second is the world in which K. exists but does not bear witness. This is the same reality as that which forms the ironic structure of literature in that tradition, i.e. the world that author and prospective reader are assumed to share, and share too with the fictional central character (which he might recognise if he could stop distorting it). The third 'reality' is the one in which Franz Kafka lived and wrote stories that are being discussed several decades after his death.

Kafka has placed the reader in a position that a supreme being would occupy if in existence. It is only through being on the outside that the reader has the power to recognise horror as a truth about Joseph K.'s society. If we want to evaluate that society we can begin from the point where we might ask whether or not particular horrors are 'necessary' but we need not argue about whether or not horror exists. In the world of Joseph K., Franz Kafka has presented the existence of horror as a fact about it, and if we do not 'see' horror as a fact then we are ignoring important things that are going on in the novel. Once we have recognised that there are these horrific aspects of the society in which Joseph K. lives, then it provides the basis upon which we can judge whether or not he is guilty.[7]

When he hurries through the streets and into Titorelli's tene-ment, he is managing to ignore what lies under his nose, he sees but does not see. In this instance he does not see the 'infant . . . belly down on the ground bawling'. This to me indicates the foundation of his guilt. He is under no obligation to lift the baby up from the ground. Moral obligations do not enter into the matter; in Kafka's fiction such entities can be likened to 'official decisions' made within *The Castle*, and these are as 'shy as young girls'. Joseph's only obligation is to bear witness to the fact that the baby exists at this moment in time amid the reality of these surroundings. (He might also notice that three boys are working in the most appalling conditions.) Once he bears witness to that fact he might form a judgment to the effect that here is at least one aspect of society, the treatment of children, which is not good. He might even describe it as 'horrible' (at a later stage of rationalisation perhaps he could judge it a 'necessary evil').

On the same day he meets a group of girls upstairs in the tenement building. He is intimidated by them. There is one in particular 'who had a slight spinal deformity and seemed scarcely thirteen years old [who] nudged him with her elbow and peered up at him knowingly.' This girl wears 'abbreviated skirts [and is] prematurely debauched.' The group includes her younger sisters and others who also are younger than her, yet 'their faces betray the same mixture of childishness and sophistication.' They are provocative, making him 'run the gauntlet between them'. An older man appears from an apartment 'wearing nothing but a nightshirt.' Titorelli himself is barefoot, his clothes in disarray, but neither male resembles in the slightest degree an aggressor. Later, in Titorelli's room, Joseph is overwhelmed by the heat and claustrophobic atmosphere and he takes off his jacket. He is witnessed by one of the girls who is outside peering in through cracks in the wood. Titorelli tells Joseph how another girl was hiding in his room and made a grab for his leg when he was 'climbing into bed'. Titorelli treats the girls only as children, children aware not of their own sexuality so much as sexuality in general and that their very presence may, somehow, effect a situation. But also he tells Joseph that 'these girls belong to the Court', whether as Wards of Court only – excluding the more sinister implication – is left unclear.

If K. sees the rottenness at the core of his own society and ignores it then he is guilty of ignoring reality, which is tantamount to authorising 'bad news' by default. His only defence seems to rest on the hopeless task faced by one individual in the face of such an authority as society (the combined power of all other individuals within society). Yet he cannot be absolved of all responsibility.[8] He is a member of society. Ignorance is not a valid defence, although it forms the basis of his when confronted by the priest in the Cathedral. He now can accept he is no longer innocent:

> 'But I am not guilty,' said K.; 'it's a misunderstanding. And if it comes to that, how can any man be called guilty? We are all simply men here, one as much as the other.' [p. 232.]

Such a plea could be offered on behalf of a naughty infant. The irresponsible act of a child may only be irresponsible in the context of an adult value-system. If we are going to punish one child for committing a certain act then we should go and punish all children because if they are children they will at some point have committed the act; if not, they must commit it in the future. Children are to be punished for committing acts that the vast majority of adults recognise as irresponsible. But the recognition is from that adult perspective, it does not belong to the world of children. Children cannot see it, thus they are to be punished for being children.

Joseph K. is seeking absolution on the grounds that he is only a man. As far as the priest is concerned, what he has said is 'true . . . but that's how all guilty men talk' (p. 232). He is seen now as a hypocrite, for he has been living his life on the assumption that nothing exists outside society, or if it does it is irrelevant to the way society functions; nor does this entail greater responsibility on the part of K. or any other adult, rather it allows an abnegation of responsibility, perhaps on the grounds of 'imperfection'.

Although Joseph has been arrested on an unspecified charge, the others he meets on trial are 'accused of guilt' (p. 74) and all, including himself, are either middle- or upper-class products. By the time any have reached the Court they have had to pass from the bottom of society (another of Kafka's concrete realizations of conventional images) to the attics. If they are already aware of the 'bad news' in their society and are willing to concede a degree of accountability, no matter how minimal, then they are entitled to be 'accused of guilt'. Perhaps, if they had been able to rationalise it as a necessary but incidental evil, they would have escaped arrest. Perhaps not. It makes no difference. Innocence is just about impossible. The episode in which Titorelli tells K. about Court procedure is ample evidence of this. Only three methods of acquittal operate: 'definite', 'ostensible' and 'indefinite'. 'Definite' is only granted to those who are innocent, but in the painter's experience nobody has ever been known to be innocent although he has heard 'legendary accounts of ancient cases' (p. 171). Both 'ostensible' and 'indefinite' acquittals are the only methods to avoid the Courts but the guilt of those acquitted is *a priori* established.

The case of Joseph K. is different. He is the only accused individual of whom we know whose trial reaches the ultimate conclusion. He is the only person we know to be ignorant of the Law's existence. But he was genuinely ignorant prior to his thirtieth birthday. He was not having 'lies' told about him: he was living a lie. He assumed that the values of 'his' society (middle- and upper-class) were the supreme authority of humankind and then discovered they were subservient to a greater power, that of the Law which allowed his social inferiors to assume authority over him. Everyone else knew about the sham. They also assumed that he did.

He is incapable of truly accepting it all even while the executioners call for him, but he is content to 'insist on playing it to the end'. He still does not believe anything exists outside society as he knows it. And according to the text, his lack of belief is perfectly justified. If the layers of the Courts were eventually to be stripped away, there is no evidence to suggest that anything would be left. It is probable that the ignorant K. is the only individual who recognises that possibility; those who regard themselves as instruments of the Law may simply be deceiving themselves. The figures in whom authority is thought to be invested may, unwittingly, be the actual authority in itself.

Everything about this mysterious Law suggests it is under the control of human reason. Yet it is a peculiar form of reason. It seems to be attempting to translate something that must remain outside human understanding into a form which human beings can understand.

After the parable of 'Before the Law' the priest is giving the exposition to Joseph that he might arrive at some form of understanding. But one of the major hurdles to understanding is his failure to grasp what is nothing more than a logical point, a syllogism: if it is impossible for any individual to understand the Law then it is impossible for Joseph K. to understand the Law.

It is stated repeatedly that the door-keeper is incapable of understanding. And if so, how can he be expected to convey an understanding to the man from the country? The best he can do is convey his inability to so do. This Law operates by a mixture of 'mystery, miracle and authority'.[9] No route exists towards true understanding. Whether the 'supreme being' or 'supreme power' actually exists cannot be discovered:

> If God stops a man on the street, calls him by a revelation and sends him out to the other men armed with divine authority – then they say to him, 'From whom art thou?' He answers, 'From God.' But lo, God cannot help his ambassador as a king can who gives him an accompaniment of soldiers or policemen, or his ring, or a letter in his handwriting which everybody recognises – in short, God cannot be at men's service by providing them with a sensible certitude of the fact that an apostle is an apostle . . .[10]

Joseph K. is approaching enlightenment. When he leaves the Cathedral he has understood that the Law need not appear 'just' in the eyes of man in order to be 'just'. The appearance does not have to correspond to the reality – a reality which must always remain beyond an ordinary mortal. Those authorised to serve the Law can be corrupt but this does not mean that the Law itself is corrupt. Nobody would call God a thief if a priest stole a coin from a collection-box. It is at this point Joseph and Ivan Karamazov[11] become brothers, for the former is still seeking a logical proof, while being offered an absurd form of reasoning. He is to accept that 'corruption' can be 'integrity'; that 'good' can be 'evil'; that 'truth' is 'falsity'. The argument is based on the premise that an ordinary individual is incapable of distinguishing that which is from that which is not. And, in common with Dostoevski's 'hero', Joseph K.

rejects that point of view . . . for if one accepts it, one must accept as true everything the door-keeper says. But you yourself have sufficiently proved how impossible it is to do that.' 'No,' said the priest, 'it is not necessary to accept everything as true, one must only accept it as necessary.' 'A melancholy conclusion,' said K. 'It turns lying into a universal principle.' [p. 243].

The warders arrived on his thirtieth birthday and his executioners on his thirty-first. His trial has lasted a year. If there is a flaw in the construction of the novel it lies in the timespan[12] and the many gaps that appear in the narrative. That is an effect of the author's presentation of the reality of K.'s society. It would have been extremely difficult, for example, to give a fuller account of the bank clerk's personal history. Kafka's presentation of that reality only works if the reader is there when the action is occurring, bearing witness to the central protagonist manoeuvering his way through life. Informative detail has to be worked in somehow. As it is, the snatches we do hear about Joseph's history are usually from dialogue, or reported dialogue. This is also why Kafka's prose is full of 'stories within the story'; it is a method of escaping the technical exigencies brought on by his working of reality, thus detail can be compressed and selected. When detail is selected it ceases to become value-free. But Kafka's internal stories are usually open to interpretation, not only for the reader but for the characters them-selves. It is recognised that a 'story' is not 'reality'. Expositions are therefore necessary to get beyond the evaluations, to discover 'the truth'. His characters never quite reach any conclusions about that though, no matter the amount of time they spend on it.

Between the executioners and Joseph K. is an underlying sense of the absurdity of the occasion. His initial reaction is a mixture of fear and contempt. He sees them as he saw the warders and describes them as 'tenth-rate old actors' (p. 245). It is possible that the outfit worn by the pair is their own interpretation of what 'real' executioners would wear under authorisation from a genuinely supreme power. The charade continues. He plays along and is taken by the pair on the journey to the place of execution. On route he sees Fräulein Bürstner or an image of her. From this time on he regards the two men as 'his companions'; he is seeing them as men who are having to fulfil a function of society. This factor crucially reveals the transformation in Joseph K. since the warders arrived a year ago.

When he intuits that suicide is expected of him he will not wield the knife. His refusal to take this responsibility is not a defeat. He is aware of the sham of society. At the same time he has no faith in there being any external source 'behind' the Law. Those who exist in the knowledge that the values of society are not the reality, are existing under a different illusion, they believe that something exists beyond reality itself.

After Fräulein Bürstner's appearance, Joseph admits his guilt: 'I always wanted to snatch at the world with twenty hands, and not for a very laudable motive, either' (p. 47). The admission is oddly ambiguous and tends to distance K. from individual guilt by his use of a cliché, the kind of phrase 'Everyman' might make. But he is prepared to accept an individual's responsibility and not simply in a vague general sense.

He is also aware of other individuals apart from the two men who have the job of executing the final demand on him. A window opens and a person appears 'and stretched both arms [forward], a human figure, faint and insubstantial' (p. 250). He tries to see if it is 'a friend . . . a good man . . . one person only.' His thoughts turn back on himself and he concludes the thought by wondering if 'any arguments . . . had been overlooked'. He replies to himself 'of course . . . logic is doubtless unshakable, but it cannot withstand a man who wants to go on living.'

The last statement could only be made by someone who has recognised the value of other individuals in themselves, as ordinary human beings. Those readers who find *The Trial* ultimately pessimistic will be pessimistic about individuals in general.

Part 3   *The Castle*: Ignorance and Freedom

Amerika was episodic but its last chapter indicated a movement towards greater creative freedom in the author's abandonment of conventional reality in favour of 'celestial witchery'. *The Trial* shows how Kafka developed a different reality. Again the narrative was dual-purposed but the third-party narrative, when not giving an indirect account of the characters' psychological life and actions, was so value-free it was approaching the purity of an objective presentation of reality in itself. Not of the world as we know it, the world in which Franz Kafka's books exist, but the world of his fictional characters. Kafka depicted the reality of the world inhabited by Joseph K. not just in the manner it appeared to him. There was nothing to suggest that anything existed outside society except, somehow, the Law. Yet without society the Law would not exist. As readers we were elevated into a position generally occupied by 'supreme beings'. We could make value-free judgments and did so on at least one occasion, at the entrance to the building where Titorelli lived and painted pictures. We bore witness to Joseph K. and acknowledged his guilt as a valid condition in terms of the society in which he was a member. Here we have a man who is so ruthlessly selfish that he can step over a baby lying unprotected at a gutter in order to go more swiftly about his business.

The Trial is a remarkable novel, although it is possible to judge it structurally defective, which would be harsh. When we remember that the timespan of the story is a period of one year we may respect the enormity of the problem faced by the writer. It was incumbent upon him to present the action as it happened, or find a method of avoiding that. If within the third-party narrative there had been a pause for a report of past actions it would have become, in effect, the *perception* of a 'narrator', a 'third-party voice'. Even had this narrator remained 'unbiased' it would still have amounted to a perception of reality; not the image of reality but a report of its appearance. This is a primary technical factor in Kafka's use of 'a story within a story', it solves the problem of how to impart historical and other information indirectly, i.e. without having to present it dramatically, with immediate effect. The use of dialogue is a common method writers adopt to that end, where the characters themselves 'fill in the gaps', providing personal histories and so on.

Described as the 'best integrated'[1] of the three novels, *The Castle* is perhaps the most coherent. The Land Surveyor's quest lasts for about a week. There are no time-gaps. The author is able to use such primary techniques as having the central character go to bed, stop for a meal, be with his girlfriend, etc., in order to make his way from scene to scene without any hiccups. In this manner the novel becomes a continuous unit, in effect one long scene of action. James Joyce was born the year before Kafka and was working on *Ulysses* at roughly the same period as Kafka on *The Castle*.[2] Both were having to work out their own methods, resolving formal problems, in order to reach similar goals involving time and reality. Essential elements of the Epiphany envisaged by the Irishman may not be too far away from what the Czech was after in a scene like the tenement entrance to Titorelli's lodgings.[3]

While Kafka overcomes the difficulty in *The Castle,* it is not so much that he provides an answer to the problems he faced in *The Trial.* Instead he simply shelves reality in itself; there is no attempt to present it.[4] The narrative is concentrated into the perception of the Land Surveyor. It is not dual-purposed. Before getting fully into the story, Kafka made a few beginnings, alternating between first- and third-party narrative. Eventually he settled on the third but it mostly resembles a sort of interior first. Far from the plane of 'supreme being', the reader is to find his or herself in a state similar to the Land Surveyor: ignorant.

The author's use of the subjunctive mood is well known. Within *The Castle* almost all judgments are contingent and the mood is essential. Since the narrative keeps pace with K., his lack of certainty must be embedded in it, thus we are constantly being told 'it would seem' and 'it would appear' and 'it was as if'. We are seeing things as they are and the world as it is, but not in order to arrive at a further evaluation. If individuals are to act decisively, appearances may be the only 'evidence' required. The major obstacle in approaching *The Castle* is the lack of external reference.

Our own knowledge as readers is not greatly useful, perhaps of value in terms of negation. We seem to be seeing the world over the Land Surveyor's shoulder. And, never having seen anything like the Castle before, 'if K. had not known that it was [one] he might have taken it for a little town' (p. 19). He cannot know the Castle by its appearance alone but does have some prior knowledge, enough to recognise it anyway. But once again we are grounded in that crucial area of struggle within Kafka's work: appearance versus reality.

Here within the vicinity of the Castle, not even the time of day can be stated with any degree of certainty:

> When by a turn in the road K. recognised that they were near the inn, he was greatly surprised to see that darkness had already set in. Had he been gone for such a long time? Surely not for more than an hour or two, by his reckoning. And it had been morning when he left. And he had not felt any need of food. And just a short time ago it had been uniform daylight, and now the darkness of night was upon them. 'Short days, short days,' he said to himself, slipped off the ledge, and went towards the inn. [pp. 29–30.]

Temporal vagaries may be worthy of comment but are only of incidental interest, incapable of furthering his quest; he is content to describe how things are rather than waste any time on why they should be as they are.

The Land Surveyor is a man in a hurry, nor is he lacking in ruthlessness, a characteristic shared by the central characters in each of the novels. If Karl Rossmann was a male on the threshold of manhood, K. can be regarded as an individual who has had his chances and decided that, for better or worse, he must do something before it is too late. Why such a decision should have been resolved by coming to the Castle remains problematic. While K. never quite admits to having made the journey entirely of his own volition, the Castle authorities will never admit to having summoned him. In the early pages we are given a little information. K. has flouted Castle authority by being sarcastic to Schwarzer, the son of an 'under-castellan'. Schwarzer phones the Castle to find out whether they know about him and learns that nothing at all is known of him. Before he quite gets to the stage of throwing K. back over the bridge, the Control Bureau phones back to advise that there has been an error.

> K. pricked up his ears. So the Castle had recognised him as the Land Surveyor. That was unpropitious for him, on the one hand, for it meant that the Castle was well informed about him, had estimated all the probable chances, and was taking up the challenge with a smile. On the other hand, however, it was quite propitious, for if his interpretation were right they had underestimated his strength, and he would have more freedom of action than he had dared to hope. And if they were expecting to cow him by their lofty superiority in recognising him as Land Surveyor, they were mistaken; it made his skin prickle a little, that was all. [p. 15.]

Coming so early in the tale, this information seems extremely valuable. It *is* extremely valuable. But gradually its significance will become lost in a welter of ambiguity. In retrospect it has the appearance of a miniature account of the quest in abstract. The actual quest itself could be reduced to an all-encompassing portrait. Nothing exists to assist us in following the trail. We have to fix our sights on K. and by the time we enter the latter stages of his quest we are beginning to gain an overall picture: but by this time, of course, we have just about read the novel. Eventually he confides to Olga that he 'was engaged to come [to the Castle] yet that was only a pretext, they were playing with me . . . I came of my own accord' (p. 244). That he has always realised his responsibility for his own actions marks his maturity as an individual when we compare him to Joseph K. As I mentioned earlier, the Land Surveyor is more akin to young Rossmann; his method of arrival is paralleled by the the latter's entry into 'The Nature Theatre of Oklahoma'.

What little we know of the Land Surveyor's background (which gives him an advantage over the reader) is more than adequately compensated by our experience of reading Kafka's other prose.

We are familiar with the idea that people are willing to remain subject to the authority of a supreme power even while knowing that the power itself is no longer existent.[5] We are prepared to hear of a mysterious Count whose power is so great that after the opening pages his name need never be referred to again. The source of the Castle authority is as shrouded in ambiguity as was that behind the Law in *The Trial*. Whether Count Westwest exists or not is beyond the realm of discussion; such a question never arises for the inhabitants of the Castle province. All that matters is the existence of the Castle and the supremacy of its authority.

During K.'s first few hours in the village we glimpse this authority through the reaction of the peasantry to him; as a stranger he is treated contemptuously, then when his link has been established to the Castle he commands immediate respect: he is the superior of everyone else at the Bridge Inn.

It is seen that individuals have no basic rights; their value – or individual authority – is a function of the strength of their link to the Castle. As will become evident, those outside the Castle have absolutely no authority, they are peasants. Within the Castle a pecking-order does appear to exist but it is virtually impossible for an outsider to gain any knowledge of it. We are following the Land Surveyor, we are outsiders. We can never even be sure that Castle servants are inferior to Castle officials. 'According to Barnabas . . . the higher-grade servants are even more inaccessible than the officials . . . perhaps they are even of higher rank' (p. 214). The more remote a functionary is from view, the greater is his power, or so the peasantry believe.

Barnabas is only the Land Surveyor's intermediary; he is a messenger with no way of knowing the significance of his messages, for he does not belong to the interior of the Castle; he is a messenger removed from authority. Although his uniform had impressed K. at first sight, it proves to be one of his own design; he is only an 'ostensible' messenger. This mistake of the Land Surveyor is one of the few he makes. He is not a person to be cowed by a uniform. Everybody he has direct dealings with he treats as individuals. He has grasped the distinction between authority-figures and authority in itself. His cavalier approach to the Castle officials is a straightforward expression of that knowledge, officials are mere individuals, just like himself.

If an overall authority does exist, then K. is disinclined to believe it is Count Westwest. This continual disregard for the proprieties of Castle life shocks the villagers, and exasperates a few. Schwarzer is aghast at his jocular reference to the Count. But it is his disregard for conventional attitudes that allows him to conduct his quest on a plane outwith their ken. Towards him the attitude of the villagers fluctuates between dread and hero-worship. K.'s boldness may derive from ignorance but it gives him the freedom to behold even the mighty Klamm as a mere man.

Although we cannot be certain, Klamm appears to be the highest official in the Castle, and people regard him in that light. His name is invoked as though he was a god (p. 142). Ironically, whenever Klamm visits the village, the traits he displays are those of a timid wee fellow. If remoteness is a sign of power perhaps Klamm is less powerful than people imagine. The common denominator among the officials is the fear of seeing a stranger or, even worse, being seen by one. Klamm carries it to absurdity; he cannot stand to see a stranger's footprints. Now he has to cope with the fact that a strange Land Surveyor has just absconded with his mistress.

In this place where K. is truly an outsider. He neither belongs to the Castle officialdom nor yet to its village workforce and peasantry. But he does not want to remain beyond the Castle walls. His quest is to gain entry.

Klamm's mistress has been impressed, perceiving 'something concerning himself . . . which he had not known to exist' (p. 52). Whatever it was is enough for Frieda to cut loose from her existing link to the Castle. She ceases her relationship to Klamm. While that mighty official sat in an adjacent room she was in the arms of the Land Surveyor, 'among the small puddles of beer and other refuse gathered on the floor' of the taproom (p. 59). She gained a strength from K. that both allowed her to defy existing authority, and to glimpse beyond the existing horizon. Seldom can 'the south of France or . . . Spain' (p. 72) have received such poetic force which this girl obtains by the mere mention of the place-names amid the bleak surroundings of the village schoolroom.

As an outsider the Land Surveyor reflects the big wide world beyond and Frieda is not the only woman attracted to him, so too are Olga and Pepi, and even Amalia. The older women are not immune. It is only with K. that the landlady of the Bridge Inn can confide her feelings for Klamm while she of the Herrenhof finds it possible to discuss her secret vice with him: three wardrobes full of elaborate dresses.

K. is symbolising freedom, but only for the villagers. As readers we are too aware of his motives, that he is content to exploit everyone he meets to achieve his purpose. He is *bound* to the quest, and is not interested in other people except incidentally. Both landladies have recognised this in him, and one will eventually call him 'either a fool or a child or a very wicked person' (p. 386). This description carries a fair amount of significance: typically it is applied to individuals who are thought subversive, a danger to the existing socio-political order.[6]

Coincidentally it transpires that there has been unrest among the village workmen. A cobbler by the name of Brunswick was the ringleader, an outspoken member of a group who was in favour of 'summoning . . . a Land Surveyor' (p. 89) some time ago. The most obvious connection would concern actual land itself since land surveying concerns the measurement of land. It is a mistake to ignore the connection simply because it is so obvious. In Kafka's prose problems often dissolve by recognising reality from its appearance.[7] Much of the Land Surveyor's strength is derived from his capacity for stating the obvious, and not seeking 'hidden truths'. In the passage above concerning the mysterious nature of time within the Castle, the Land Surveyor was content to describe the fact of 'short days' as 'short days'; he did not solve any problem, it evaporated upon utterance of the reality.

When so much in the author's work is left unsaid, it would be foolish to seek the overtly political. If we go to his life we see his political beliefs outlined quite clearly. But in the writing itself not only is there no comment from the author, it is very difficult to find anything pushed covertly. This latter might appear not by intention, but always in the language itself, discovered in its unchecked values. There are very few authors who have managed to sustain such value-free narratives.

On the other hand, it can be argued that Kafka's three novels contain nothing but politics, that they are so saturated with injustice and appalling inequalities that to talk of anything else is preposterous: it is to ignore the reality of the texts themselves. It is to make precisely the same error as those of his characters who search for a 'supreme source' in order to impose order on a terrible reality – so terrible that a way must be found to stop bearing witness to its appearance, whether intentionally or otherwise.[8] Reality is not easily shoved to one side. In the tale of 'Metamorphosis' Gregor Samsa's immediate reaction on discovering his transformation was to go back to sleep. Unfortunately for him, when he next woke up he was still an insect.

If we seek political awareness among the village workmen then we seek in vain. Nor do we find, given Kafka's own political sympathies, 'personal' statements hidden within their dialogue; he is the most unobtrusive of writers. Brunswick, the former ringleader of the workmen, hardly appears in the story and we hear of no current political issues. The reader who seeks any cause for unrest among the villagers has to judge for him- or herself. But we have had experience of this from *The Trial*.

Olga tells us that all villagers and Castle employees are 'supposed to belong to the Castle . . . and that may be true enough on ordinary occasions, but . . . not true when anything really important crops up' (p. 240). What she says is correct. In *The Trial* the lower orders did have a saving grace, the Law existed. One of the consequences of this Law was that it nullified that authority of society which is based on middle- and upper-class values. This is not an interpretation of mine, nor is it an evaluation. It is simply a summary of much of that Law's procedure within the text. In *The Castle* there is no such saving grace for the peasantry and the rest of the villagers. There is only the reality of Castle authority. The distinction between the villagers and the Castle employees is quite basic, the former have none of the authority, they simply belong to 'it'.

Earlier, when the Land Surveyor met the cobbler without realising it after blundering into a peasant's cottage, a different sort of distinction was suggested. By referring to himself and the other peasantry as 'we small people' (p. 25) Lasemann the tanner seemed to imply a very concrete physical if not racial difference between the two factions. That K. notices himself as the 'biggest man in the room' is an additional factor. But this line should not be taken too rigidly in relation to the Castle. Barnabas has been inside and he says of 'the higher grade servants [that] it's a marvellous sight to see these tall and distinguished men slowly walking through the corridors' (p. 214). Sortini, the official who makes the lewd proposal to Amalia, turns out to be a tiny individual. Just to confuse matters further, Sortini should not be confused with Sordini, 'the real authority' and the man K. thought responsible for bringing him to the Castle in the first place. No other official is described as tall. Another reference to height arrives by way of a faded photograph of Klamm as a youth, part of whose training for Castle work consisted in doing 'high leaps' (p. 102). Although not racial, the gulf remains enormous bteween villagers and Castle inhabitants, as though impossible to bridge. It has the rigidity of a caste system and yet it is not one. An individual's potential is *almost* governed by birth, but not quite.

There is an interesting parallel between Brunswick's situation and that of Amalia. Both are guilty of interference; each has disrupted Castle protocol through their own personal affairs. The cobbler has married a 'girl from the Castle' who spends her life brooding about it, and wants desperately to return. Amalia, the daughter of the old village cobbler, has refused Sortini's proposition. K. regards both Brunswick and Amalia as little short of enemies and wants nothing to do with them; in their own way each is also an outcast. K. has recognised and is fearful of becoming such a thing himself. He had earlier noticed the peasantry looking as though they 'really wanted something from him' (p. 40). He offers nothing. The Land Surveyor is no political revolutionary arrived to unite the people. His quest concerns 'only and no one else' but himself (p. 142). In this he is quite willing to exploit

Brunswick's son, in the hope of enlisting the services of the 'girl from the Castle'. Again the distinction between the two groups belonging to the Castle is emphasised by the son who is

> willing to accept K. even in his present state. The peculiar childish-grown-up acuteness of this wish consisted in the fact that Hans looked on K. as a younger brother whose future would reach further than his own. [p. 188.]

Hans might here be said to have recognised *a priori* limits being imposed on him by the functionalism of life within the Castle. His potential as an adult is already restricted by virtue of his 'role' in society as the son of the village cobbler. Even as the offspring of a sort of mixed marriage he will never have the freedom held by K. as a right, as the right of a total outsider. The boy is as convinced as K. that his job as janitor is strictly temporary.

The Land Surveyor may have taken a job in the village but, at this stage, no one could properly describe him as a village workman. Before being given the janitor's job by the village Superintendent he had turned down a similar offer from Klamm. K. had quickly recognised the 'danger . . . in sinking to the workmen's level' (p. 36). As a man without a label he is retaining a form of authority and, at best, is the equal of anyone. Once he has accepted a role he must risk being defined by it. Agreeing to become a village workman would have been tantamount to accepting Castle authority in whatever form it chose to present itself, whether via officialdom or simply by his having to defer to villagers like the teacher, Momus the secretary or the Superintendent among others. In agreeing to become janitor the Land Surveyor was agreeing to become an 'ostensible village worker whose real occupation was determined through the medium of Barnabas' (p. 38). The irony is that he has yet to discover that Barnabas is only an 'ostensible' messenger.

The preoccupation with messages and messengers receives a more concrete expression in the shape of Amalia's brother. In Olga's 'story' there is page upon page of exposition on the role – or life – of Barnabas. But the search for a logic will end in absurdity. Each individual case demands separate criteria, the logic is always internal, of little value in helping resolve other cases. While her brother's lifestory is being related, Olga also gives information on the workings of the Castle and a history of her sister Amalia which has as its kernel the message from the official.

Olga's 'story within the story' takes up nearly 25 per cent of the first published edition of the novel.[9] Before Amalia's misfortune the family were respectable peasants, the father village cobbler, and things were going as well as could be expected for folk subject to the Castle and its authority-figures. After the misfortune the family have become paupers. Their life is now structured around the misfortune. Barnabas hopes that by attaching himself to the Castle he can in some way get the authorities to bestow favour on the family.

Amalia's real fault, as Olga appreciates, was to have insulted the messenger, obstructing Castle protocol. By making her body available to every servant from the Castle who has the desire, Olga hopes to come into contact with the individual who delivered Sortini's lewd proposal. Meantime the father has entered an early senility because of his struggle to erase the stigma; his 'fighting' method is based on a wish to be punished. If the family can be punished then it will be over and done with, surely. Unfortunately he cannot establish the grounds on which the family are guilty and he becomes convinced that this 'guilt was being concealed from him because he had . . . paid only the established taxes' (p. 260).

Part of the tragedy of this family is that their very respectability has become the prime factor behind their continuing decline. They could have acted as though nothing had happened, or 'suddenly put in an appearance with the news that everything was settled' (p. 254) even though this had not happened in reality. Everyone was looking for a way 'to avoid mentioning the matter' but the family was unable to fulfil it. They have had to act as if something terrible happened and because of this are shunned by former friends, plus everybody else; they all want 'to avoid hearing about it or speaking about it or thinking about it or being affected by it in any way' (p. 255).

Once the reader starts to rationalise the several factors in Olga's story about her family, there is a glaring trap. This trap also existed in *Amerika* when Karl is seen as guilty of insulting Mr Green over the letter. It would have existed in *The Trial* should Joseph K. have borne witness to the reality at the entrance to the tenement, *and then rationalised it* in a particular way. The problem arises when the recipients of the bad news disappear from the equation. The reality of the tenement entrance is that a baby is 'belly down' in the middle of winter in a scene of total horror. In *Amerika* a sixteen-year-old is being banished yet again, sent 3,000 miles away to the other side of the continent, with no money and no prospects, and all for having disobeyed a societal code. In *The Castle* Olga's family are being punished (whether the father grasps it or not) for having behaved as human beings.

The reader who has rationalised those 'cases', and started considering how the characters might have avoided their present condition, has fallen into the trap. The reasoning stems from a kind of logic which should be confined to cases involving ventriloquists' dummies. The reader who is ignorant of Castle procedure might want to ask why any girl should have been subjected to the treatment received by Amalia; and why her sister should feel obliged to give herself to all and sundry. The deeper into the Castle we progress the less easy such questions appear. Gradually they dissolve altogether as we become more sophisticated in applying

Castle logic. The reality remains: Amalia's family are peasants and this is why they have been treated as less than human, they have neither authority nor the basic rights of individual human beings. The Land Surveyor is aware of this and he tells Olga:

> Fear of the authorities is born in you here, and is further suggested to you all your lives in the most various ways and from every side, and you yourselves help to strengthen it as much as possible. Still, I have no fundamental objection to that; if an authority is good why should it not be feared? [p. 225.]

This last proposition is tricky. Should we accept it? Perhaps we are to regard it with caution, a caution similar to that which the priest tries to instil into Joseph K. during *The Trial,* in reference there to the door-keeper. Occasionally the door-keeper sounds the very embodiment of common sense. But the priest points out

> '. . . that [the door-keeper] is a little simple-minded and consequently a little conceited.' Take the statements he makes about his power and the power of the other door-keepers and their dreadful aspect which even he cannot bear to see – I hold that these statements may be true enough, but that the way in which he brings them out shows that his perceptions are confused by simpleness of mind and conceit. The commentators note in this connexion: 'The right perception of any matter and a misunderstanding of the same matter do not wholly exclude each other.' [pp. 238–9.]

It would be a mistake to regard the Land Surveyor as the one truly wise man of the novel, for in his own way he is as blinkered as the other folk of the Castle. His strength, after all, derives from a form of ignorance. This is why the villagers, as well as being attracted to him, are repelled by him. The landlady of the Bridge Inn tells him that his 'ignorance of the local situation is so appalling that it makes my head go round to listen to you and compare your ideas and opinions with the real state of things' (p. 75). The Land Surveyor agrees but with typical bravado declares 'an ignorant man thinks everything possible'. Up to a point this has been true for K. He has had no 'fear of the authorities' through his capacity to conceive of them as individuals in whom Castle authority is invested. But he is mistaken to conclude that these same officials have no authority as such. It is irrelevant where the authority derives, for the fact remains that Castle officials are exercising it.

The Land Surveyor has seen his main task as reaching Klamm and then to advance beyond him 'further yet, into the Castle' (142). It is now becoming evident that the existence of this official cannot be taken for granted. One 'who is so much sought after and so rarely seen is apt to take different shapes in people's imaginations' (p. 223). The incident in the Herrenhof Inn courtyard only heightens the ambiguity. There was no evidence to suggest that the man was even there. If there was a person answering to the name of Klamm this does not mean a thing. The 'real' Klamm could have been elsewhere. Names count for very little indeed. The landlady has already advised K. of the difficulty. She told him that because Klamm used to shout the name 'Frieda' it should not be taken for granted that he was calling for Frieda. He might simply have been shouting the word in an arbitrary fashion. And even if Frieda answered such a call, it did not mean she had actually been called upon by Klamm.

When Erlanger informs K. that she must return to work at the Herrenhof it transpires that neither Erlanger nor anyone else knows if Klamm wants her back. It is the officials themselves who want her to return, for their own 'peace of mind' (p. 331); they are disturbed by the possibility that Klamm *might* be disturbed. Frieda has by this time left K. for one of his assistants. This means he is absolved of a certain responsibility. When he asks her to remain with him he makes it plain that he is not too bothered one way or the other. Thus we are uncertain as to whether he would have been prepared to defy the authorities. But one thing we do know: the Land Surveyor is not the man he was.

There is a conventional view of Kafka's work which presumes it bleak and by implication humourless. It is a misguided view. Kafka can induce the range of emotions. In *The Castle* in particular he brings as much delight to bear on the bumblings of bureaucracy as Gogol or Dickens. That marvellous episode in which K. observes the 'files' being 'distributed' is an exercise in comic invention. Unfortunately for the Land Surveyor, it reveals a decline in him. While watching the procedure with detached amusement he begins to infer the significance of certain details; he finishes by imposing order on chaos. He is committing a cardinal error: no longer is he capable of seeing reality.

Had he witnessed the chaotic scene a week earlier, he would have seen it through 'ignorance' and judged it chaotic, as would any outsider. Gradually he has become less ignorant of the ways of the Castle and has learned to appreciate its protocol. In doing this he concedes its authority. He no longer has the power to recognise reality from its appearance. And he offers a logical explanation for an occurrence that should be regarded as nonsensical, as ridiculous. And that was something Joseph K. managed to resist to the end.

Absurd logics can only really 'work' if people accept supreme sources of authority. The Land Surveyor always has faith in such an entity, right from the moment he paused on the bridge into the Castle grounds. He did not see an 'emptiness'. He saw an 'illusory emptiness' (p. 11). Yet judging by the experiences of Barnabas, had the Land Surveyor succeeded in obtaining entry behind the Castle gates he would have had to face countless other doors and barriers. There has been nothing to suggest the existence of any supreme source.

But K.'s failure to rely on the evidence of his own eyes during the 'file distribution' should not have surprised us too much. This because it follows immediately upon a section where he was incapable of using his own ears.

The fault was not entirely his. In a scene strongly reminiscent of Joseph's meeting with Titorelli in *The Trial*, the Land Surveyor has the misfortune to blunder into the bedroom of a master rhetorician. Burgel is a 'liaison secretary' who can only sleep when villagers are bringing their complaints to him. Let me repeat, Burgel is a 'liaison secretary' who can only sleep when villagers are bringing their complaints to him. But it is 4 a.m. and there is a possibility that K.'s blunder may be advantageous because it is still night and

the secretaries have the following qualms regarding the night interrogations: the night is less suitable for negotiations with applicants for the reason that by night it is difficult or positively impossible completely to observe the official character of the negotiations . . . the allegations of the applicants take on more weight than is due to them, the judgment of the case becomes adulterated with quite irrelevant considerations of the rest of the applicants' situation, their sufferings and anxieties, the necessary barrier between the applicants and the officials, even though externally it may be impeccably maintained, weakens, and where otherwise, as is proper, only questions and answers are exchanged, what sometimes seems to take place is an odd, wholly unsuitable changing of places between the persons. [pp. 318–19.]

The 'liaison secretary's' monologue lasts for about fifteen pages and is quite a remarkable piece of work. During this period he totally demolishes the last remnants of physical endurance the Land Surveyor may have had left in him. The writing itself is full of the repetitions, fractured syntax and wearisome semantics that Burgel employs deliberately to beat down the listener. Coupled with never-ending sentences in which all sight of a principal clause is lost amid a welter of irrelevancies, this ensures the poor Land Surveyor is out of his depth; he does not notice that this 'changing of places' is happening right under his nose. It is his own 'judgment' we see weakened by 'considerations' that should only apply to 'officials' and have nothing to do with 'applicants'. He falls into a doze and eventually leaves through 'a sense of the utter uselessness of staying any longer' (p. 330). In so doing he has missed what might have been his one and only opportunity of slipping in the back door to the Castle.

I mentioned earlier how the villagers saw in him something approaching a symbol of freedom. Paradoxically, freedom has been the one thing of which the Land Surveyor has been in dread. After the débâcle of his attempt to confront Klamm in the snow-covered courtyard, he was full of terrible forebodings, 'as if now in reality he were freer than he had ever been, and . . . there was nothing more senseless [than] this inviolability' (p. 137). In fact he has given here a fair assessment of Amalia's predicament and that of her family. It is worth recalling how quickly he set himself in opposition to Amalia. She had noticed the extent of his commitment to the quest, and treated him contemptuously because of his interest in petty details concerning the Castle. She implies she had thought K. beyond such trifling. ' "On the contrary," said K., ". . . and more-over people who don't care for such gossip and leave it all to others don't interest me particularly" ' (p. 251). His reply is true, but not true insofar as he is suggesting that his motives are altruistic: we already know how self-centred he is.

At the point where their dialogue occurs, the 'naïve' questioner may well be surprised by how strongly the Land Surveyor reacts to Amalia, perhaps still expecting the girl's position to be seen as justified overall. But there is no 'overall'. There is the reality of this Castle's authority and the internal logic of its procedure, but nothing else. And as K. points out to Olga, 'it was himself that Sortini shamed', not Amalia (p. 236). Later he is more criticial of the girl and describes how initially he was 'repelled by . . . her cold hard eye'. Now he knows 'on reflection [that he] can't take Sortini's passion for her very seriously' (p. 252).

In this land where 'work gains the ascendancy' (p. 277), no appeals are made to those unseen universal truths that may allow for equality of the spirit, but not much else. Such entities are never referred to. Within the reality of the Castle, Amalia is guilty. She insulted a messenger. She insulted the individual who carried the message from Sortini.

The Land Surveyor is in favour of 'authority' if it is 'good'. What horrifies him is the abuse of power. He does not question the right to hold such power. He has accepted that peasants are subject to authority. Thus he is placed beyond the 'naïve' questioner who might want to ask why people should be in such a position in the first place.

Yet even by his own criteria there has been nothing to suggest that this particular authority is 'good'. Once again we can see the distinction between Land Surveyor K. and Joseph K. of *The Trial*. The former has revealed his readiness to accept corrupt authority-figures, and that this does not entail the corruption of authority itself. He would have accepted that absurd reasoning of the priest in the Cathedral for whom 'it is not necessary to accept everything as true . . . only as necessary' (p. 243, *The Trial*). From a man who could recognise 'short days' from their appearance, the Land Surveyor has learned to believe that there *has to be* order in chaos.

There is an extraordinary irony in this also; if the Land Surveyor had not been in the corridor in the first place, then the 'file distribution' would have taken place in a reasonably orderly fashion. His presence indicates how disruptive a 'free' man can be. But there again, he has never sought freedom. In a sense he might be said to have exploited even that, the thing Frieda saw in him. He was always wanting admission into the place of authority.

Kafka did not complete the novel as he wanted. His intention had been that the Land Surveyor was to find 'partial satisfaction': the Castle authorities were willing to let him live and work in the village; he was to have been advised of this while about to die 'worn out' by the quest.[10] Such an ending contains a consistency that I think is entirely appropriate to the ending we have. K.'s gradual awareness of the subtleties of Castle protocol has been accompanied by an increasing respect for its figures of authority. And there is no question that the Castle bureaucrats are extremely capable workers, as Burgel demonstrated so well. K. is only one individual, the task he set himself proved mammoth.

In his biography of the author, Max Brod tells of a letter he received in which Kafka quoted at length from Kierkegaard:

As soon as a man appears who brings something of the primitive along with him, so that he doesn't say, 'You must take the world as you find it,' but rather, 'Let the world be what it likes, I take my stand on a primitiveness which I have no intention of changing to meet with the approval of the world,' at that moment, as these words are heard, a metamorphosis takes place in the whole of nature. Just as in a fairy story, when the right word is pronounced, the Castle that has been lying under a spell for a hundred years opens and everything comes to life. [p. 171.]

If the Land Surveyor began his quest in the manner of such a man, it was no guarantee of success. It is not so much that *The Castle* is not a fairy story, just that it contains a different reality. In the situation confronted by K. the 'primitive' strength of one solitary individual might never have been enough. Yet he did believe he could make it on his own. And while he also believed that no man had to be subject to the authority of another, he seems to have assumed that *all* men have to be subject to something, and this something may be divorced from men. Oddly enough, the rest of the peasantry never bothered about drawing such fine distinctions. Like the townsfolk in Dostoevski's fifteenth-century Spain, they were content to remain subject to the authority-figures alone,[11] never mind whence their authority derives.

As with *The Trial,* an optimistic note can be discerned. The Land Surveyor appeared a free man but it was an effect of his ignorance. The more he became educated in the workings of the Castle, the less able was he to see reality. In one sense this is cause for pessimism, but only if ignorance is a valid goal in life. During his painful encounter with Burgel, the Land Surveyor was told to

> pay attention, there are sometimes after all opportunities that are almost not in accord with the general situation, opportunities in which by means of a word, a glance, a sign of trust, more can be achieved than by means of lifelong exhausting efforts. [p. 317.]

At this stage K. had almost passed into unconsciousness through exhaustion, so perhaps he could not take in the advice being offered. We readers can read the reality and judge for ourselves.

It could be argued that 'overall' he was correct to be wary of the 'inviolability' of Amalia, such inviolability resembles that of a leper. Through no fault of her own she found herself in a situation which might not have occurred had her family been other than peasants. But she has also refused to help her family except by attending to the immediate physical needs of her parents. She could be said to have rejected life itself because of her pride, which is never a good thing to do in Kafka's fiction. She is more than willing to 'leave it all to others' just as K. said. Olga is different, possibly the nearest we have to a heroic character in the novel; this in her basic instinct not to accept reality but to see it and confront it.[12] She does her utmost to secure the survival of her family in the most practical way she can.

If K. has lost much of his 'primitiveness', he has at least retained some capacity for recognising aspects of reality. Through listening to Olga he has to face the fact that Barnabas is not an official messenger, just a youth trying to act like one in the hope that he might eventually be so accepted. K.'s hopes have been completely misplaced, yet he would not

> forget Olga either, for still more important to him than the messages themselves was Olga, her bravery, her prudence, if he had to choose between Olga and Amalia it wouldn't cost him much reflection. And he pressed her hand cordially once more as he swung himself on to the wall of the neighbouring garden. [p. 283.]

The qualities he sees in the girl are those of 'a good [person] . . . someone who sympathized . . . someone who wanted to help' (*The Trial*, p. 250). He is seeing Olga for what she is, as one human being, not as a person whose value is determined by her link to the Castle. If the Land Surveyor was really involved in a quest for 'good' and not just a 'good authority' then perhaps Olga has shown that 'more can be achieved' by her means than by other kinds 'of lifelong exhausting efforts'.

Endword

I have avoided becoming involved in Kafka's life in this essay, in particular his relationship with his family. For an understanding of his work I do not believe a knowledge of his life is necessary. I think it is worthwhile and important but to regard it as necessary I think is presumptuous. At the same time our awareness of certain aspects of his life may stop us from further presumption.

I have been arguing that one essential aspect of his work, as it occurs within the three novels, is the conflict between 'mere' individuals and authority; his preoccupation with messages and messengers is a crucial element of this. Kafka read philosophy and was influenced by Søren Kierkegaard but his fictional characters seem unacquainted with any of that and none reveals faith in spiritual transcendence. Within the texts I find nothing to suggest the existence of any source of 'supreme authority', e.g. God, gods or a god; the opposite is more likely, that nothing exists outside of mankind itself. The Land Surveyor came closest to holding such a belief insofar as his quest implied a power beyond that of ordinary men and women. Perhaps such a power did exist but if so it was confined behind the Castle doors, and they never opened for him. Eventually, when his quest had failed, he was revealed to have begun in ignorance.

At the end of both *The Trial* and *The Castle* Joseph K. and the Land Surveyor K. have developed awareness of the value of other individuals. Readers who regard the author's work as bleak and pessimistic perhaps are guilty of bringing their own prejudices to bear. Maybe they think human beings would be in a terrible state if they were not being guided around by external agencies of a benign nature.

A Marxist criticism could develop from Kafka's 'failure' to offer any transcendence through the considered actions of a community of individuals: the state, for example. This can be answered. Kafka's central characters are in conflict with any authority which seeks to impose itself on individuals by appealing to necessity in the face of what cannot be recognised as true. It makes no difference if the source of the authority is religious or not.

Yet to regard his work as a doctrine of pure relativism would be a mistake; and it is, in my opinion, another mistake to see his 'place' in the modernist tradition. In Kafka's work reality *can* be posited; it can remain 'unseen' or it can be 'ignored' – and Karl Rossmann, Joseph K. and the Land Surveyor are guilty of doing both – but, in spite of the wishes or dreams of the central characters, it can be posited. Marxist critics should simply read the work and find the reality. Kafka read Hegel, and he read Bakunin, Belinsky, Herzen and Kropotkin.

The distinction between relativism and existentialism may blur at times but the distinction remains all the same. The author's 'place' in literary terms is within the existential tradition and his formal development offers the evidence of this. He posits a synthesis: the individual's perception of reality and reality 'in itself', transcended by the world in which Franz Kafka created literary art, and the most concrete example is *The Trial*. The possibility was suggested decades earlier in James Hogg's *Confessions of a Justified Sinner* and was an implication of the existential tradition in literature as it progressed in Europe.

Kafka's achievement is possible to underestimate because of its deceptively simple style. Simplicity had to be the method. In order to present a reality 'in itself', language had to be pared of value to as great an extent as possible; this in the knowledge that what was left had to be readable would have been reasonable grounds for despondency in any writer. As the *Diaries* illustrate, his belief in his work fluctuated between despair and great elation. Finally Franz Kafka left instructions that in the event of his death all of his unpublished writings were to be destroyed. His executor waived the instructions, and gradually the writings – including the three novels – were published.

It was a complicated affair. That Max Brod happens to have been the author's closest friend made it the more so. They had known each other close to twenty-five years, since they were about nineteen years old, which is not to say everything was always fine between them.[1] A few options were available. If Brod decided to perform the 'role' of executor on behalf of the 'testator' (i.e. Kafka) then he was obliged to destroy the manuscripts, this because he had accepted the 'role', and presumably its obligations. If he decided to act strictly as a friend the manuscripts might yet have been destroyed, for the demands of friendship carry their own authority and Franz had given his instructions. On the other hand, Max could have decided against destroying them and still felt he was acting out of friendship. As a further complication, he was also a writer and, in the best interests of literature, could have decided his 'real duty' was to preserve his colleague's work. At the same time, still acting strictly as a colleague, he might have gone ahead and destroyed the manuscripts after all because individual writers know best where their own work is concerned.

Whether Franz would have been content with the outcome can never be answered. More secondary works have now been written about him than any other writer aside from Shakespeare and Goethe. Maybe that would have baffled him. Yet it seems safe to say that the irony of the affair would have amused him. It contains the elements of a fine 'messages and messengers' interlude. When Edwin Muir refers to Kafka's central characters as 'not mere individuals' he meant it as a compliment but he was expressing a view of life Kafka would have found abhorrent. Although the outcome of his old friend Max Brod's judgment is not certain to have pleased him, perhaps Kafka would have been satisfied that one solitary individual was prepared to face a variety of 'authorities' and, for better or worse, arrive at his own decision.

BIBLIOGRAPHY

Franz Kafka: *Amerika, The Trial, Metamorphosis and Other Stories, Wedding Preparations in the Country and Other Stories* (all translated by Willa and Edwin Muir). The editions I used are in the Penguin Modern Classics series. For *The Castle* I used the Secker & Warburg 1953 edition, with its additional material as translated by Eithne Wilkins and Ernst Kaiser.

Edited by Max Brod: *The Diaries of Franz Kafka* (Penguin Modern Classic, 1972).

Anders, Gunther: *Kafka* (Bowes & Bowes, 1960).

Brod, Max: *Franz Kafka* (Schocken Books, New York, 1960).

Flores, Angel (ed.): *The Kafka Debate: New Perspectives for Our Time* (Gordian Press, New York, 1979).

Politzer, Heinz: *Franz Kafka: Parable and Paradox* (Ithaca, 1962).

The three essays of Georg Lukàcs can be found in *Marxists on Literature* (edited by David Craig for Pelican Books, 1977) and in *20th Century Literary Criticism* (edited by David Lodge for Longman, 1972).

The essays by Kierkegaard I read towards this essay can be found in *Existentialism from Dostoevsky to Sartre* (edited by Walter Kaufmann, New American Library, Meridian Books, 1975).

Social Diversity and the
New Literary Order

EQUALITY IS THE very essence of democracy and as it applies in the greater society so too must it apply within our artistic and cultural communities. None should expect favour as of right, whether God-given, ideological or otherwise. These are fundamental principles. Who would gainsay them? We have not yet reached a stage where the sanctity of individual human life is itself called into question, where in order to be adjudged worthy of imagined existence a character must eke out an existence on the inner city streets, afflicted by HIV syndrome. We have no personal axes to grind at the perpetual aggrandisement of those bereft of economic opportunity, an increasing minority of whom, in an urban setting, are forced to resort to crime, drugs and drunkenness that they may the better cope with the exigencies of the new millennium.

Every area of Scotland's culture exists to be celebrated. Whether that area is a recent cultural phenomenon or as tried and tested as the Standing Stones of Orkney is of little significance to us. It is doubtless amusing to some of our more radical 'voices' when they hear a few timid souls call for 'the great Morningside novel' or 'the great Kelvinside epic poem'. Yet however fanciful we might find the idea, at base the concept is legitimate, given that the citizens of both these urban environments are deemed unworthy of aesthetic consideration by our fashionable 'realists' since, it would appear, they do not experience social deprivation. Yet even were this the case, surely no true Scots man nor woman ever was ashamed of any aspect of our society. None among us would set store by the 'tartan and haggis' ethic these days but that is a far cry from advocating its exclusion from the cultural arena. It is proper for any society that its various communities are imaginatively represented by its artistic practitioners. It is also proper that the artefacts produced by its creative people are available for general consumption, both at home and overseas. But a healthy market is diverse in nature and the producers of these artefacts should not remain uncognisant of what is, arguably, undeniable.

Presently, the imaginative manifestation of one area of Scottish society, that of the urban under-classes, is being accorded much literary attention. It is no small source of local pride that, for some of these writings, this value is placed from beyond our borders. At the same time it would be unwise if we as a nation – and we are a nation, whether within or without the United Kingdom is of little consequence to all but the politically pedantic – were disinclined to adopt a self-critical approach. It is never an act of disloyalty to pose the awkward question when and where that question requires to be posed, no matter that those to whom it is posed are our own compatriots. Self-appraisal is the signal of intellectual maturity.

It is to the credit of many of our home-based literary critics that they subject their own field of endeavour to the most stringent scrutiny with great relish and enthusiasm. Indeed the view is now being expressed that our contemporary literature is perhaps in a less healthy state than conventional wisdom would have us believe, given the occasional clamour from excitable foreign sources. They argue that there is nothing *inherently* wrong with much if not most of the 'school of urban realism'; and clearly questions of this form belong to another context. Their concern is that the current preoccupation with this one community is in danger of presenting an imbalanced picture not only of our national literature but of the larger Scottish culture. This branch of our literature (for it is certainly that), initially Glasgow-based, has spread eastwards and further north. Nowadays one confronts it as a matter of course in most every contemporary literary magazine or anthology one cares to peruse. We have a fair sprinkling of it within the libraries of certain of our more up-to-date, not to say fashionable, senior schools, as well as those of our broadly based universities and higher-education colleges. It is fitting that this should be so. The danger would arise from a disproportionate time being spent on its perusal; our students have these days a demanding academic syllabus.

It is important that each and every area of our richly diverse Scottish society is encouraged to explore itself artistically. It is equally important that we acknowledge the inherent right of each and every area to that artistic exploration. No single social arena has a claim greater than another.

Much of our country is rural. Very many of our people earn their crust far from the madding thunder of city traffic, whether by farming the land or the seas surrounding our rugged coastline. Those areas of our contemporary Scottish society are every bit as ordinary (or extraordinary) as those pertaining to the urban under-classes; they are of equal social and cultural merit. None among us would argue that areas of society might exist that are deserving of greater value than the indigenous under-privileged. Yet in the larger literary context might we not look for the poem devoted to the Hebridean shepherd, the dramatisation of the Minch fisherman whose life is daily at risk?

There is little question that for the under-classes urban existence is less than easy, often harrowingly so. Elsewhere it is equally tough, perhaps tougher. These things are relative. Clearly our new-found neighbours from overseas would not have arrived seeking

337

sanctuary if life, formerly, had been easy. It is time to examine more closely what constitutes a healthy, not to say egalitarian, literary culture as fully reflective of the reality of Scottish life. It is not inconceivable that a more balanced approach would better enable a national literature that might reflect the deep-rooted vitality of Scottish culture as a whole.

None would recommend, reasonably, that our creative literary artists should consider extending their range of social experience. But is it not the case that all persons at liberty in this country have one contact or another with individuals of a differing social order? Who has not stood in the queue at the local supermarket and marvelled at the breadth of its cultural diversity, reminiscent of the communal plurality of the old-town tenement in eighteenth-century Edinburgh. Here too was the then unfashionable 'urban setting' yet did not Sir Walter succeed in exploring its every social dimension? Two hundred years on we are at a loss to find such unexceptional riches within the pages of our dour but contemporary littérateurs. Is it not a peculiar phenomenon? In any society in any of the world's continents we will distinguish economic difference. At the same time we will distinguish an exciting variety of other social features. Even our well-publicised, homeless young people are forced to consult a doctor or dentist, perhaps visit a headmaster's study or be called in front of an examining magistrate. Must this fact of societal experience slip through unacknowledged by our new literary realists?

Neither is it a mark of disloyalty to our currently fashionable authors if we remark that a youthful friend (a very bright post-graduate student whose larger family resides in an outer-city housing-scheme) has advised us that 'people don't live that way at all, and they don't swear all the time either'. He and his young colleagues are of the opinion that a preponderance of poetry and prose fiction features the imagined lives of an indigenous underclass that exists in a form of rarefied urban limbo, what a few of our more adventurous home-grown critics have perceived as 'a cultural vaccum'. The question of language and veracity we shall hold for a later date. At present we are inclined merely to wonder if the creative products pertaining to this one particular social area are in fact truly representative even of themselves.

Yet if it is true that people do not exist if they do not exist imaginatively, then Scottish society as a whole is in danger of being rendered null and void or, at best, absent. Oddly, we do have writers who strive to operate from a broader cultural church. This more fulsome branch of our contemporary creative writings is, however, something of a literary secret. Within its pages we encounter sundry social strata; we eavesdrop on the private conversations of diplomats, men and women of the world; we journey on the trampships of South-East Asia, peruse the natives of exotic sub-tropical villages, the pin-striped denizens of London's Canary Wharf; we share the urban bohemias of the Parisian artist, the New York jazz musician, the Berlin cabaret performer. For our part, the mystery of literary fashion remains for ever obscure, surrounded as we are by the new literary order, our 'school of urban sameness'.

Throughout the years we have strived to maintain an open-door policy to afflicted overseas communities; one thinks of the Irish, the Polish, the various Russians, the Jews, the Romanians, the Bosnians and so forth. Of course this has not been one-way traffic. Those who would argue for tighter controls may have the material argument on their side but let them visit our craggy coastal regions where innumerable ruined cottages exist to haunt the national psyche, bearing witness to the tragic but historically fated upheavals of the past three or more hundred years. Let us never forget that a minority of our own Scottish people has endured past suffering, past hardship. They too travelled the world in search of greater opportunity, for themselves and their families. In a majority of instances they earned their right to be there by working twice as hard as the majority of their indigenous brethren (who would take issue with the Andrew Carnegies of the world?). Not only did they integrate successfully within their new-found business communities; frequently, by dint of hard-won study, they took leading positions within their respective intellectual circles, whether artistic or academic.

Every Scottish schoolchild is doubtless instructed by our generally hardworking, modern-day teachers, that for several centuries our thinkers and scholars have sojourned from Paris to Rome, from Vienna to St Petersburg and beyond. Those thinkers and scholars were skilled in many languages, and tested these skills in appropriate writings. That cosmopolitan bent of the Scottish democratic intellect – much prized – has been a primary commodity of our larger society, and may it continue to be so. On occasion those early itinerant intellectuals, our forebears, were content to publish abroad if the need arose; just as in the present day not a few of the current crop have made as their publishing base the Southern Counties of England. This has been an effect of natural constraints rather than ideologies and may be regarded as an additional source for pride.

Yet it remains an unfortunate consequence that beyond our own border there is a growing fear that the present fashion will come to be viewed by foreign clients as representational. In the wider overseas arena the Scottish people are in danger of being perceived as one homogenous mass, what the politically incorrect of our grandfathers' day would have termed (erroneously, in our opinion) 'the great unwashed'.

These are controversial matters. It is not expedient to discuss the natural influences of one's personal background in the present social climate. It may well be to the benefit of the majority that a few traditions of our old people are held to have been prejudicial; they now lie in disrepute. None would counter this, seriously, as a good thing. Yet it is scarcely the fault of individual human beings, and literary practitioners cannot be exempted, that they chance to be born in one economic, geographic or – dare we say it – linguistic setting, as opposed to any other.

Or is a writer's merit to be evaluated in relation to the circumstance of birth? Must the value we wish to place on a writer's literary output become a function of our own ideologically based opinions of the social influences experienced by that writer *a priori*? What price the sense of starry-eyed wonder of the highland-born lad or lass endeavouring to perfect the intricacies of Latin declensions in order that he or she may gain entry to his or her chosen profession? Is such a life to be deemed an unfit subject for general literary consumption? Must the trials and tribulations of the Inverness-born chartered accountant or, for that matter, the Perth businessman, be hidden from imaginative existence?

None of us is ashamed of our own family background which, in many instances, was as down-to-earth, not to say 'working-class', as that of any stalwart of the new literary order. Through the good offices of our parents and schoolteachers we were encouraged to keep a free and unfettered mind. By virtue of one tiny piece of ink-smudged cardboard we gained access to the wider universe: a junior ticket to our local public library; freely given, gratefully received. No silver spoon was necessary. Like countless ill-clad boys before us, we unsparingly exploited this traditional channel of the Scottish democratic intellect. We were enabled both to comprehend and to come to love the mysteries of that vaster global culture, feasting our imaginations on the glorious exotica of humankind. Here lay riches beyond our childish dreams, beyond the stunted vision of our local parish leaders. We were granted access to an empire of untapped wealth and resources, resources of a quite startling diversity, yet a diversity that neither precluded nor negated its ultimate totality.

Here lay true equality. We experienced a multiplicity of cultural influence. We were not glued to the gin-sodden back alley of the intellect. Our boyish instincts knew no boundaries, fired by the pioneering spirit of the Martin Rattlers, the Jim Hawkinses, the Prester Johns. Yet too was the heightened sensitivity of our youthful manhood counterbalanced by the fierce but meditative passion of the young Keats or Byron, now aroused by the sonnets of William Shakespeare, becalmed by the wisdom of a John Milton. Later we came to know and respect the literary products of our own countrymen, the Henrysons, the Dunbars and others of that ilk, down to such as Burns or MacDiarmid. These were unfettered and majestic imaginations, internationalists all, yet Scottish to the very marrow of their being.

There is no political ideology being espoused from this quarter, for these are uncertain times, yet there exists an underlying danger lurking in the paucity of social experience reflected within our new literary order. It is the evil of cultural insularity, that tarted handmaiden of xenophobes the world over.

Large numbers of people of diverse racial and cultural origins have settled in Scotland, the overwhelming majority of whom have set up home in urban districts. We are by no means alone in expressing pride that they should have chosen our country as their destination, temporary or otherwise. We further propose that the cultural artefacts produced by our immigrant communities be encouraged. It would be churlish to seek otherwise. Our new neighbours will learn to create their own products. These are exotic influences and can act towards the integrated growth of the Scottish body politic. We may go further: it is our humane duty to encourage these endeavours. We look forward with interest to seeing how this will be reflected within the pages of our national literature.

Yet no matter how worthy of encouragement a particular area of our larger Scottish society appears to be, it will be deemed an error if it were so encouraged to the detriment of another; nor yet if it should undermine, and possibly exclude, one or more of its fellow cultural areas. At the same time it should be ensured that our larger society, in all its indigenous heterogeneity, is accorded an equal cultural value. Indeed the logicians among us might favour a greater cultural value, it being an obvious point that, while without the latter the former could not exist, the converse, strictly speaking, cannot apply: parts are never greater than a whole.

Contemporary Scottish literature has arrived on a plateau. Our critics and creative writers can remain at a standstill or, if they so choose, scale further imaginative peaks. It would seem to us an error were we to return to a time when the under-classes did not make their presence felt within our literature. Indeed, ample inventive energy has been expended on espousing the validity of this very argument; it is nowadays accepted, freely, that the literary presence of these people is warranted. None would propose that the battle was unwarranted. It is more difficult to sustain an argument for its continuation. The old school has thrown up its hands in surrender. Our exponents of the new literary order may rest assured that the niche they have carved for themselves is not under threat.

But now is the time to move forward. Our compatriots are charged to consider the position maturely. If the creative burden is too onerous then the future of Scottish literature is itself under threat.

Militarism and the City

It is important that we monitor and try to resist the ways in which control is exercised on urban populations, including the introduction of video cameras on the streets, another attack on the public; but maybe it is a mistake to lay too heavy an emphasis on the distinction between city and State, given that draconian measures are often sneaked in via local bylaws, e.g. the notorious Glasgow curfews or the criminalisation of people who are partial to a drink out-of-doors, the assorted attempts to criminalise even more groups of young people. The Labour Party is of course the majority political holding in Scotland, including its control of local Government in Glasgow and the rest of the central belt. It would be good if the left began monitoring the work the Labour Party does in local Government on behalf of the State in the implementation of these and other domestic security measures. Maybe some of this monitoring is already happening and such information will be made available to the general public

The British State has increased both its attacks and the violence of its attacks on its own citizens over the past few years. It is quite remarkable what they have achieved since the 1970s. Coupled with the capitulation of the orthodox left – the mainstream Labour movement – tens of thousands of people are now stranded, people who would want to offer some resistance to what is happening;

many seem overwhelmed by the sheer scale of the assault. There is no need to enumerate these attacks, they range across the spectrum.

When a State steps up its domestic terrorist activities, usually it also attempts to instil fear and panic within the population at large. This is done in at least two ways, (1) by conjuring up evil foreign tyrants and evil foreign empires (e.g. Gaddafi, Saddam Hussein, the Soviet Union, Arab peoples, Muslim peoples). And (2) by conjuring up evil forces on our own doorstep; preferably 'infiltrators', ranging from any foreigner, immigrants, asylum-seekers, through sleeper-members of the IRA; but not only infiltrators; 'anti-social elements' such as 'aggressive beggars', 'street-drinkers', 'rowdy teenagers', truanting schoolchildren, prostitutes, 'drug addicts', homeless people, etc.

The first way the State instils fear in its domestic population – the existence of malevolent foreigners – offers signal benefits to the armed forces and security services, also the munitions and defence industries (one of our strongest exports is instruments of torture to despotic regimes). The second way the State instils fear is, like I say, on the domestic front itself – the malevolent ones are lurking right on our own doorstep – and an immediate result of this is greater power and resources given to punitive institutions and agencies such as the police and prison authorities, the immigration department, judiciary, the DSS and the other internal security organisations.

The concept 'civic identity' is used in a similar manner to the State's manipulation of the concept of patriotism in times of war. It serves to 'unite the people' as a front against 'the alien'.

It is all fairly obvious once you think about it. The interesting part is how our politicians and media as a rule manage to avoid reference to these outrageous attacks on civil liberty and freedom. People generally are becoming more aware of how the west, led by the USA, has used these different methods of control over the past decades; some have been documented and clarified by Noam Chomsky, Philip Agee, Howard Zinn, Edward S. Herman and others.

Language is a crucial tool of State. At the same time as the US-led western powers have conducted their own imperialist terrorist activities, they shift the blame on to the victims, and one aspect of this has been to name the victims as 'terrorists' and themselves as 'defenders', and meanwhile name the indigenous populations as 'aggressors'. Even when thousands of US-led troops conduct their wars on foreign soils, still they describe themselves as 'defenders' while the indigenous soldiers get described as 'terrorists'.

Here in Britain the State is quite ruthless, prepared to do most anything to maintain its authority. It both victimises and criminalises different communities: workers, immigrants, beggars, refugees; black people, young people, gay people; unemployed people, football supporters; people who go to raves or else just like to stay up enjoying themselves after midnight; then of course sick people, people suffering and dying of industrial or environmental disease; single parents, elderly people. These and other groups and communities are among those victimised and/or criminalised by the State, and of course if need be the State has the machinery by which it kills or causes the death of its own citizens. I am not saying anything new; most people here are aware of all this.

When these acts of domestic terrorism, often described as 'political measures', are being carried out by a State it is only with difficulty we can call it democratic. However, in this country, within mainstream intellectual circles, you find it assumed that the system we have is democratic. Maybe it would be fair enough if the people in these circles were content to call Britain a Greek democracy; I mean by that a State where a form of democracy operates within the ruling élite.

Personally I am not bothered about whether or not we can call the British State a democracy. Maybe it is and maybe it isn't. The fact remains that a great many sections of the people are under attack and whether or not we describe these attacks as anti-democratic is irrelevant. But maybe if we carry on stating the obvious – that these attacks are anti-democratic – then we are playing into the hands of the powers-that-be.

In other words, if it is enough for you to argue that the domestic terrorism being carried out by the State is anti-democratic then why not just contact your local MP and ask him or her to 'represent' the question for you at Whitehall. The politicians will be happy to take on such a chore because it is the kind of semantic nonsense that our political system exists to exploit.

You can imagine a left-wing MP at Westminster (or is this a contradiction in terms?) being invited by The Speaker to stand up and make his or her point. Yessir Mister Speaker, sir (or madam), the measures being carried out by the British State are anti-democratic!

It is doubtful if there would be any gales of laughter even from the Opposition benches. They would just look at each other.

Racism and the Maastricht Treaty

I HAVE NOT studied the Maastricht Treaty, nor have I taken part in any debates on the matter, although I doubt that I am alone in that. When decisions of crucial national interest are taken by the State the news breaks to the general population in one way or another and the outcome is meaningless hogwash, a public-relations exercise. In cases like the ratification of the Maastricht Treaty, a variety of 'experts' appear on television and radio discussing the decision, giving arguments for and against. But such discussions are meaningless, the 'expert debate' occurs publicly but does not involve the public. It is one of the current methods that allow us to think we live in a genuine democracy. Since the 'discussion' takes place within the media it is in front of the general public and is then said to be 'taking place in public'. An impression is gained that the arguments that took place in strict privacy between influential individuals within the State are the same arguments that would have occurred among the general public had they been allowed entry.

Perhaps the most dangerous tendency in Scotland, as elsewhere in Europe, is the rise of racism and racist violation. We should be clear that racist violation is not the violent outcome of a 'struggle between the races'. Has such 'racial' struggle ever existed? The concept 'race' is so ill-defined that beyond trivial lines of argument it becomes almost worthless. The violation is, and almost always

Racism and the Maastricht Treaty

has been, directed by white people against black people. Where violence occurs the other way round it takes the form of self-defence (often in response to police or other State brutality). Unprovoked, arbitrary brutality from black to white is so exceptional in this country that it is difficult to give examples. What we can predict is that if such violence does occur then the news will be broadcast from Land's End to John o' Groats.

Yet from across Europe (including Scotland) there are attested daily reports of savage crimes, including murder, being perpetrated by white people against black people. At the same time State forces of law and order show themselves unwilling to defend – or incapable of defending – the victims. The crimes are suppressed; distorted, misrepresented, not reported or not recorded. The mainstream media and educational systems simply pump out propaganda and disinformation.

The grim reality of what it is to be a black person in Europe (including Scotland) is not something the authorities wish to see broadcast. If this did happen black people would be seen as victims and this does not fit in with State policy. Instead black people are to be recognised as 'the problem', they are criminalised, shown as the anti-social elements, the violators, the perpetrators of crime and various abuses. Thus over the years there have been general anti-social or criminal charges levelled against the black communities, so much so that certain crimes have been seen as 'black', e.g. drug dealing, mugging, living off prostitution; social security scrounging and petty fraud, tax evasion; exploiting labour by forcing children and others to work long hours for 'slave-wages'; rent-racketeering, etc. And when black people are murdered by white racists, i.e. when people are murdered for no other reason than the colour of their skin, they are thought to be somehow resonsible for 'bringing it on themself'. Their colour is 'the problem'. They become the cause of the violation being perpetrated against them.

The one so-called 'crime' that the European State authorities want to lay upon black people is 'terrorism'. The grounds are already prepared for this.

The actual *right* to self-defence has never existed; it must always be contested, not just domestically, as in Glasgow when Scottish–Asian youths were condemned by the authorities for 'attacking their attackers', i.e. defending themselves, or as happened in England ten years ago with the so-called Bradford Twelve – that right must also be fought for internationally. So we have the brutal immigration laws and the horrific restrictions placed on asylum-seekers. It has reached the stage where people do not have the right to get out of the firing line. On the home front, black youths who fight back are transformed into the aggressors. Abroad, the fact that a mercenary army enters your country, executes the Government, and starts killing everybody in sight is no longer a justifiable cause to grab your children and run.

There is a general point and it is nothing new: victims are not allowed to be victims; instead they are victimised or otherwise stigmatised, until the point is reached where the concept 'victim' loses its meaning and we have difficulty in stating to whom or what the term refers. Obviously the USA and its client states (e.g. Israel, Turkey, the UK) prefer that the people on the receiving end of official foreign policy are not seen as the victims of horrific, inhuman brutality. So they suppress the information. The mercenary army gets transformed into a local liberation front (the Contras, UNITA, Renamo, etc.) and the people fighting for liberation become 'terrorists' (PLO, ANC, PKK) or else we wind up with a 'civil war'.

But that systematic transformation of language and reference is crucial. A brief look at the recent history of concepts like 'torture', 'human rights', 'freedom' and 'terrorism' is illuminating. The ratification of the Maastricht Treaty clears the path for the State doctrine that victims do not exist. No doubt 'Victims; the Concept' will be formulated as a new field of endeavour within universities, and many academics will forge ahead; the first couple of decades will be spent discussing the concept, then generations of students will have excited boozy arguments down the pub about whether or not there exist grounds that allow of the proposition 'victims are existent human entities'.

If we want to get beyond the official version we must take into account the machinations within the power bases of the right during the past twenty-five or so years. A great deal has come to light on this and related aspects, including the covert policies of the USA and its client states. Much of it has been distorted or marginalised, as in the case of the writings and analyses of western commentators such as Noam Chomsky, Edward S. Herman, Peter Dale Scott, Philip Agee and others. On the other hand, apologists and theorists of the far right are employed and empowered by State authorities. Their writings are reviewed and given prominence, turned into seminal manuals for the use of the police and the military everywhere, e.g. propagandists like Yonah Alexander and Paul Wilkinson, Sterling, Clutterbuck, Crozier, Kirkpatrick, etc. Their opinions and value-judgments appear on television and radio, and feature in newspapers and journals in one guise or another.

The right has manipulated the concept 'terrorism' in a striking way, strengthening the domestic-control industry quite markedly. The situations in Northern Ireland, the Middle East, Africa and Central America have been of prime importance. Again it is back to the fact that the right to self-defence no longer exists, nor do the grounds for national liberation. Nowadays anyone is a 'terrorist' who seeks to overthrow State authority – any State authority, no matter how illegitimate, barbarous or murderous it might be. 'Terrorists' engage in 'terrorism' for its own sake. The primary purpose of 'the terrorist' is the creation of 'terrorism'.

It is no coincidence that the expressed concerns of European State authority are immigration, terrorism and drugs. This has been the central focus of right-wing apologists and theorists for years past. Black people in Europe are not victims but potential terrorists, every last one of them. The international controls curtailing freedom of movement render this official. Once this is accepted generally and has become the conventional wisdom of the European public, the next stage is the systematic imposition of greater domestic controls. It has already started. What follows is the tightening of the net, the widening of those international and domestic controls, bringing in other 'potential terrorists': political activists, trade-unionists, 'known dissidents', unemployed migrant workers; in fact anybody at all who tries to fight back, or is thought to have the potential for so doing.

Some people on the left appear to take a sort of pro-Maastricht line. The reasons for this, as far as I can see, are to do with an anti-xenophobic breaking down of boundaries and barriers, greater freedom of movement, establishing solidarity networks and so on, with a view to the interests of humanity in general. But it is absurd to think that such stuff was anything to do with the original State decision.

The establishment makes much of the fact that the parliamentary right and left are aligned in opposition to the Treaty. This juxta-position is designed to ridicule and subvert ALL opposition as either 'extremist' (Norman Tebbit v. Tony Benn) or 'opportunist' (the Labour Party as a whole). It is pointless becoming inveigled in the politics of the right, whether the authoritarians are giving way to the libertarians or whatever. It is also pointless to discuss whether or not Tony Benn is a member of the left (as opposed to the Labour Party left, which is something else entirely). The State is in control and will use whatever means it must to keep it that way. Where possible it prefers to be seen as 'moderate'. The so-called alignment of the so-called 'extremist' right and left factions allows this.

If the British State wants something then this something is not in the interests of the general public. And by rule of thumb the general public should therefore assume an oppositional role. The something is always pushed in 'the national interest' but there is no such thing as 'the national interest'. On this occasion there seems a split within the party of Government but since the 'rebels' are not in power we must assume that the desire of the State currently is being expressed by John Major's frontbench.

John Major's statements last June left little to the imagination and there is little point in trotting them out here. It should be enough to say that, in justification of his proposals to curb 'the flood of illegal immigrants', Major said: 'if we fail in our control efforts we risk fuelling the far right'. Of course, instead of 'fuelling the far right', our Prime Minister is appeasing them. Immediately he had finished his speech in Luxembourg last June, who was the first group to give him the firmest backing? What formation in the whole of the United Kingdom was the first to wire him with its warmest greetings? Who else but the Monday Club.

It is worth reminding people here today about the kind of Government that is supposed to be representing us, the various populations of England, Wales, Scotland and the North of Ireland:

a memo leaked in late September . . . revealed proposals from ministers Michael Heseltine and David Mellor at a secret ministerial meeting on asylum that Britain withdraw altogether from the 1951 Geneva Convention, from which international obligations toward refugees are derived, and which 103 countries have signed . . . The Foreign Office proposal, as an alternative 'solution', was to send all asylum-seekers back to 'international camps' or 'safe havens' in their countries of origin, in which claims could be assessed.

I have quoted this from the journal *Statewatch*. The proposal came from Her Majesty's Government in full knowledge of the mass murder that has taken place in so-called 'international camps' and 'safe havens' from Beirut to Turkey. And Her Majesty's Minister, Mr Michael Heseltine's justification for the secret ministerial meeting was the 'pressure on housing' created by refugees.

This is not irresponsible, it is merely an example of the British State at its most ruthless; and questions to do with morality are irrelevant, it is just a kind of functional barbarism. How can you argue morality in such a context? Every government has duties and responsibilities; to whom it is responsible is the only practical question. And a quick look at the way the British State treats its own people supplies an answer, whether we examine the workings of domestic law enforcement, the immigration service or the Department of Social Security. We need quite a hefty pair of blinkers to suggest that Her Majesty's Government sees its primary duty lying in service to the citizens of the country. And if it does not, then at least we can define the question of responsibility in a negative way, we know to whom the British Government is not responsible: the vast majority of the British population.

Of course some might say – and I am thinking here of certain groupings, e.g. the permanent State, the secret service and the armies and the domestic security forces, polis and shit, prison wardens, civil servants, blah blah blah, all of that kind of thing – that their primary duty is to the Queen or whoever the first monarch happens to be at any particular time; the citizens do not come into it, not even officially.

A word here about the Monday Club, the ones who gave Prime Minister John Major their warmest applause. Apparently this was not the old Monday Club which sections of the media ask us to regard as cuddly and lovable in the style of a crabbit old uncle who has secretly got a heart of gold. This was the new, so-called 'hardline' Monday Club. The old cuddly and lovable one was formed thirty years ago to oppose 'the dismantling of the British Empire', and was strongly 'stimulated by Enoch Powell's rivers of blood speech' in the late 1960s. Those in control presently are linked directly to the authoritarian group known as Western Goals (UK), 'a London-based right-wing organisation devoted to the preservation of traditional Western values and European culture, and it opposes communism, liberalism, internationalism and the "multi-cultural society"' (*Observer*, 24 February 1991). Of its many cuddly patrons, one name to note is Roberto D'Aubisson, leader of the El Salvador death squads.

Western Goals has close links with the Front National in France, now 'demanding the establishment of "jus sanguinis", the law of blood, or nationality through parentage and not birth on French soil.' The French Front 'plan to re-examine all naturalisations of foreigners pronounced since 1974.' Western Goals (UK) is also linked to the Republikaner Partei in Germany, and various other racially pure European beings, right from Johannesburg to Washington DC. They have 'contacts with right wing forces in Namibia, Angola and Mozambique' and of course South Africa itself. 'In 1988 [they] helped organise a visit to Britain by Joseph Savimbi of the Angolan UNITA, and held a briefing with him in the House of Commons, attended "by 20 Western Goals (UK) MPs".'[1] The group's vice-president is Gregory Lauder-Frost and he is now political secretary and chairman of Monday Club foreign affairs. 'I don't believe [second-generation immigrants] are British,' he said. 'Just because they were born here is of no consequence. They're not interested in being British, they're interested in wearing saris and so on.'

Let us define 'being British', or 'being a member of the British community-at-large', or 'being a native-born British person'. On the other hand . . .

There is an argument that the reason Britain does not have the same problem with neo-fascism and/or 'ultra-right ultra-nationalism' as elsewhere in Europe is because the Tory Party performs a role that keeps the extremists in check. It is the party of Government and has 'always kept doors open to the right radical underworld': why 'vote for Mosley or Colin Jordan when you can vote for Enoch Powell or Norman Tebbit'? A deadly nightshade by any other name. But to sustain such an argument you need to introduce concepts such as 'right–left', and arrive at the point where you nod sagely when folk on the liberal–left as opposed to liberal–right remark that in the person of John Major 'Conservative rhetoric has swung back leftwards to the party's centre of gravity'.[2]

There must come a time when we look at what exists rather than what the State tells us exists.

There is one principle we can hold, that the aims and objectives of the State are diametrically opposed to the interests of the general population. We can go further, that the ratification of the Treaty is in line with these aims and objectives and firmly grounded upon the desire to set ever firmer restrictions on the freedom of the general population to damage State interests. The people of this country should oppose the Maastricht Treaty in as meaningful a way as possible. The Government exists to serve the interests of the State and we must begin by assuming that the Cabinet decision to ratify the Maastricht Treaty is in line with the wishes of that élite body. Therefore there are no grounds the left can offer in its support. No matter what is presented to the public, the only consideration is increased private profit with increased security in its pursuance. In other words, if the British State wishes to go with the Maastricht Treaty it is because profit and capital can be secured and increased. Yes, there are solid grounds for believing that the wealth of the wealthy can be increased vastly, without resorting to physically robbing people in the streets which is not only unpredictable but liable to retaliatory acts by the victims.

The rise in racist violation may well represent a breakdown or failure in society but does not represent a failure of the political system within the 'European democracies'. Perhaps the European State authorities are powerless to halt the rise but so what, what does that even mean when most, if not all, European states are themselves racist anyway. In Great Britain the attitude of the authorities is amply demonstrated by the behaviour of the police and the immigration service. Both act as servants to the permanent State and the permanent State is permanently right-wing, permanently authoritarian. Street brutality is consistent with State policy. But the left need not be powerless. The first thing we must do is admit reality then show solidarity with the victims: white people must align themselves with black people, they must assist and support in their self-defence.

I have some questions to pose myself:

To whom does the military belong?

What purpose can a military serve if no enemy exists?

'The Communist threat' no longer exists: what was 'the Communist threat'?

Whom or what did 'the Communist' threaten?

Does 'the Communist' exist if 'the Communist threat' doesn't?

What is 'the Arab threat'?

Who or what is threatened by 'the Arab'?

What does 'the Islamic threat' mean?

What does 'international terrorist' mean?

Who or what can be terrorised 'internationally'?

Who or what can terrorise 'internationally'?

What does 'internal security' mean?

To whom does the police belong?

What do we mean by 'policing'?

357

Can 'the police' have 'enemies'?
Is 'crime' the purpose of 'the criminal'?
What is 'a domestic terrorist'?
Is 'terrorism' the purpose of 'the terrorist'?
Explain 'the necessity of increasing internal security'.
Can the internal security forces exist without enemies?
Who can these enemies be?
Is 'containing the public' a realized or potential concept?
Distinguish between 'migrant' and 'immigrant'.
Is a person 'an asylum-seeker'?
What does 'to seek asylum' mean?
What does 'we' mean?
What does 'national interest' mean?

Literary Freedom and Human Rights

TASLIMA NASRIN IS not safe inside her own country and, like countless other human beings, has been forced to seek sanctuary abroad. She is now living in exile in Sweden. Only months ago I attended another meeting here in Edinburgh held on behalf of a writer: Ken Saro-Wiwa, now in detention in his own country of Nigeria. I suggested then how it might occur to some people to wonder what would happen should the Nigerian writer manage to escape and somehow land here in the United Kingdom in search of asylum. Would he get further than passport control? I doubt it. And if he landed at Heathrow Airport probably they would call Securicor or whatever private force is winning the contract these days. They would come and dump him straight into Pentonville Prison. Then, having been refused entry by the British immigration department, he would be returned into the hands of the Nigerian authorities, the very forces he had escaped originally. But maybe not, maybe he would have been found dead in a Pentonville Prison cell, in mysterious circumstances, like so many other black people. Or perhaps because he was a writer his case would be taken up by individuals with a modicum of political or media clout. So he might well have been been granted sanctuary at long last, and released on to the streets of Great Britain, maybe to land here in Edinburgh, like Ahmed Shekh, another asylum seeker. No, better not like Ahmed Shekh; he was murdered by racists only about a mile away from this very building.

We should not fool ourselves when we consider the plight of somebody like Saro-Wiwa, or like Taslima Nasrin, our guest this evening. It is within the context of present-day reality that meetings such as this should take place. Unfortunately that context cannot be guaranteed at meetings. Far too often certain myths are allowed to go unchallenged, like the one that says literary freedom and human rights are part and parcel of the British way of life. In this country we are bedevilled by myths and propaganda, and disinformation, and the revision of history. Almost every debate or discussion programme that appears on television or on the radio is premised on that fallacy – to repeat, that literary freedom and human rights are part and parcel of the British way of life. And unfortunately many meetings hosted by well-intentioned bodies cannot break out of that thinking and when we sit down and listen to people talk we become aware that such is the presumption, here we are in the land of the free! Oh, aye, okay.

But there is so much extraordinary nonsense being peddled via the mainstream media that you sometimes wonder right enough. What the hell is going on? People in high places come out with the most outrageous crap yet it goes unchallenged. We now have a new President of the International Bar Association. No doubt we should feel proud of the fact he is Scottish, only the third president ever chosen from the UK in fifty years. I saw him quoted in a recent newspaper article where he said that 'the problems in other countries put everything at home in perspective.' Oh yeah, okay, fine. And, drawing a lesson from a recent trip he had made to Turkey, he concluded with the following comment: 'one sees clearly throughout the world that it is lawyers who are the last bastion of liberty.' I beg your pardon? What did that guy just say there? Let me draw a breath.

Communication can be difficult when we meet up with writers and activists from other countries. Some of them suffer the same delusions about life in the United Kingdom. Some who are a bit more realistic still manage to suppose that, okay, we might have our problems, but really, in the face of the iniquities being faced in other parts of the world, what goes on here does not matter all that much.

Yeah, tell that to a black or Asian family living on a British housing estate.

Unless we content ourselves only with the fate of individual writers suffering oppression, as opposed to each and every individual human being, then it is difficult to see how anything of lasting significance can ever be achieved. Nothing truly worthwhile can happen until the debate is opened up properly, until we face the reality of life in our own country for the black and Asian communities, and in overseas countries the reality of British intervention and British aggression.

Of course there is censorship and of course there is suppression, here in Scotland just as there is in the UK as a whole; there is distortion, there is disinformation, and it is surprising we still have to keep saying it at public meetings such as this, that we are not allowed to take this as given, that we have to spend valuable time stating what should be obvious. We have a variety of Government departments and State institutions issuing their daily doses of propaganda, designed to disguise reality, whether historical or actual, and of course we have the media to contend with, aiding and abetting the State at every level, the diverse ways in which they collude towards the manipulation of public discourse.

On BBC Radio Scotland yesterday afternoon (6 April 1995) a forthcoming programme was being advertised and the voice-over referred to a few countries where freedom of speech is suppressed and went on to remark how in this country people have the

"And the judges said . . ."

freedom to 'speak out' – in fact I think that was the name of the radio programme, 'Speaking Out'. It was quite odd, though, listening to this guy. As I say, that was yesterday afternoon, while I was taking a break from my work on this paper. Even now, beyond the imposition of the Criminal Justice Bill, there are still many many people who insist on the existence of freedom as a premise of everyday reality in this country and get irritated when you suggest otherwise. Often they refuse to discuss the matter or else they accuse you of nitpicking, of being pedantic, of always complaining, and they ask how you would like to be a writer in Turkey – well, not Turkey, usually they choose a tyranny that is not supported by the British State.

No doubt the radio broadcaster who was referring to the freedom to 'speak out' just never thinks about what he is saying. There again, maybe he believes what he is saying. In that job he will have been university-educated to a high level and Chomsky is probably correct that the most indoctrinated community in society are those who have gone through the higher reaches of the education system. It seems logical enough, given the ideological nature of the education system, that those who have spent so much of their life subject to it will be the more influenced.

I was invited on to a live-radio programme to discuss a new feature-length documentary film on the life of Noam Chomsky (*Manufacturing Consent*). Often what happens in live-interview-style programmes is that the interviewer will discuss things with you beforehand, giving an outline of the questions, then when the actual programme starts s/he will hit you with something that was never discussed earlier, something they hope will leave you high and dry. I have had first-hand experience of this tactic on a couple of occasions. On this one, the opening bolt-from-the-blue question was designed to pre-empt any blast from myself *re* the block on freedom of expression. So the first question thrown at me was along the lines of why does Chomsky complain about media suppression all the time when he seems to be appearing everywhere and anywhere saying whatever the hell he likes. And while we are on the subject, Mister Kelman, if it comes to it, why do you continually complain about the same thing when here you are sitting in a BBC studio doing a *live* broadcast and thus have the freedom to say whatever you want?

Only days before this I had been along to the Edinburgh studio doing another BBC radio programme in which I was to read a brief section from my last novel.[1] There were only a limited number of sections I could read because of what media people describe as 'the sweary-word problem'. They use infantile phrases like that to dismiss 'the problem', suggesting that people like me are being childish for insisting on using language we know to be offensive to other people. Anyway, to give an example of the lack of freedom of expression, I explained how it had not been possible to read honestly from the novel. I would have had to censor myself. So, for this current programme I suggested to the interviewer that I read from any page I opened at random in the novel. He conceded that it would be better if I did not do that, 'sweary-words' were not quite the thing.

It sounds as though I had proved the point. In a sense I had. The trouble is that media people in general deny that the issue is important; some even deny that the suppression of 'sweary-words' is suppression. They are surprised when people take the matter seriously and regard them as a bit silly, which is consistent with their use of childish language, downgrading the issue as one unworthy of mature debate.

Of course genuine creativity is by its nature subversive, good art can scarcely be anything other than dissident. It challenges convention, not by intention necessarily, but simply because good art is also the expression of one individual's perception, it cuts through cliché and stereotype; and our society is premised on stereotype. Hierarchies like ours can only exist by taking advantage of that, by exploiting difference.

We should accept that a great many people who genuinely are supportive of Amnesty International have swallowed these myths about freedom, human rights and the British way of life. These people believe that what happens here in Scotland or the United Kingdom as a whole is insignificant in relation to our guest this evening, Taslima Nasrin, who has had her work banned by her Government and has been condemned to death by a section of her home community. However, I am arguing that there will never be an end to these brutal assaults on freedom of expression unless we begin from what exists under our nose. I am talking primarily about two things, the absence of freedom in this country, and the reality of racist violation.

Some people become upset when you make these points. When they are not accusing you of living in a fantasy world, etc., they accuse you of being unpatriotic. Yes, freedom does exist in this country, if we restrict ourselves to literature. But this is not the rule, it is the exception. It will be argued against me how come I spend time discussing freedom and suppression when here I am able to stand up in public and say whatever I want. In other words we not only can write what we like, we also have freedom of speech and so on and so forth. This is that same sort of argument that searches for a particular and makes it a general principle, it seeks out the exception and calls it the rule.

When we talk about rules in regard to literary freedom there is only one: that writers are free to uphold the cultural values of our dominant ruling élite. Once we try to challenge these values then freedom can no longer be taken for granted. It can still exist but it has to be fought for, and it is not a battle that ends with someone else's victory. As in so many spheres of civil life, precedents go for nothing, you might think you have won a war but you have not. It is a continuing struggle and one which perhaps must be fought for in every generation, for as long as governments continue to rule as servants of the rich and powerful, whether in Britain or Bangladesh.

Now when it comes to human rights we should also be clear about what we are talking about, or what we are not talking about. I quote from Rajani Desai of the Federation of Organisations for Democratic Rights (in a recent edition of *Inqilab*, the journal of the South Asia Solidarity Group):

> There are certain basic differences between human rights, civil liberties and democratic rights. Human rights is a term best left to refer to what the United Nations has incorporated in the Charter of Human Rights and to understand the motives within that Charter. It relates to the notion that certain atrocities should be objected to on grounds of humanity.
>
> But if you actually look at its history and practice, it has been associated with the determination of the imperialist countries, or the more advanced countries as they are called, to use the human rights' issue in order to negotiate better terms, or to impose something on third world countries or on one of their own members with whom they may be having some problems.

Desai also says of civil liberties that

> they are mentioned in the Constitution of India which is actually an 80% replica of the British Act of 1935 for colonial India, which Nehru said at the time was a document for imposing slavery on the Indian people. But the 'fundamental rights' in the Constitution of India are not available to 95% of the Indian people today . . .

But through these distinctions we can see that the area of democratic rights might be a way of reaching the real crux because 'it asserts the rights of the people to struggle against exploitation or oppression'. We are now talking about something extremely urgent and extremely political: the right to self-defence, the right to defend yourself under attack. This goes much further and much deeper than the basic pursuance of either civil liberties or human rights. It offers empowerment, self-determination.

Desai also argues that 'the democratic rights' movement cannot be a movement of intellectuals only. It has to have for its backbone the working-class and the peasantry, employees, women and students – working people generally.'

Now generally it is not the right of oppressed people to defend themselves under attack. This right is typically denied them. Instead it is the duty of powerful élites to defend them. Or to treat them well. Whatever. That duty takes the form of a moral obligation. Yes, and enough said for anybody who ever had a look at the state of Anglo-American moral philosophy and its effect on the world order, either now or historically. No matter what these powerful élites might decide, well, it is their decision; the rest of the world just has to suffer the consequences.

One other obvious point, in line with the argument offered by Rajani Desai: as opposed to the majority of the population, the educated élite are seldom if ever under personal grievous attack at all, they have armies and security forces and Government agencies to safeguard them, on top of that they already have most of the trappings of freedom. Apart from securing these trappings their only obligations are moral.

Meanwhile victims of their security never have to worry about morality and ethics, they are too busy finding ways of defending themselves; and defending themselves in the main against the culture that produced the Human Rights Commission. Yes, our culture, the dominant culture of the west.

There is evidence that 'the Bangladesh Islamic fundamentalist party, the Jamat-e-Islam, slaughtered thousands of progressive writers, artists and scientists on the eve of Independence back in 1971.' And also, that in tandem with 'its current campaign of violence against women and its recent growth in power it has been openly supported by the West via Saudi Arabia.' We can further hazard a guess that many fundamentalist groups did not exist in any real strength prior to the work of agencies like MI6, CIA and their forerunners and counterparts.

So maybe we should face the fact that the tens of hundreds of thousands of people who are under attack in so many countries throughout the world, are under attack by forces overtly or covertly fuelled and supported by the USA and satellite states such as the UK, Israel, Saudi Arabia, Turkey. For this controlling interest it never really matters which brand of tyranny it is; despotic monarchies or brutal totalitarian regimes, religious fanatics – who-ever, whatever, it makes no difference, just that the effects of the tyranny will both secure and advance its own wealth and power.

This used to be described as 'providing a bulwark against Communism'. Nowadays and for as long as it is expedient, we have moved through the bogey of Arab expansionsim into 'confronting the Islamic Threat'.

In fact conventional western wisdom would have us believe that Islam and fundamentalism are synonymous, that it is not possible to be both tolerant and Muslim at the same time. Christian, Jewish or Hindu fundamentalists do not seem to count, not even when they are massacring people. When Muslim people are being massacred in India these days, we can look for it being reported in the west under the heading of communal riots.

The danger here is – just as it was, and remains, in the case of Salman Rushdie – that support can be given to Taslima Nasrin blindly; because she is a writer somehow she is seen as *one of us*. If this happens it is at the expense of the victims of racism here in the United Kingom, it will serve to reinforce the current criminal-isation of the wider Muslim community, both at home and abroad wherever it suits the west and causes minimal diplomatic upsets with the oil-producing kingdoms. This blindness will not admit what is happening right on our own doorstep to those who are arriving constantly in this country in search of asylum, and throughout Europe and all the other so-called liberal democracies. So of course we have to support Taslima Nasrin, but not at the expense of domestic reality.

Into Barbarism

TWO YEARS AFTER the killing of their teenage son, Neville and Doreen Lawrence have had no respite. In their struggle for justice the Committal Proceedings will be seen as a qualified success. Yet this has been a further twist in their own private nightmare: being forced to endure publicly a blow-by-blow account of the horror perpetrated on their boy, while given daily reminders of the callous indifference of the authorities, personified by the continuing cant of the Crown Prosecution Services (CPS). The media debate on the result of the Committal Proceedings has centred on the difficulties people have with the CPS generally. This is to miss the point. What the media have so far failed to tackle is the record of the CPS in dealing with racist crimes in particular.

Now it appears that if there is a successful outcome at the end of the Committal Proceedings the CPS will try to move in and prosecute the case when finally it comes to trial. The family is opposed to that. Stephen's mother tells us that 'We have come this far without the CPS' and we have to listen, and we have to urge the authorities to listen. The whole affair is shameful. If within the CPS there are individuals who retain some integrity, they must exert their own pressure, whether upwards or down-wards, and allow the Lawrence family 'to continue to the end without their involvment'.[1] For black people the Lawrence

Family Campaign is a matter of extreme urgency; for some it is life or death.

Contrary to official information, the private criminal prosecution launched by the family has been unprecedented. While it may be the fourth (in 130 years) in relation to the charge of murder, there are aspects of the case that are certainly unique. From the outset it has been made clear that the campaign is not about 'law and order', it is about justice. 'Unlike the CPS the Lawrence family and their legal team intend to mount an "enlightened prosecution", respecting the rules of evidence and the right to be considered innocent until proven guilty.'[2]

A shocking thing about the history of racism is how little known it is among white people. For Stephen's father there can be no rest until 'the killers and the hidden perpetrators of all racial attacks and murders are brought to justice, and for the whole truth to be known.' And when he speaks of 'the whole truth' he refers to what the political establishment in this country has failed so dismally and consistently to acknowledge, let alone confront. It is what people from the black communities have known through experience and alternative channels of information for many many years but only now is beginning to percolate down through society at large: the British State advances the cause of racism directly through such agencies as the police, the immigration service, the DSS and so on; and throughout the legal, judicial and education systems; and so on. It is accomplished in such a systematic manner that to describe it as 'unintentional' is to award the authorities not only the benefit of the doubt, but a lack of foresight so extreme as should disqualify them from office.

The death of Joy Gardner served to highlight the horrific reality of one such Government agency where acts of terror and torture may be enacted against black people in the name of who knows what, but officially it's called the Department of Immigration.

About the only policy-adjustment to have occurred since this tragedy is one that will increase the probability that such so-called 'accidents' will occur again and again. An entire range of public-sector workers (health workers, school teachers, job-centre clerks, ambulance drivers, etc.) is being conscripted into our State security system as informers, 'trained to identify illegal immigrants'. It will be part of their unofficial job-description that they are racists, paid racists from 9 till 5; this if for no other reason than that in the identification of illegal immigrants racial origin is the primary piece of 'circumstantial evidence'.

Five officers of the British State were involved in the killing of Joy Gardner, acting on behalf of the immigration services. They 'handcuffed her, attached leg, thigh and body belts to her, and gagged her with 13 ft of sticky tape wrapped seven times round her head while her five-year-old son Graeme looked on. She collapsed and . . . died four days later as a result of brain damage.'[3]

Is being paid to be a racist thug the same as being paid to be a bus-driver? What happens afterwards, outside working hours? When does somebody who is paid to be a racist stop being a racist? Will those tens of thousands of State employees 'return' to humanity on their way home from work, become 'normal' human beings when they get off-duty? Off-duty police officers in Manchester were discovered 'relaxing', having a beer and a laugh, in the privacy of a night-club owned and run by the British 'comedian' Bernard Manning; he whose loathsome, racist verbiage is excused by the mainstream media as a form of humorous eccentricity (those who voice their disapproval are pilloried as priggish spoilsports).

Towards the end of 1994 three of the officers involved in the horror perpetrated on Joy Gardner were sent for trial on man-slaughter charges 'but . . . acquitted in June 1995 after claiming that [she] was "very very strong".' And later on the police authorities

371

made their own ruling, that 'the officers could not be disciplined after being acquitted by the courts'.[4]

State agencies themselves, aided and abetted by the British Government, will do their best to ensure that employees and colleagues will not – preferably *cannot* – be held responsible for their actions individually. Where possible accountability is contained within the ranks. The Home Secretary[5] has said that 'lawful residents in Britain will not be affected and have nothing to fear' from the expansion of our State security system by means of 'civilian' conscription. Will this modify the extreme fear that afflicted Kwanele Sziba to such an extent that she fell to her death while attempting to escape 'interrogation'? In the case of Kwanele Sziba no doubt the immediate response of the Home Office was to enquire if the dead woman was 'legal'. And what about Ibrahima Sey, was he 'legal' when he was 'unlawfully killed' at Ilford police station in London? Evidence to the inquest established that while the man was

> on his knees, with his hands cuffed behind his back, and surrounded by over a dozen police officers in the secure rear yard of the police station, he was sprayed by CS gas, and then, upon being taken into the police station, he was restrained face down on the floor for some 15 minutes or more until he had stopped breathing . . .

The inhumanity of this treatment was illustrated when one of the officers involved told the inquest how he had swapped the handcuffs he placed on the man with those of a colleague because he did not want to do the overtime involved in accompanying the prisoner to hospital. It is reckoned that Ibrahima Sey would have been dead by that time anyway.[6]

But that lack of regard for a fellow-human being is consistent, revealed in off-the-cuff comments, as much as the actions, of the police and security agencies. Those who commit, aid and abet these outrages are spurred by a form of prejudice that dehumanises the individual. Of course if the victim is less than human then moral questions do not arise. Dispense with humanity, the responsibility people have one for the other as a first principle of human behaviour. Dehumanise the victims and debase the perpetrators, and morality will not enter the frame. The history of imperialism is the history of barbarism.

Obviously not every white member of the armed forces, the police or the immigration department is a racist thug. But nobody who carries out – or is party to – the racist operations of the British State can be excused on the grounds that s/he is only doing a job. Who can be excused from being a human being? On a balance of probability, anyone who operates on behalf of the State will collude in the cause of racism. If these people are not racist let them use the little power remaining to them and be responsible for their actions. More than half a century has passed since the Nuremberg Trials.

And we have arrived at the stage where if the police are charged with criminal misconduct they will be entitled to withhold evidence against themselves. In the months following the launch of the Lawrence Family Campaign, the Home Secretary proposed that prosecution documents need never be submitted. This may be little more than a blatant attempt to claw back the small gains derived from such blatant miscarriages of justice as that affecting Judith Ward where 'the High Court was so shocked that it ruled the defence must in future see virtually all the material held by the prosecution'.[7] But it also means that the burden of proof has been reversed and is now on the heads of the victims and their families. The guilty are now innocent; the innocent 'guilty', until proving otherwise.

Any racist killing is a political killing, as people may be aware who know the work of human rights' agencies and bodies such as Amnesty International:

> Political killings are carried out by order of the government or with its complicity in different parts of the world and in countries of widely differing ideologies . . . [We call] these unlawful and deliberate killings political because victims are selected by reason of their real or imputed beliefs or activities, [their] religion, colour, sex, language or ethnic origin. [It] flouts the absolute principle that governments must protect their citizens against arbitrary deprivation of life, which cannot be abandoned under any circumstances, however grave. It is [their] duty not to commit or condone political killings, but to take all legislative, executive and judicial measures to ensure that those responsible are brought to justice. Governments are responsible for these crimes under national and international law.[8]

This is not the place to discuss the number of mysterious deaths of black people while held in prison or police custody[9] but if the British Government has 'a duty not to commit or condone political killings, [and] to take all legislative, executive and judicial measures to ensure that those responsible are brought to justice' then patently the British Government has failed. Not only are the authorities not 'taking measures to prevent further deaths', on the contrary, the measures they are taking will set the conditions to ensure the situation deteriorates further, that more people will die, that more 'extrajudicial executions' will go unpunished.

They were cowards who killed Joy Gardner with such brutal disregard for her humanity. The cowards performed the act on behalf of the British State using practices and procedures laid down by the British State. Not only does the British State commit acts of terrorism in the privacy of overseas countries, it commits acts of terrorism at home upon its own black population, upon immigrants and upon refugees.

The base motive of European colonisation and imperialism was greed; side by side, or slightly behind, came the rationalisation, which includes concepts like law, ethics and religion. The gunboats and armies engaged in wiping out anyone who got in the way of capital expansion. Meanwhile officers of the various branches of intellectual endeavour, e.g. philosophers and theologians, deliberated on such weighty topics as whether or not there are grounds to assume that a human being is a human being.

Any society emerging from tyranny has to cope with successive generations of brutalised children. This has been the case in decolonised Africa and the Sub-Continent, in Palestine and the Middle East generally; and in far too many other parts of the world, including Northern Ireland. If the outrages that occur on the streets of the United Kingdom are an extension of state policy, *official* estimates put the number of racist assaults at around 140,000 per year. Joy Gardner and Stephen Lawrence were targeted – one by the State and one by a streetgang of racist thugs – because they were of black non-European extraction. If either had been of white European extraction, no matter which country they or their parents or grandparents had come from – Jamaica, New Zealand, Iran, Canada, Bangladesh, Ghana, Singapore or wherever else in the world you care to name – it would have been irrelevant: if they had been white neither tragedy would have occurred. Those responsible for the killings are psychologically damaged and the effects of institutionalised racism, historical and contemporary, are material to that damage. Until the white population face up to this, the savagery that has devasted so many families will not only continue, it will increase.

Racial Harassment in the Community

PEOPLE IN THE United Kingdom are being forced to live what the vast majority would regard as some sort of horrific nightmare. They are being terrorised in their own home by people from their own area, often neighbours. They are bullied and humiliated, subject to sickening physical assaults that have ended in death. They are forced to witness their children being attacked and beaten, not only by other children but by adults.

Horrific, yes, also shameful. From babies in prams to elderly and disabled people, none is exempt from attack. Each member of the family is a potential victim to acts of abuse and brutality. Parents go to bed at night and try to sleep in the anticipation of worse to follow; a petrol bomb shattering a bedroom window, lighted rags being pushed through their letterbox, their children being murdered.

There is a consistent failure to acknowledge, let alone alleviate, the suffering of these people, whether by act or omission, by those in a position to offer immediate support. One of the most common psychological phenomena in the face of human suffering is *denial*. The means to support victims in a diversity of ways often lie within the statutory duties and powers of the authorities. In many cases local authority agencies, by their negligence, are in total breach of statutory duties. But so what? Even where these breaches are evident and admitted as such, there is no remedy. We might expect that admitting liability would lead to some form of action being taken either to punish the culpable or ensure that such glaring examples of the dereliction of duty would not occur in the future. But clearly to expect any such thing is naïve.

The responsibility to ensure that statutory duties are carried out rests on the shoulders of individual officials and employees. There exists little or no internal monitoring, no process capable of ensuring that these duties and powers are implemented. If we dwell too much, however, on the failure of local political authorities, we are in danger of ignoring the reality of the past decades' attack on local democracy by national Government.

But nothing at all will happen while those wielding authority, whether political, administrative, legal or judicial, continue to deny reality. This is the fundamental requirement. Suffering cannot be alleviated until it is acknowledged. These families are in crisis and they are in jeopardy. A clear line of consistency is apparent within the submission of the victims, that the officials will not be convinced of their plight, that the officials continue – often wilfully – to place the burden of proof on to the victims. This in itself is a breach of the guidelines: the fundamental requirement of the so-called 'victim-centred' approach is to act on the assumption that the victim is stating the case, i.e. telling the truth as s/he sees it.

Yet the victims have almost no political clout at all. The checks and balances that local or national Government should provide on their respective administrations scarcely exist. Those who come to their support do so from a position of basic humanity, there is no other obligation.

The evidence demonstrates that those in political power are not committed to the alleviation of the suffering of these people. There are remedies within the law to effect real change; yet whether or not those who have statutory duties and powers decide to implement them is neither being checked nor monitored adequately, not within the agencies themselves, and not by those holding political office. It is left to external agencies to do that work, some voluntary, others such as the Commision for Racial Equality (CRE).

One of the more glaring inadequacies is the general lack of the multi-agency or corporate approach. To take just one example, children are being denied their rights under law. This applies not only to the offices of the Social Works Department but also to the departments of Education, Health and Welfare whose obligations are statutory. (What possible grounds can there be for not referring a psychologically damaged, emotionally distressed or physically abused child to the relevant authority?)

The law is being breached, civil and criminal. Crimes are committed in a discriminate and methodical way. The perpetrators either believe themselves not to be acting in a criminal manner, or assume that nobody 'who matters' is concerned. They regard themselves as untouchable and assume that the section of the community they attack is open to such victimisation. Apart from isolated examples, the response from the authorities would vindicate the assumption that black people are easy targets. They are not protected by the law. The statistics on the legal remedies taken against perpetrators validates the use of the term 'isolated'; the vast majority of perpetrators have no action taken against them. We also find that victims are themselves punished, e.g. they may be removed from the community.

This is the situation as it exists. The submissions put forward during the day by the police, the Crown Prosecution Services (CPS) and local agencies concentrated largely on policy, strategy, etc. At best that may offer hope to *potential* victims but it offers no remedy at all for those suffering right at this moment. Unfortunately the CPS would not discuss on-going cases with the People's Tribunal. Nor were they willing to discuss any other examples. In my opinion the representative from the CPS concealed his contempt for the proceedings only with the greatest difficulty.

Surely the primary issue to be resolved is how to support the victims. It is important to consider *potential* victims, obviously. But if we stay with the concerns of existing victims perhaps the matter of potential victims will be accounted for in the process itself. This is also a reason why the emphasis is laid on dealing with the perpetrators of these crimes; not so that the interests of law enforcement are carried out, but to ensure that the guilty are stopped from wreaking further havoc on innocent people. Punishing culprits is a means to that end. Individuals involved in racial harassment have ended up murdering people.

It would be pointless to look for racist motivation from within the ranks of officialdom, the various authorities, i.e. the police and the CPS; the Housing, Education and Social Works departments, etc. We know and accept that racists are employed in different spheres of the public sector throughout the United Kingdom. From people at the higher echelon of State or Government authority down through policemen on the beat or clerks at the local Housing Office. This is self-evident from their own pronouncements. The point surely is to ensure that their racism has no detrimental effect on people There are individuals within every agency and Government department who are motivated by prejudice; given the endemic nature of racism and racist attitudes within society, it would be surprising if this were not the case. Attempts to root out individual racists are a waste of time, and time is integral to the support of victims. It would not remedy the situation as it exists. And Government encourages racism in its own employees by its ruthless behaviour toward immigrants and asylum-seekers of non-white European extraction. Ruthless individuals are promoted.

It is presumptuous of individual agencies to adopt as a strategy a development of such notions as 'racial harmony'. The effects of this can be damaging, even at executive levels of authority. It is usually a red herring, an attempt to disguise the fact that agencies under the control of local authorities are in breach of statutory duties. It has us looking for *general* factors within society to account for the existence of racial harassment, and therefore avoids the reality of what is happening right now to tens of thousands of people throughout the country.

Gross misunderstandings of the crisis may arise through certain side-effects of that approach, allied to the development of notions of 'community'. In the submissions by the different agencies, I was struck by the recurrence of terms such as 'feuding', 'tit-for-tat', 'neighbourhood dispute', etc. which I found quite perverse in face of the evidence. It indicates the degeneration that can occur from parallel notions of 'impartiality', 'objectivity', 'balance' and so on, implying there are 'two sides to every story'. What nonsense. We are here talking about set patterns of violence. Surely local authorities must ensure that such developmental notions are stopped from serving as *substitutes* for the implementation of statutory duties and powers.

What possible grounds can there be for referring a victim of grievous bodily harm to the police Community Liaison Officer? It is absurd. Would we expect the judiciary to come out with the suggestion that a murderer and the parents of the murdered child shake hands? The function of the Community Liaison Officer needs clarification for outside agencies, and for individuals working within the police-force.

Those in a position to alleviate the suffering of people under racist attack must look to what is available and be prepared to disregard the irrelevant, even where well-intentioned. Some laws are 'good', they exist to support victims; other laws are bad; others again are immaterial, unless put to use. As a matter of interest, given that the police have no *statutory duties*, what would lead individual officers to make use of a power that enables them to arrest and charge somebody who has just suffered a violent assault, somebody who is a known victim? ('known victim' as determined under Appendix B of *Metropolitan Police Guidance*; OG 11/83/41 (T030)). Is any monitoring done to see whether or not these force directives are applied?

When somebody reports racial harassment the officials typically respond as though the victim has to convince them; the burden of proof is on the victim who offers his or her evidence, and the official sits in judgment. It is shocking to find that, in a great number of instances, instead of sympathy victims are treated with outright hostility, as troublemakers, nuisances, people who complain all the time. People are lumped together into a group which in itself can fuel prejudice, their behaviour is regarded as group behaviour, e.g. 'they complain all the time'. Beyond a trivial level it is a mistake to lump together the victims of racial violence and harassment. It also may prejudice the seriousness of these crimes. It further may lead to a major error, where the cause of violation is sought in the victims. It is worth pointing out that not only do the perpetrators usually go free in one way or another, their crimes are rewarded. Often it is the victims who are punished, they are taken out of the community. In some cases the victims have been prosecuted. The punishment or prosecution of perpetrators is a means to an end, to bring to a conclusion the suffering of these people under attack.

As a strategy, the 'victim–centred approach' offers obvious potential. Authorities do not require to substantiate the veracity of a victim's story in order to offer support. An allegation of racial harassment is sufficient. This attempts to redress the crucial problem of the burden of proof. In theory nobody needs to prove that s/he is a victim before action is taken to tackle the crisis.

Unfortunately this potential is not being realised. There is great confusion about such an approach, technical confusion, not only for members of the police. Individuals in positions of power appear confounded by the concept that a person does not have to offer proof. Unfortunately the 'victim–centred approach' does not operate everywhere and at all levels. Where it does exist as policy it should be practised.

It is surely obvious that victims would not report racial harassment until recognising that that is what it is. And this recognition is a process, based on *a series of acts* against them. People are not going to leap to false conclusions about something like that. They will need to be sure as to what it is, and will identify act after act of abuse; and only when convinced that these acts are not random will they report their conclusion to the authorities; that they are suffering racial harassment within their community. Seeking police help or advice is often a last resort.

But a crime cannot be solved until it is acknowledged as having taken place, or as taking place. When racial harassment is reported, it means that racial harassment is taking place, not that it has taken place. It is important to grasp this.

The phrase 'racial harassment' is generic, applying to a class or group of activities that are in breach of the law, whether civil or criminal. Unfortunately there is a tendency to think of the concept as a thing in itself. Thus when a victim reports racial harassment and identifies a perpetrator, individuals expect to discover evidence to show that 'the crime of racial harassment' has been committed.

The United Kingdom is in a state of moral and civil degeneration and if we gear our greater energy towards stemming this 'politically', e.g. lobbying for a change of leadership in the Government or some such foolishness, then we run the risk of withdrawing all hope from the tens of thousands of people who are already victims.

The past twenty and more years has seen a withdrawal of what the majority of the population assumed to be part of an evolutionary process, the widening and strengthening of democratic rights, the spread of social justice. The difficulty we have in raising issues concerned with human suffering is that it immediately becomes a political matter. Our opponents prefer it that way, they are then entitled to toss it out of court, condemning us for political bias.

This charge cannot be avoided. It is an integral part of the reconstruction that has taken place. To be an opponent of human suffering to the extent that we might propose – or put into practice – ways of alleviating some of the suffering, is to be biased, to be motivated by something other than the *need* for natural justice. Yet some would argue that this need for natural justice is part of what it is to be a human being, that contemporary society educates this need out of us. We have lost the right not to stand back and let other people suffer. Those who attempt to do something about it are no longer lumped under labels like wishy-washy, politically correct do-gooders, but are described as 'political activists', a legitimate target of the internal security forces, no doubt; any political activist is potentially a 'domestic terrorist' in the perception of the State.

State authorities find the concept of altruism difficult, though much of its rhetoric is premised on quasi-universals such as 'human nature' and 'basic human values'. Those in executive power either do not share the values held in common by the public at large (i.e. people with no access to power), or else believe that such values do not and should not impinge on how they (or anyone else) operate in their '9 to 5', functionary capacity. They reject the implications of the Nuremberg Trials with their constant attempts to reinstate the 'I was only following orders' argument. In a sense this is the nub of the distinction in respect of the State's use of the concept 'policy', allowing a withdrawal of responsibility by Government ministers.

We have to face up to reality, we must assume that those in political office lack the will or commitment to effect change. If we do not assume this then we cannot support the victims of racial harassment. Whether or not we believe that change will come about by the transference of authority from one party to another, it remains the case that a large section of the adult population is presently being attacked. Perhaps one question to ask is what can we do – as citizens – to ensure that changes are effected in society no matter who occupies the seats of authority, even those who appear to act against the common good by intention.

The 'Freedom for Freedom of Expression' Rally
Istanbul, 10–12 March 1997

The arrogance of [the Iranian King] Jamshid had set his subjects in revolt against him, and a great army marched towards Arabia from the highlands of Iran. They had heard that in Arabia there was a man with a serpent's face that inspired terror and to him they went in order to elect him as their king. Zuhak eagerly returned with them and was crowned . . . Jamshid fled before him, and for a hundred years was seen by no man, till Zuhak fell upon him without warning in the confines of China and put him to death. Thus perished [Jamshid's] pride from the earth.

For a thousand years Zuhak occupied the throne and the world submitted to him, so that goodness died away and was replaced by evil. Every night during that long period two youths were slain [whose brains provided food for the serpents that grew from Zuhak's shoulders] . . . It happened that [there remained two men of purity, of Persian race who] succeeded in entering the king's kitchen. There, after no long time, they were entrusted with the preparation of the king's meal, and they contrived to mix the brains of a sheep with those of one of the youths who was brought for slaughter. The other one they saved alive and dismissed secretly, saying to him: 'Escape in secret, beware of visiting any inhabited town; your portion in the world must be the desert and the mountain.'

In this manner they saved two hundred men, of whom is born the race of Kurds, who know not any fixed abode, whose houses are tents; and who have in their hearts no fear of God.

Abul Kasim Mansur Firdawsi[1] (AD 935–1025)

THIS THREE-DAY event, the 'Freedom for Freedom of Expression Rally', was organised and hosted by the Freedom of Thought initiative, a 200-strong group of artists and activists. There is a multiple trial in progress in Istanbul; writers, musicians, actors, journalists, lawyers, trade-unionists and others are being prosecuted by the State Security Court. Twenty international writers attended the rally; most are members of PEN but three travelled at the invitation of Amnesty International (AI), including myself.

More writers are imprisoned in Turkey than in any other country in the world[1] but 'the real question [is] not that of freedom for a writer. The real question is that of the national rights of the Kurds.'[2] The annexation of Kurdistan, the attempted genocide and the continued oppression of the Kurdish people are three of the major scandals of this century. Historically, the British State, if not prime mover, has had a pivotal role.[3] At one point 'we' needed a client state 'to secure ['our'] right to exploit the oilfields of Southern Kurdistan', and so 'we' created a country, gave it a king, and called it Iraq.[4] 'Our' active participation in the assault on the Kurdish people continues to the present where 'we' retain a leading interest in diverse ways, e.g. client state of the USA, member of NATO, member of the European Union, etc. Turkey itself 'is now the number two holiday destination for U.K. holidaymakers thanks to superb weather, great value for money accommodation, inexpensive eating out and lots to see and do.'[5]

Prisoners are routinely tortured and beaten in Turkey, some-times killed. Rape and other sexual violations occur constantly. In the Kurdish provinces the mass murders, forced dispersals and other horrors practised by the security forces are documented by many domestic and international human rights' agencies. People have been made to eat excrement. From Kurdish villages there are reports of groups of men having their testicles tied and linked together, the women then forced to lead them round the streets. There are files held on children as young as twelve being subject to the vilest treatment. This from a 16-year-old girl detained not in a Kurdish village but by the police in Istanbul:

> They put my head in a bucket until I almost drowned. They did it again and again . . . They tied my hands to a beam and hoisted me up. I was blindfolded. When I was hanging I thought my arms were breaking. They sexually harassed me and they beat my groin and belly with fists while I was hanging. When they pulled down on my legs I lost conscious-ness. I don't know for how long the hanging lasted . . . They threatened that they would rape and kill me. They said I would become paralysed. The torture lasted for eight days.[6]

The young girl was later charged with being a member of 'an illegal organisation'. Germany, USA and the UK compete to supply war and torture implements to the Turkish security forces who learned about the efficacy of the hanging process from their Israeli counterparts. A student we were to meet later at Istanbul University was once detained for twenty-four fours and during that period she too was tortured.

There exist '152 laws and about 700 paragraphs . . . devoted to regulating freedom of opinion.' The Turkish Penal Code 'was

passed in 1926 . . . [and is] based on an adaptation of the Italian
Penal Code . . . [Its] most drastic reform was the adoption in 1936
of the anti-communist articles on "state security" from the code of
Mussolini. Only in April 1991 were some changes made through
the passage of the Law to Combat Terrorism.' Before then, and up
until 1989

court cases against the print media had reached a record level
with 183 criminal cases against 400 journalists . . . at least 23
journalists and editors in jail with one of them receiving a
sentence of 1,086 years, later reduced to 700 on appeal. The
editor of one [well-known journal, banned by the Ozal
dictatorship] was prosecuted 13 times and had 56 cases brought
against her. She was in hiding at the time the journal[7] appeared
in July of 1990. One of her sentences amounted to 6 years, 3
months. Despite international appeals and protests the Turkish
government refused to reverse her sentences. No left-wing or
radical journal was safe from arbitrary arrest, closure or seizure
of entire editions. Police persecution extended into the
national press and included daily newspapers. Authors and
publishers of books were victimised. In November 1989 449
books and 25 pamphlets were burned in Istanbul on the orders
of the provincial governor . . . [Until] 1991 189 films were
banned . . . [and during the following two years came] the
liquidation of journalists, newspaper sellers, and the personnel
of newspaper distributors, as well as bombing and arson attacks
against newspaper kiosks and bookstores . . . [In 1992] twelve
journalists were murdered by 'unknown assailants' [and] in
most cases, the circumstances point to participation or support
by the state security forces. [In 1994 writers and journalists
were sentenced to] 448 years, 6 months and 25 days . . . There
were 1162 violations of the press laws [and] a total of 2098

persons were tried, 336 of whom were already in prison . . .
The security forces interfered with the distribution of press
organs, attacked their offices, and arbitrarily detained publishers, editors, correspondents and newspaper salesmen.[8]

Shortly before the last military coup, in the spring of 1991, I
took part in a public meeting organised by the Friends of
Kurdistan.[9] I intended publishing a version of my 'talk' in written
form but it never worked out. In the talk I looked at parallels in the
linguistic and cultural suppression of Kurdish and Scottish people,
and that was a mistake.[10] Parallels between the two may be of some
slight functional value from a Scottish viewpoint but when we
discuss the Kurdish situation now and historically we are discussing
the systematic attempt to wipe from the face of the earth a nation
of some thirty million people. It is doubtful if any form of oppression exists that has not been carried out on the Kurdish people and
I think the scale of it overwhelmed me. I combined some of the
elements of my 1991 talk with those of others of the same period,
and published an essay.[11] I now give an extract from my notes for
that talk, as a brief introduction to how things were for Kurdish
people before the 12 September military coup back in 1980:[12]

*The Turkish Republic set up its apparatus for the repression of the Kurdish
people soon after it was founded. Following the War of Independence,
during which they were acclaimed as 'equal partner' and 'sister nation', the
Kurdish people found their very existence was being denied. The authorities
have since sought to destroy everything which might suggest a specific
Kurdish identity, erecting an entire edifice of linguistic and historical
psuedo-theories which supposedly 'proved' the Turkishness of the Kurds,
and served as justification for the destruction of that identity.*

*These theories have become official doctrine, taught, inculcated and
propagated by the schools, the universities, the barracks, and the media.*

The authorities banned all unofficial publications that tried to even discuss the subject. Historical or literary works, even travellers' tales published in Turkish and other langauges, were all removed from public and private libraries and for the most part destroyed if they contained any reference to the Kurdish people, their history or their country. All attempts to question official ideology were repressed.

It is estimated that 20 million Kurds dwell in Turkey and the Kurdish language has been banned there since 1925. In 1978, of all Kurdish people over the age of six, 72 per cent could neither read nor write. The publication of books and magazines in the language is illegal. The Turkish authorities purged the libraries of any books dealing with Kurdish history, destroyed monuments and so on.[13] All historical research into Kurdish society was forbidden. An official history was constructed to show the Kurdish people were originally Turks. Until 1970 no alternative research could be published. Thus officially the Kurds are purest Turk.

The Turkish authorities have systematically changed the names of all Kurdish towns and villages, substituting Turkish for Kurdish names. The word 'Kurdistan', so designated from the thirteenth century, was the first to be banned; it is regarded as subversive because it implies the unity of the scattered Kurdish people. Kurdistan is colonised not by one country but by four: Turkey, Iran, Iraq and Syria whose Chief of Police

published a Study [in November 1963 which] set out to 'prove scientifically' that the Kurds 'do not constitute a nation', that they are 'a people without history or civilization or language or even definite ethnic origin of their own', that they lived 'from the civilization and history of other nations and had taken no part in these civilizations or in the history of these nations.' [He also] proposed a 12-point plan:
1) the transfer and dispersion of the Kurdish people;
2) depriving the Kurds of any education whatsoever, even in Arabic;
3) a 'famine' policy, depriving those affected of any employment possibilities;

4) an extradition policy, turning the survivors of the uprisings in Northern Kurdistan over to the Turkish Government;

5) divide and rule policy; setting Kurd against Kurd;

6) a cordon policy along the lines of an earlier plan to expel the entire Kurdish population from the Turkish border;

7) colonization policy, the implantation of pure and nationalist Arabs in the Kurdish regions to see to the dispersal of the Kurds;

8) military divisions to ensure the dispersion;

9) 'collective farms' set up for the Arab settlers who would also be armed and trained;

10) a ban on 'anybody ignorant of the Arabic language exercising the right to vote or stand for office';

11) sending Kurds south and Arabs north;

12) 'launching a vast anti-Kurdish campaign amongst the Arabs'.[14]

Media organs are the property of the official language in Turkey, and the Kurdish people are kept starved of outside news. Kurdish intellectuals are expected to assimilate, to reject their own culture and language, to become Turkicised. A person from Kurdistan cannot be appointed to fill a post without the prior approval of the political police. Kurds are not nominated for jobs in the Kurdish provinces; the authorities try always to separate them from their own country.

All business is conducted in the language of state and Kurdish speakers must use interpreters. Literature produced in exile, beyond the Turkish borders, is not allowed into the Republic. Kurdish writers and poets have had to write in Turkish, not simply to ensure publication but because they were unfamiliar with their own forbidden language and culture.

A group of Kurdish students once published a tract demanding that incitement to racial hatred be made a punishable offence and were charged with having claimed that there was a Kurdish people, thereby undermining national unity. They published the tract in response to various anti-Kurd threats made publicly from right-wing sources, including one nationalist journal implicitly threatening the Kurdish people with genocide.

For a brief period a group called the Organization of Revolutionary Kurdish Youth (DDKO) was tolerated by the authorities; this group set out to inform public opinion about the economic, social and cultural situation; organising press conferences and public briefings, publishing posters, leaflets etc., focusing attention on the repression within Kurdish areas; its monthly ten-page information bulletin had a print run of 30,000 which was distributed among Turkish political, cultural and trade-union circles, as well as in Kurdish towns and villages. Eventually 'news' about what was happening to the Kurds filtered through to the media and the public and there were protests against the repression. Six months before the military coup of March 1970 the leaders of the organisation were arrested and after that all 'left-wing parties and organisations were outlawed'.

But from 1975 new youth organisations formed, known generally as the People's Cultural Associations (HKD), concentrating on educating their members and helping peasants and workers who were in conflict with the authorities in one way or another. A policy of terror and ideological conditioning was implemented by the Ankara Government which in the words of Turkish sociologist Ismail Beşikçi managed to 'make people believe he who announced "I am Kurdish" was committing a crime so heinous that he deserved the death penalty.' Dr Beşikçi was put on trial for the crime of 'undermining national feelings' and 'making separatist propaganda'.

In the same talk I drew attention to an interview Ismail Beşikçi had given while in prison awaiting yet another trial. He had remarked of the German prosecution of the Kurdish Workers' Party (PKK), that the one thing established was the existence of a 'secret agreement between the NATO alliance and Turkey, in relation to Kurdistan'. Germany has now fallen into line with the Turkish State and has declared the PKK an illegal organisation, even to sport their colours is a criminal offence. The victimisation of Kurdish people has spread outwards, we are witnessing the attempted criminalisation of the entire diaspora.[15]

Throughout Europe there are incidents being reported by monitoring agencies. In November in Belgium '100 police and members of the special intervention squad . . . raided a Kurdish holiday centre . . . The Ministry of Justice claimed [it was] used by the PKK as a semi-military training camp.' Nobody at all was arrested. But forty people were deported to Germany. On 2 February of this year (1997) 'the Danish television station, TV2, revealed that the Danish police intelligence service [PET] had written a 140-page report on meetings of the Kurdish parliament-in-exile which took place in Copenhagen in March 1996 [and the] transcript . . . ended up with the Turkish authorities.'[16]

Here in the UK Kani Yilmaz is halfway into his third year in Belmarsh Prison, London. He came from Germany in October 1994 at the direct invitation of John Austin-Walker MP, to meet with British MPs and discuss cease-fire proposals between the PKK and the Turkish armed forces. In a shameful act of betrayal the British State responded by arresting him. Germany wants him extradited and Turkey waits in the wings. Sooner or later they will find a way to sort out 'the extradition problem', thus the British can hand him back to Germany who can hand him back to Turkey. Or else they might just cut out the middle man, this would be their ideal situation.

Olof Palme of Sweden was assassinated more than ten years ago; it so happens he was also the only European leader who ever confronted the Turkish State at the most fundamental level, by 'recognising the Kurdish people as a nation and [committing] himself to attaining recognition of their rights.'[17] It would be comforting to suppose that the British and other European governments and state agencies act as they do through sheer cowardice. Unfortunately I doubt if this is the case. The Turkish

State has in place the means of authoritiarian control for which many Euro-state authorities would cut off their left arm. In certain areas they draw ever closer, for example in matters relating to asylum and immigration; their punishment of the most vulnerable of people; the torture that takes place in prisons and police-cells, the beatings, the killings. And not too long ago

> on 14 February 1997, the [British] government attempted to introduce a private members' bill, the Jurisdiction [Conspiracy and Incitement] Bill, which would have had the effect of criminalising support for political violence abroad. It was only defeated when two left Labour MPs, Dennis Skinner and George Galloway, unexpectedly forced a vote on the third reading and caught the government unawares, as they were relying on cross-party support for the Bill.[18]

In October 1996 came the *Lloyd Report*, published 'with very little publicity and only a brief press-release, an inquiry into counter-terrorist legislation . . . set up jointly by Home Secretary Michael Howard and Secretary of State for Northern Ireland Sir Patrick Mayhew. Such is the terrorist threat,' says the report 'that not only is permanent legislation desirable to combat terrorism, but past powers need to be further widened and strengthened.' The expert commissioned by Lord Lloyd 'to provide "an academic view as to the nature of the terrorist threat" [was] Professor Paul Wilkinson of St Andrew's University.' His 'academic view' provides Volume 11 of the report whose

> new definition of 'terrorism' is modelled on the working definition used by the FBI: 'The use of serious violence against persons or property, or the threat to use such violence, to intimidate or coerce a government, the public or any

section of the public, in order to promote political, social or ideological objectives.'[19]

No later than one month after its publication, 'amid allegations of financial losses', the *Mail on Sunday* named the professor as 'terrorist expert in college cash riddle'. Then came the more interesting information that Professor Wilkinson was 'believed to work for the British security services and the CIA'. There is one thing established by the fact that Wilkinson is still commissioned for work as sensitive as the *Lloyd Report*, this is the contempt held by the British State not just towards the public but its elected representatives.

His connections were something of an open secret before this; readers of *Lobster* magazine have known of his pedigree for at least ten years, in particular his 'inept role in the state's attempt to discredit Colin Wallace in the 1980s.'[20] This was when 'disinformation was run into the Channel 4 News office' by Wilkinson, two members of the UDA plus 'a former colleague of Wallace' at the Information Policy unit in HQ Northern Ireland.[21]

Notwithstanding any of this, the 'terrorist expert's' credibility is undiminished, and as I write, following the day of transport stasis in London,[22] one of Scotland's two 'quality' daily newspapers, the *Glasgow Herald*, again features the Professor's 'academic view'; on this occasion he proposed that 'to defeat their terrorist tactics, British and Irish security must target the godfathers of the IRA's crimes' and not give into such tactics as 'bringing a complex transport system to a halt . . . Any group of clever dicks in an open society could achieve that . . .'

The juridical system in Turkey may be complex but its central purpose seems straightforward enough, it sanctifies the State and protects it from the people. Following the 1980 coup and throughout the next decade changes in the law took place, the mechanisms for the suppression of Kurdish people altered. For the Kurds it became one nightmare after another. The level of State-sponsored terrorism degenerated to a point where sometime between 1981 and 1983, in Diyarbakir prison, forty Kurdish youths were tortured to death for refusing to say 'I am a Turk and therefore happy.'[23]

We have to respect the fact that it was not until 1984 that the Kurdish Workers' Party began its armed struggle. If we do not then we play into the hands of the Turkish propaganda machine. The new constitution had come into existence in November of 1982 and an indication of the potential repression is available there, e.g. this from the opening preamble:

> no thought or impulse [may be cherished] against Turkish national interests, against the existence of Turkey, against the principle of the indivisibility of the state and its territory, against the historical and moral values of Turkishness, against nationalism as defined by Atatürk, against his principles, reforms and civilising efforts . . .

Not only is the possibility of democracy denied at the outset, it is illegal even to think about something that might be defined by the constitution as 'against Turkish national interests'. The system is so designed that any Turkish government, courtesy of the constitution, is in thrall to a higher authority: the National Security Council (i.e. the military).

Some might argue that 'Turkish democracy' is designed solely to suppress the Kurdish population and it would be presumptuous of me to argue the point, especially with Kurdish people. But if justice is ever to be achieved by the Kurds in Turkey perhaps it will come about through the will of the majority of the people, and the majority is Turkish. Münir Ceylan, one of the contributors to the *Freedom of Expression* publication, makes the point that if you analyse the Anti-Terror Law carefully, it is obvious that [it] is intended to destroy the struggle for bread, freedom and democracy not just of the Kurdish people but of our entire working-class and working masses.

It seems that among Turks there has been an increase in solidarity with the Kurdish people, and also a willingness on the part of many to confront one of the world's most ruthless state-machines. The courage and perseverance of Dr Beşikçi surely have been crucial in this. Next to Abdulla Ocalan, president of PKK, the National Security Council appears to regard the sociologist and writer as its most dangerous enemy. Beşikçi is not Kurdish, but Turkish. Since 1967 he has been in and out of court and has suffered 'arrest, torture, jail, ceaseless harassment and ostracism'.[24] Now fifty-seven years of age, he has spent nearly fifteen years of his life in prison. Each time an essay, book or booklet of his is printed he is given a further term and so far the aggregate stands at more than 100 years. Under Turkish law his publisher is prosecuted simultaneously and to date has received sentences in the region of 14 years. Less than two years ago the two men 'were abused [and] physically assaulted while being conducted from prison to the court . . . [and their] documents . . . rendered useless.'[25]

There is a distinction between the people of a country and its ruling authority. The Turkish State is not representative of the Turkish people and neither is the British State representative of myself or Moris Farhi from England who was there in Istanbul on behalf of PEN International Writers-in-Prison Committee. My invitation to the Freedom for Freedom of Expression Rally came from Amnesty International (UK), by way of Scottish PEN. Although not a member of either body, I was glad to accept. There were twenty foreign writers present and each of us would have been conscious of the relationship to Turkey held by our individual

397

countries: Netherlands, Germany, UK and Sweden supplied two apiece; one each from USA, Mexico, Canada-Quebec, Finland and Russia; one writer represented Palestinian PEN, whereas six writers came from Israel.[26] The multiple trial of writers, artists and others which is now in process derives from January 1995 when

> Yaşar Kemal was tried in Istanbul's No. 5 State Security Court regarding one of his articles which was published in *Der Spiegel* magazine. On the same day, intellectuals gathered outside the court in support [and] decided to collude in the 'crime' by jointly appending their names to [that and other] articles and speeches alleged to be 'criminal'. The 'Initiative Against Crimes of Thought' was born [and] a petition started. Within a short time the signatures of 1080 intellectuals from various fields had been collected [and they] co-published a volume of articles entitled *Freedom of Expression*. Under the Turkish Penal Code Article 162: Republishing an article which is defined as a crime is a new crime, and the publisher is to be equally sentenced . . . On 10 March 1995 the 'co-publishers' voluntarily presented themselves before the State Security Court to face charges of 'seditious criminal activity'.[27]

Thus the State authorities were challenged at a fundamental level, leaving the Turkish Government 'with the old dilemma: either democratise the law and the Constitution or face the opposition of Turkish and world democratic opinion, and the stench of another major scandal.'[28]

There is scarce room for bureaucratic manoeuvring in the Turkish system and if a 'crime' has been committed there is little option but to prosecute. If not then the Prosecutor himself is open to prosecution.[29] So far the Freedom of Thought initiative has forced the hand of the authorities to the extent that the State Security Court has had to bring to trial 184 people. It is known as the 'Kafka Trial' and has been described as 'the most grotesque farce in Turkish legal history'. Even so, the State makes use of its power and 'for the accused [it is] likely to result in twenty months' prison sentences.' Some of them are already in receipt of suspended sentences for earlier 'criminal' thoughts or statements and their periods of imprisonment will be even longer.

The next step taken by the campaign organisers was to produce an abbreviated form of the *Freedom of Expression* publication, and then invite international authors to sign up as 'co-publishers'. In principle, the repressive nature of the Turkish legal system does not allow foreigners to escape the net, even on foreign soil. By using a network based on PEN International Writers-in-Prisons and other human rights' agencies the campaign's organisers managed to obtain the signatures of 141 writers as 'co-publishers' of the booklet. But this time the State Security Court declined to prosecute 'on the grounds that [they] would not be able to bring [the international writers] to Istanbul for trial . . . because such an "offence" does not exist in US or English law.' (Perhaps not yet. I take nothing for granted.)

So the campaign organisers moved a stage further; they invited some of the international writers to come to Istanbul in person, and present themselves at the State Security Court. Again using the network of PEN and other human rights' agencies, they asked that invitations be issued on their behalf. The twenty of us present included poets, film-makers, novelists and journalists. Interest in the 'Kafka Trial' has escalated within Turkey; at each public engagment there was a full-scale media presence.

On Monday morning more than half of us were in court to witness the trial of an actor, one of the 1,080 Turkish writers, artists and others who signed as 'publishing-editors' of the original

Freedom of Thought, the collection of writings by authors either already in prison or due to stand trial. Yaşar Kemal has received a twenty-month suspended sentence for his own contribution to the book. But the actor's trial was postponed until May, presumably when no international observers will be present. Meantime he continues rehearsing a joint production of Genet's *The Maids* and Kafka's *In the Penal Colony* and hopes to be at liberty to take part in the performances.

Following the postponement, some of us were due at Bursa Prison; the authorities were allowing us to visit with Dr Beşikçi and his publisher, Ünsal Öztürk. Others were scheduled to meet IsIk Yurtçu, a journalist imprisoned at Adapazara. Then permission was reversed by the authorities; we could make the journey if we wanted but we would not be allowed to speak to the prisoners. It was decided we would send a 'symbolic' delegation. A majority of us volunteered to make the journey but places were limited to three, and two went to Bursa Prison. Louise Gareau Des-Bois was nominated to visit Adapazara. She is Vice-President of Canada-Quebec PEN and also speaks a little Turkish; seven years ago the Quebec centre seconded a Kurdish PEN resolution concerning Dr Beşikçi. When she arrived at the prison the authorities reversed their previous reversal and she was allowed to talk with IsIk Yurtçu through a fenced area for nearly twenty minutes. What disturbed her most was the great number of young people behind bars, some little more than boys.

We were in court for a second occasion with Moris Farhi who was signing his name to the abbreviated version, *Little Freedom of Expression*. The State Prosecutor dismissed his declaration out-of-hand. The third time we arrived at the State Security Court a dozen of us were there on our own behalf. But a heavy contingent of police had been instructed not to let us enter the gate. The prosecuting authorities were refusing to accept our statements, not even if we sent them by registered post. We held a press conference outside on the main street and signed our statements in front of the television cameras. Münir Ceylan was there with us. He is a former president of the petroleum workers' union and from 1994 served twenty months' imprisonment for making statements such as the one quoted above. Recently he received a further two-year sentence and expects to be returned to prison any day now. His case has been taken up by Amnesty International, supported by the Scottish Trades Union Congress. He and others walked with us to the post office, in front of the television cameras, where we sent our signed statements by registered mail.

If the authorities continue to refuse our names alongside those of the Turkish writers and other artists who have been on trial, then the initiative's organisers will attempt to have the State Prosecutor charged with having failed 'to fulfil the constitutional commitment to equality of treatment.' It is a bold campaign and puts individuals at personal risk; some have been threatened already, some have experienced prison, others expect it sooner or later. On the same afternoon we had a public engagement at Istanbul University. A forum on Freedom of Expression had been organised by students and a few sympathetic lecturers. About twenty young people came to meet us then escort us to the campus; four of their friends are serving prison sentences of 8 to 12 years for 'terrorist' activities.[30]

Every day at Istanbul University between one and two hundred police are on campus–duty and the students have their bags searched each time they enter the gate. Along with us on the bus came Vedat Turkali,[31] a famous old writer who spent seven years in prison for political activities. He remains a socialist and is now domiciled in England. When we arrived we discovered not only had the forum been cancelled by the Security Forces, they had shut down the actual university. More than two thousand students had gathered in protest outside the university gates. We were instructed to link arms and march as a body, flanked by students on either side, straight to the gates of the university.

Hundreds of police in full riot-gear were also present. The cancelled forum on Freedom of Expression had become the focus of a mass student demonstration, the underlying concerns being the current withdrawal of subsidised education and the continued victimisation of the student population. I could not see any tanks although occasionally they are brought in on student protests. When we got to the gates at the entrance to the university the riot-police circled and sealed us off. Some student representatives, lecturers and the media were allowed into the circle with us. A few held banners, an act of 'terrorism' in itself, and were requested to fold them away, not to provoke the situation.

After negotiations with the Security Forces it was agreed that an abbreviated press conference could take place with the inter-national writers, and that statements might be broadcast to the students via a loud-hailer. Demonstrations are illegal in Turkey unless permission has been granted by the Security Forces. Most people have given up seeking permission; instead they organise a press conference and invite everybody. A female student opened the meeting then Şanar Yurdapatan[32] spoke, calling for everyone to stay calm, no blood should be spilled under any circumstances. Next to speak was the lawyer of the four imprisoned students, Pelin Erda, one of whose own relatives was raped during a period of detainment. Only about a dozen of the twenty international writers were present at this 'press conference' and each one was intro-duced. The situation was extremely tense and time restricted. Joanne Leedom-Ackerman (Vice-President International PEN) and Alexander Tkachenko (President of Russian PEN) were delegated to speak, and they were given a great ovation by the students. Then we had to leave at once, linking arms to stay as closely together as possible, returning quickly the way we had come.

There was no news of any bloodshed although we did hear that a disturbance and arrests had taken place in the area of the post office, after we had left the scene earlier in the day. That evening we attended a reception held for us by the Istanbul Bar Association. A few lawyers are among those openly expressing their opinions on the issue of freedom of thought and expression. We met Eşber Yagmurdereli, lawyer, writer and playwright, at present 'appealing against a 10-month sentence [for referring] to the Kurdish minority'. He is also under suspended sentence from an earlier case; if he loses the appeal he will face 'imprisonment until 2018'.[33]

It was at the same reception we heard that Ünsal Öztürk, Beşikçi's publisher, had just been released from prison. He came to our last official engagement, described as 'a meeting of writers and artists', organised by Turkish PEN, the Writers' Syndicate of Turkey and the Association of Literarists. However, there was little opportunity of a meeting as such. Twelve or more people spoke from the platform during the two hours, including some of the international writers. For some reason Öztürk was not invited to speak. Nor for that matter was Vedat Turkali. I mentioned to a member of Turkish PEN that it might have been worthwhile hearing what Turkali had to say and was advised that in Turkey there are 'thousands like him', whatever that might mean.

I thought it also of interest that Şanar Yurdatapan was not invited to speak. Yurdatapan and his brother, his secretary and a translator were our four main hosts and escorts throughout the four- to five-day visit, ensuring we remained together in the various awkward situations. He is one of the central organisers of this campaign and has served previous terms of imprisonment. He also led an international delegation to probe the notorious Güclükonak massacre of 'eleven men travelling in a minibus'.

According to official sources they were killed by the PKK, but the 'investigations left little doubt that government security forces carried out the killings.'[34]

We also met Ünsal Öztürk and his wife socially on the last night. They sat at our table for a while, giving information through an interpreter to Soledad Santiago of Mexico–San Miguel PEN who was hoping to take up his case through the PEN International Writers-in-Prison Committee, although he is a publisher and not a writer. Like Münir Ceylan and others, Öztürk is liable to re-arrest at any moment and I found it difficult to avoid watching his wife who seemed to be doing her best not to watch Ünsal too often and too obviously.

The next morning it was time to fly home to 'freedom and democracy'. For the flight into Turkey I had been advised to take nothing that might be construed as political – especially 'separatist' – propaganda. For the flight to Glasgow via Amsterdam on Thursday afternoon I was also careful. During the past days students had given me diverse literature to take from the country but the situation by this time had become extremely sensitive. In the lounge of our hotel that morning only four of the twenty writers remained, passing the time before being driven to the airport. There were people showing more than particular interest in us, and doing it in shifts. I thought it better not to take chances, and so I dumped the diverse literature.

When we left I bought three English-language newspapers. One carried a report on the introduction of torture in USA prisons; the other had a front-page lead on the arrival of a new prison-ship off the south coast of England – which may prove opportune for Turkey's justice minister who recently complained of

a negative atmosphere about Turkey. But now we will monitor human rights in Europe. The only thing Europe does is criticise Turkey. However, from now on we will criticise Europe.[35]

In Article 18 of the *Statutes of the Human Rights Commission*, the language itself is exclusive, where 'we' have 'a duty to encourage ethnic groups' whose culture is under attack but the 'ethnic groups' under attack are somehow left out of the equation. Perhaps 'we' do have a duty, but it is to stand aside and let 'them' fight back in whatever way 'they' deem necessary. Perhaps the real duty 'we' have is not to interfere when 'they' resist oppression.

I also accept the significance of the distinction between 'democratic rights' and 'human rights': 'democratic rights' – unlike civil liberties or human rights – 'assert the rights of the people to struggle against exploitation or oppression'; the right to defend yourself under attack, it allows of empowerment, of self-determination. I accept the right to resist oppression and that this right is inviolable. The people of Turkey and/or Kurdistan will resist oppression in whatever way they see fit. I can have criticisms of the form this resistance sometimes takes but I am not about to defend a position that can only benefit their oppressors.

Almost nothing of contemporary Turkish writing is available in translation via English-language UK or USA publishing channels. As far as I know, not even Beşikçi's work has managed to find a publisher.[36] At Glasgow's version of a press conference, organised by Amnesty International (Scotland) and Scottish PEN on the morning after my return from this extraordinary event in Istanbul, only one journalist turned up. This was an embarrassed young guy from *List* magazine, a fortnightly entertainment listings magazine. A couple of weeks before my visit to Istanbul, the *Scotsman* newspaper had included the following snippet in a rare UK report on Turkish domestic affairs:

Turkey's armed forces have intervened three times in the past 37 years to restore law and order in the country and to safeguard its secular nature.

Em Hene![1]

SOME PEOPLE FIND it possible to support campaigns on behalf of writers imprisoned for their political beliefs without worrying about the substance of these beliefs, why the writers are imprisoned in the first place. They know next to nothing about the writer's culture, community or society and manage not to regard such knowledge as fundamental to the campaign. It follows that they agitate for the cessation of human rights' abuses without inquiring why the rights of these particular human beings are being abused in the first place. At this time of writing, in Turkey there are many writers in prison but if one writer is being victimised for daring to give expression to a 'dangerous thought', it is likely that tens of hundreds are in the same plight, perhaps tens of thousands, with none but their family and friends to fight and campaign on their behalf. The writer and sociologist Dr Ismail Beşikçi has spent nearly fifteen years of his life in prison. He argues that those who campaign on his behalf must recognise that the campaign cannot be about one writer, it is about the existence of Kurdistan, it is about justice for Kurdish people.

Abdullah Ocalan is President of the Kurdish Workers' Party (PKK) and until his capture in Italy was one of the most wanted men in the world.[2] For the majority of the Kurdish people he is a hero. Beşikçi has maintained that Ocalan is a legitimate leader of the Kurdish people. In the first report I read of Ocalan's capture, the pro-Turkey bias was blatant, straight from the public relations department of the National Security Council. It is still a surprise when distortion and propaganda of this magnitude come unchallenged in the mainstream media. This example arrived via Associated Press (AP) thus would have appeared not only in the US but in the UK and elsewhere in the 'free' world. One comment sticks with me, that there have been 'no executions in Turkey since 1984'. That kind of rubbish is just disgraceful. Who knows the number of executions committed in Turkey since 1984. State executions are also 'extrajudicial', defined as the 'unlawful and deliberate killings of persons by reason of their real or imputed political beliefs, ethnic origin, sex, colour or language, carried out by order of a government or with its complicity [and] take place outside any legal or judicial process.'[3]

Human rights organisations will have approximations of the number. There can only be approximations. It is estimated that between 1991 and early 1997 there were 'more than 10,000 "disappearances" and political killings.'[4] Each Saturday in Istanbul women and girls gather in the famous old thoroughfare of Galatasaray to bear witness to the 'disappearance' of husbands, boyfriends, fathers, sons and brothers. The courage of these women and girls is quite something, there are hundreds of them. Most are Kurdish but a few are Turkish. Sometimes the police just wade in and batter them with riot-sticks, whether observers are there or not.

Football fans will recognise Galatasaray as the name of a leading Turkish football club. The stadium is not too far away and this area is at the heart of Istanbul's tourist quarter. Holidaymakers and football fans are surprised that the women are battered right out in the open. Some look the other way. This is encouraged by the British political authorities who, when they are not supporting the Turkish

State in a less passive manner, take care not to look themselves. It is only a few months since the end of that other sorry saga, the British Government's cowardly, but ruthless, treatment of Kani Yilmaz.[5]

In the above AP news item, mention was made of the German authorities 'seeking Ocalan on a 1990 warrant'. This refers to the time the German State prosecuted the PKK which up until then was a legal political party. The Turkish State was doing its utmost to have the PKK criminalised throughout Europe as a terrorist organisation. Their Deputy Chief of Staff on 1995 stated, 'We'll finish terrorism but we are being held back by democracy and human rights.'[6] Around that time there had been a horrible massacre 'in the village of Geri [when] 30 people, mainly women and children, were brutally killed.' This massacre was reported as the work of PKK 'terrorists', and the Turkish authorities 'showed video-footage for days to members of the European Parliament', in an attempt to discredit the PKK and to have its leadership outlawed as 'terrorists'. Subsequently a delegation from a human rights association went to the village of Geri itself and came up with somewhat different findings. Members of the delegation 'included the President of the now banned Socialist Party' and also Hatip Dicle, 'ex-MP of the Democracy Party [DEP], currently serving 15 years' imprisonment alongside Leyla Zana and three other DEP MPs.'[7] In Dicle's opinion, 'shared by all the members of our delegation . . . this massacre was an act of the contra-guerrillas.' But even though discredited, the Turkish State would regard its work of that period as highly successful, given that the German prosecution of the PKK resulted in its being banned.

Ismail Beşikçi was awaiting trial in a Turkish prison that same year. In an interview with Amnesty International he commented on the German prosecution, that the one thing it did establish was the existence of a 'secret agreement between the NATO alliance and Turkey in relation to Kurdistan'.

The Turkish State resorts to terrorism to achieve or maintain its ends and one large area of Turkey, the south-east, has been under martial law for years. The south-east of Turkey is the north-west of Kurdistan. Kurdish people have been executed summarily in this area for decades. The savagery of the Turkish military has been such that Kurdish people have crossed the Iraqi border. They would rather face Saddam Hussein than the monstrosities of the Turkish military.

During the 1960s there was a strong students' movement in Turkey as in different parts of the world and Abdullah Ocalan emerged from this. The political system of that time has been described as 'democratic Fascism'. Even that was too liberal for the military and they conducted a coup in 1971. The young Beşikçi had been doing his own sociological research from the early 1960s, coming up with certain findings in relation to the Kurdish people that did not suit the establishment, academic or politicial. He was by turn marginalised, victimised, excluded from academic work, had his work censored and suppressed; later he was brought before the law and imprisoned. It is ironic that a couple of the present Turkish Government were also rebellious students of the period, to the extent that they were imprisoned.

If Beşikçi was Kurdish and not Turkish he would be dead already. In the western 'democracies' he would neither be imprisoned nor murdered, just marginalised. There are different ways of suppressing the work of writers and it is doubtful if even one country in the world exists where freedom of expression can be taken for granted. Ismail Beşikçi's writings are suppressed by the Turkish authorities but people also need to pay attention to the fact that his work is not available to the English-speaking public of the world. None of his thirty-three books has so far been published in the English language.[8]

There is a block on information about Kurdistan. The UK

media are either silent or party to the different forms of propaganda issued on Turkey's behalf. The situation is epitomised by the UK travel industry which, under the nose of HM Government, tries to sell us 'summer sunshine holidays' in a war-ravaged police-state. The Turkish propaganda is often blatant but masquerading as news, as in the notorious article run by the *Observer* in September 1997, attacking 'the PKK in particular and the Kurdish community in general [which] consisted of a series of unsubstantiated allegations ranging from the perverse to the bizarre made by a young Kurd who had either been terrorised or disorientated or compromised by Turkish intelligence.' Harold Pinter and Lord Avebury were among those who condemned the newspaper publicly and many people were outraged to discover that such blatant disinformation circulates in one of the top 'quality' newspapers. It was important that the *Observer* should have been condemned but those who were too outraged might be suffering delusions about the UK media; it indicates the depth of untruth to which they have become accustomed.

Of course this is a time when the public receives images of starving children in Africa as adverts for national charities; the images themselves are structured on disinformation, much of it racist. These charities are headed by a vanguard of millionaire celebrities; members of the aristocracy, rock stars and movie stars; football stars, dashing young captains of industry, and so on. In their wake the public is supposed to donate money as a moral duty – or perhaps not quite, the money is to be given on the understanding that the suffering experienced by the starving children has to do with the inherent nature of Africa itself. It has nothing to do with politics, nothing to do with the foreign policy of external forces, not interest rates and not the movement of capital, nothing to do with 'guidelines' that may be enforced by the IMF or the World Bank. None of that. Instead the suffering is to be seen as a sort of physical attribute of the African continent, perhaps of the 'African character'. If the African adult population could learn to plan more efficiently and devise better strategies then they would take better care of their children. Until that indefinite point in the future the charities of the western democracies have to do the job for them, self-determination is not an option, not yet, and YOU can help!

The peculiar relationship the UK media have with the public was in evidence a few weeks ago (26 April), again in the *Observer*, this time it was a feature article by Norman Stone, 'renowned Oxford historian'. It was little more than a public relations exercise on behalf of the Turkish State. Professor Stone is currently at the Department of International Relations, Bilkent University, Ankara. Stone's views are of the far-right variety and he is open in praise of the 'true heroes' of our time, e.g. Brian Crozier.[9] For very many years Professor Stone's 'hero' was an 'operative of the CIA', and a leading figure 'within the whole panoply of right wing . . . intelligence and propaganda agencies' including straight CIA-funded projects such as the Congress for Cultural Freedom and Forum World Features.

Crozier was also a founding member of the secretive but highly influential Pinay Circle, 'an international right-wing propaganda group which brings together serving or retired intelligence officers and politicians with links to right-wing intelligence factions from most of the countries in Europe . . .'[10] In the UK he founded the Institute for the Study of Conflict, 'part of a network of right wing bodies . . . lecturing on subversion to the British Army and the police.'[11] This network included Common Cause, the Economic League and bona fide agencies of the British State such as MI5, much of whose 'intelligence work was inspired not by the demands of security but by extreme right-wing political ideas.'[12] Another colleague was Brigadier Frank Kitson who in 1969 'was seconded to Oxford University for a year to read and synthesize the literature on counter-insurgency. His thesis was published in 1971 as *Low Intensity Operations*, and a year later he was given command of a brigade in Belfast to test his theories.'[13]

Crozier is one of an international group of 'terrorist experts' who argues for 'the concept of internal war . . . and the parallel . . . between the situation of a country at war with an external enemy, and the country faced with a situation like Ulster, or Vietnam, or Turkey or Uruguay.' If the general public in these countries can swallow the idea that they are at war then all kinds of 'emergency regulations' can be introduced.[14] As with Professor Stone, he is an apologist for the brutalities of the Turkish military. 1971 was a crucial period in recent Turkish-Kurdish history, 'when the army overthrew the Demirel Government . . . and thousands of people were arrested and tortured in counter-insurgency centres which had been set up by Turkish officers trained by the U.S. in Panama.'[15] This is interpreted by Crozier as a 'military intervention to force the creation of a government determined to restore order.'[16] In response to an article critical of 'allegations of ill-treatment during interrogation in Ulster' he wonders why people were 'so distressed [by such] relative mildness . . . What if it [had extended] to the grim horrors reported during . . . the early 1970s in Turkey?'[17] Then he justifies the barbarism of the Turkish State Security forces on the grounds that it 'undoubtedly helped to provide the security forces with the intelligence they needed [to smash the Turkish People's Liberation Army] as an effective instrument of revolution.'

I think if I was Kurdish I would have become a wee bit tired hearing European writers and others urging the Turkish State to change its ways. It is difficult to think of one country in Europe that does not collude with Turkish ruling authority in one way or another. 'Turkish ruling authority' is just another name for Turkish

National Security which is just another name for the Turkish military. Beyond the *Observer* and the mainstream media in general, the contempt for the UK public is in evidence elsewhere, including at the highest levels of Government, as when the previously discredited academic, Professor Paul Wilkinson, was commissioned by Lord Lloyd 'to provide "an academic view as to the nature of the terrorist threat."'[18]

It would be of more value to the people of Kurdistan that we let our own governments know that we are aware of the reality, that we know what is happening behind the closed doors of power, we know of the cowardice of our own politicians and academics, and of their complicity, both at the present time and historically. We should accept responsibility and challenge those who hide in the shadows. If we expect media coverage of this 'dirty war' and the atrocities being perpetrated against the Kurdish people, we do so in the knowledge that weapons and torture implements used by the Turkish State are supplied by the Scottish and British business community, as well as those of USA, Germany and France.

While Professor Stone praises Turkey as the 'fastest-growing economy in the European region', another academic has now spent around fifteen years of his life in prison. Dr Beşikçi is being punished as an example to other writers, to other activists, to other academics, to other sociologists, to other scientists and – most crucially – to other Turks. During one trial speech he made the basic point that it was not he who was on trial but science itself. How can the science of sociology exist as a valid field of study until he is released from prison and his work made freely available? Until then the entire subject is contaminated, not only in Turkey and in Kurdistan but elsewhere throughout the world.

When I Was That Age Did Art Exist?

for Mia Carter

(a) addressed to students of sixteen, fifteen and fourteen years of age

ON MY WAY from Austin on board the plane I found myself worrying: just who is it am I talking to? sixteen-, fifteen- and fourteen-year-olds? What do I remember from that age? Okay, freshmen and sophomores, that's what they get described as. And I thought, God, I don't even know what freshmen and sophomores are. Where I come from we don't have these words to describe people of your age-group. I hate to say it but I don't think we have any words at all to describe you – horrible teenagers is about the nearest thing.

So at least here in Dallas, Texas as opposed to your compadres back in Glasgow, Scotland you get a little bit more respect from people, having your own distinct names for your own distinct age-groups. But maybe that doesn't please everybody. Not everybody wants to be categorised. Some of us prefer being total individuals. I suppose if you were a mature eleven-year-old and somebody called you a freshman then you would take it as one of the mightiest compliments you could ever be given. On the other hand if you were a seventeen-year-old male and somebody called you a freshman you might take it as a bit of an insult, you might want to take them outside and give them a sharp talking to.

And what if you were a seventeen-year-old female, what then? If somebody called you a sophomore, or a freshman? I have two daughters myself; if I had ever called one of them a freshman . . . well, they would just have given me a look, my daughters could give me the meanest of looks, even when they were babies.

So, who knows, freshman or sophomore, I don't. But you all do. Which is kind of weird. The only person in this entire auditorium who doesn't know what these words mean is me. And I'm the one up here talking! I'm the one that was invited here to talk, the respected writer, the one who's supposed to know about the nuts and bolts of language!

In so many different parts of the world we speak the same language, which is English, but that doesn't mean we all know what each other's talking about, we don't. Think about something as simple as football. If you talk about football here in Texas or anywhere else in the United States, or Canada, then you're talking about a bunch of enormous big guys all wearing crash helmets, all with big padded shoulders and various other paraphernalia, all charging about knocking each other down at every opportunity. But if you talk about football in my country and in almost every other country of the world then you're not talking about that game at all, you're talking about soccer. We call soccer football, and your kind of football we call American football.

We may speak the same language but that doesn't mean we all know what each other's talking about. In fact we often can't seem to 'hear' what it is the other person is saying.

There was a movie playing in Austin a couple of weeks ago called *My Name Is Joe*. It is set in Glasgow. The native language there – as far as I know, and I live there – is English, yet here in Texas the movie was playing and it had English subtitles. You know what subtitles are? In foreign-language movies you see a translation into English and it's written at the lower end of the screen – subtitles. So here was a movie set in my hometown with my people speaking the same English as they usually speak, but this English – my English – was being translated into another English, for the sake of all you movie-going people who live over in this part of the world.

It is interesting. I'm acquainted with at least four of the actors in that movie, and three of them have acted in plays of mine; when I go home to Scotland in May I'll be telling them that their English isn't fit to be heard in Texas. Yeah, interesting. Well, it is to me anyway. Of course I'm very aware that perhaps only half a dozen people in this auditorium have ever heard a real live Scottish person speaking in a real live Scottish accent, and for the rest of you it must be difficult, especially if I forget and speak *too* quickly.

But . . . I . . . am . . . trying . . . to . . . speak . . . slowly, slowly and clearly, trying to speak slowly, and clearly, but if I speak too slowly slowly and too clearly clearly then . . . I . . . will . . . start . . . seeing . . . you . . . all yawning and before long some of you will be falling asleep, right in front of me, falling asleep, your guest speaker!

No no, you would be far too polite to do that, no matter how boring I was.

It is only recently that I've been able to think about being sixteen, fifteen or fourteen years of age at all. Writers work so much from memory but being in that age-band seemed to have slipped from my own, even though as a writer I could be writing stories from the point of view of boys and young men and in my new collection of short stories[1] this is what I was doing for much of the time. But really, my own past is different from my stories, I'm talking about my own personal stuff. I don't make stories from my own direct experience, not in the way you might think. Some writers do. I am one of the ones who don't, I just make them up as I go along. Honest, yeh, like a kid would do, that is how I do it.

But take the age of fourteen, for a long time I hardly remembered it at all except in a general way as a sort of living hell. But when I tried to think What was hellish about it? it no longer seemed like a living hell at all, more like a bad dream. Not a nightmare, it was too boring to be classed as a nightmare, it was just a bad dream, a boring bad dream.

The truth is that from the age of twelve I went my own way to quite a large extent. I was earning my own money delivering newspapers. My parents didn't have time to worry about me. I have four brothers. As the second oldest I had to be a kind of minor adult myself, looking after the younger brothers and all that stuff, some of you'll know the feeling. But – and this is a fair confession – I didn't always manage to avoid temptation, sometimes I just ditched them along the way, I'm talking about my brothers, I would vanish round a street-corner, I didn't want them cramping my style. What a terrible way to behave, but all too common among siblings.

Let me pass beyond that, right to the major confession of this morning. Yes, I'm talking about the *major* confession, my career as a highschool student: it was lousy. My career as a highschool student was so lousy you couldn't describe it as a career at all. It was totally damn dreadful, it really was. This guy who has been invited here to talk to you. Yeh, it was farcical, highschool career, what a joke. I left as soon as it was legally possible, which was at the age of fifteen. Yes folks, the good old days. I can tell you're all jealous as hell. Fifteen was the age you were legally entitled to finish with school for ever and get yourself a full-time job in the world of adults, and that's exactly what I did.

My parents were surprised when I told them. No wonder. I hadn't given them any advance warning. But they didn't raise any serious objections. And as far as my teachers were concerned, well, I don't think any of them noticed. That includes after I was out the door, they didn't know I was gone. I was not the kind of guy they would prefer to see gone. Or even to see present. I was unnoticeable. I had not sparkled as a student, not even as a villain, not until what became my main accomplishment, getting sent home a couple of times because I insisted on wearing certain articles of clothing that were frowned upon by the authorities.

Shoes with pointed toes to be precise.

At that time in Glasgow, Scotland for guys of my age and background there was nothing more neat than black leather shoes with pointed toes, nothing more stylish, not in regard to footwear; you could wear them with laces or you could wear them with buckles, either way was good, either way was against the law of that school and the authorities took great exception to them. These authorities regarded the wearing of pointed-toe shoes as a sign of rebellion. They felt such footwear might lead to revolution. And as with authorities everywhere, those in the education department of Glasgow spent much of their time searching for the least sign of revolution, and then stamping on it severely. Any sign of rebellious behaviour; the authorities would stamp it out at all costs. So when I turned up for class wearing the cool footwear the registration teacher sent me to the headmaster's office and the headmaster despatched me home at once, never to darken the doorstep ever again, not in these shoes anyhow.

Yeh, I kept getting sent home from school. Some punishment! It was great! Freedom. My punishment was freedom!

My father started out with the same attitude as the school authorities. Even worse, when I first came home wearing these stylish pointed-toe shoes he threatened to burn them. I told him how can you burn them? They're not yours to burn, they're mine, I bought them out my own money.

And so I had, as I might have mentioned earlier: since the age of twelve I had been earning my own money from my seven-day-a-week job delivering newspapers. I bought the black leather shoes from my own wages and also certain other marks of juvenile rebellion back in the late 1950s, I'm talking about jeans. Yes folks, believe it or not, back in the olden days, authorities everywhere regarded jeans not just as evil but as a major subversive practice, they thought jeans were highly dangerous to the entire social order. It was simply out of the question to wear them to school, even for real rebels, and I'm not talking about myself now but the seventeen-year-olds, yeh, if you had had the gall to wear jeans to school you got the distinct impression the school authorities would have sent for the cops – in fact if they had had the choice these authorities would have sent you to prison, locked you up and thrown away the key.

But no matter how evil and subversive the Scottish educational authorities thought my pointed-toe shoes were, I was proud of them and, like I say, I bought them out of my own wages. Eventually my father accepted my argument. But not the headmaster. Although I do recollect him giving me to understand that we were both men of the world, and if I was in his position I would do the selfsame thing to me as *he* was doing to me.

But no, no, I wouldn't, I disagree. I definitely do not think I would have done what he did at all. For one thing, remember how I said I enjoyed the punishment. I mean if I was going to punish somebody I would try and make sure I didn't give the culprit something they enjoyed. My punishment was not to be locked up in school. Yeh, freedom. Freedom! Can you imagine it? Freedom to roam the streets, wherever whatever, instead of being locked up in school! A punishment!

No, I can't say I ever regretted getting myself a job and leaving the place at the very first opportunity.

But out in the world of adults there are some very strange things, occasionally difficult not so say dangerous things that can happen to young people, whether males or females, and most of you can make a few guesses about what I'm referring to. Many adults cannot cope with hearing about it, they turn their head from reality. They much prefer to stick with cartoons and fairy tales about growing up, nice little fantasy yarns about fluffy animals and all that sort of stuff.

It does bother me, as also it will bother most of your teachers that, unless things are dramatically different here from my country, adults seldom feel free enough to talk to young people about the difficult stuff some of you have to face up to. And what I'm really talking about here, as most of you may have guessed by now, is abuse. There are some horrible, really horrible, and shameful, abuses, as everybody here knows and there are people of your age and much much younger, little kids, who are forced to endure these horrible shameful things, most often on their own, unable to talk to anybody, not to their brothers and not to their sisters, not to their closest friends. And even *within* families these abuses can occur. Yet to talk about it is awkward and difficult, and too often it just is not socially acceptable. You start trying to discuss the situation and you can tell immediately everybody wishes you would shut up, people don't want to know, they switch off, turn their heads from you.

And talking about the home, without going as far as the question of abuse in the home, it is a weird thing to me how we've always got to pretend families are wonderful. Sometimes I look back and I think no, not wonderful, crazy – insane! families are insane, you have to be insane to live in a family, like the old joke goes, if you aren't insane to begin with then living in a family drives you to it.

When I was around your age group I remember the subject of family insanity could sometimes crop up in conversation with close friends; for example, the peculiar eating, drinking and general living habits of one's grandparents. If you mentioned that sort of stuff somebody would guffaw immediately then get self-conscious and start wondering how come you knew all their embarrassing family secrets, had you been spying on them or what? Of course also we had the extraordinary habits of fathers to consider; those provoked much discussion among us boys. In fact when people went silent in the company during that kind of conversation it always made me think, My God their old man must be even worse than mine!

Yeh, and that was among the boys . . . So the discussion must have been even worse among you girls. And here I'm now speaking as a father of two girls myself. I hesitate to even imagine what girls have to say on the subject of fathers and their peculiar behaviour, which is a good title for a story: 'The Peculiar Behaviour of Fathers'. If I ever see a movie or a novel or a poem or short story with that title in future years then I'll know the writer is probably a girl, probably from Highland Park Highschool here in Dallas, and probably attended this morning; and, like most future writers, kept her mouth tightly closed while her eyes and ears were as widely open as humanly possible.

But once you start to think about family life . . .! My God! And everybody in this room will have their own stories to tell. But stop! Don't tell them to me! I've got my own.

You must have noticed by now, surely, that soon as you start to talk about your troubles every last person has their own. And even worse, they want to tell them to you. Yeh, even when it's you that's doing the talking. Even when you're *already* doing the talking; even right in the middle of a sentence damn it they want to butt in with their tales of woe.

In fact, as soon as you even begin talking you'll notice that the person you're supposed to be talking to isn't listening, not at all, they're too fidgety. They're going from foot to foot, they're hopping about the place — hyper-tense, all twitches, nerve-ends jingle jangling, they can't even hear you they're so nervous, it's all they can do not to scream in their impatience, waiting for *you* to finish with *your* story so they can jump in with theirs, to tell you about all that's happened to them, in particular about how crazy their own family is! You think your family is crazy? Wait till you hear about theirs! They've got the craziest family in the entire universe.

So there you have it, one reason why you should all become writers, every last one of you; just so you can speak without being interrupted; so you can tell *your* stories without being interrupted.

I never thought of that before, when I'm writing one of my stories that is that, and nobody can butt in to tell me theirs.

Well of course even that depends, if you're living in a family, especially a family of kids, when you're working at the computer and some child comes bursting into your room: Daddy she hit me.

Excuse me oh daughter, I'm trying to write the masterpiece novel of the century.

Yes but daddy she hit me.

Oh yeh? That's your story.

I'm going to hit her back.

Okay . . .

Some of you here have reached sixteen years of age. I'm not sure of the situation in Texas but if you were in my country you would be legally entitled to get married without the permission of your parents. I'm speaking only of Scotland — not the United Kingdom as a whole — we have our own legal system. As far as marriage goes it is a more relaxed position. So other sixteen-year-olds from neighbouring countries like England and Wales have eloped north to our place. Traditionally, yeh, sixteen-year-old boys and girls run away from home to get married in Scotland. It really is romantic!

Except once they get there and discover it hasn't stopped raining for the past twenty-five years and when it does, well, we also have mosquitoes, we call them midges, pesky little blood-sucking varmints just like yours, all waiting to pounce. As soon as the rain stops out they come. But I suppose young love puts up with mosquitoes.

In some parts of the world it can be younger than sixteen to get married, at least for girls. Many years ago, when he was twenty-one years old, a famous rock musician married a girl of thirteen. This took place in one of your neighbouring states here, southern states. It caused a huge commotion. Even across the Atlantic Ocean myself and my friends all knew about it. At that time, I think I was younger than thirteen, but maybe the same age. I can tell you that it was a strange feeling to hear the news, like suddenly you had one less place to hide.

Growing up is not easy, to put it mildly, but it's also very personal, and that's sometimes forgotten by people, how personal an experience it is. We all do it, we all grow up, and yet we all do it differently, or so it seems. And about that young girl of thirteen who got married, in a sense it was like she was suddenly out there in the world with nowhere to turn, nowhere to go, nowhere to have her own space; these are the kinds of feelings I think I had back then.

Thinking about that makes me think about stories and story-telling, how we have our own stories, each of us, we have our own personal stories. It's slightly embarrassing to talk about but sometimes we've got to be honest. You know these stories about yourself. And no one else has access to them. I remember as a boy if I was walking down the road sometimes I would think of a song I liked and play it in my head. Yeh, at the same time as I was walking. Maybe I wasn't the coolest guy I knew but –

– nah that's a lie, of course I was: without question I was the

424

coolest guy I knew. Even if nobody else knew it. And nobody else did seem to know it. But when I was walking down the street with that song going in my head one thing it did help me get, I think, was a wee drop of respect, self-respect, no matter how minute that drop was.

But can you imagine being a parent at sixteen years of age, mother or father, and somebody not only expecting to treat you like a kid, but expecting to get away with it? Expecting *you* to just let them treat you like a kid when you're the mother or father of an actual kid yourself? It's weird.

A couple of boys I knew did get married at sixteen and were trying to raise their own kids with their own girlfriends who were now their wives. Not only were they entitled to think of themselves as adults, in a way so were the rest of us, us that were the same age. We were entitled to think of ourselves as adults as well, and we were entitled to whatever respect went along with it. That was how I felt. I still feel that way.

But even before I turned sixteen years of age there were things happening in my own life that I felt entitled me to respect, if not as an adult then damn close to it, at least as a responsible person with opinions of my own, and my opinions had as much value as those of anybody else. That was how I felt, even before leaving school to start work in the factory, I was having to deal with issues that are difficult to deal with, issues that can leave a mark on your life. Many young people have to deal with similar issues and a few have to deal with much more complicated issues, ones that most people here would find horrible. There were three things that kept me sane during my different troubles: friendship, sport and art.

Now I must quickly point something out here as far as art is concerned: I'm not talking only about painting and drawing, the visual arts; when I use the word art in this context, it is to cover *all* the different artistic areas that we can be involved in. Not just painting or drawing but also sculpture, and then there is dance and there is music; and movies, watching a movie, going to see a play, acting in a play, writing a play; writing a poem, reading poems; writing songs, song lyrics, composing your own music; reading stories, writing stories: all of these different activities – and others – come under the heading of art. So when I talk about art I'm talking about any or all of these different things, different activities.

And that was what it was that made life bearable for me, that was the one thing. Art. I'm talking about when I was sixteen, fifteen, fourteen years of age. If you put art together with sport and friendship then yeh, like I said, these were the three central things in my life, they made it bearable, they were mine. These three things were with me in my own time and in my own space, I chose them. Whatever ones I chose, it was me that chose them. I remember my mother finding one novel that I had chosen, I was either fourteen or fifteen at that time, and she dumped it into the fire. All I found when I came home from school that day was a pile of ashes. That was such an invasion of my privacy; as you can see more than thirty-five years later it still rankles. Yet I also remember that her finding the novel – okay there was quite a lot of sex in it, I confess – but it did not embarrass me that she had found it, and I mean that honestly, because I really did feel that I was not a child and had a right to be treated as an individual.

Art, sport and friendship. Some of you might think I've missed one out. And I'm including the parents and teachers here this morning, some of you might think I've missed out religion. Well, it's true, and so I have missed out religion. The things that kept me sane were, like I say, friendship, sport and art. These were the things that I was drawn to, that I chose. I chose them. So in that sense they were my things and not things imposed on me. My own feeling about religion was, when I was a boy and on into my teens, that like school and medicine you had to put up with it, you just had to accept or trust what the adults told you, that in the long run it was going to be good for you. But when I managed to get my own space and my own time it was not religion, I either opened a book or else I got the music on.

And maybe it was music more than anything else that kept me sane. It was music helped me keep my own secret life, helped me keep my own secret stories about my life. At the age of fourteen I could hear songs on the radio that sent shivers through me. I don't mind saying that to you. I don't know what I did when it happened. The songs I'm speaking about didn't have to give me thoughts. I don't think art does have to give you thoughts. Maybe all it does is make it that bit more enjoyable to sit staring into space, or at the wallpaper, or the paint on your ceiling; staring at nothing at all, I don't know. But without art, and for me in particular music and books, and I'm speaking here about your age, when I was your age, it would have been very difficult to cope with life. Sure it's a big thing to say. But art can be a life saver. There is no doubt about it. And that gets missed by people, just how crucial it is for you. That goes right throughout your entire life, but I have to say this as well, sometimes I think that it never means more to you than now, when you're into the age you are right at this moment.[2]

Let me say briefly about sport, I still love sport, not only watching others but doing it myself. One of the difficult things for me in getting old is not being able to play certain sports myself, and I'm talking especially about soccer. I wasn't particularly good but I loved playing it. Unfortunately you can't always play the sport you like. I mean if I had loved basketball as a wee boy, slowly but surely, never having grown beyond five foot nine inches, I would have been forced out of competition. And your brand of football, what we call American football, that would have been a problem too because I was not tall and not built like a tank and it's like you have to have certain physical characteristics to play that game, mostly dependent on whether or not you've lived on apples, milk and T-bone steak all of your life for breakast dinner and evening meal, and what happens to vegetarians is maybe another question.

But what if I was a skinny little Japanese boy and I loved Sumo wrestling? Even worse, if I was a skinny little Scottish boy and loved Sumo wrestling. Or what if I had the build of a Sumo wrestler but I loved tennis? Or ice-hockey, or athletics, long-distance running? And then of course what if I had some debilitating physical condition, what if I was confined to a wheelchair or, I don't know, if I became blind and I loved playing baseball, or nine-ball pool, and so what happens, could I ever again participate? And what if I had been born a girl, how would that have affected me, the whole way in which I looked at sport, would it change completely?

There is no question that there are these things about sport that at a certain level are in-built into them, and what they do is exclude a very wide variety of people. Whole groups of people cannot get involved in particular sports as players, simply because of their physicality, and I include gender and age in that.

It means that sport is not as equal as people like to make out. And not only that, other things enter into it, like money. In my country some sports are only open to you if your parents have cash. They never seem like real sports to me, even nowadays they don't seem like real sports, because so many of the population just cannot hope to play them. I won't waste time on examples, they vary from culture to culture. Let me just say that in most countries in the world you have to have money to play golf, only rich people play golf, but not in my country, golf is much easier to get into, and not too difficult in some parts of Texas as far as I'm aware, so it does vary from culture to culture.

I'm going to speak now about trust and how you come to trust art. Usually we associate trust with friendship. Sometimes I think we place too much emphasis on friendship. Yeh, it's great to have friends and without them life would be very difficult indeed, and sometimes we do need to rely on them. But without friends it is possible to survive. I know it sounds a bit strange. I'm saying that without friends it is possible to survive.

It isn't that friends let us down so much as sometimes they just don't have choices. Nobody wants to let people down. But there are times you don't have a real choice. Maybe there's a clash of loyalties, maybe you're forced to put your family first. Those of you with brothers and sisters might have experienced this. Also there's the other side of the coin; your family is your family, but sometimes we need to be with friends from outside the family, and then we get those feelings of disloyalty, we start thinking how selfish and unnatural we are because we prefer the company of friends rather than brothers or sisters. But I don't see that as unnatural at all, I see it as perfectly natural. We should not feel that we're selfish, it's a really natural thing. I have four brothers and I have two daughters so I have always been aware of that problem. We do need our own space and so often that's easier to get with friends than with family. What I find is that your family can become friends, but that tends to happen as you get older. Yeh, it's great to have friends, but it is possible to survive without them. And for some people I think it is an amazing thing to discover. I set great store by my friends. I always have done. But discovering you can survive without them, that is something.

I think all I'm saying here is that when the going gets tough, maybe the only thing left for you at a real basic level is art. One of the things about it is how it just seems to require you, just you yourself. You've had a really bad day, and eventually you get home, you vanish into your room if you're lucky enough to have one and don't have to share it with other members of your family. But whatever, even if you don't have your own room, you maybe can find your own space somewhere, just enough to get into your own head, get on your own music. Or maybe you discover that little bit more energy, just enough to open the pages of a book, and that writer may lead you into another story altogether, somebody else's story. And all you have to do is *open* the book. If the writer is any damn good they'll force you to turn the pages. Sometimes that turns out to be what good writing is, if ever you want a quick definition – to pass an exam or something, impress a new teacher. Good writing is the thing that stimulates you into turning the page. But it's only a quick definition. It gets tricky after that. In fact I would be wary of this one altogether, so why did I even bother saying it!

But there is something going on in art that drew me to it right from an early age, and whatever else it had to do with it also had to do with freedom and truth, and integrity, and no hypocrisy.

There were always things that sickened me in life and I want to draw attention to two of them; the first is bullying and the second is hypocrisy. And by hypocrisy I mean people acting or saying one thing, but doing another. And not just so-called adults. In a strange way, in my early and mid-teens, I expected hypocrisy from adults. But not from people my own age, especially friends and close acquaintances, somehow I didn't expect it from them, so when it did happen it sickened me.

No, I wasn't blameless myself, it is difficult to stand up for what you believe. Most of the time I took the easy way out, not standing up to the bully, whatever form it took. I preferred not standing out, not drawing attention to myself, even though I would be all too aware that some people just don't get that option, unlike me they couldn't hide. I was one of the lucky ones in that sense, I could hide. But not everybody is lucky, maybe to do with race or religion, the colour of people's skin, whatever the bully's prejudice happens to be, kids do get picked on, whether at highschool or on the street. Even at home within the family, it's amazing how much bullying goes on inside families. Throughout society you come to find so much is dominated by bullies, and the more you go into it the more you see the extent it happens. It's not only kids but all kinds of people who get picked on and who get harassed and bullied and victimised within society; racism is probably the worst, yeh, but other things are there too. But just so many areas in our society are dominated by bullies, by out-and-out bullies.

Freedom and truth, and integrity, and no hypocrisy. For some of you it might sound a strange way to think about music, stories, or the theatre, or poetry, painting, dance, the movies, other forms of art in that way. Most of you are used to thinking about art in a different way, as a form of entertainment, maybe high-class entertainment but only as entertainment all the same. But I don't see it that way. On its own I don't think 'entertainment' is powerful enough to describe what our relationship to it is, the way that we respond. When you think about it, how could it be? How could entertainment be enough to help you through these difficult times, to survive these horrible traumas? But that is what art does. Of course art can be entertainment, but it is so much more. And although I may not have said it in these words, I think what I've been saying just now is close to what I felt those many years ago, back at the age you all are. I trusted stories, and music. I trusted them, and other forms of art too. And I still trust them.

(b) addressed to students of eighteen, seventeen and sixteen years of age

The vast majority of you are eighteen, seventeen and sixteen years of age. As you know I'm also talking to students younger than yourselves, sixteen-, fifteen- and fourteen-year-olds, and I've been finding it interesting to look back on these two age bands myself, seeing whether I really can separate them. You'll all be pleased to hear that I can. I'm sure you don't want to be told by some old guy like me that life at eighteen years of age is hardly different from life as a fourteen-year-old.

I turned fifteen during the month of June, a couple of weeks before the long summer break from school, and less than three months later I had left and was out into the world of adults, working full-time in a factory.

I wasn't any good at school. I didn't like it at all. The career-guidance people used to come round and speak to us in class occasionally and at other times you were invited to go and see them. Because this meant you could miss an ordinary school period I took the opportunity whenever possible. One time they asked me if I found anything of interest that they were talking about in school, surely there was some one thing that interested me. I don't think they were being sarcastic. I told them that the art classes did interest me, just a wee bit. So they got me an interview for a job connected with art, what they thought I thought was art. The job they got me an interview for was in a printing factory. I suppose the career-guidance people were thinking of graphics and so on, to give them the benefit of the doubt. I never gave it a thought, I was just amazed, and glad, to be out in the world of adults.

In different parts of the world, other cultures and other societies, that's how things are to this day, not just for fifteen-year-olds but children half that age, they have to work to find money to survive on their own account, little kids under ten years of age, their parents are unable to take care of them, for whatever reason, and the proper authorities either do not or cannot accept responsibility for their welfare. It's one reason why we can buy cheap clothes and stuff down at the local mall, because it's just kids making them and their employers just pay them a kid's wage. But in my own case I've never regretted finishing with school at fifteen. Not then not now. I preferred working in a factory. That's how bad school was for me! Working full-time in a lousy factory was my preferred option.

I know school is much much better nowadays and that you'll all be perfectly content and satisfied . . . Not one of you will ever have wished you could just run away and join a circus. Well, maybe a couple of years ago.

But my parents were surprised when I told them I was leaving for ever on Friday and starting work first thing Monday morning. They were wise enough not to raise any serious objections. With five boys in the family things weren't easy economically, I'm speaking about finance. From the age of twelve anyway I was working seven days a week delivering newspapers. And I enjoyed spending the dough I earned. The marks of juvenile rebellion, all these rebellious articles of clothing, I bought them out of my own wages. It was my business, or, as I might have put it as a wordly-wise fifteen-year-old, it was between me and my tailor.

I'll be impressing some of you with my youthful manliness and maturity and all that kind of nonsense. Other manly and mature habits of that period included smoking. How manly and mature smoking is can be seen from the fact that I began when I was nine years old and had the habit well and truly developed by the age of twelve.

But when you think about it, there I was working like crazy as a wee twelve-year-old newspaperboy and these gigantic worldwide tobacco corporations were already screwing me week in week out, extracting a regular percentage of the pittance I got for a wage and sticking it into their own multi-billionaire corporation coffers, in the full knowledge that they were damaging my health into the bargain. Talk about shameful!

I'm serious, it's quite amazing the different ways young people get exploited. When I started working life in the printing factory I was paid even less money than I was delivering newspapers. Yeh, for my first full-time work I had to take a drop in wages from what I earned as a schoolboy doing all my deliveries. Of course I knew I couldn't be a newspaperboy all my life. And even if I did, the wages were unlikely to rise in keeping with my age which was going to increase at its usual rate – which I found a staggering truth in itself, I just mean the idea that I was getting older every single day of my life. I'm talking about all the time! What an extraordinary thing. Every solitary minute of the day I was growing older!

Sometimes I couldn't sleep at night thinking about it.

And then suddenly I would be dead in my coffin!

That is, if I was lucky enough to afford a coffin, because even back in the olden days, dying was an expensive business. So expensive you had to save up your money. That was what I heard anyway, from all the coffin-box makers and their advertisers. Anybody who's been to Los Angeles, that's what I recollect, everywhere you looked it was adverts for mortuaries and cemeteries and gardens of remembrance. But maybe if I spent all my dough in advance, maybe if I went into debt, I don't know what they would do, I'm talking about the coffin-box industry, these gigantic worldwide mortuary and undertaker corporations, maybe they wouldn't allow me to die if I still owed them money for their product, their gold-lined, feathered-nest, lap-of-luxury coffins and their nice wee plots of land overlooking tasteful, scenic views.

Some imagination. How did I get into this?

Working in a factory.

Yes. So, working in a printing factory was my strategy. I got a job as an apprentice compositor, learning how to fill in these rectangular blocks, so that when each was printed it would make up into a proper book page or else a printed form of some sort.

Probably nobody here knows what a compositor is.[3] One way to think of it is that it was the compositor's job to compose the pages of print. If you think of a page of print, any one page of print – say in a book, for example – how each word is composed of letters and between the words there are spaces, and between the lines there are other spaces; think of one page as an entire block that requires to be filled, and the compositor fills it, with letters and all kinds of punctuation marks and symbols, and also spaces.

Each individual letter, punctuation point or number, and each individual bit of space that you get between words and lines, each had its own individual bit of lead. Think of one line of one page of print. Most of you will already be working on computer. Think of the different fonts, not a big typeface like 'New York' but a small font like 'Times', and now think not of a 9- or 10-point face, think of a 6-point face, yeh, we used to work with tiny little 6-point typefaces and each one of these tiny little letters had its very own tiny little piece of lead type. Imagine it.

Okay? So maybe some of you'll get an idea of how finicky the job of compositior could be, piecing all these tiny bits of lead type together to make a whole page ready for printing – just one page. You would feel sorry for these huge big guys with big thick, beefy fingers, trying to sort out these tiny little bits of lead type; really, it was very painstaking and very precise. Yeh, when you think about it, it was quite a dainty job.

Take one page of a broadsheet newspaper, say the *New York Times* or the *Dallas Herald*, and now imagine all the different things that go to make up that one page. All of what goes to make up just one page of a broadsheet newspaper, imagine it, the different fonts, the different style of fonts, the different sizes of the words; the size of headlines, the size of the classifieds, the style of words, italics, bold-face, shadows, outlines, underlines, and so on. Now add in the photographs, and whatever else. Those of you who are into graphics could tell me so much more. So okay, add in all your graphics. And cartoons, what about cartoons! Yeh, throw in the lot. Now get it into a proper rectangular shape and give it a frame.

In the old days what you get there on each page of a newspaper was put together by the compositor. It was an incredibly complicated business. The compositor was preparing the way for the printer. It was the printer who would receive the framed blocks you had put together. You gave them to him one by one and away he went to prepare for the inking, then he would place them one at a time into the printing machine. And eventually out of all that process would come a complete broadsheet newspaper.

I hope some of that makes sense.

Anyway, after going through all of that with you, it is now my duty to tell you that my old job of compositor no longer exists, not in our society anyway. It's been killed off by computer technology. In some countries with much less developed technologies than ours, compositors still exist but there will come a time when the trade will die out altogether.

For those who have an interest in the way old newspapers used to be with these old printing offices – like you'd imagine in a Sherwood Anderson or Ernest Hemingway story, or O'Henry – I recommend you make a visit to what is probably the earliest road in North America: El Camino Real, the Old Spanish Trail from Mexico to the Florida coast, via San Antonio and Natchitoches, Louisiana, 'the main thoroughfare across Texas'. Head along there to the town of Alto in Cherokee County and, with a bit of luck, the

436

reporters' offices and entire compositors' caseroom and printing works, lock, stock and barrel of the *Alto Herald* will still be there. You expect old Thomas Mitchell to come walking out smoking a cigar. The *Alto Herald* newspaper no longer exists but the place does. The newspaper amalgamated with the *Cherokee Sentinel* and is now known as the *Cherokee Herald*. When it closed down some thirty years ago the folk there just locked the door, and they left everything. And the place is still there. It is on Main Street. But Main Street is no longer the main street, it was bypassed years ago. Nowadays Main Street is a little backwater. But let me tell you that one of the twentieth-century heroes of the Texas newspaper business worked there at the *Alto Herald*. And she did so for something like sixty years. She was a real compositor: Mrs Mamie Lee Carter.

The town I come from is Glasgow and it used to be quite a good place for newspapers. Not now, but once upon a time. Glasgow was one of the first industrialised cities in the world and was known for its shipbuilding for close to a hundred and fifty years. Very different from the fantasy world most of you associate with Scotland, based on cartoon movies like *Braveheart*, *Rob Roy* and *Highlander*. I think of them as the tartan equivalents to the Irish dancers doing their *Riverdance* stuff. I never quite believe it. But maybe that's just me . . .

Back when I was a boy in the far-off 1950s a few of the famous old shipyards remained in existence and it was still a bustling place. Of course you could no longer catch a boat direct to New York harbour. At one time you could, about ninety years ago, you could buy a one-way boat ticket from Glasgow to New York at the cost of five pounds sterling – then about twenty dollars. Maybe the most appropriate way of working out what that amounts to in present-day terms is to consider that five pounds sterling would have equalled about five weeks' wages for a labouring man doing an ordinary unskilled, labouring job.

"And the judges said . . ."

You may remember me saying how as a fifteen-year-old I told my career-guidance teacher about a vague interest I had in art. It's true. The art class was the only one that I would have gone to of my own free will. I remember one basic thing about it, that the teacher there assumed you wanted to do it, and then she left you alone to get on with it. My teacher was a woman, she was older. I recollect that her name was Miss Harper and that she treated me as a responsible human being. That is how good she was. I thought it then and I think it now.

Okay when I spoke about art I was thinking about the visual arts, painting and drawing, especially figure drawing; I used to like doing hands and fingers, legs, shoes, and heads; but not so much faces, I always had trouble with faces, especially the faces of girls and women. I cannot remember ever getting anything that was like a real girl or woman's face. Mainly it was males I drew and painted, although even with males I had difficulty with faces. But I enjoyed it, I could spend time doing it. I also enjoyed looking at the paintings and drawings done by other people.

I had four brothers and no sisters so obviously I was curious about the difference between males and females; figure paintings and life drawings did attract me and not always because of the art so-called. I confess it! The facts of life were a taboo subject in my home. Nobody spoke about things like that. I don't know how my four brothers got on, but for me it was a bit of a headache.

Even at this vaguely humorous level you can see how art becomes something more than entertainment for a lot of young people, more like a life saver, at least for boys without sisters in a house full of taboo subjects. Scotland used to be a fervently religious place. And that can make it tricky for young people, you end up with some very weird ideas about cabbages and apples and I'm sure without encountering art I would have looked even more of a fool.

When I Was That Age Did Art Exist?

The work of the artists helped me with my education, the kind that somebody often provides informally, like an uncle or an aunt, an older cousin, maybe even your grandparents – somebody older and more experienced, somebody that you can trust to tell you the truth and who isn't hung up on taboos the way your parents can be. And whoever it is you know you can trust them, even if they deceive you, you know it isn't done intentionally, they are doing their best, they have integrity; if they go wrong it is not deliberate.

We can come to art at an early period in our lives, much earlier than most people think. It is worthwhile thinking this one out, why that should be the case; I think it has to do with indoctrination myself, we are taught that we have to be educated in order to appreciate art. Well, whether that is true I don't know. But one thing I do know is that in order to love art no education is necessary at all, none.

Eventually in the visual arts my own interest extended to other things beside the bodies of males and females, moving beyond the beauty of the human form. And the reason was not always to do with me. Sometimes the artists didn't allow me any choice. They *forced* my attention to other subjects, subjects of their own choosing. They took control. That is what happens in art, the artist takes you places; into areas of experience outside yourself, into ways of life that otherwise you might never encounter, not personally, not in ten lifetimes.

Around that same age of fifteen I found a little book on the French Impressionist painters and next to the prints of the paintings there were snippets of biographical detail. I found the lives of these artists interesting. In fact I found their lives extremely exciting. They were standing up for what they believed in, many of them had nothing, they went without food, they had a tremendous commitment to what they were doing. And the authorities didn't like it. That was a rule of thumb for me, if the authorities didn't like it then it might be interesting. From there I became interested in the lives of the artists and I used to love reading biographies of the French Impressionists, including some who were not French and some who, strictly speaking, were not even Impressionists.

Van Gogh and Modigliani were two early heroes of mine, and Cézanne. I thought Cézanne was the greatest. In his entire lifetime that guy never managed to sell one painting but what a painter! Look at the way he changed everything about. He and the writer Émile Zola were close friends in their youth. They had a row later on. As far as Cézanne was concerned that was that, he wanted nothing more to do with Zola. Zola felt differently, he wanted to patch up the quarrel. I was so into their work and their lives and that whole environment that I took a position on the feud! I would get quite carried away and want to travel across to Montmartre and see Cézanne, forgetting the guy had been dead for sixty years: 'Come on Paul, Émile just wants to end the feud . . .' As you can see at the age of sixteen, seventeen, I was a total romantic. I read Zola quite thoroughly but then into my late teens or early twenties I got totally nauseated, and I haven't read him since.

In Forth Worth just now there is an exhibition by two other great painters, Matisse and Picasso, and if you don't know their work, well, I recommend it. Most of you have heard all about it by now and some of you will even have been to the exhibition. Picasso is one of the best-known and best-loved artists of this century. He can be an interesting artist for other artists to consider. There's a museum in Paris devoted to his work. So much of his stuff is available to the public that you can get some idea of his working methods. Maybe not just of his but of artists, you can pick up ideas on how artists might work in general. I'm not only talking about painters. I think writers can also benefit, and musicians, every kind of artist. Be aware that when I use the term 'artist' it usually covers every kind, from sculptors to dancers; musicians and actors, playwrights and poets, novelists, makers of movies; all of these different individuals come under the heading of artists the way I'm using it here.

Original, innovative artists like Picasso can get a lot of hostility because they move away from representational art, by which I mean ordinary, naturalistic pictures; scenes from day-to-day life as everybody seems to know it and to live it. A thing to remember about many great artists when they are young, and Picasso was one of them, he was already painting like some of the great masters, doing very fine figurative paintings and life-drawings. There's only so long you can carry on doing that. And why should you anyway, if somebody's already done it? Why paint like Rembrandt since Rembrandt's already done it. No great artist is ever content to stand still. It's boring! My God! Why keep doing the same old thing! No artist ever *wants* to do that. Great artists certainly don't, they extend themselves. Even although most critics can't cope with it and hate it when the artists do it, still the artists go away and they do it anyway. Sooner or later the critics try to catch up with them, but they don't always succeed. And what you find is that many great artists are unknown even up to when they die and like Cézanne, Van Gogh and so many others, they don't really sell anything except to friends and family.

If you follow the work of individual artists they can lead you on to things you never thought about before. Picasso, Matisse, artists of this and earlier periods. From an early interest in the shapes of human beings, they can lead you into an interest in shape itself, believe it or not, abstract shapes, triangles, squares, cubes; they can get you interested in the way that light bends, in science, in mathematics, in philosophy. Look at the influence Cézanne had on Picasso and Cubism.

If you are prepared to go along with it, then artists can bring you from elemental aspects of humanity into a much more complex world, a mysterious haunting world. You see so-called ordinary portraits by artists from 200, 300, 400 or 500 years ago and they take you into the depth of humanity, from portraits of these individual human beings, walking out of history, you look at these paintings and you're into the complexity of human existence, even into the depths, the darker recesses of the mind, reminiscent of the stories of that great writer and fellow-countryman of yours, Edgar Allan Poe, these strange tales of imagination and mystery. Poe's step-father was Scottish and as a boy young Edgar spent a little bit of time in Ayrshire. He enjoyed magazines such as *Blackwood's* which published writers like James Hogg. Well, there is only one James Hogg so I don't know why I'm using the plural. Many of James Hogg's stories are full of ghosts and demons and strange psychological musings. My country's always been okay for that kind of stuff . . . strange psychological musings . . . the darker recesses . . . etc., etc. It ain't necessarily a good thing. But on the other hand . . .

I was saying earlier that sometimes we get into the work of somebody – it can be any sort of artist; a musician, a writer, dancer, sculptor, whatever – and then we find ourselves moving and developing. That happens because we allow ourselves to get into their work properly, we are open to it; we haven't gone into it with our own agenda, with our prejudices to the fore. We have been open to these artists and they have taken us to a different level. It can be that we don't have any choice in the matter, the artists have forced our attention to somewhere else. And we don't have to look at the work of the master artists, we can use more basic examples. I recall again from my mid-teens, fourteen, fifteen, sixteen, that I was reading books by the cowboy author Louis Lamour. Yeh, this was back in Scotland, the cowboy tradition interests males quite a bit in Scotland. But I confess that other cowboy writers just bored me. Louis Lamour was one of those writers like Raymond

Chandler who sometimes can lead people away from genre fiction, and by genre fiction I mean cowboy stories, sci-fi stories, horror stories, love stories, private-eye stories, cops and robber stories, hospital stories, and so on, where there are set ideas about things. And it can be difficult for writers to break out of that.

At a younger age though it wasn't painting and literature so much that excited me, it was music. From before the age of fourteen, myself and other young folk in the main cities of the United Kingdom were listening to people like Buddy Holly, Fats Domino, Brenda Lee, Connie Francis, Del Shannon, Sam Cooke, the Everly Brothers. Later came major bands from some of our own UK cities and this is not long after I turned sixteen years of age, I remember it quite well. There were two crucial influences on these bands from here in the United States, one was blues, great music being produced by working-class black people, a few of them Texans; the other was country and western music, great music by working-class white people, mostly from the south, and a few of them were also Texans.

As I have said elsewhere, these musicians, black and white, had a striking impact on the young people of my country. They sang of their own lives and in their own voice, from their own emotion, whether rage, hatred or love. They didn't try to be something they weren't, and neither were they ashamed of what they were. At the root of what they were about was self-respect, as I see it, they had respect for themselves and each other, respect for their own culture and their own people. And another thing that is important to recognise, the people I'm talking about, black people, white people, working-class people, they had assumed the right to create art. They just went out and did it. They made no apologies for how they played, how they sang, how they dressed, how they spoke, none of that – in fact the opposite, they took a pride in it.

This I see as the essential thing young people in my own country were learning, especially young working-class people. It's crucial to understand and appreciate that point: the people who were learning self-respect through the art of music were people who were used to being taught their own inferiority. Yes, and I'm referring here to the education system every bit as much as society in general. As a working-class white boy in my country I was used to hearing about how inferior such a background was. In different ways it was tough, yeh, but so what, as far as these black musicians were concerned, and also white working-class musicians. Okay, life could be better but you still had the right to enjoy art and even more than that, you had the right to make it. You had the right. Nobody gave you that right, nobody was ever going to give you that right, you just took it; that was what you had to do, you had to take it, you exercised freedom. Nobody gives you freedom, it's there for the taking.

And relate that to me talking about pointed-toe shoes earlier on. These people exercising their freedom to make music in whatever way they wanted were also exercising another freedom and it was to do with style or – to award it greater status – how *to be in the world*, how to dress. This also came out of the 50s into the 1960s, that among us working-class young people we started dressing as we wanted. And we wore clothes in which middle-class people would not have been seen dead, at least not to begin with. Later on, around the mid-1960s, young people from the middle-class thought it was cool, and no doubt rebellion also was part of that, and they started to dress in a similar way to working-class kids, it's no coincidence that the young middle-class people were associated mainly with art colleges.

It took a while before I found anything comparable in literature to what was happening in music, and not from living writers. I did find writers from earlier generations whose work I found extremely exciting, dynamite. But these were either from the last century or else from earlier this century. I never found work by contemporary writers that had anything resembling the impact of contemporary rock music, which more than anything kept me sane. But later on I started to find that writers were also doing strong things, they also were working in ways that attracted me strongly.[4]

There is a difference now because for the past twenty-five or more years I have practised art myself, and I've tried to live by it. In my case I've been a writer of stories. That is what I do for a living. How lucky can you get! People pay me to make up stories! Sometimes I can still find that amazing. I heard a musician, a local Texas guy, I think it was Ray Wylie Hubbard, he was talking a couple of months ago on the Austin Music Network, and the interviewer was asking him something along the lines of, 'Does it not bother you that hardly any people beyond the Texas border have ever heard of you?' He just shrugged and told the interviewer how he had made a living out of writing and playing music for the last thirty years. There was never anything else he ever wanted to do, so what was wrong with that.

Exactly.

That goes for me too. I can make up whatever stories I like, the most outrageous yarns, it doesn't matter. I can use whatever language I want. It just depends on the story. It is up to me, all up to me. I make the decision.

There is one thing integral to what I'm saying and that is

freedom. More than anything maybe that is what it comes down to. Art is one of the only places on the planet where you can find freedom; remember that.

Notes

INTRODUCTION

1 The essay was published in the Glasgow-based *Variant* magazine, vol. 2, no. 2, spring 1997.

2 From *Situations Theoretical and Contemporary* by Tom Leonard (Galloping Dog Press, Newcastle, 1986), reprinted in his *Reports from the Present: Selected Work 1982–94* (Jonathan Cape, 1995).

3 *Busted Scotch* (W. W. Norton Ltd, New York, 1997), for US publication only.

4 'Artists and Value' and 'The Importance of Glasgow in My Work', from my collection *Some Recent Attacks: Essays Cultural and Political* (A. K. Press, 1992).

5 Published by Clydeside Press, Glasgow, 1988.

6 George Eadie and John McLaughlin.

7 Other writers who took part in support of the miners include Norman McCaig, aonghas macneacail, Freddie Anderson, Agnes Owens, Alasdair Gray, Jeff Torrington, Tom Leonard, Anne Tall, Liz Lochhead; musicians included Danny Kyle, Roy Miller, Jim Dailly, Ewan MacVicar, Nancy Nicholson, Rab Noakes and Allan Tall.

8 See note 2 to my essay 'Opening the Edinburgh Unemployed Workers' Centre'.

9 Edited by Brian Filling and Susan Stuart (Aberdeen University Press, 1991).

10 Author and publisher; also editor of *Daughters of Africa; an International Anthology of Words and Writings by Women of African*

447

Descent from the Ancient Egyptian to the Present (Jonathan Cape, 1992).

11   The Anti-Apartheid movement was always active in Glasgow; and see Brian Filling's essay 'Nelson Mandela and the Freedom of Scotland's Cities' for information on the Scottish movement as a whole, included in *The End of a Regime?* (Filling, op. cit.).

12   See *South Africa: The Struggle for a Birthright* by Mary Benson (Penguin African Library, 1966; reprinted 1985 by The International Defence and Aid Fund for Southern Africa).

13   *The Struggle for South Africa: a Reference Guide to Movements, Organisations and Institutions* by Rob Davies, Dan O'Meara and Sipho Diamini, vol. 2 (Zed Books, 1984).

14   In his essay 'Call to Revolution' included in *Apartheid: A Collection of Writings on South African Racism*, edited by Alex La Guma (Lawrence and Wishart, 1972).

15   Rob Davies, Dan O'Meara and Sipho Diamini, op. cit.

16   Nelson Mandela, quoted by Mary Benson, op. cit.

17   See *Sechaba*, July issue 1983, Harold Wolpe's article.

18   The accused were a microcosm of the country: six Africans, three whites (of whom one was quickly freed with charges withdrawn) and an Indian. See pp. 254–8 *South African: The Struggle for a Birthright* by Mary Benson. Only seven were sent to Robben Island, no white men.

19   UNISON nowadays.

20   The idea for the pamphlet came from Cathie Thomson, Alasdair Gray did a smashing job with the original artwork while Tommy Kays and the people at Clydeside Press gave their usual solid support. Tommy is a hero. For years he and his team have been just about the only left-wing printers in Glasgow.

21   Edited by James Peck (Serpent's Tail, London, 1988).

22   Edited by Peter Kravitz, then published by Polygon Press, a branch of Edinburgh University Students' Union.

23   In a paper on David Hume that he delivered in response to Noam Chomsky's opening contribution at The Self-Determination and Power Event, Govan, Glasgow, 1990.

24 John Stuart Mill was a central figure in the study of philosophy when I was there but his connection north of the border, however remote, was never remarked upon. It would have been of value to know that his father, the philosopher James Mill, was Scottish: son of a shoemaker who initially trained to become a minister, a radical who educated his son independently and was a founder of University College, London; and, apparently, exerted a little influence on Karl Marx.

25 Peter Kravitz published it in *Edinburgh Review*, 1988.

26 Of the many who got involved I recollect Statia Rice, Keith Millar, Malcolm Dickson, Ramsey Kanaan, George Gallacher, James Ferguson, William Clark, Peter Kravitz, Carole Rhodes, Cathie Thompson, Alistair Dickson. All the catering was done by Brendan and Maureen of the Scotia Bar.

27 Held in the Pearce Institute, Govan, Glasgow.

28 See the Conclusion to *Noam Chomsky: A Life of Dissent* by Robert F. Barsky (MIT Press, 1997).

29 In the Edinburgh magazine *Cencrastus*. Kenneth White's essay, or a version of it, has been reprinted in his collection *On Scottish Ground: Selected Essays* (Polygon Books, 1998).

30 Duncan MacLean published my response to White's attack as a pamphlet, *Tantalising Twinkles; or, There Is a First-Order Radical Thinker of European Standing Such That He Exists*, in the series entitled *Emergency Eye Wash* (Emergency Eyewash Press, Breckan, Stromness, Orkney, 1997).

31 October 1992.

32 *The Keelie* was a radical little journal published for a couple of years by the Workers' City group. A copy or two may still be discovered down the Briggait in Glasgow, if you ask the hawkers nicely.

33 The manager of Aberdeen Football Club at that time was Alex Smith. I used to support the club way back in the glory days, and I'm talking here not about when they were managed by Alex Ferguson but way way back. I was brought up in Govan and whenever Rangers scored at Ibrox you could hear the roar of the crowd. It was silence that Saturday afternoon, the day of my conversion, sometime

in the 1953–54 season when the good old Dons thrashed Rangers 6–0 in the semi-final of the Scottish Cup. A wee footballing pal of mine in Govan was the nephew of one of that fine team, which included Harry Yorston, Ally Young, 'Gentleman' George Hamilton, Paddy Buckley and Jackie Hather. (Back to reality in the final when Celtic won 2–1, in front of a record crowd of 134,000.)

34 The writer and educator Roxy Harris, chiefly responsible for *Language and Power*, originally put together by the Inner London Education Authority Afro-Caribbean Language and Literacy Project in Further and Adult Education, published eventually by Harcourt Brace Jovanovich, 1990.

35 Gus John and Ian Macdonald QC compiled *Murder in the Playground; the Report of the Macdonald Inquiry into Racism and Racial Violence in Manchester Schools* (Longsight Press, 76 Stroud Green Road, London, 1989).

36 Where Marie Connors and myself were married in 1969.

37 Published by New Beacon Books Ltd, 1992.

38 And also William Clark, Malcolm Dickson's successor as editor of *Variant*; he it was who accomplished the work of transcription.

39 George Galloway MP shared the platform.

40 I remember that Tom Leonard and myself took part in the 1989 event, also L. K. Johnson, Jean Breeze and many other writers and musicians whose names I cannot recall. Ten years later, on the 20th Anniversary of the murder of Blair Peach, it was reported that the friends of the schoolteacher from New Zealand once again were calling for an inquiry. See *Statewatch* of May–August 1999.

41 See my essay 'ATTACK NOT RACIST, say police' for more information.

42 See the article 'Tragedies that Shaped Perceptions' by Libby Brooks, *Guardian*, 26 February 1999.

43 This information is not difficult to find; perhaps the best place is London's Institute of Race Relations, also *CARF* magazine [the Campaign Against Racism and Fascism] publishes a back-page diary of 'race and resistance'.

44 See *Statewatch*, vol. 6, no. 1 and vol. 6, no. 4 for further information.

45   Various sources; see also the 1991 publication *Deadly Silence: Black Deaths in Custody* (Institute of Race Relations).

46   *Statewatch*, vol. 5, no. 3, 1995 and, vol. 6, no. 4, 1996.

47   See *Statewatch* vol. 5, no. 6; also vol. 6, no. 1 and vol. 6, no. 6. For further information on the inquest see *CARF* 36, February / March 1997 and Amnesty International's report of 8 August 1996. In her 'Inquests: The Solicitor's Role', Louise Christian writes 'in cases where the deceased and the deceased's family are black people there may be particular concern about the racial composition of the jury. In the inquest into the death of Brian Douglas who died after being hit with truncheons by police officers there was a verdict of [death by misadventure] by an all-white jury despite the fact that the deceased was black. The Coroner has power to summon the jury. However, in practice in London the jury are not actually selected by the Coroner or his officer but are taken supposedly randomly from jury panels at Crown Courts or the Old Bailey. However, if a jury panel comes from a particular area of London where there are no black people living, it is clearly far more likely that it is going to be an all-white jury. It is believed the Brian Douglas jury came from the Croydon area. Although the Coroner will state he has no power over jury selection it may be worth making representations about the area from which the jury is to be selected. Note also that although only the Coroner has the power to object to a juror, he has a very wide discretion whether to do so and representations can be made to him in the absence of the jury about the basis on which he should exercise this power.' [see *Two Garden Court Criminal Law Seminars*; No. 6, 25 November 1999]

48   In a BBC news report of Thursday, 30 July 1998, 'The Master of the Rolls, Lord Woolf, said: "the present inquest has performed in an exemplary manner the important purpose of investigating the facts and little more could be achieved by subjecting all concerned to the considerable expense and stress of a further inquest." [He] accepted there may have been "just sufficient evidence" to leave unlawful manslaughter as a possible verdict [but] did not consider there was

any evidence of gross negligence. But the ruling was rejected by Mr Douglas's family, who said they have been "denied justice". Wayne's sister Lisa Douglas-Williams said: "We are particularly upset by the judge's remarks about the expense of holding a further inquest. A proper verdict on my brother's death is far more important than money." The first inquest into his death found he had been held face-down with his hands cuffed behind his back on four separate occasions. The jury found, by an 8–1 verdict, that his death from heart-failure had been an accident, despite acknowledging that it was caused by police methods of restraint.'

49 The other panel members were the writer Yasmin Alibhai Brown and Ratna Dutt, Race Equality Officer; Professor Gus John, former Director of Education in the London Borough of Hackney, and Herman Ouseley, then Chairman of the Commission for Racial Equality. Ian Macdonald QC was to chair the Tribunal originally but in the event he could not attend. In his absence I became 'acting-Chair'. The reasoning behind this was simply that others had far more to say as ordinary panel members.

50 *Arming Repression: U.S. Arms Sales to Turkey During the Clinton Administration*, by Tamar Gabelnick, William D. Hartung, and Jennifer Washburn, with research assistance by Michelle Ciarrocca, a Joint Report of the World Policy Institute and the Federation of American Scientists, October 1999.

51 *Report on the State of Emergency Region*, 1992, by the Human Rights Association branches and their representatives; this extract from the pamphlet *Gathering in Istanbul for Freedom of Expression: March 10–12th, 1997* (published by the Freedom for Freedom of Expression Initiative, 1997).

52 See the pamphlet *Gathering in Istanbul for Freedom of Expression: March 10–12th 1997*, op. cit.

53 See note 26 to my essay 'The "Freedom for Freedom of Expression" Rally'.

54 The campaign journal of Amnesty International.

55 For a full account of this, see 'Byzantine Politics: The Abduction and

Trial of Abdullah Ocalan' by William Clark, published as a *Variant* magazine supplement.

56 Ibid. citing the *New York Times*, 20 February 1999.

57 See the *Kurdish Observer*, 28 November 1999.

58 See the campaign literature for Ocalan's fight for freedom (the international appeal to writers and artists of February 1999).

59 For fuller information on the abduction, trial and all surrounding events, see the essays by the writer Sheri Laizer, available through the internet.

60 Also present on these occasions were writers and poets Alasdair Gray, Agnes Owens, Tom Leonard, Bernard Mac Laverty; Sandie Craigie, Gordon Legge and aonghas macneacail; Neville Lawrence, Suresh Grover, the Kurdish musician Newroz, and the Sativa Drummers. The events were supported strongly by Edinburgh's only radical bookshop, Word★Power Books.

61 In London and Wales among the participants were Moris Farhi, Vedat Turkali and Jack Mapanje (Malawe), and musician Dafydd Iwan. It is good to report that in Autumn 2001 Dr Beşikçi had been released from prison. He continues to write, but cannot publish under threat of immediate arrest.

62 Robert organises Wordspace Arts in Dallas, with his wife Adrienne and a group of enthusiasts.

"AND THE JUDGES SAID . . ."

1 From *Situations Theoretical and Contemporary* by Tom Leonard (Galloping Dog Press, 1986), reprinted in his *Reports from the Present: Selected Work* (Jonathan Cape, 1995).

2 See *Ris a' Bhruthaich: Criticism and Prose Writings* by Somhairle Mac Gill-eain, edited by William Gillies (Acair Ltd, Stornoway, Isle of Lewis, 1985).

SHOUTING AT THE EDINBURGH FRINGE FORUM

1 Richard Demarco, who at that time had a gallery down Edinburgh's Canongate. Other writers appearing with me (fellow-members of

the Glasgow Print Studios Press) were Liz Lochhead, Carl McDougall, Tom Buchan, Alan Spence, Alasdair Gray, Tom Leonard and aonghas macneacail.

OPENING THE EDINBURGH UNEMPLOYED WORKERS' CENTRE

1 See my essay in *Some Recent Attacks: Essays Cultural and Political* (A.K. Press, 1992).
2 A few years later the centre was still operating, run on a voluntary basis. I took part in a benefit night held at The Venue in Edinburgh, on 26 September 1994. Writers and musicians on the 'Artists in Solidarity' bill that evening were Michael Marra, Gill Bowman, Irvine Welsh, Davey Steele, Black-Eyed Biddy, Long Fin Killie, Dawson, Badgewearer, Dominic Waxing Lyrical, Sativa Drummers.

ALEX LA GUMA (1925–1985)

1 Published in *Cencrastus* magazine, autumn 1981.
2 In her essay found in *Aspects of South African Literature*, ed. C. Heywood (Heinemann, 1976).
3 *Cencrastus* (autumn 1981).
4 *Tasks and Masks* by Lewis Nkosi (Longman, 1981).
5 Ibid.
6 See Ian Fullerton's article in *Cencrastus*, summer 1980.
7 The Hungarian critic Georg Lukàcs has written the seminal work on Kafka and 'modernism'.
8 In his *Twelve African Writers* Gerald Moore says differently. He believes La Guma's short stories are technically inferior to his novels, which I dispute here.
9 Two of his poems can be read in the *Race Today Review* of February 1986.
10 *Edinburgh Review*, number 69 (1985).

ATTACK NOT RACIST, SAY POLICE

1 *Evening Times*, 30 August 1990.
2 *Independent*, 13 October 1990.

Notes

3   In the pamphlet *The New Cross Massacre Story: Interviews with John La Rose* (Alliance of the Black Parents Movement, Black Youth Movement and the Race Today Collective, London, 1984).

4   *Recorder*, 3 August 1990.

5   Ibid.

6   *Guardian*, 13 December 1989. 'Ramesh K' was the name given to the father of the family to conceal their identity.

7   Ibid.

8   Page 28, chapter 2 of *White Law: Racism in the Police, Courts and Prisons* by Paul Gordon (Pluto Press, 1983).

9   Ibid.

10   See the *Independent*, 13 October 1990.

11   See chapter 5 of *White Law: Racism in the Police, Courts and Prisons* by Paul Gordon (Pluto Press, 1983), and for further information on the racism of the judiciary.

12   Ibid., chapter 2.

13   Ibid., pp. 51–2 especially.

14   Page 78 *Under Siege: Racial Violence in Britain Today* by Keith Thompson (Penguin Special, 1988).

15   Page 106 *White Man's Country: Racism in British Politics* by Robert Miles and Annie Phiizacklea (Pluto Press, 1984).

16   See the *Independent*, 13 October 1990.

17   Ibid.

18   See chapter 2 of *White Law: Racism in the Police, Courts and Prisons* by Paul Gordon (Pluto Press, 1983). There was an 'Unofficial Committee of Enquiry set up by the National Council for Civil Liberties [which] came to the "inescapable conclusion" that Peach had been killed by a blow deliberately inflicted by a member either of Unit 1 or Unit 3 of the Metropolitan Police Special Patrol Group.'

19   Ibid. The inner quotation here is from 23rd April 1979, *Southall Rights 1979.*

20   Wednesday 6 December 1989; this report from *Newlife* (Asian newsweekly), Friday 3 August 1990.

21   *Guardian*, 22 January 1990.

FIGHTING FOR SURVIVAL: THE STEEL INDUSTRY IN SCOTLAND

1   Kuldip Singh Sekhon; see the essay 'ATTACK NOT RACIST, say police'.
2   I cannot find the source of this quotation but I think it must come from a *Lobster* magazine of this period.
3   See *Lobster* magazines of this period for fuller information on the issue of the use made of such groups by the British State and far right in general.
4   Then convenor of the Ravenscraig workforce, responsible for the 'hanging himself on somebody's else's cross' statement which I quote later; he made the comment in response to the criticism the steelworkers received for their lack of support for the miners.
5   Then Secretary of State for Scotland.

A READING FROM THE WORK OF NOAM CHOMSKY AND THE
SCOTTISH TRADITION IN THE PHILOSOPHY OF COMMON SENSE

1   I thank Noam Chomsky for his response and comments, also George E. Davie. It is crucial to mention the conversations I've had with Tom Leonard over the past fifteen years or so, and here with particular reference to the 'existential voice' in literature and related problems of time and space. There is a fine essay by P. G. Lucas – collected in *Philosophy: Man's Search for Reality*, ed. I. Levine (Odhams Books, London, repr. 1963) – entitled 'Some Speculative and Critical Philosophers (1600–1750)' which helped greatly to clear my head.
2   This and all other unaccredited quotations throughout the essay are by Chomsky, taken from *The Chomsky Reader*, edited by James Peck (Serpent's Tail Press, 1988). My review of the book developed into this essay.
3   My editor points out that there was 'tremendous opposition to the war on university campuses (Berkeley, etc.), partly inspired by Chomsky . . .' In context I don't think students enter into it here; if so it is to a very limited extent.
4   *Chomsky*, John Lyons (Fontana/Collins, 1970).
5   Ibid.

Notes

6 Harry S. Truman.

7 The Managua lectures which comprise both Chomsky's *Language and Problems of Knowledge* (MIT Press, 1988) and *On Power and Ideology* (South End Press, 1987).

8 See Bertrand Russell's biased account of Rousseau in his *History of Western Philosophy* (Allen & Unwin, 1961).

9 Lyons, op. cit.

10 (6.52) *Tractatus Logico-Philosophicus* (Routledge & Kegan Paul, 1961).

11 J. R. Lucas *The Freedom of the Will* (Clarendon Press, 1970), in his essay of the same name.

12 Lyons, op. cit.

13 President of the UK's National Union of Mineworkers, famously during the great strike of 1984–85, when the miners fought so bravely against the British State.

14 Chomsky pointed this out to me in a letter, and I quote here from that.

15 *Language and Problems of Knowledge*, Chomsky, op. cit.

16 See his *Structuralism* (Routledge & Kegan Paul, 1971).

17 See note 14.

18 *The Scottish Enlightenment*, published as a pamphlet from the Historical Association, London, 1981, and now collected in *The Scottish Enlightenment and Other Essays* (Polygon Books, 1991).

19 *A History of the Scottish People*, T. C. Smout (Collins, 1969).

20 *The Scottish Enlightenment*, George E. Davie, op. cit.

21 'The Social Significance of the Scottish Philosophy of Common Sense', essay by George E. Davie (the Dow Lecture delivered before the University of Dundee, 30 November 1972), later collected in *The Scottish Enlightenment*, op. cit.

22 *The Scottish Enlightenment*, George E. Davie, op. cit.

23 *The Crisis of the Democratic Intellect*, George E. Davie (Polygon Books, 1986).

24 'The Proof of the Mince Pie', essay contained in *Intimate Voices: Selected Work 1965–1983*, Tom Leonard (Galloping Dog Press, Newcastle, 1984).

25 *Towards a New Cold War: Essays on the Current Crisis and How We Got There*, Noam Chomsky (Pantheon, New York, 1982).

26 See *Lobster* magazine, issue 16.

27 'On Reclaiming the Local or The Theory of the Magic Thing', essay by Tom Leonard, published in *Edinburgh Review* magazine (77); later collected in his *Reports from the Present: Selected Work 1982–94* (Jonathan Cape, 1995).

28 'The Proof of the Mince Pie' by Tom Leonard, op. cit.

29 For this and the other quotations in this area see 'The Rafferty File' in Peter Taylor's *Beating the Terrorists* (Penguin Books, 1980).

30 *Introduction to Philosophy*, Oswald Külpe (Sonnenschein, 1897).

31 'Berkeley, Hume and the Central Problem of Scottish Philosophy' by George E. Davie (uncollected essay).

32 Thomas Reid in his essay 'Of the Sentiments of Bishop Berkeley', in *Inquiry and Essays*, ed. Ronald E. Beanblossom and Keith Lehrer (Hackett Publishing Co. Inc., Indianapolis, USA) p. 166.

33 Quote from George E. Davie in the Church and State section of his pamphlet *The Scottish Englightenment*, op. cit.

34 See George Berkeley's Introduction to his *The Principles of Human Knowledge; with Other Writings* (Fontana, 1982).

35 Ibid.

36 Reid, op. cit.

37 J. S. Mill, cited in John Passmore's *A Hundred Years of Philosophy* (Penguin Books, 1968).

38 See Fr. Copleston's *A History of Philosophy*, Vol. 5 Part 11 (Image Books edition, 1964).

39 As Davie points out.

40 In *The Crisis of the Democratic Intellect*, Davie speaks of the 'well-known lines, in which [the poet] remarks that our blind spots are due to its being impossible for us to see ourselves as others see us, a phrase which he directly borrows from . . . Adam Smith's *Theory of Moral Sentiments* (a book admired by Burns).'

41 Predating James Audubon. Wilson was tossed in to the dungeon for lampooning local politicians. When he landed in the USA he took various jobs, including schoolteacher. He later developed his interest

in art, in particular drawing birds, and nowadays is regarded as the 'grandfather' of American ornithology. In his lifetime he published seven of the final nine volumes of his collection of the birds of America. He travelled throughout the country, where possible drawing the birds in their habitat whereas Audubon had the birds brought to him. All of Wilson's collection eventually was published in four complete volumes and this beautiful work can be seen, with permission, in Paisley Central Library, Renfrewshire. At the same location, also with permission, you can see that other beautiful work, James Audubon's magnificent collection, in four mammoth volumes.

42   This disinformation, unfortunately, is found in Peter MacKenzie's history of Glasgow. Instead of honouring individuals such as James 'Purly' Wilson, or for example John Baird and Andrew Hardie, the political establishment in Scotland, led as usual by the Labour Party, continues to pay its public respect to such as the so-called 'Glasgow Merchants', individuals who made extreme fortunes in the slave trade and by the employment of their personal enslaved workforces in the tobacco industry.

43   Goethe's work is of interest in this connection, for both his prologue and the later added epilogue to *The Sufferings of Young Werther*. Hogg translated writings by Goethe who seems also to have been influenced by the Christian mystic Johan Hamann referred to later in this piece. An early unpublished essay by Tom Leonard on Hogg's *Confessions of a Justified Sinner* has been essential to my own understanding and appreciation of the novel in this context.

44   22 March 1988 in a BBC television programme.

45   *Radical Renfrew* by Tom Leonard (Polygon Books, 1990); see his introduction.

46   *Einstein*, Jeremy Bernstein (Fontana, 1973).

47   Cited by Chomsky in *Language and Problems of Knowledge*, op. cit.

48   Cited by Isaiah Berlin in his *Against the Current* (OUP, 1981).

49   Bernstein, op. cit.

50   Cited by William Weaver in his study *William Carlos Williams* (CUP, 1971).

51 'On Reclaiming the Local or The Theory of the Magic Thing', essay by Tom Leonard, op. cit.

52 *On Formally Undecidable Propositions of Principia Mathematica and Related Systems* by Kurt Gödel (Dover Publishing, Inc., New York, 1992).

53 Selected extracts from *Gödel's Proof* by Ernst Nagel and James R. Newman (Routledge, 1989).

54 Chomsky pointed out, in the same letter as in note 14, in relation to his 'critique of the stucturalist approach. This really has nothing to do with incompleteness. The problem is that Harris, Bloomfield, and others were seeking a system of analytic taxonomic procedures that could carry them from a text from some language to a description of that language, and we now know that such procedures simply do not exist. My critique was essentially based on that observation.'

55 Passmore, op. cit.

56 Bernstein, op. cit.

57 'The Social Significance of the Scottish Philosophy of Common Sense' by George E. Davie, op. cit.

58 'Husserl and Reinach on Hume's "Treatise"', George E. Davie (uncollected essay).

59 Or 'epistemology'; the term was first coined by James Ferrier, according to Davie.

60 *Language and Problems of Knowledge* by Chomsky, op. cit.

THERE IS A FIRST-ORDER RADICAL THINKER OF EUROPEAN STANDING SUCH THAT HE EXISTS; OR, TANTALISING TWINKLES

1 Thomas Reid.

JUSTICE IS NOT MONEY

1 I saw it myself alongside the then Chairperson of the CAA group, and two local community workers.

2 This campaign was successful.

SAY HELLO TO JOHN LA ROSE

1 Nor at the present time, in the autumn of 2001.

Notes

AN INTERVIEW WITH JOHN LA ROSE

1 Cheddi Jagan was then leader of the People's Progressive Party (PPP) and Chief Minister of the Government of Guyana (at that time British Guiana). The PPP and the West Indian Independence Party, of which John La Rose was a leading member, were close allies in the Caribbean.

2 César A. Cui (1835–1918), Alexander P. Borodin (1833–1887), Nicolai A. Rimsky-Korsakov (1944–1908), Modest Petrovich Mussorgsky (1839–1881), Mili Alexeyevich Balakirev (1836–1910).

3 James Maxton (1885–1946) from Barrhead, near Glasgow; socialist MP from the first half of the twentieth century; chairman of the Independent Labour Party. He also wrote a fair bit, including a biography of Lenin.

4 In his *Low Intensity Operations*, Kitson 'argued that far too much military strategy was geared to fighting an enemy whom everybody could identify: the Russians, or the Chinese. The real threat . . . came from subversives inside the country who were doing the Communists' work for them.' See Paul Foot's *Who Framed Colin Wallace?* For some information on Kitson and his contemporaries within the British State security agencies, see *Lobster* magazines of the late 1980s through the 1990s.

5 For further information, see *The New Cross Massacre Story; Interviews with John La Rose* (Alliance of the Black Parents' Movement, Black Youth Movement and Race Today Collective, London, 1984).

THE CARIBBEAN ARTISTS MOVEMENT 1966–1972

1 See also *Kaiso, Calypso Music*, David Rudder in conversation with John La Rose (New Beacon Books, 1990).

A LOOK AT FRANZ KAFKA'S THREE NOVELS
(For publishing details of books referred to below, see Bibliography at the end of the essay.

Introduction
1 Quoted by Kierkegaard in his essay 'That Individual'.

2 Edwin Muir regards the character in this light, see his Introductory Note to the novel.

3 The two stories are found in *Wedding Preparations in the Country and Other Stories* under the titles 'Conversation with the Supplicant' and 'Conversation with the Drunken Man'; they were published in 1909, three years before he started on *Amerika*.

Part 1 *Amerika*: Innocence and Ignorance

1 Peter Heller in his essay 'On Not Understanding Kafka', *The Kafka Debate*, p. 24.

2 *The Diaries of Franz Kafka*, p. 388.

3 Which is how Muir describes the author's central protagonists in his Introductory Note to the novel.

4 A couple of months before embarking on the novel, Kafka experienced a most vivid dream about arriving in a crowded harbour that he realised was New York. See his entry for 11 September 1912.

5 See his study *Franz Kafka: Parable and Paradox*, p. 122.

6 Muir's description of Karl.

7 See Lee Baxandall's essay 'Kafka as Radical', *The Kafka Debate*, p. 122.

8 See Muir's Introductory Note.

9 Brunelda bears a resemblance to the character in the later short story 'Josephine the Singer, or the Mouse-folk' (in the collection *Wedding Preparations in the Country and Other Stories*).

10 Kafka's description of the means by which Karl was to escape his bleak situation; see Muir's Introductory Note.

11 See Lee Baxandall, op. cit.

Part 2 *The Trial*: Ignorance and Guilt

1 On the subject of the significance of Kafka's naming of people, places and objects, Ronald Gray's essay 'But Kafka Wrote in German' (*The Kafka Debate*) is of particular interest.

2 To enter further into this would be beyond this essay's scope.

Notes

3 None of Kafka's family, as far as I understand, survived the genocide in Europe during the 1930s and 40s.

4 See Politzer's *Franz Kafka: Parable and Paradox*, p. 177.

5 Ibid.

6 As does Gunther Anders in his *Kafka*, and by implication so too does Georg Lukàcs whose three essays mentioned in the bibliography I enjoyed very much. His opinion of the author alters for the good eventually but he still sees him through a Hegelian cloud of 'state transcendence'. He is fundamentally wrong to say that Kafka does not create 'any new means of expression' ('Franz Kafka or Thomas Mann') as I hope to have shown here; this could also be the basis of an argument against Lukàcs's ideas on realism in art. When an artist appears as 'simplistic' in method as Kafka did to Lukàcs it should make a critic applaud, and then reach for the microscope; Lukàcs does the former alright but forgets the latter.

7 We do not have to get involved in the life of Kafka, see note 4.

8 Karl Rossmann was always hoping for that too, but he is not an adult.

9 This is the description of how to hold the people 'captive', according to Ivan Karamazov's 'Old Inquisitor'.

10 Kierkegaard, in his essay 'Dread and Freedom'.

11 Ivan rejects God because of 'His' good being evil, etc.

12 The episode in which K. tells of his visits to Huld is the most obvious example. This indirect reportage is at odds with the dynamic of the novel and is surely a flaw. Yet it is around this point that Brod got involved in tidying up the manuscript for publication. (See Epilogue.)

Part 3 *The Castle*: **Ignorance and Freedom**

1 Politzer, p. 226.

2 Joyce was a year older. *Ulysses* was published in 1922 although he began work on the novel in 1914. Kafka had begun *The Trial* the same year. He started on *The Castle* in 1921 and stopped work on it

463

in 1922.

3   Presenting reality 'in itself', of course, has to capture the moment. Although Kafka uses the past tense, he often puts pen to paper to record the dramatic present, but the very act of putting pen to paper sets the moment in the past, the immediate past.

4   Actually, the problem has evaporated. Kafka's solution is involved with appearance and reality; it is necessary that no such thing as reality 'in itself' is presented, while on the other hand nothing else is being presented. In a sense K. is making reality. See the next paragraph in context.

5   'The Great Wall of China', in particular.

6   Examples from the British media of 1983–84, the period when I was writing this, would be so-called radicals like Ken Livingstone, Tony Benn, Arthur Scargill and Vanessa Redgrave; each of these at one time or another has been vilified after that fashion. It altered somewhat in the case of Vanessa Redgrave who was marked by the media and political establishment as 'simple-minded' and/or 'easily led'.

7   See note 4.

8   Maybe some of the critics who rush to describe Kafka's work as allegory, myth, parable, metaphor etc., are committing a similar error.

9   The section translated by the Muirs.

10 This information is contained in the Publisher's Note to the definitive text and is taken from Max Brod's Editor's Note to the first edition.

11 In 'The Grand Inquisitor' section from *The Brothers Karamazov*.

12 The distinction between Olga and Gregor Samsa, for instance.

Endword

1   In a diary entry of January 1912, for example, Franz writes of an occasion he 'felt . . . [Max was] almost not my friend'.

Notes

RACISM AND THE MAASTRICHT TREATY

1   See *Lobster* 21, the article by Mike Hughes; the quotations were
    taken mainly from a press release by Western Goals itself, at a fringe
    meeting organised during the 1989 Tory Party Conference.
2   All the quotes not accredited here are from the *Observer*, 24 February
    1991.

LITERARY FREEDOM AND HUMAN RIGHTS

1   *Hate late it was, how late* (Secker & Warburg, 1994).

INTO BARBARISM

1   Eventually the CPS allowed the family to continue on their own.
2   From a campaign press release.
3   There's a great deal of stuff available on the web. The case is notorious.
    Entries from the World Socialist web site (socialequality.org.uk) tell us
    that 'Five police officers and an immigration official forced their way
    into her home . . . She died as a result of the restraint methods
    employed by three officers from the Alien Deportation Group . . .
    The ADG was a secretive police unit that specialised in forcible
    deportations. Its activities were controlled and authorised by the
    Home Office and the Home Secretary.' There is a book referred to
    here entitled *A State Murder Exposed: The Truth about the Killing of Joy
    Gardner* (Mehring Books, 1998).

    According to a United Kingdom Report on Human Rights
    Practices for 1996 released in USA by the Bureau of Democracy,
    Human Rights, and Labor on 30 January 1997, 'A police tribunal
    dismissed a case of neglect of duty against a senior police officer who
    supervised the police squad involved in the death of illegal immigrant
    Joy Gardner. This brought an end to all disciplinary proceedings in
    the case of Gardner, who died of brain damage in 1993 after police
    officers gagged her with adhesive tape when she resisted arrest. The
    Home Office no longer permits mouth restraints to be used in the
    removal of people under Immigration Act powers.'

    There was a BBC report of 7 November 1998 in which Sir Paul

Condon 'said the case had "horrified" him, although he was not attributing individual blame.'

4 See *Statewatch*, vol. 4 no. 6, November–December 1994. See also 'Tragedies that Shaped Perceptions', an article in the *Guardian*, 26 February 1999, by Libby Brooks.

5 At that time the Tory MP Michael Howard.

6 The incident took place in March 1996, see *Stateswatch* 3, vol. 7, no. 6, Nov–Dec 1997 for a report on the inquest.

7 Ibid., in the words of Mike Mansfield QC.

8 *Political Killings by Governments*, introduced by Theo C. van Bowen, former Director of the United Nations Division of Human Rights (Amnesty International, 1983).

9 See *CARF* magazine and the journal *Race and Class* for detailed information on this.

THE 'FREEDOM FOR FREEDOM OF EXPRESSION RALLY',
ISTANBUL, 10–12 MARCH 1997

1 Current report from PEN International Writers in Prison Committee.

2 Dr Ismail Beşikçi's *Selected Writings: Kurdistan & Turkish Colonialism* (see note 36).

3 With France and Iran (Persia); the USA stayed somewhat in the background.

4 Ismet Sheriff Vanly's 'Kurdistan in Iraq', collected in *People Without a Country: the Kurds and Kurdistan*, see note 12.

5 *Evening Times*, Glasgow, 21 April 1997, encouraging its readership to 'fly to Turkey this autumn'.

6 Amnesty International report.

7 *Voice of Kurdistan*, whence this information is taken.

8 *The Kurds and Kurdistan: Thinking is a Crime*, a report on freedom of expression in Turkey, published by the International Association for Human Rights in Kurdistan (IMK E.V.).

9 At Edinburgh University.

10 In mitigation, I had prepared for an audience I assumed would consist almost exclusively of Scottish people, but roughly half were

Kurdish exiles.

11 'Oppression and Solidarity', in the collection *Some Recent Attacks* (A. K. Press, Edinburgh, 1992).

12 Except where stated, and with apologies to Kendal, the information here is lifted directly from a collection of essays published by Zed Press in 1979, reprinted a year later after the fall of the Shah of Iran, with an extra section: *People Without a Country: the Kurds and Kurdistan*, edited by Gerard Chaliand; Kendal's essay is entitled 'Kurdistan in Turkey'.

13 Among the literary works I presume proscribed in Turkey is my 1949 Penguin edition of Xenophon's *The Persian Expedition*. In his translation Rex Warner not only refers to 'Kurdistan', he refuses to censor or suppress Xenophon's account of his encounters in BC 400 with the 'Kardouçi' (which is spelled 'Carduchi').

14 See Nazdar, 'The Kurds in Syria', *People Without a Country*, op. cit.

15 For evidence of this read almost any issue of *Statewatch* journal (take out a subscription, c/o PO Box 1516, London N16 OEW). A public meeting was held in 1997 in London on the issue of 'the Criminalisation of the Kurds in U.K. and Europe'.

16 Information from *Statewatch* vol. 6, no. 6.

17 For a discussion of a South African/Turkish connection in the murder of Olof Palme, see *PSK Bulletin*, number 6, November 1996.

18 *Statewatch*, vol. 7, no. 1.

19 Ibid., for an extended discussion on this.

20 *Lobster* 32, for its comment on the *Mail on Sunday* report.

21 Linked directly to the British security services (MI6 in the early 1970s, MI5 after that). See *Lobster*s 16, 19 for information on Paul Wilkinson and see also *Lobster*s 10, 14 and others for a fuller account of the whole murky area. Wilkinson is erstwhile colleague of far-right 'terrorist experts' such as Brian Crozier and Maurice Tugwell. Subscribe to *Lobster* c/o 214 Westbourne Ave. Hull HU5 3JB, UK.

22 On 22 April 1997.

23 See Dr Ismail Beşikçi's *Selected Writings: Kurdistan & Turkish Colonialism* op. cit.

24 Ibid.

25 Amnesty International report.

26 It may be an oversight but I note that none of the six Israeli writers is listed as having 'knowingly and willingly consent[ed] to the publication of the Mini Freedom of Expression booklet'.

27 Press releases by the Freedom of Thought initiative.

28 From the introduction to the *Mini Freedom of Expression* booklet.

29 This is only as I understand it, as a layperson.

30 As I recall, this involved students unfurling a banner in parliament.

31 A pseudonym adopted by the writer.

32 Famous Turkish musician and composer; former journalist; a leading human rights' activist over the last two decades.

33 A. I. report, *Turkey: No Security Without Human Rights.*

34 *Kurdistan Information Bulletin* no. 34, Jan 1997. Just more than four weeks after the event, on 16 April, Yurdatapan was detained at Istanbul airport then held at the Anti-Terror Branch of police HQ.

35 Ibid.

36 An introduction to his work, *Selected Writings: Kurdistan and Turkish Colonialism* by Ismail Beşikçi, published by the Kurdistan Solidarity Committee and Information Centre, London.

EM HENE!

1 From the Kurdish, *Em hene* translates into English as 'We exist!'

2 See my Introduction for more on this. It is worth noting that Italian politicians of the left, in recent years, have been open in their support of the Kurdish people, and in the mid-1990s a major conference took place in Rome, attended by members of the Kurdish Parliament-in-Exile.

3 Amnesty International report.

4 Ibid.

5 As mentioned in the essay 'The "Freedom for Freedom of Expression" Rally', Kani Yilmaz was arrested on his way to address a meeting in London. It was not until the summer of 1997 that he was finally extradited to Germany to face charges of organising

attacks on Turkish businesses and properties, after Home Secretary Jack Straw ignored campaigners' pleas and upheld the court order for his extradition. Yilmaz had spent almost three years in detention in Belmarsh prison. The decision, following the House of Lords' rejection of his petition against the extradition, was a slap in the face to supporters who believed that Straw would carry his opposition convictions into government; Straw was one of several Labour MPs who protested strongly when Yilmaz was arrested and detained for deportation on 'national security' grounds on his way to a meeting at Westminster in October 1994. The arrest caused embarrassment to the Tory Government because Yilmaz had been allowed into the country freely days beforehand: the German Government's action in seeking his extradition was widely seen as too convenient, particularly since Yilmaz, a refugee from Turkey, had spent much time in Germany, where he had stayed quite openly and there was never any attempt to charge him with criminal offences . . . [The original intention of Yilmaz, John Austin-Walker and others was] to discuss finding a peaceful solution to the war in Kurdistan and self-determination for the Kurdish people. He [later] said he will not seek judicial review of the Home Secretary's decision, having had his confidence in the British judicial system severely undermined by the courts' passive endorsement of the extradition request. But he will use the German courts as an opportunity to present the case of the Kurdish people and to expose the collaboration of Europe's governments with the Turkish state. [*Statewatch*, Vol. 7, July–October, 1997.]

6   General Ahmet Çörekçi, quoted in an Amnesty International briefing entitled *Turkey: No Security Without Human Rights*.

7   See *The Kurdistan Report* number 27 for Hatip Dicle's report on this example of Turkish 'contra-guerrilla activity'. He makes the point that whenever anything sympathetic to the Kurdish struggle is happening 'on the eve of important international gatherings', the Turkish State will move to undermine and subvert the Kurdish case.

8   If not for *Selected Writings: Kurdistan and Turkish Colonialism*, the little

booklet put out by the KSC–KIC in 1991 in London, we would have nothing at all.

9   Who was himself responsible for describing the Oxford historian as 'renowned'.

10 See *Lobster* magazine 17 (1988), the essay 'Brian Crozier, the Pinay Circle and James Goldsmith', which quotes at length from *Der Spiegel* No. 37 [1982] in an article called 'Victory for Strauss'. See also *Lobster* 18, 'The Pinay Circle and Destabilisation in Europe'.

11 Ibid.

12 Former MI5 agent Cathy Massiter, on why she 'had been required to resign from MI5', see Paul Foot's *Who Framed Colin Wallace?*

13 See *Covert Operations in British Politics 1974–78, Lobster* 11. Note also John La Rose's reference to Kitson in my 'Interview' with him.

14 For the extended discussion of this, see Crozier's *A Theory of Conflict* (Hamish Hamilton, 1974), the chapter on 'The Problem of Subversion'.

15 Kemal in his 'Kurdistan in Turkey', see *People Without a Country: The Kurds and Kurdistan* (Zed Books, 1980); see also Crozier's *Free Agent: The Unseen War 1941–1991* (HarperCollins, 1993).

16 See Crozier's *A Theory of Conflict*, op. cit.

17 *Sunday Times*, 17 October, 1971.

18 I refer to this more fully in 'The "Freedom for Freedom of Expression" Rally, Istanbul, 10–12 March 1997'.

WHEN I WAS THAT AGE DID ART EXIST?

1   *The Good Times.*

2   I borrowed this section from the talk I delivered to the sixteen-, seventeen- and eighteen-year-olds.

3   A boy came up afterwards and told me his old man was a compositor and what I was saying just sounded the same.

4   I borrowed this section from the essay entitled ' "And the judges said . . ." '

Index

asylum-seekers, 11, 22, 42, 345, 350, 359; government behaviour, 379
Atatürk, Kemal, 396
atomism, 174, 183
Austin Music Network, 444
Austin-Walker, John, 393
Australia: asbestos, 207; Wittenoom miners, 211
authority(ies), 31, 271, 277, 279–81, 283–5, 287, 291–3, 313–4, 318–19, 322–3, 331–2; authorisation, 307; conventional reality, 288; defiance, 315; figures of, 305, 320, 328; 'good', 327, 330; school, 420; societal, 294, 302, 304, 317; specialist critics, 47; state, 383; 'supreme', 269, 324; voice of, 86
autonomous organisation, 248
autonomy denial, 152–3, 247
Avebury, Lord, 411
Ayckbourn, Alan, 77

Baird, John, 176
Bakewell, Joan, 3
Bakunin, Mikhail, 332
Balakirev, Mili Alexeyevich, 237
Baldwin, James, 226
Ballantyne, R.M., 58
'Baltimore Judgement', USA, 212
Bangladesh, 365; fundamentalists, 367
Barbados, 230, 234
barbarism, functional, 354
Barbican building site, 220–5
'batmen', 60–1
Beatles, the, 37
Beckett, Samuel, 181
Begley, George, 171
behaviourism, 151–2, 155; ideological, 164
Belgium, Kurdish repression, 393
Belinsky, Vissarion, 332
Bellow, Saul, 165–6
Belmarsh prison, London, 24–6, 393; court, 28
benefit nights, 23
Benn, Tony, 352

Berger, John, 242
Berkeley, George, 164, 172–5, 179, 188
Berry, Chuck, 37
Beşikçi, Ismail, 34, 392, 397, 400, 403, 407, 409–10, 414
Bilkent University, 412
Billy Elliot, 69
bipartisan campaigns/united front, 121–3, 125, 127, 129, 131–2, 134
Black Education Movement, 239
Black Panther Movement, 242
Black People's Assembly, 252
Black Power, 262
Blair Peach Anniversary Committee, 118
Blake, William, 179, 269
Bloomfield, Leonard, 149–50; behaviourism, 151
Bloomsbury, publishers, 70
Blow Out, 17
Blues Poets, the, 24
Blues Council, the
Blues music, 37, 442
Blythswood Shipbuilding, 197
Blyton, Enid, 57
Bogart, Humphrey, 7
Booker Prize, 55, 242
Borodin, Alexander P., 237
Boswell, James, 190
Boyd, Eddie, 2
Boyle, Peter, 204
Bradford Twelve, 350
Bragg, Melvyn, 81
Brando, Marlon, 90
Brathwaite, E. Kamau, 18, 233–4, 240–1, 261, 263
Brazil, carnival, 248
'breathlessness', 214
Brennan, Thomas, 123
Britain (UK), 32, 155, 350, 367, 398, 405; colonialism, 231, 233, 236, 245–6; covert operations, 122; law, 399; racism, 368; rock music, 37–8; state, 42, 109, 229, 346–7, 353–4, 356, 362, 370, 373–5, 386, 393, 395; state surveillance, 344;

Index

'terrorist' legislation, 394; torture supplies, 387, 414

British Broadcasting Corporation (BBC), 69, 84, 121, 238, 363; Newsnight, 203; Radio Scotland, 361

British National Party (BNP), 115

British Steel, 130

Brixton: 1981 riots, 247; police, 248

Brod, Max, 328, 333

Brothers Karamazov, The, 266, 306

Brown, Robert, 180; Brownian motion, 181

Brown, Thomas, 191

Buchan, John, 58–9, 61

bullying, 430; families, 431

bureaucracy, 324, 328

Burns, Robert, 81, 176, 245, 342

Burroughs, William, 240

Bursa Prison, Turkey, 400

Busby, Margaret, 7

Busconducter Hines, The, 20

Busker, The, 85

Byron, George, 342

Cairney, John, 81

Calder, John, 240

Callaghan, James, 167

Cambridge University, 233

Campaign Against Racism and Fascism (CARF), 109

Campbell, Clifton, 263

Camus, Albert, 19

Canada, Canada-Quebec PEN, 398; Indonesian investments, 146

cancer, lung, 211

Cape Town, District 6, 96

capitalism, 275; capital, 282

Caribbean: Artists Movement (CAM), 18, 229–30, 233–6, 239–44, 258, 260–3; Federation, 229; 1930s, 247; theatre, 241

carnival, 248–50; democratic, 251

Carter, Mamie Lee, 437

Carter, Mia, 415

Castle, The, 19, 265, 285, 287, 294, 301, 309–31

Castro, Fidel, 152, 251

Cattigan, Lillian, 79

Cézanne, Paul, 53, 181, 440

censorship, 68, 138, 361; media, 120–1; South Africa, 100; -self, 65, 69–70, 86

Central Intelligence Agency (CIA), 412

Ceylan, Münir, 396, 401, 404

checks and balances, 160

Chaggar, Gurdip, 115–16

Chancer, A, 19, 125

Chen, Acham, 237

children, 271, 300–1, 321; brutalised, 375; exploited, 433

Chomsky, Noam, 13–15, 140–6, 147, 149–51, 155–9, 164–6, 171, 175, 179, 184–6, 346, 351, 362–3

Churchill, Winston, 234

Cipriani, Captain, 232

Citizens Rights Office, Edinburgh, 5, 11, 88–9, 92

civil law, 210; liberties, 365–6

Clancy, Tom, 59

Cleaver, Eldridge, 226

Cliff, Jimmy, 223

Cloyne, Ireland, 173

Clutterbuck, Richard, 351

Clydeside Action on Asbestos (CAA), 16–17, 195–6, 200–4, 209, 213–14

coal: 'free world' market, 128; miners' strike 1984–5, 123, 126, 131

Cobb, Lee J., 90

Cobbett, William, 163

Coker, Steven, 106

colonialism: British, 231, 233, 236, 245–6; experience of, 234, 242

Coloured People's Congress, South Africa, 101–2

Commission for Racial Equality, 378

'committed art', 39–40

Committee for the Release of Political Prisoners in Kenya, 238

Common Cause, 122, 412

Common Sense philosophy/tradition, 14–16, 140, 160, 164, 175, 177, 179, 184, 191

473

Index

Index

Harris, Roxy, 18
Harris, Wilson, 261
Harris, Zelig, 144, 149–50
Harvey-Jones, John, 128
Hausa language, 219
Havana, 102
Haynes, Jim, 240–1
Heathrow Airport, 12, 106, 359
Hegel, G.W.F., 189–90, 332
Heidegger, Martin, 189
Heinemann African Writers Series, 98, 227
Hemingway, Ernest, 226, 436
Hendry, Joseph D., 226
Henry, O., 436
Henryson, Robert, 342
Herman, Edward S., 346, 351
Herzen, Alexander, 332
Heseltine, Michael, 353
hierarchy(ies), 164, 184, 364; fallacies, 51
Hiroshima, 142
Ho Chi Minh, 247; autonomy denial, 152
Hobbes, Thomas, 14
Hogg, James, 177–8, 182, 269–70, 300, 332, 441
Holly, Buddy, 37, 442
Hölderlin, Friedrich, 189
horror, societal, 299–301, 321
'houghmagandie', 73
House of Commons, 90, 254
How late it was, how late, launch, 24
Howard, Michael, 394
Howe, Darcus, 236, 256
Hubbard, Ray Wylie, 444
Human Rights Commission, 366
Humboldt,, Wilhelm von, 160
Hume, David, 13, 164, 175, 179–80, 187–8, 190
humiliations, daily, 72
Hungary, 128
Hunterston terminal, 131–2, 134
Hurd, Superintendant, 117
Hussein, Saddam, 345, 410
Husserl, Edmund, 16, 184, 189, 191
Hutcheson, Frances, 171

hypocrisy, 303, 430–1

Ibn Rushd, 192
ignorance, 272, 287, 290, 295, 297, 303–4, 314, 323–4, 329
immigrant communities, Scotland, 342
Immigration department, Britain, 116, 345, 354, 359, 370–1, 373
imperialism: dogma, 152; think-tanks, 151
Impressionist painters, 53, 439
Imrali Island prison, Turkey, 34–5
Independent Broadcasting Authority (IBA), 121
In the Fog of the Season's End, 99
In the Night, 4, 76, 79, 81
'In the Penal Settlement', 285, 293, 400
India: Communist movement, 238; Congress movement, 237; Constitution, 365; Hindu fudamentalism, 367
Indian Congress, South Africa, 102
Indian Workers' Association, UK, 114
Indonesia, US arms supply, 146
Industrial Research and Information Services, 122
inferiorisation, 242
information access, 165
informers, Britain, 371
Inqilab, 365
inquests, 255–6
Institute for the Study of Conflict, 412
Institute for the Study of Terrorism, 139
insurance: claims, work, 54; insurers, 206, 209–10
intellectualisation, 243
'intentional fallacy', 298
International Bar Association, 360
International Monetary Fund, 411
International Working Men's Movement, 232
intuition, 147, 165
Iraq, 386, 410
Irish Republican Army (IRA), 345
Iron and Steel Trades Confederation (ISTC), 132

Index

Index

Nigeria, 359; state authorities, 42
Nkosi, Lewis, 98
Nkrumah, Kwame, 261
Nolan, Paul, 89, 91–2
North Athlantic Treaty Organisation
    (NATO), 386, 392, 409
Nortje, Arthur, 102
'Nose, The', 291
Notes from Underground, 268, 300
Nuremberg Trials, 373, 383

Observer, The, 411–12, 414
Ocalan, Abdullah, 35, 397, 407–8, 410
Ogoni people, Nigeria, 42
oil, business, 128
OILC, offshore oilworkers union, 17
On the Waterfront, 90–1
Organization of Revolutionary Kurdish
    Youth (DDKO), 392
ornithology, 176
Orton, Joe, 241
out-of-court-settlement, 196, 198–201,
    203, 205
'Overcoat, The', 268, 291
overtime, 220–1, 372
Owens, Agnes, 70, 74
Oxbridge, leadership specialization, 163
Oxford University, 413
Ozal, Turgut, 388
Öztürk, Ünsal, 36, 400, 403–4

p'Bitek, Okot, 227, 239
Paine, Thomas, 89
Paisley Writers Weekend, 102
Pakistani Action Committee, Southall,
    114
Palestine, children, 375; PLO, 350
Palme, Olof, 393
Pan-Africanist Congress of Azania, 9
Paris, 176
Pathfinders, the, 37
Pavarotti, Luciano, 133
Peach, Blair, 24, 117
PEN, 386: International Writers in
    Prison Committee, 22, 31, 397,
    399, 404; Russia, 402; Turkish, 403

Penton Street, labour exchange, 19
Pentonville prison, 359
People's Cultural Association, Kurdish,
    392
People's Tribunal on Racial Violence
    and Harrassment, 28–30, 378
performance: plays, 241; poetry, 240;
    writers, 240
Peru, 240
Piaget, Jean, 159
Picasso, Pablo, 440
Pinter, Harold, 411
Pissarro, Camille, 53
Pittodrie Park, Aberdeen, 133
plantation society, Caribbean, 230
Plato's Problem, 155, 171
play-readings, 80
Poe, Edgar Allan, 441
poetry, performance, 240
Poets, the
Poland, 128
police, 370, 372; Community Liaison
    Officers, 380; Complaints
    Authority, 27; filming, 27;
    inhumanity, 372; Inquest power,
    255; media strategy, 257; resources,
    345; victim blame, 110–12
politics: -art separation, 43, 244–5;
    effective tactics, 93
Politzer, Heinz, 275, 298
poll tax, 247; campaign against, 133
Polmaise: The Fight for a Pit, 131
Port Talbot, 126
Powell, Enoch, 115, 248, 355–6
Prague, 274, 276, 279–80, 282
prejudice, 273; elitist, 66
pride, 330
'primary qualities', 172–3
Principia Mathematica, 182
printing, 435–6
*Private Memoirs and Confessions of a
    Justified Sinner*, 177, 269, 300, 332
professional politicians, 5
proof, burden, 381; burden reversal, 373
prose, formal advances, 100
Proudhon, Pierre-Joseph, 190

Index

steel industry, 128, 131; Scotland, 120,
123, 126–7, 130;
workers, 129, 134
Steel, David, 81
Stein, Gertrude, 181
Stephen Lawrence Family Campaign,
23–5, 28, 30, 373
Stepps, distillery workers, 134
stereotyping, 364; black people, 349
Sterling, David, 351
Sterne, Laurence, 269
Stewart, Dugald, 175
Stoke Newington, police station, 26
Stone Country, The, 98–9
Stone, Norman, 412–14
Stonehaven, 135
'stories within the story', 307, 309, 320
Strathclyde Police, PR Dept, 105
Strathclyde Regional Council, 132, 133;
low pay, 123
Strathclyde University, 13, 139;
philosophy department closure, 12,
136
street surveillance, cameras, 344
structure, theory of, 159, 174
'structuralism', 142
sub judice law, 109, 111, 256
Sufferings of Young Werther, The, 269
Sun Yat Sen, 237
'supreme authority', 331
'supreme source', 316, 325
Sweden, 22, 359, 393, 398
symbolism, 275, 297, 315, 326; sexual,
284
Syntactic Structures, 141, 155
Sziba, Kwanele, 372

taboos, 439
Tagore, Rabindranath, 232
Tall, Allan, 79–80
Tambo, ('Comrade O.T.'), Oliver, 7, 9
Tannahill, Robert, 176
Tebbit, Norman, 352, 356
television: dominance, 85; self-
censorship, 86
'terrorism'/'terrorists', 346, 350–2, 375,

383, 401–2, 409, 413
Thatcher, Margaret, 115, 130, 132;
immigration scares, 116;
'Thatcherism', 122, 125
*The Caribbean Artists Movement
1966–1972*, 18
*The End of a Regime? An anthology of
Scottish-South African Writing Against
Apartheid*, 6
Them, 37
The Maids, 400
theatre, 240; Caribbean, 241; 'loss share'
productions, 2; 'profit share', 76;
Scotland, 52, 76
Thomas, Hywell, 12
Thomson, Cathie, 2
Thomson, Karen, 24
Three Glasgow Writers, 225
Time of the Butcherbird, 99, 101
time, luxury of, 41
Timex workers, Dundee, 23, 247
Tkachenko, Alexander, 402
To Jerusalem and Back, 165
torture, 170, 387; concept definers,
167–9; implements, 414; refugees
reports, 166; Turkey, 394, 397
Torturer's Charter, 167
Tory Party, 130, 356; Scottish, 133
trade unions, 210; branch meetings, 222;
movement, 209; officials, 211, 221
Trades Union Congress (TUC), 8, 122,
131
Trammell, Robert, 36
Transport and General Workers' Union
(TGWU), 121, 220–1, 223–4
Traverse theatre group, 240
Trial, The, 265, 271, 284–5, 287–9, 293,
296–8, 300, 304, 308, 313, 317,
321–2, 325, 327–31
Trinidad, 230, 238, 242, 256, 258; 1937
General Strike, 238; carnival,
248–9; elections, 250; Labour
Party, 232; oil, 231, 246; Workers'
Freedom Party, 261
Trocchi, Alexander, 240
Turgenev, Ivan, 53

Index